Productive failure

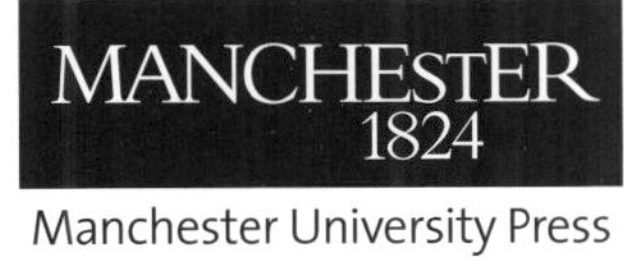

Manchester University Press

rethinking **art's** histories

SERIES EDITORS
Amelia G. Jones, Marsha Meskimmon

Rethinking Art's Histories aims to open out art history from its most basic structures by foregrounding work that challenges the conventional periodisation and geographical subfields of traditional art history, and addressing a wide range of visual cultural forms from the early modern period to the present.

These books will acknowledge the impact of recent scholarship on our understanding of the complex temporalities and cartographies that have emerged through centuries of world-wide trade, political colonisation and the diasporic movement of people and ideas across national and continental borders.

Also available in the series

Art, museums and touch Fiona Candlin

The 'do-it-yourself' artwork: Participation from fluxus to relational aesthetics Anna Dezeuze (ed.)

Fleshing out surfaces: Skin in French art and medicine, 1650–1850 Mechthild Fend

The political aesthetics of the Armenian avant-garde: The journey of the 'painterly real', 1987–2004 Angela Harutyunyan

The matter of miracles: Neapolitan baroque sanctity and architecture Helen Hills

The face of medicine: Visualising medical masculinities in late nineteenth-century Paris Mary Hunter

Glorious catastrophe: Jack Smith, performance and visual culture Dominic Johnson

Otherwise: Imagining queer feminist art histories Amelia Jones and Erin Silver (eds)

Photography and documentary film in the making of modern Brazil Luciana Martins

After the event: New perspectives in art history Charles Merewether and John Potts (eds)

Women, the arts and globalization: Eccentric experience Marsha Meskimmon and Dorothy Rowe (eds)

Flesh cinema: The corporeal turn in American avant-garde film Ara Osterweil

After-affects|after-images: Trauma and aesthetic transformation in the virtual feminist museum Griselda Pollock

Vertiginous mirrors: The animation of the visual image and early modern travel Rose Marie San Juan

The paradox of body, building and motion in seventeenth-century England Kimberley Skelton

The newspaper clipping: A modern paper object Anke Te Heesen, translated by Lori Lantz

Screen/space: The projected image in contemporary art Tamara Trodd (ed.)

Art and human rights: Contemporary Asian contexts Caroline Turner and Jen Webb

Timed out: Art and the transnational Caribbean Leon Wainwright

Performative monuments: The rematerialisation of public art Mechtild Widrich

Productive failure

Writing queer transnational South Asian art histories

Alpesh Kantilal Patel

Manchester University Press

Copyright © Alpesh Kantilal Patel 2017

The right of Alpesh Kantilal Patel to be identified as the author of this work has been asserted by him in accordance with the Copyright, Designs and Patents Act 1988.

Published by Manchester University Press
Altrincham Street, Manchester M1 7JA
www.manchesteruniversitypress.co.uk

British Library Cataloguing-in-Publication Data
A catalogue record for this book is available from the British Library

ISBN 978 1 7849 9254 5 hardback
ISBN 978 1 5261 3252 9 paperback

First published by Manchester University Press in hardback 2017

This edition first published 2018

The publisher has no responsibility for the persistence or accuracy of URLs for external or any third-party internet websites referred to in this book, and does not guarantee that any content on such websites is, or will remain, accurate or appropriate.

Typeset
by Toppan Best-set Premedia Limited
Printed
by Opolgraf S.A., Poland

Contents

Plates

Plates appear between pp. 170 and 171.

1 Anish Kapoor, *1000 Names*, 1979–80. Wood, gesso and pigment, dimensions variable. Museo Nacional Centro de Arte Reina Sofia AD00005. © Anish Kapoor.

2 Cy Twombly, *Ferragosto II*, 1961. Oil, oil crayon and pencil on canvas, 64¾ × 78⅞ in. (164.5 × 200.3 cm). Hirshhorn Museum and Sculpture Garden, Smithsonian Institution, Washington DC. Gift of Joseph H. Hirshhorn, 1966. Photography by Lee Stalsworth. © Cy Twombly Foundation.

3 Natvar Bhavsar, *VAATRI*, 1969. Pigment, oil and acrylic on canvas, 108 × 192 in. Photo: Janet Brosious Bhavsar. © Natvar Bhavsar.

4 Natvar Bhavsar, *THEER-A-THEER-A*, 1969. Pure pigment, oil and acrylic on canvas, 81.5 × 360 in. Photo: Alessandro Allegrini. © Natvar Bhavsar.

5 Stephen Dean, Stills from *Pulse*, 2001. Video installation, sound, 7:20 min. Whitney Museum of American Art, New York 2002. 140 © Stephen Dean.

6 Mario Pfeifer, *A Formal Film in Nine Episodes, Prologue & Epilogue*, 2010. 35 mm film transferred to HD video; stereo, 52 min; multiple projections for exhibition space (variable). Hindi, Tamil with English subtitles. Courtesy of Mario Pfeifer & [blackboardfilms], © 2012. Installation view: MMK Museum für Moderne Kunst, Frankfurt am Main 2012–13.

7 Adrian Piper, *The Color Wheel Series, Second Adhyasa: Pranamayakosha II. 102 (Adrian Piper)* (7/31/01). 8.25 × 10 in., 600 dpi. Pantone #5767 CVC, 287 CVC, 1385 CVC. Photo: Maurice Berger. Detail of page project for *Art Journal* 60, 3 (2001). © Adrian Piper Research Archive Foundation Berlin.

8 Kehinde Wiley, *Femme Fellah*, 2010. Oil on canvas, 45 × 36 in. © Kehinde Wiley.

9 Kehinde Wiley, *Bonaparte in the Great Mosque of Cairo*, 2010. Oil on canvas, 60 × 72 in. © Kehinde Wiley.

Figures

Every effort has been made to obtain permission to reproduce copyright material, and the publisher will be pleased to be informed of any errors and omissions for correction in future editions.

Preface: Productive failure, cruising and affirmative criticality

When this book was in its nascent stages, I would say to anyone who asked about its content that it was concerned with writing transnational South Asian art histories and visual cultures. Even though I used 'transnational' in favour of 'diaspora' – which British sociologist Paul Gilroy notes assumes an 'obsession with origins, purity and invariant sameness' – what I found was that most would presume that my book was organized around genealogy anyway.[1] They could not imagine I would be discussing the artworks of Cy Twombly or Kehinde Wiley (as I do in Chapters 3 and 4, respectively); or a public art memorial commemorating the death of Brazilian Jean Charles de Menezes in London and Adrian Margaret Smith Piper's work on the slain African American Trayvon Martin (both of which I explore in Chapter 7). This response, of course, seems unsurprising from a non-academic, but I was taken aback that art historians, too, were not able to conceive of my project outside of bloodlines.

When I began to introduce the book as a 'productive failure' *before* indicating that I was 'writing transnational South Asian art histories', the responses were quite different. I do not mean to imply that I managed to get art historians to think I would explore the aforementioned artists' works and visual cultural material, but I did pique these scholars' imaginations. I got them to think that my book project was perhaps not only about genealogy. 'Failure' in 'productive failure' is strategic and could be characterized as a 'queer failure' as articulated by queer theorist and gender studies scholar Jack Halberstam in his important book *The Queer Art of Failure* (2011).[2] While I fail to uphold a strictly genealogical approach to writing transnational South Asian art histories – which I am indicating most people assumed the book to be exploring – I succeed in writing more radical ones.

At the same time, there is a history of how the word 'failure' and its variants have been mobilized in relation to 'non-Western' art histories with which I have to contend. To explain, consider this disclaimer that *New York Times* art critic Holland Cotter provides to readers of his review of a 2015 Guggenheim Museum exhibition of abstract paintings by V. S. (Vasudeo Santu) Gaitonde

(1924–2001). He asked readers to keep in mind the following paradox when they visit:

> Many Western abstract painters in the early 20th century – Albers, Kandinsky, Mondrian – were deeply influenced by Asian art and philosophy, though no one dismissed them as Orientalists. Their cosmopolitanism was a point in their favor, and proof of Modernism's wide embrace. By contrast, if Asian artists showed signs of absorbing Western models, their work was disdained as derivative, inauthentic and evidence that Western Modernism was the only true one, the source that supplied the world.[3]

That Cotter has to point out the above to readers of *The New York Times* – who we could assume are largely well informed – illustrates what is at stake when I use 'failure', which is a synonym for Cotter's usage of 'inauthentic' and 'derivative'.

I would argue, though, that the contemporary art world does not have a problem legitimizing art histories dealing with the transnational or the non-West, but the discipline of art history still seems to lean towards only doing so through a multiculturalist approach that homogenizes difference. So, the fear should not be that the histories I write will be reinscribed as inauthentic by mobilizing the word 'failure'. Rather, by not invoking 'failure' the histories I write will be construed as authentic but in only the most reductive manner. To be clear, I see no problem in this book being categorized under the label of South Asian art history – or a variant of it – in a library, but I hope that my writing will help expand what artworks could fall under the label 'South Asian art history'. Therefore, 'productive failure' as a concept signals that the art histories I write have broad ramifications for how we might write transnational South Asian art histories both *with* and *beyond* genealogy.

Art historian Simon Ofield-Kerr's theorization of 'cruising' as a mode of research is one way through which I more effectively accomplish this goal. Drawing on Roland Barthes, he writes that cruising is a 'productive not reductive process' and that it 'has an inbuilt potential for diversion, irregular connections and disorderly encounters'.[4] In short, cruising refers to being open to *not* finding what you are looking for and being open to 'something you never knew you wanted, or even knew existed'.[5] Cruising could refer to surfing on the internet but it also can refer to looking for sex. Given the focus on issues of sexuality in this monograph as well as descriptions of my own walks in urban space (as in Chapter 5), the erotic element embedded within the genealogy of the term is something I do not wish to abstract in my usage of the concept here. I do not wish to cloak my desires as an art historian for my objects of study, either.

London-based artist Anish Kapoor's *Svayambh* (2007) provides insight – even if unwittingly – for *doing* (art) history, too. Weighing approximately 7 tons, the work consists of a large block of red paint, wax and Vaseline, set on a plinth that imperceptibly and noiselessly moves over a track system set above the floor.[6] The Musée des Beaux-Arts in Nantes, France, and Haus der Kunst in Munich, Germany, co-presented the work in 2007 (Figures P.1 and P.3). The work was also in Kapoor's survey exhibition at the Royal Academy of Arts in London in 2009 (cover image and Figure P.2). The passageways through which

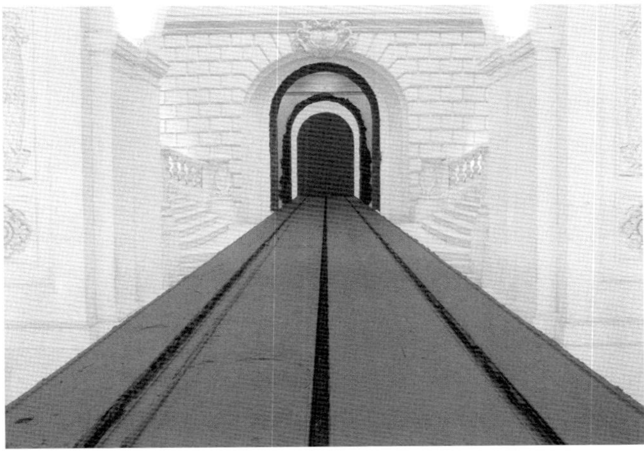

Anish Kapoor, *Svayambh*, 2007. Wax and oil-based paint, dimensions variable. Installation view: Musée des Beaux-Arts de Nantes, 2007. **P.1**

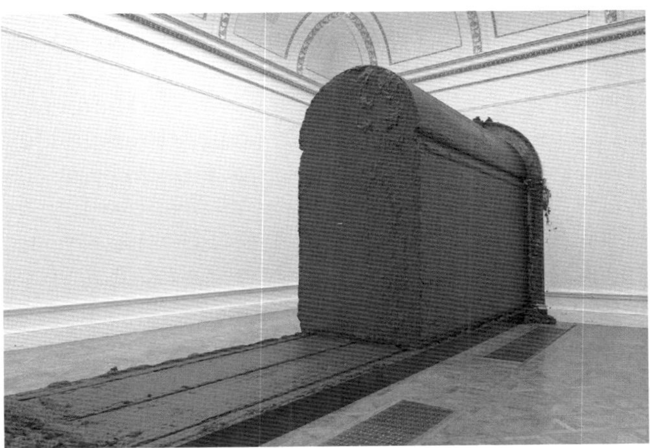

Anish Kapoor, *Svayambh*, 2007. Wax and oil-based paint, dimensions variable. Installation view: Royal Academy of Arts, London, 2009. **P.2**

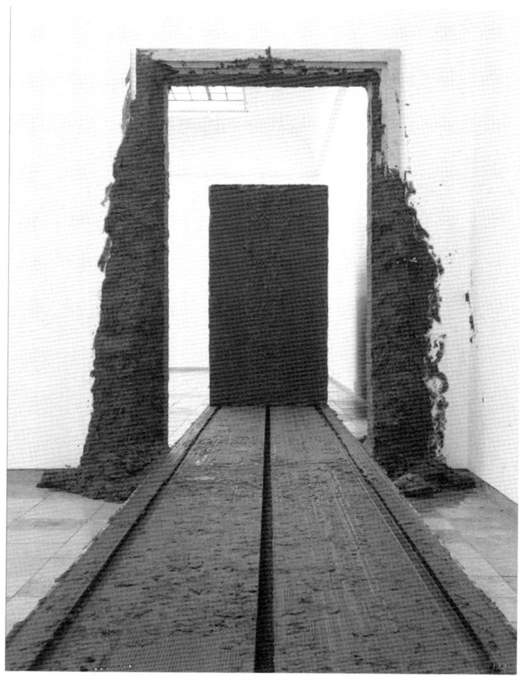

P.3 Anish Kapoor, *Svayambh*, 2007. Wax and oil-based paint, dimensions variable. Installation view: Haus der Kunst, Munich, 2007.

the block traverses in these buildings would mould or carve its final shape. In Nantes and Munich, the work might conjure up Nazi trains of deportation. The former is the city from which many Jewish people were taken on trains to the death camps and the latter's Haus der Kunst is the first monumental propaganda building of the Third Reich.[7] However, as art historian Karen Lang writes in the context of her experience viewing the work in Munich, '*Svayambh* quickly departs from expected meaning … as a physical object, *Svayambh* brings to expression the Haus der Kunst's history of violence. As a perceptual object … it initiates more intimate and associative connotations: trains of thought.'[8]

One of the 'associative connotations' or 'trains of thought' the work brings up for me is that the physical door frames of the buildings in which Kapoor's work are installed shape the block of viscous material in much the same way conceptual frames which art historians use – such as form, authorship and subject matter – construct histories of art. Of course, as *Svayambh* moves across the galleries, chunks of red Vaseline ooze out onto both the door frames and contiguous walls: the building is not left untouched. In a similar way, paying attention to – rather than attempting to foreclose – the slippage between the frames I use and the evidence I attempt to shape into histories of art is of vital importance. Each chapter begins with a fairly conventional mode of organizing artworks – as well as visual culture in later chapters – but that which I attempt to shape inevitably demands a slight shift in my framing device or evidence. For example, in Chapter 5 I use space and site as frames to better articulate the lesbian, bisexual and trans* collective Sphere's public artwork in Manchester, England. In the end, though, writing *with* the work ultimately took me in directions that I had not anticipated – everything from including my own walks through the spaces of the city as well as queer club flyers and marketing materials as integral to the writing of a queer feminist transnational South Asian art history. Just as Kapoor's work makes both the object and subjective experience of the viewer uncertain, I attempt both to make the objects under investigation and the art historian and his frame of reference remain somewhat precarious, unresolved and entangled though not indistinct.

Feminist postcolonial literary scholar Gayatri Chakravorty Spivak in 1987 said: 'It is the questions that we ask that produce the field of inquiry and not some body of materials which determines what questions need to be posed to it.'[9] I agree with this but I would update it to suggest that the 'field of inquiry' is one that is negotiated between the 'questions that we ask' and the materials we think are – but may not end up being – appropriate for answering them. Put another way, I argue that critics and historians should implicitly configure the artwork as a subject, which materializes as a subject-in-making with, and through, their personal investments – and sited engagement – rather than as an object to be explained. Lang implies as much in her essay on Kapoor's *Svayambh*. She writes that the work 'so straightforwardly referential at first view' in the end is anything but that; it 'depends on the presence of a beholder to set it in motion'.[10] Kapoor's works instantiate my call for critics and art historians – special kinds of beholders – to acknowledge the role they play in creating meaning. I discuss my investments in more detail in the Introduction and in Chapter 2, I explore the fraught nature of authorship as a frame through the lens of the art criticism of Anish Kapoor's work.

This notion of a subject-in-making is embedded in the genealogy of the title of *Svayambh*. The word *svayambh* is an adaptation of the Sanskrit word *svayambhuv*, which roughly translates into 'self-generated' in contradistinction to *rupa*, which refers to a human-made form.[11] Indeed, Kapoor's sculptures often appear as if they materialize without human artifice – that they had always been there – but of course, they have been laboriously fabricated. *Svayambh* engenders a space for the viewer in which this paradox is felt and where subject and object, nature and artifice and thinking and feeling are all blurred. This space is generative and generous, allowing for multiple meanings, and thereby underscoring that meaning-making and the writing of art histories can be nothing but provisional.

The argument, of course, is that this is tantamount to saying that an artwork can mean anything and everything and there are no standards through which to filter it. However, the default model in which the historian or critic constructing histories of art remains largely invisible has the unfortunate, if largely unconscious, effect of producing narratives that claim 'objective' truth value but in fact are shaped by the writer's myriad concerns, investments and desires. Those interested in having a dialogue with art, I would argue, need to make their personal investments and the methods of their engagement more explicit – the nature of our dialogue is imbricated with the histories we write with and through art. To do so is to engage in the practice of what art historian Marsha Meskimmon describes as 'affirmative criticality', where aesthetics and ethics meet.[12] She writes that in contradistinction to negative critique – which attempts 'to analyse and interpret things as they are or have been (present, past)' – affirmative criticality as a mode or praxis 'engage[s] actively with the constitution of the future'.[13] A practice-led project in the form of curating I describe in Chapter 6 attempts to imagine and bring into being an incipient, more ethical future. Indeed, the second half of the book, especially, begins to move towards making my own entanglements more palpable and explicit with the histories of art I write as well as the visual culture with which I engage. At the same time, 'the constitution of the future' with which affirmative criticality is concerned could also involve a reconstitution of the past. In Chapter 3, for instance, I re-imagine post-Second World War abstraction.

Affirmative criticality and productive failure, in fact, are well paired as broad conceptual frameworks that articulate my approach to writing art history. Affirmative criticality does not translate into a less critical mode of engagement in the same way productive failure does not minimize the importance of genealogy in writing transnational South Asian art histories. Rather both demand a slight adjustment to the way we practice art history and thereby produce the possibility of a more ethical and responsible writing with and through art. Moreover, cruising as an overarching method is how I try to accomplish this goal. In the end, my approach is to aim to write art histories as slippery, subjective and entangled with each other and me.

Notes

1 Also, one of my case studies deals with the production and consumption of art in the subcontinent, which the term 'diaspora' tends to exclude. For the Gilroy quotation, see Brent Hayes Edwards, 'The Uses of Diaspora', *Social Text* 19, no. 1 66 (20 March 2001): 63, doi:10.1215/01642472–19–1_66–45. It is not my goal here to set up a Manichean debate between 'diaspora' and 'transnational',

though. In fact, the genealogy of the latter is already deeply intertwined with that of the former. For instance, British cultural studies scholar Stuart Hall has theorized 'diaspora' in a manner that addresses the implications of fixed origins and destinations that Gilroy references. He defines 'diaspora experience' as determined not through 'return' and 'not by essence or purity, but by the recognition of a necessary heterogeneity and diversity; by a conception of "identity" which lives with and through, not despite, difference'. See Stuart Hall, 'Cultural Identity and Diaspora', in *Identity: Community, Culture, Difference*, ed. Jonathan Rutherford (London: Lawrence & Wishart, 1990), 235.

2 Judith Halberstam, *The Queer Art of Failure* (Durham, NC: Duke University Press, 2011).

3 Holland Cotter, 'V. S. Gaitonde Retrospective at the Guggenheim', *The New York Times*, 1 January 2015, www.nytimes.com/2015/01/02/arts/design/v-s-gaitonde-retrospective-at-the-guggenheim.html.

4 Simon Ofield-Kerr, 'Cruising the Archive', *Journal of Visual Culture* 4, no. 3 (1 December 2005): 357, doi:10.1177/1470412905058353.

5 Ibid.

6 These details are from the website of Aerotrope, the company in charge of the structural design of this and many of Kapoor's monumental works. See http://aerotrope.com/what-we-do/art/svayambh-anish-kapoor-france-germany-uk.html.

7 On 18 July 1937 Adolf Hitler opened the 'House of German Art' (renamed 'Haus der Kunst' in 1946 to ' "denazify" the historically troubled building') as the first 'Great German Art Exhibition' and a day later the vilified show *Degenerate Art* was opened in the rooms of the then Archeological Institute in Munich. See 'Haus Der Kunst – FAQs', *Haus der Kunst* accessed 26 July 2016, www.hausderkunst.de/en/research/history/faqs/. Information on Nantes culled from the following: Julia Weiner, 'Interview: Anish Kapoor Is the Biggest Name in Art', *Jewish Chronicle Online*, 24 September 2009, www.thejc.com/arts/arts-interviews/interview-anish-kapoor-biggest-name-art.

8 Karen Lang, 'Anish Kapoor's *Svayambh*', *X-Tra: Contemporary Art Quarterly* 11, no. 2 (Winter 2008): 60–3. Online version consulted was unpaginated: http://x-traonline.org/article/anish-kapoors-svayambh/.

9 Irit Rogoff, *Terra Infirma: Geography's Visual Culture* (London and New York: Routledge, 2000), 31. As paraphrased by Rogoff from a discussion after a lecture given by Gaytri Chakravorty Spivak at Harvard University's Center for Literary and Cultural Studes in 1987.

10 Lang, 'Anish Kapoor's *Svayambh*'.

11 Ibid.

12 Marsha Meskimmon, *Contemporary Art and the Cosmopolitan Imagination* (London; New York: Routledge, 2011), 91.

13 Ibid.

Acknowledgements

Two anonymous peer reviewers carefully read both the proposal for the book and the manuscript. I am so grateful to them for engaging with my text; their feedback has certainly elevated the content. My greatest intellectual debt, though, goes to Amelia Jones and Marsha Meskimmon, the editors of this series of which this book is a part. Of course, I am aware that any attempt to acknowledge the contributions of both of these brilliant scholars will always fall short. Indeed, Amelia and Marsha have been involved in various aspects of my training as an art historian since practically the beginning of my postgraduate education. It is only their capacity for generosity and friendship that could rival their intellect.

Also, this book has also been deeply impacted by my participation in the National Endowment of the Humanities (NEH) 2012 summer session 'Re-imagining American Art History: Asian American Art, Research and Pedagogy', organized by the trailblazer art historian Margo Machida and Alexandra Chang. My many thanks to them as well as the wonderful scholars who participated and who I thank throughout the book.

Conference papers I have delivered and panels I organized at the annual conferences of many professional organizations—in particular, College Art Association (CAA), Association of Asian American Studies (AAAS), Performance Studies International(PSi), and Association of Art Historians (AAH)—became an important mode through which I experimented with many of the ideas in this book. Panels of which I was a part include in chronological order: 'Live Art and Performance in History and the Politics of Inclusion', cochaired by me and Amelia Jones (PSi, 2012); 'New Trajectories in Asian American Art and Criticism', chaired by Laura Kina and Jan Bernabe (AAAH, 2013); 'Abstraction and Difference', cochaired by David J. Getsy and Tirza T. Latimer (CAA, 2014); 'Colour Me Queer', coaired by me and Natasha Bissonauth (AAH, 2014); and 'Contemporary Art History and Queer Transnational Flânerie', chaired by Natasha Bissonauth (AAAH, 2015).

My gratitude to scholars who invited me to write chapters for anthologies that provided me an opportunity to work through concepts I explore more fully in this book. These books include *Creolising Europe: Legacies and Transformations*, coedited by Encarnación Gutiérrez Rodríguez and Shirley Anne (Liverpool University Press, 2015) and *Queering Contemporary Asian American Art*, coedited by Laura Kina and Jan Bernabe (Washington: University of Washington Press, May 2017).

The following artists, the works of whom I try my best to write *with* rather than about, have provided so much inspiration for this book: Natvar Bhavsar; Stephen Dean; Anish Kapoor; Adrian Margaret Smith Piper; Mario Pfeifer; and Kehinde Wiley. Lastly, I will be forever grateful to the artists who were a part of the *Mixing It Up* exhibition, especially Sphere collective's Jaheda Choudhury.

Many of the artists, collectors, and galleries were kind enough to waive fees for permissions to reproduce many of the images. Danielle Damas ably assisted me in photography permissions research and Kelley Antoniazi-Taksier graciously edited some of the photographs. Also, Meg Kaplan-Noach, Libby Hruska, and Susan Richmond provided crucial editorial support at various stages of this project. I, of course, take full responsibility for any mistakes in the book.

I have been fortunate to have many friends who have been important sounding boards for my ideas and who kept me laughing: William Burke, Jacek J. Kolasiński, Noelle LaForest, Susan Richmond, and Przemysław Strożek. My core support remains my family. I am thankful to my parents Kantilal and Lalita without whom this book would simply be unthinkable; to my brother Satish and sister-in-law Smita, who I consider a sister, for their ongoing support. I dedicate this book to my family which includes my nieces Niya, who was born a decade ago when the book began to take more concrete form, and Rayna, who was born shortly before I submitted my book proposal.

Finally, it is wonderful to be publishing this book with Manchester University Press since the city of Manchester features heavily in it. I lived in Manchester from 2005 to 2008 and that time and place impacted this book in innumerable ways. Indeed, the city was a muse of sorts and the people I met a source of inspiration.

Introduction: towards *creolizing* transnational South Asian art histories 1

> Even the History of Art at the End of the Universe is not as far out as its proponents have claimed ... Not every artwork made ... is visible, and it is possible that there are many more that have not been counted, even by their curators or by art historians, simply because they have never been seen. When considering anything in deep space it is essential to remember a fundamental maxim of inter-planetary travel – *L'essentiel est invisible pour les yeux* ('What is essential is invisible to the eye'). (Raqs Media Collective)[1]

This book project pivots around a seeming paradox or contradiction: my desire to construct the unwritten history of artworks by artists of South Asian descent produced in the transnational space bound by British colonialism and the impossibility and even problematic nature of such a project, however well intentioned. I have begun to provisionally map out a history of artworks by such artists in the post-1980s period who remain marginalized in the American and British context, but does making them visible achieve the inclusivity that is implied in such a project?[2] French philosopher Jacques Derrida's conceptualization of the supplement is instructive in this regard. He writes, 'the supplement adds itself, it is a surplus, a plenitude enriching another plenitude [...] But the supplement supplements. It adds only to replace.'[3]

Supplementing hegemonic art history, then, can never fully deliver on its promise of inclusivity; it will always fall short of becoming complete. New Delhi-based artists, curators and self-described 'philosophical agent provocateurs' Raqs Media Collective insinuate just as much.[4] In the extract from a presentation they gave as part of the conference *Art History in the Wake of the Global Turn*, with which I begin this chapter, they suggest that there always will be artworks that are invisible to the art historian.[5] Rather than suggesting that histories attempting inclusivity should be avoided merely because they are implicitly unfinished, this project aims to move away from *only* considering genealogy and writing art histor*ies* (plural) and thereby to make apparent their inherent supplementarity.

Visual culture and queer studies scholar Gavin Butt meditates on the word 'paradox' – a word I use in my first sentence in this introduction – in relation to art criticism; I want to consider this idea in the context of writing art histories. In his introduction to his edited volume of essays, 'The Paradoxes of Criticism', Butt writes:

> This book considers criticism, then, in a defining relation to the paradoxical. Not paradox as in the strict sense of being logically contradictory … Rather that criticism, in order that it *remain* criticism, of necessity has to situate itself *para* – against and/or beside – the *doxa* of received wisdom.[6]

Art history is not art criticism, but I do want it to remain critical in the manner Butt describes: to situate itself 'against and/or beside' the normative or 'received wisdom'. In this way – and slightly reworking what he writes – I work against the 'constantive, reportive dimensions of … [hegemonic art] historical inquiry'.[7] Indeed, I am not reporting facts but arranging them as evidence to create palpable fictions as history.[8] In this way, paradox can be productive and generative: it can open up the multiple histories of art.

I approach art history as a performative *doing* rather than understanding it as the creation of stable, inviolable narratives that reveal the truth of the past. Precisely by *not* succeeding in producing conventional art historical narratives, a redefinition and reorientation of what art history can *do* – rather than *be* – is possible. German art historian Michael F. Zimmermann ends his introduction to the edited volume *The Art Historian: National Traditions and Institutional Practices* (2003) by similarly noting that 'Art history … should less define itself on the ground of what it is, than of what it does'.[9] His statement is meant as a rebuttal to what he describes as the endless claims of the death of art history. He writes that he 'favors radical contingency' for the discipline.[10] In this way, it is constantly in a state of *becoming* knowledge. Aware that the death of art history has at least partially to do with its xenophobia and racism (among other issues), Zimmermann cautions that he is '[n]ot arguing against ethnological or post-colonial approaches' to art history. Rather, he implies that these approaches are themselves part of the radical contingency that marks the discipline at its best.[11] Interestingly, he further notes that his particular notion of 'radical contingency' as a polemical point is perhaps too general and 'thus in itself not contingent' at all.[12] Given my specific interest in writing transnational South Asian art histories, this project can be seen as enacting the radical contingency of art history about which Zimmermann compellingly writes.

Defining transnational South Asia as the 'Brown Atlantic'

To theorize the space of my analysis, I invoke British sociologist Paul Gilroy's theory of the Black Atlantic. Gilroy's theory draws upon and makes more specific French philosopher Michel Foucault's theories of genealogy, discourse and heterotopia through the specific optic of theories of black identity. My reworking of Gilroy's theory here is more of a lateral move to another space bound by a different set of power dynamics: it is the 'Brown Atlantic' to which both Asian American studies and film scholar Jigna Desai in her *Beyond Bollywood* (2004) and queer and South Asian cultural studies scholar Gayatri Gopinath in her *Impossible Desires* (2005) loosely refer in their scholarship.[13]

As Gilroy describes in his now epochal *The Black Atlantic: Modernity and Double Consciousness* (1993), his intercultural theorization of the Black Atlantic is not tethered to identitarian notions of ethnicity or nationalism.[14] He famously invokes the metaphor of slave ships 'in motion across the spaces between Europe, America, Africa, and the Caribbean' to theorize black diasporic identities and to 'focus attention on the middle passage'.[15] Gilroy refers to this 'middle passage' as the 'Black Atlantic', which he argues avoids the implications of the classical notion of 'diaspora'. According to him, in an interview with philosopher Timmy Lott, the latter assumes an 'obsession with origins, purity and invariant sameness'.[16] Instead, the Black Atlantic is a theoretical model that underscores identity as always in flux.

The post-structuralist underpinnings of the Black Atlantic have allowed it to be reworked and adopted by scholars to theorize other more focused spaces – such as the 'Lusophone Black Atlantic', the geographical area bound by the slave routes between Portugal, Brazil and Africa.[17] In connection to a 'Brown Atlantic', Gopinath writes, 'Such a mapping of South Asian diasporic movement suggests the differences and similarities between the experiences of racialization of South Asian immigrations in North America and the UK.'[18] The 'Brown Atlantic' could refer to a broad range of nations beyond the latter, such as Pakistan and the Caribbean (Jamaica, Trinidad, Tobago and Guyana) as well as former British colonies such as Fiji, South Africa and Mauritius to which South Asians migrated in the late nineteenth and twentieth centuries. However, I deal here primarily with the transnational space including the United Kingdom, United States and India which is bound by British colonialism.[19]

My own 'roots and routes', as Gilroy pithily refers to his Black Atlantic model, approximates the space of my analysis: I am a UK-born, US-raised and currently Miami, Florida-based subject whose family emigrated originally from Gujarat, India.[20] Also, much of the second half of this book was researched while I lived in Manchester, England. The case studies reflect these routes in that I focus largely on the United States and England with some attention to India. At the same time, my identification as 'queer' has added traction to a simplistic mapping of my personal history onto the space I have otherwise sketched out. In the next section, I expand on how I approach my authorship as well as how I attempt to prevent it from becoming stabilizing or even wholly knowable in the context of writing transnational South Asian art histories.

The self-fiction (not self-exposure) of the art historian: queer and towards queering

One of the ways in which this project tries to perform art histories as shifting and ever changing is to make clear that they are always a product of the people who write them. Because the discipline of art history predominantly follows a model in which the historian or critic constructing histories of art remains largely invisible, this has the unfortunate (if largely unconscious) effect of producing narratives that claim 'objective' truth, which are in fact shaped by the writer's myriad concerns, investments and desires. As art historians Amelia Jones and Andrew Stephenson write in their groundbreaking, coedited book *Performing the Body/Performing the Text* (1999), which examines the performativity of art history and art criticism: 'one must locate the "professional spectator" (the art critic and art historian) within the operative discursive operations and a distinctive Western taxonomy … which serves to authorize and naturalize his readings as "truthful"'.[21] They are partly referring to what they note are the now well-rehearsed problems with American critic Clement Greenberg's formalist approach to art criticism of the 1950s and 1960s, which effectively veiled the critic's interestedness in the objects about which he wrote. I will thus interrogate how my own authorship – not only my aforementioned roots and routes but also my identification as queer – has an impact on the histories I write; by doing so I thereby make explicit the *subjec*tivity of art history. That is, this monograph does not try to disentangle the writing of art histories from my own history and biases.

At the same time, Jones and Stephenson caution that the need to fix value and meaning to artistic endeavours extends to 'even the most seemingly enlightened and most radical varieties' of art historical and art critical practices, as well.[22] They clarify:

> Even as Euro-American art history and art criticism have by and large shifted away from a value system based on abstract aesthetic ideals to one based on political efficacy (in terms of Marxian, structuralist, feminist, and other radical agendas), the majority of supposedly 'anti-' or 'post-' modernist analyses continue to veil the investments at work in posing particular values and meanings for works of art.[23]

Moreover, as art historian Michael Schreyach notes in his introduction to the edited volume *The State of Art Criticism* (2007), 'admitting one's preferences and investments is self-exposure, not self-criticism'.[24] While he is referring to what he describes as the 'endless acknowledgement of positionality', or frames of reference, since the 1960s, this can just as well be applied to the insertion of the critic's or art historian's biography into his writing.

To prevent my writing from becoming self-exposure, I do not offer my personal anecdotes as autobiographically anchored 'facts', but as the kind of 'self-fiction' women's and gender studies scholar Nancy K. Miller theorizes.[25] French philosopher Roland Barthes, in his 'autobiographical' sketch *Roland Barthes by Roland Barthes* (1977), also rigorously refused to revert to an underlying reality or essence by revealing the construction of subjectivity itself as a product of language.[26] He wrote, 'This book consists of what I do not know: the unconscious and ideology, things which utter themselves only by the voices of others. I cannot put on stage (in the text), *as such*, the symbolic and the ideological which pass through me, since I am their blind spot.'[27] In this way, I undermine any full sense of power or authority I have as a critic-historian. To be clear, my provisional readings in the forthcoming pages should not be construed as being non-committal, nebulous or indistinct; I present what I believe are lucid arguments in connection to works that cohere into a specific legibility but without concretizing them.

To make palpable and visible this project's Barthesian 'blind spot', I mobilize 'queer' as both a noun and a verb. That is, queer as an identification and a subjectivity is important to my writing of transnational South Asian art histories, but it also functions as a destabilizing agent meant to acknowledge the complex entanglements of *other* identifications such as gender and class with sexuality. I draw here on legal scholar Kimberlé Crenshaw's theory of intersectionality that points to the importance of considering constructions of gender, race/ethnicity and class as constitutive of one another.[28] Queer theorist and cultural studies scholar Jasbir K. Puar argues that intersectionality 'holds fast as a successful model of political transformation', but it needs to be supplemented as a tool for political intervention.[29] For Puar this has meant a focus on assemblage but she does not jettison intersectionality as a concept completely. She notes that intersectionality is 'a much more porous paradigm' than is generally acknowledged and her conceptualization of the 'becoming of intersectionality', in which there is an emphasis on motion rather than points of meeting, is particularly provocative.[30] Crenshaw's cogent description of cars meeting at an intersection, which Puar notes is suggestive of intersectionality being an 'event', is instructive.[31] Puar writes:

> As Crenshaw indicates in this description [the analogy of cars], identification is a process; identity is an encounter, an event, an accident, in fact. Identities are multi-causal, multi-directional, liminal; traces aren't always self-evident. In this 'becoming of intersectionality', *there is emphasis on motion* rather than gridlock; on how the halting of motion produces the demand to locate.[32]

One way to avoid 'gridlock' is to attend to the '*event-ness* of the critical encounter' between the critic and the objects he addresses 'to revivify the practices of contemporary criticism'.[33] British architectural art historian and feminist art critic Jane Rendell brilliantly elaborates on the latter in her important book *Site-Writing: The Architecture of Art Criticism* (2010), which considers 'the construction of texts – essays and installations – architectures of art criticism – that write the sites' of her encounter with artworks.[34] For her, 'the sites' broadly refer to the 'material, emotional, political, and conceptual – of the artwork's construction, exhibition and documentation, as well as those remembered, dreamed and imagined by the artist, critic and other viewers'.[35]

The 'otherwise' of queer transnational South Asian art histories

As perhaps is clear by now, an important thread running through the chapters of this book is not to jettison art history as a discipline wholesale but to think it *otherwise*. I invoke 'otherwise' in the spirit of how art historians Amelia Jones and Erin Silver use the word in the title of their 2016 anthology *Otherwise: Imagining Queer Feminist Art Histories*, especially given this project's interest in queer subjectivity and theory. While this book does not purport to be concerned exclusively with women's artistic practices or those of lesbian, gay, bisexual, trans*, queer, questioning and intersex-identified subjects, it does increasingly engage with them in the second half.[36] In her introduction, Jones writes that 'queer theory and feminism are "otherwise" to each other, as well as to art history, but also to the ways in which they both deal with the "otherwise" of sexual and gender identifications in relation to (in this case) visual culture'.[37]

Borrowing and reworking this felicitous language of Jones's, this monograph is enmeshed in how queer theory and transnational, diaspora and related theories are otherwise to each other and to art history; and how they deal with the otherwise of a queer and transnational South Asian identification in relation to visual culture. To clarify, the critiques queer and diaspora bring to each other do not necessarily 'sustain a more perfect union or, in this case, a more perfect oppositionality', as Puar perspicaciously argues.[38] For instance, Gayatri Gopinath, like Puar, notes the masculinist tendencies of both queer and diaspora theories: the title of her path-breaking book *Impossible Desires* (2005) refers partly to the occlusion of queer feminist desire in these theoretical models.[39] Queer and diaspora theories do not necessarily enfold other intersecting issues, such as class and faith, either.[40]

The discipline of art history has remained silent on the broad range of queer feminist South Asian visual culture and artistic practices that Gopinath has begun to brilliantly examine.[41] Indeed, the incorporation of queer theory and feminist critique into the growing literature that explores art history in the context of the 'transnational', 'global', 'world' and 'diaspora' – all slippery terms, of course – has been sorely lacking.[42] An important exception is *Women, the Arts and Globalization: Eccentric Experience* (2013), edited by art historians Marsha Meskimmon and Dorothy C. Price.[43] In the introduction, they point out that 'Contemporary artists traverse the same routes as empowered, metropolitan elites and the economic migrants left in their wake, and, arguably, the territories described by these global circuits are always, already gendered.' In this way, they situate the importance of gender not as an additive frame but as integral to understanding contemporary art in the context of globalization.[44]

Art historian Aruna D'Souza writes that, though global art histories 'draw upon the language of a particular strain of visual culture studies (a critique of disciplinarity)', they do not embrace the latter's other imperatives, such as an 'attention to a broader array of media and non-art forms … as a way of rejecting the limiting category of art'.[45] Indeed, given this project's focus on not only identity but also artworks in relation to other kinds of material visual culture, this investigation is closer in spirit to the concerns of visual culture and is indebted to a genealogy of work going back to the Birmingham Centre for Contemporary Cultural Studies, which celebrated its fiftieth anniversary in 2014 and was headed by British cultural studies scholar Stuart Hall.[46]

At the same time, in her essay 'What Is a Theorist?' visual cultural studies scholar Irit Rogoff compellingly writes that, though her initial transition from art history to visual culture was to shift from a discipline to a 'less disciplined place', visual cultural studies has begun suspiciously to function much more like that which it aimed to supplant.[47] In this way, the invocation of 'art histories' in this book's title is not meant to be a counterpoint to visual culture. The conscious choice of the term 'art histories', however, is to signal that a strong impulse behind this project is to make visible histories of artworks that remain marginalized – something that perhaps is less obvious under the umbrella of visual cultural studies even as I am arguing that the divisions between these disciplines are not so clear cut.

Each subsequent chapter takes a variety of different approaches to examining the visual. Some are fairly conventional for art history – such as authorship (Chapter 2), form (Chapter 3), and subject matter (Chapter 4). These provide critical modes of close analysis of artworks and the visual *tout court* that cultural studies approaches (even if not purposefully) often sidestep. I also consider 'practice-led' approaches, such as auto-ethnographic narratives relating experiential knowledge of space/site (Chapter 5), curatorial knowledge-making via exhibitions (Chapter 6), and the affective knowledge generated by encounters with visual culture (Chapter 7). Affect can be loosely described as feeling before cognition and while it has been embraced by cultural studies scholars, only a handful of art historians – especially Jill Bennett and Marsha

Meskimmon – have begun to think about its potential.[48] I illustrate that all of these frames can be powerfully queer – that is, destabilizing – and radical tools to examine the transnational.

To further clarify what I hope to achieve through the above, the following statement by Stuart Hall is suggestive, even if it does not explicitly deal with transnational South Asia. Here, Hall expands on curator and writer Gilane Tawadros's use of 'fault lines' as a frame to explore 'the postcolonial and geo-political situation of the work of contemporary African artists' that were part of her exhibition *Fault Lines: Contemporary African Art and Shifting Landscapes* at the 50th Venice Biennale (2003):

> Of course, fault lines, like other relations of power (as Michel Foucault would remind us) are also *productive*. Those escaping the vertical lines of force forge new lateral connections. New formations appear where older ones disappear beneath the sand. Borders, which divide, become sites of surreptitious crossing. Separate and inviolable worlds meet and collide. Where only the pure, the orthodox, were valorised, a new universe of vernaculars and creole forms comes into existence. Multiple logics of identification and translation operate.[49]

If we consider transnational South Asian art history organized through the frame of genealogy as a singular fault line attempting to disrupt the 'pure', 'orthodox' and dominant white art history, then the aforementioned frames of authorship, form, subject matter, space/site and affect can be seen as other fault lines to organize or analyse artworks. These fault lines can be seen most '*productive*' when, per Hall, 'new lateral connections' are made across (or trans) fault lines. In this way, each chapter is only *initially* framed through one singular frame; eventually lateral connections are made to other frames that result in 'a new universe of vernaculars and creole forms' of art histor*ies* to emerge. By 'creole forms', Hall is describing new hybrid forms that cannot be mapped back to an origin or to its components, which are themselves hybrid.

Creolizing transnational South Asian art histories

It was not until January 2002 – a year before the *Fault Lines* exhibition – that the mainstream contemporary art world explored 'creole' as a term. That year, as part of Documenta 11, an exhibition which takes place every five years, curator Okwui Enwezor incorporated a series of seminars and discussions at various sites in addition to, and outside, Kassel, Germany, where it traditionally takes place. One of these sites was St Lucia where 'Platform 3' titled 'Créolité and Creolization' took place.[50] Participants, one of whom was Stuart Hall, explored the genealogy of the titular terms as well as a third term, 'Creole', and their potential to describe phenomena beyond their historically and geographically specific origins to the contemporary art world.

Interestingly, this platform took place only a few months before the Sterling and Francine Clark Art Institute conference 'The Art Historian: National Traditions and Institutional Practices', organized by art historians Michael Ann Holly and Mariët Westermann.[51] However, there is no overlap between these two gatherings in terms of ideology or participants.[52] Platform 3 did not address art historical practices and was largely populated by visual culture scholars, curators and artists, while the Clark conference eschewed discussions of creolization, diaspora or migration, with the exception of a brief discussion of global art history.[53]

I hope to bridge the divide exemplified above. First, I describe the terms 'Creole', '*créolité*', and 'creolization' before considering how they are useful to theorizing writing transnational South Asian art histories. As Hall notes, 'Creole' is 'an exceedingly slippery signifier'.[54] Linguistically, it is often used to describe the vernacular language that emerged in the colonies of the Caribbean which typically included mainly European and African languages.[55] Sociologically, 'Creole' was initially used to describe 'white' settlers (mostly French and Spanish) in the Caribbean who their European peers felt had spent so much time there that they had forgotten how to be proper gentlemen. Over time, the term was used to refer both to white Europeans and black populations born in the colonies.[56] However, to underscore the term's complex usage, 'Creole' is used to distinguish between Indians and blacks in Guyana and Trinidad. Creoles in this context are blacks. Hall further points out that 'Creole' has been defined as a kind of racial mixing in many dictionaries. He clarifies, though, the term has never really referred to mixing bloodlines but rather *cultural* mixing.[57] One particularly appealing – if implicit – feature about 'Creole' is that embedded within it, whiteness and blackness are imbricated with rather than external to conceptualizing the mixing that results in cultural formations such as the focus of this investigation: transnational South Asian art histories. Whiteness, in particular, is the unacknowledged ground of all racialized art histories. I explore the latter in more detail in all the chapters but especially Chapter 4.

In his expansive understanding of 'Creole', Martinican-born poet and theoretician Édouard Glissant refers to the term (as summarized by Hall) 'to describe the entanglement – or what he [Glissant] calls the "relation" – between different cultures forced into cohabitation in the colonial context'.[58] Glissant is referring to the shared space in which colonialists lived with slaves, indentured servants and their descendants.[59] Comparative literature scholar Mary Louise Pratt refers to these entanglements as 'contact zones', or 'social spaces where disparate cultures meet, clash and grapple with each other often in highly asymmetrical relations of domination and subordination.'[60] Indeed, power asymmetries are key to the 'relations' brokered between colonizer and colonized.[61] However, rather than characterizing the colonizer and colonized as binary, Hall conceptualizes them as 'mutually constituting' and ongoing or processual: one imprints on the other and vice versa.[62] He further notes that rather than 'newer and more contemporary cultural formation[s]' emerging from entanglement, the configuration brought about 'can no longer be disaggregated or restored to their originary forms, since they no longer exist in a "pure" state'.[63]

Hybridity often assumes that the components that created it can be segregated. The concept of entanglement, on the other hand, suggests that the components are not only *not* identifiable but are hybrid themselves given the ongoing flux associated with 'entanglement'. Glissant refers to the processual nature of 'entanglement' as 'creolization', the second term in the Platform's title. He distinguished between 'Creole' and creolization by noting the latter is constantly changing in contradistinction to the former. He also writes that creolization can refer to a broader set of sociocultural processes not only in the Caribbean but also 'all the world' (*tout-monde*).[64]

Irit Rogoff has proactively invoked the second term in the 'Platform' title *créolité* as an approach to visual cultural studies in her essay 'What Is a Theorist?'.[65] Martinican writers and intellectuals Jean Bernabé, Patrick Chamoiseau and Raphaël Confiant developed the concept of *créolité* in their 1989 manifesto 'Éloge de la Créolité' (translated in 1990 into English).[66] It specifically was meant to describe the cultural production in the French Caribbean. Drawing on Hall, however, Rogoff suggests that *créolité* can more broadly reference the construction of a literary or artistic project out of creolizing processes.[67] The transnational South Asian art history explored in this book can be considered such a project, I argue. Of course, the construction of this art history can never be complete given creolization is itself processual. Indeed, this monograph hopes to realize the potential of Rogoff's wish for visual culture – that I extend to art history – to become a 'field of complex and growing entanglements that can never be translated back to originary or constitutive components'.[68]

Writing creolizing transnational South Asian art histories means considering artworks by artists who are white, of South Asian descent and of African descent to be seen in one frame – not as equivalents but as entangled. These art histories exceed yet are not completely disconnected from notions of kinship or bloodlines or the construct of the nation-state. Art historian Donald Preziosi notes that 'style' has historically been tied to kinship.[69] He writes that the works act as 'surrogates or "*representations*" of connections or differences between their makers'.[70] Creolization demands that constructions of art history move away from that to which they have been historically tied: bloodlines and the nation. In addition, moving beyond kinship means moving beyond heteronormativity and reproduction. Indeed, Rogoff mobilizes creolization beyond race, ethnicity and nationality to consider gender and sexuality, both of which are important to my investigation.[71] While a creolizing approach makes visible transnational South Asian art histories beyond fixed notions of identity/genealogy, this does not imply that those histories chiefly concerned with artwork by artists of South Asian descent are retrograde. Rather, creolization demands a deeply relational and non-hierarchical approach to art histories, genealogical and otherwise.[72]

Finally, I am interested in creolizing transnational South Asian art histories that are 'both multiple and One, and inextricable'.[73] The latter is Glissant's explanation of 'globality' as distinct from the neo-imperialism of 'globalisation'. Per Glissant's logic, while these histories are multiple they are not necessarily mutually exclusive. Following his logic, strands of the multiple often intertwine and overlap and thereby cohere collectively around – but never quite approximate – the 'One', in this case a singular transnational South Asian art history.

Summaries of case studies

Chapter 2 explores authorship. In particular, I examine the writing about the work of Anish Kapoor, one of the most critically and commercially successful artists of Asian descent in the West. Kapoor's career has spanned nearly four decades and has spawned numerous reviews and critical essays; this archive provides an unprecedented opportunity to explore the shifting manner in which critics and art historians have identified him and his work. This case study is partly a critique of the facile categorization and Orientalist overtones of some of the writing on Kapoor's work. More importantly, I argue that the failure to locate Kapoor in any final or fixed way suggests a subtle but important shift in how art historians could write the histories of work by artists with complex genealogies such as his. Not only should they make their stakes clear in the framing of the work and thereby write contingent rather than fixed histories, but also acknowledge that their writing is influenced by their engagement with artworks and the sites in which they are encountered.

I focus on my identification as queer and South Asian American in Chapter 3 to put pressure on the coherency of an LGBTQI art history, a history of artworks by lesbian, gay, bisexual, trans*, questioning, queer and intersex-identified subjects, and an Asian American art history, a history of artworks by artists of Asian descent living in the United States.[74] To productively open up both of these art histories beyond social constructions of identity and genealogy, I focus on connecting formal similarities of abstract work produced in the 1960s in New York City by Cy Twombly and Natvar Bhavsar. Given the dominant interpretive models for post-Second World War art movements that emphasize form at the expense of inclusion of work by artists of Asian descent, this chapter also serves to reimagine this period in art history.

Chapter 4 explores the work of artists who have all mobilized subject matter in their artworks that could be read as 'South Asian', but none of whom are genealogically linked to the subcontinent. In particular, I explore whiteness, the unstable and invisible ground on which a transnational history of artworks by artists of South Asian descent is implicitly constructed. As an integral part of this discussion, I also expand the range of authors whose work I explore by considering whiteness's other: blackness. These artists are French-born, NYC (New York City)-based Stephen Dean; German-born and NYC- and Berlin-based Mario Pfeifer; NYC-born, Berlin-based Adrian Margaret Smith Piper; and Los Angeles-born, NYC-based Kehinde Wiley. Overall, I write an art history that disrupts and keeps in play facile categories such as South Asian/non-South Asian and non-white/white.

The second half of the book, from Chapter 5 onwards, slowly shifts from deconstruction that dominates the early chapters to what could be described as 'practice-led research': a shift from analyzing the work of others to producing curatorial projects that are then critically reflected upon. Chapter 5 focuses on space and site. It pivots partly around my experience of viewing the installation *Sphere:dreamz* in spring 2006 in Manchester, England – where I lived from 2005 to 2008. The work was produced by Sphere – a collective of Manchester-based, queer-identified South Asian women – and was strategically situated near Canal Street, the epicentre of the Gay Village, an area of the city with many gay bars and restaurants. The queer feminist transnational South Asian art history within which I write about the work of Sphere, I entangle with my own material exploration of the city's spaces – both the Gay Village and Curry Mile, an area of the city so named for its many South Asian restaurants and shops. Curry Mile is about a half-hour bus ride from the Gay Village. A motive for the writing of this chapter is the relative dearth of exploration of queer South Asian sexuality in artworks and art historical writing – including my own in the first half of the book, in which queer functions largely as a theory rather than as lived experience.

Chapter 6 focuses on practice-led research, or what might be referred to as curatorial knowledge-making. In particular, I discuss the multi-site exhibition *Mixing It Up: Queering Curry Mile and Currying Canal Street* in Manchester that I organized in 2007. I embed my discussion of the *Mixing It Up* art projects within my exploration of material culture – especially the civic marketing of art and culture of the Gay Village in comparison to that of Curry Mile. I also discuss audience and critical academic responses to the projects to explore where the projects might have failed as productive points of departure.

In my final case study, Chapter 7, I draw on various theories of affect to explore artworks and visual culture in connection to three historical events: the deaths of turban-wearing Sikhs misidentified as terrorists after the attacks of 11 September 2001 – known as '9/11' – in the United States; the death of Brazilian Jean Charles de Menezes, misidentified by British police as a terrorist shortly after the terrorist attacks of 7 July 2005 in London; and the death of teenager Trayvon Martin, misidentified as a criminal by George Zimmerman, in Sanford, Florida, in 2012.[75] I consider a public art memorial designed by London-based Mary Edwards to commemorate the death of Menezes, artworks by Kehinde Wiley and Adrian Margaret Smith Piper, and a cartoon by Los Angeles-based Carter Goodrich that appeared on the cover of *The New Yorker* shortly after the terrorist attacks of 9/11. I theorize how these disparate works might engender an ethical future across racial, ethnic and national lines. At stake in this chapter is the question of how certain subjects are considered as 'belonging' and others as not; and the role of art and writing in the reconstitution of notions of 'home' and thereby transnational South Asian art histories.

Notes

1 Raqs Media Collective, 'An Ephemeris, Corrected for the Longitudes of Tomorrow: Speculations on the Orbit and Motion of Objects and Processes in Contemporary Art Today and Tomorrow', in *Art History in the Wake of the Global Turn*, ed. Jill H. Casid and Aruna D'Souza, Clark Studies in the Visual Arts (Williamstown, MA: Sterling and Francine Clark Art Institute, 2014), 19. Raqs Media Collective is composed of Jeebesh Bagchi, Monica Narula and Shuddhabrata Sengupta.
2 Alpesh Kantilal Patel, 'Queer Desi Visual Culture Across the "Brown Atlantic"' (PhD dissertation, Manchester University, 2009). See Chapter 2.
3 Jacques Derrida, *Of Grammatology* (Baltimore: Johns Hopkins University Press, 1976), 144–5. In French, *supplément* means both 'an addition' and 'a substitute'. See ibid., xiii.
4 'Raqs Media Collective', artist website, *Raqs Media Collective*, accessed 13 January 2016, http://raqsmediacollective.net/.
5 Raqs Media Collective, 'An Ephemeris'.
6 Gavin Butt, 'Introduction: The Paradoxes of Criticism', in *After Criticism: New Responses to Art and Performance*, ed. Gavin Butt (Malden, MA: Blackwell, 2005), 5.
7 Ibid., 11.
8 Historian Hayden White has noted that all histories are narratives of some kind. Also, that the key difference between fiction and history is that historians insist they are presenting truth. Hayden White, 'Historiography and Historiophoty', *The American Historical Review* 93, no. 5 (December 1988): 1193–9.
9 Emphasis in original. Michael F. Zimmermann, 'Introduction', in *The Art Historian: National Traditions and Institutional Practices*, ed. Michael F. Zimmermann (Williamstown, MA: Sterling and Francine Clark Art Institute, 2003), xx. The volume is based on the eponymously titled Sterling and Francine Clark

Art Institute conference organized by Michael Ann Holly and Mariët Westermann in May 2002. Drawing on art historian Eric Fernie's scholarship, Zimmermann writes that 'even not analysis, but questions are in the center of that insecure discipline which is art history.' See Eric Fernie, 'The History of Art and Archaeology in England Now', in Zimmermann, *The Art Historian*, 160–6.

10 Zimmermann, 'Introduction', xix.

11 Ibid.

12 Ibid.

13 Gayatri Gopinath, *Impossible Desires: Queer Diasporas and South Asian Public Cultures* (Durham, NC: Duke University Press, 2005), 70. Desai fleshed out her use of the 'Brown Atlantic' in her book *Beyond Bollywood*, but she first mentioned it two years earlier in Jigna Desai, 'Homo on the Range: Mobile and Global Sexualities', *Social Text* 20, no. 4 (2002): 86 (note 6).

14 Paul Gilroy, *The Black Atlantic: Modernity and Double Consciousness* (Cambridge, MA: Harvard University Press, 1993).

15 Ibid., 4.

16 See Timmy Lott, 'Black Cultural Politics: An Interview with Paul Gilroy', *Found Object* 4 (1994): 56–7. Of course, the genealogy of diaspora is already deeply intertwined with that of Gilroy's Black Atlantic. Explaining further the distinction between 'diaspora' and 'Black Atlantic', Gilroy says: 'Very often the concept of diaspora has been used to say, "Hooray! We can rewind the tape of history, we can get back to the original moment of our dispersal!" I'm saying something quite different. That's why I didn't call the book diaspora anything. I called it *Black Atlantic* because I wanted to say, "If this is a diaspora, then it's a very particular kind of diaspora. It's a diaspora that can't be reversed."' As American literature scholar Jonathan Elmer suggests, Gilroy's Black Atlantic has proven to be influential in academic scholarship not necessarily for sharpening the concept of diaspora, but for loosening the structures that define it. Jonathan Elmer, 'The Black Atlantic Archive', *American Literary History* 17 no. 1 (2005): 161.

17 I am referring to the exploration of the Lusophone Black Atlantic by the Centre for the Study of Brazilian Culture and Society, King's College, London. See the centre's homepage (accessed 26 September 2011) at www.clba.kcl.ac.uk/index.html.

18 Gopinath, *Impossible Desires*, 70.

19 I am specifying which sector of the 'Brown Atlantic' space I explore to avoid one of the most salient criticisms of Gilroy's mode: that it slips into *homogenisation* of interregional diasporas – and thereby conflates the diverse genealogical histories of various black diasporas. See Paul Tiyambe Zeleza, 'Rewriting the African Diaspora: Beyond the Black Atlantic', *African Affairs* 104, no. 14 (2005): 35–68; Laura Chrisman, 'Re-Thinking Black Atlanticism', *The Black Scholar* 30, nos 3/4 (Fall 2000): 12–18. Indeed, the movement of South Asians to the Caribbean as indentured servants is radically different from those who freely moved to England or the United States.

20 Gilroy, *The Black Atlantic*, 133. I have left out travelling through some of the states of the former Eastern Bloc (Estonia, Latvia, Ukraine and primarily

Poland) in the autumn of 2015 as part of a Fulbright grant. I finished much of the final writing on this monograph in these countries (which undoubtedly impacted my writing process) but the research for the book had been largely completed prior to the start of the grant period so I leave this particular 'route' off the list.

21 Amelia Jones and Andrew Stephenson, 'Introduction', in *Performing the Body/Performing the Text*, ed. Amelia Jones and Andrew Stephenson (London; New York: Routledge, 1999), 2–3.

22 Ibid., 3, 9 (footnote 7).

23 Ibid., 3. Of particular note in Jones and Stephenson's volume are the contributions of Jennifer DeVere Brody, Michael Hatt and Reina Lewis, who suggest how race, ethnicity and gender have been suppressed in modernist art historical and critical literature; see Jennifer DeVere Brody, 'Shading Meaning', in *Performing the Body/Performing the Text*, ed. Amelia Jones and Andrew Stephenson (London; New York: Routledge, 1999), 89–106; Michael Hatt, 'Race, Ritual and Responsibility: Performativity and the Southern Lynching', in *Performing the Body/Performing the Text*, ed. Amelia Jones and Andrew Stephenson (London; New York: Routledge, 1999), 76–88; and Reina Lewis, 'Cross-Cultural Reiterations: Demetra Vaka Brown and the Performance of Racialized Female Beauty', in *Performing the Body/Performing the Text*, ed. Amelia Jones and Andrew Stephenson (London; New York: Routledge, 1999), 56–75.

24 Michael Schreyach, 'The Recovery of Criticism', in *The State of Art Criticism*, ed. James Elkins and Michael Newman (New York: Routledge, 2007), 9–10.

25 Nancy K. Miller, *Getting Personal: Feminist Occasions and Other Autobiographical Acts* (New York: Routledge, 1991), 24, as quoted in Keith Moxey, *The Practice of Persuasion: Paradox and Power in Art History* (Ithaca and London: Cornell University Press, 2001), 138.

26 Roland Barthes, *Roland Barthes by Roland Barthes*, trans. Richard Howard (New York: Hill & Wang, 1977). Originally published in French (Paris: Seuil, 1975).

27 Emphasis in original. Barthes, *Roland Barthes by Roland Barthes*, 152.

28 Kimberlé Crenshaw, 'Mapping the Margins: Intersectionality, Identity Politics, and Violence Against Women of Color', in *The Public Nature of Private Violence: The Discovery of Domestic Abuse*, ed. Martha Albertson Fineman and Roxanne Mykitiuk (New York: Routledge, 1994), 94.

29 Jasbir K. Puar, '"I Would Rather Be a Cyborg than a Goddess": Intersectionality, Assemblage, and Affective Politics', European Institute for Progressive Cultural Policies, *Transversal* (2011), http://eipcp.net/transversal/0811/puar/en.

30 Ibid.

31 Ibid.

32 Emphasis mine. Ibid.

33 Emphasis in original. Butt, 'Introduction: The Paradoxes of Criticism', 7.

34 Jane Rendell, *Site-Writing: The Architecture of Art Criticism* (London; New York: I.B. Tauris, 2010), 1.

35 Ibid.

36 The asterisk refers to all transgender, non-binary and gender non-conforming identities.
37 See Amelia Jones, 'Introduction', in *Otherwise: Imagining Queer Feminist Art Histories*, ed. Amelia Jones and Erin Silver (Manchester: Manchester University Press, 2016), 1.
38 Alice Y. Hom and David L. Eng (eds), 'Transnational Sexualities: South Asian (Trans)national(alism)s and Queer Diasporas', in *Q & A Queer in Asian America* (Philadelphia: Temple University Press, 1998), 409.
39 In seeking to redress that lacuna, this project makes use of the scholarship of women of colour (such as that of Gopinath, as well as that of Cherríe Moraga and Gloria E. Anzaldúa) that stretches back to the late 1970s and early 1980s, and that 'insistently situated lesbian sexuality within a feminist, racist, and anticolonial framework', as Gopinath writes. See Gopinath, *Impossible Desires*, 198 (note 43). See also Cherríe Moraga and Gloria Anzaldúa (eds), *This Bridge Called My Back: Writings by Radical Women of Color*, 2nd edn (New York: Kitchen Table, Women of Color Press, 1983).
40 Kath Browne, Sally R. Munt and Andrew K. T. Yip, *Queer Spiritual Spaces: Sexuality and Sacred Places* (Farnham and Burlington, VT: Ashgate, 2010), http://public.eblib.com/choice/publicfullrecord.aspx?p=513923.
41 For instance, see her astute readings of the work of artists Chitra Ganesh and Allan de Souza: Gayatri Gopinath, 'Archive, Affects, and the Everyday: Queer Diasporic Re-Visions', in *Political Emotions*, ed. Janet Staiger, Ann Cvetkovich and Ann Morris Reynolds (New York: Routledge, 2010), 165–92; Gayatri Gopinath, 'Chitra Ganesh's Queer Re-Visions', *GLQ: A Journal of Lesbian and Gay Studies* 15, no. 3 (1 January 2009): 469–80, doi:10.1215/10642684-2008-032. Also see her analysis of the 2004 Malayalam-language (official state language in Kerala, India) film *Sancharram* (directed and produced by US-based Ligy J. Pullappally): Gayatri Gopinath, 'Queer Regions: Locating Lesbians in *Sancharram*', in *A Companion to Lesbian, Gay, Bisexual, Transgender, and Queer Studies*, ed. George E. Haggerty and Molly McGarry (Malden, MA; Oxford: Blackwell, 2007), 341–54.
42 Before listing samples of this literature, it is worth noting that the 'global' in the global turn in art history tends to imply a spatial one beyond Euro-America, but those artists supposedly connected to this expanded space can be found within Euro-America as part of disparate kinds of diaspora: Thomas DaCosta Kaufmann, Catherine Dossin and Béatrice Joyeux-Prunel (eds), *Circulations in the Global History of Art*, Studies in Art Historiography (Farnham and Burlington, VT: Ashgate, 2015); Jill H. Casid and Aruna D'Souza (eds), *Art History in the Wake of the Global Turn*, Clark Studies in the Visual Arts (Williamstown, MA: Sterling and Francine Clark Art Institute, 2014); Parul Dave Mukerji, 'Whither Art History in a Globalizing World', *The Art Bulletin* 96, no. 2 (2014): 151–5; Hans Belting, Andrea Buddensieg and Peter Weibel (eds), *The Global Contemporary and the Rise of New Art Worlds* (Karlsruhe, Germany ZKM/Center for Art and Media; Cambridge, MA; London; The MIT Press, 2013); Saloni Mathur (ed.), *The Migrant's Time: Rethinking Art History*

and Diaspora (Williamstown, MA: Sterling and Francine Clark Art Institute, 2011); James Elkins, Zhivka Valiavicharska, and Alice Kim (eds), *Art and Globalization*, The Stone Art Theory Institutes, v. 1 (University Park, PA: Pennsylvania State University Press, 2010); Hans Belting, Andrea Buddensieg and Emanoel Araújo (eds), *The Global Art World: Audiences, Markets, and Museums* (Ostfildern, Germany: Hatje Cantz, 2009); Kitty Zijlmans and Wilfried Van Damme (eds), *World Art Studies: Exploring Concepts and Approaches* (Amsterdam: Valiz, 2008); James Elkins (ed.), *Is Art History Global?*, Art Seminar 3 (New York and London: Routledge, 2007); James Elkins and Michael Newman (eds), *The State of Art Criticism* (New York: Routledge, 2007); John Onians (ed.), *Compression vs. Expression: Containing and Explaining the World's Art* (Williamstown, MA: Sterling and Francine Clark Art Institute, 2006); Michael F. Zimmermann (ed.), *The Art Historian: National Traditions and Institutional Practices* (Williamstown, MA: Sterling and Francine Clark Art Institute, 2003); and David Summers, *Real Spaces: World Art History and the Rise of Western Modernism* (London; New York: Phaidon Press, 2003).

43 Marsha Meskimmon and Dorothy C. Rowe (eds), *Women, the Arts and Globalization: Eccentric Experience* (Manchester: Manchester University Press, 2013). See also the catalogue accompanying the eponymously titled exhibition: Maura Reilly and Linda Nochlin (eds), *Global Feminisms: New Directions in Contemporary Art* (London; New York: Merrell, 2007). Art historian Aruna D'Souza argues that feminist art histories were often always already concerned with the global and cites Griselda Pollock as an early 'important voice' in this regard. See Aruna D'Souza, 'Introduction', in *Art History in the Wake of the Global Turn*, ed. Jill H. Casid and Aruna D'Souza, Clark Studies in the Visual Arts (Williamstown, MA: Sterling and Francine Clark Art Institute, 2014), xxii (note 8); Griselda Pollock (ed.), *Generations and Geographies in the Visual Arts: Feminist Readings* (London; New York: Routledge, 1996).

44 Meskimmon and Rowe, *Women, the Arts and Globalization*, 1.

45 D'Souza, 'Introduction', x.

46 For more information, see Kieran Connell and Matthew Hilton, 'The Working Practices of Birmingham's Centre for Contemporary Cultural Studies', *Social History* 40, no. 3 (3 July 2015): 287–311, doi:10.1080/03071022.2015.1043191.

47 Irit Rogoff, 'What Is a Theorist?', in *The State of Art Criticism*, ed. James Elkins and Michael Newman (New York: Routledge, 2007), 98.

48 Marsha Meskimmon, *Contemporary Art and the Cosmopolitan Imagination* (London; New York: Routledge, 2011); Jill Bennett, *Practical Aesthetics: Events, Affects and Art after 9/11* (London; New York: I.B. Tauris, 2012), in preface.

49 Emphasis in original. Stuart Hall, 'Maps of Emergency: Fault Lines and Tectonic Plates', in *Fault Lines: Contemporary African Art and Shifting Landscapes*, ed. Gilane Tawadros and Sarah Campbell (London: Institute of International Visual Arts, Forum for African Arts, Prince Claus Fund Library, 2003), 34.

50 Okwui Enwezor et al. (eds), *Créolité and Creolization: Documenta11_Platform3* (Ostfildern-Ruit, Germany: Hatje Cantz, 2003).

51 The proceedings for the Clark conference can be found in Zimmermann, *The Art Historian*.
52 Participants of Platform 3 included Petrine Archer-Straw, Jean Bernabé, Robert Chaudenson, Juan Flores, Stuart Hall, Isaac Julien, Dame Pearlette Louisy, Jean-Claude Carpanin Marimoutou, Gerardo Mosquera, Annie Paul, Virginia Pérez-Ratton, Ginette Ramassamy, Françoise Vergès and Derek Walcott. Among those invited to 'The Art Historian: National Traditions and Institutional Practices' were Mieke Bal, Stephen Bann, Horst Bredekamp, H. Perry Chapman, Georges Didi-Huberman, Eric Fernie, Françoise Forster-Hahn, Carlo Ginzburg, Charles W. Haxthausen, Karen Michels, Willibald Sauerländer, Alain Schnapp and Michael F. Zimmermann.
53 Okwui Enwezor et al. (eds), 'Introduction', in *Créolité and Creolization: Documenta11_Platform3* (Ostfildern-Ruit, Germany: Hatje Cantz, 2003), 16. In the book edited by Michael F. Zimmermann that was published a year after the conference, he does cite Enwezor's *Documenta 11*. See Zimmermann, 'Introduction', xxii (note 9).
54 Stuart Hall, 'Créolité and the Process of Creolization', in *Creolizing Europe: Legacies and Transformations*, ed. Encarnación Gutiérrez Rodríguez and Shirley Anne Tate (Liverpool: Liverpool University Press, 2015), 14.
55 Dominique Chancé, 'Creolization: Definition and Critique', in *The Creolization of Theory*, ed. Françoise Lionnet and Shu-mei Shih, trans. Julin Everett (Durham, NC: Duke University Press, 2011), 262.
56 Hall, 'Créolité and the Process of Creolization', 14.
57 Emphasis in original. Ibid.
58 Ibid., 15.
59 For a useful gloss on the development and use of the word 'Creole', see Encarnación Gutiérrez Rodríguez and Shirley Anne Tate, 'Introduction: Creolizing Europe: Legacies and Transformations', in *Creolizing Europe: Legacies and Transformations*, ed. Encarnación Gutiérrez Rodríguez and Shirley Anne Tate (Liverpool: Liverpool University Press, 2015), 3–4.
60 Mary Louise Pratt, *Imperial Eyes: Travel Writing and Transculturation* (London: Routledge, 1992), 4. As cited in Hall, 'Créolité and the Process of Creolization', 31.
61 Hall, 'Créolité and the Process of Creolization', 16.
62 Ibid., 15.
63 Ibid., 31.
64 Édouard Glissant, *Traité du Tout-Monde* (Paris: Gallimard, 1997).
65 Rogoff, 'What Is a Theorist?', 108–9. Two years later in 2009, she integrates her writing on creolization in this essay into her larger analysis of the work of Kutlug Ataman. See Irit Rogoff, 'De-Regulation: With the Work of Kutlug Ataman', *Third Text* 23, no. 2 (2009): 179.
66 Jean Bernabé, Patrick Chamoiseau, and Raphaël Confiant, 'In Praise of Creoleness', ed. and trans. Mohamed B. Taleb Khyar, *Callaloo* 13, no. 4 (1990): 886, doi:10.2307/2931390.
67 Rogoff, 'De-Regulation', 179. See also Hall, 'Créolité and the Process of Creolization', 20.

68 Rogoff, 'What Is a Theorist?', 109.
69 Donald Preziosi, *The Art of Art History: A Critical Anthology*, 2nd edn (Oxford and New York: Oxford University Press, 2009), 578.
70 Emphasis in original. Ibid.
71 Rogoff, 'What Is a Theorist?', 108–9.
72 Creolization as an approach, I believe, can be productively mobilized to collapse other binaries, such as Global North/South or Eastern/Western Europe that are not explored in this book. As an example, consider art historian Piotr Piotrowski's compelling essay that examines links between Eastern Europe and Latin American art histories that in turn confuse either as discrete. Piotr Piotrowski, 'The Global NETwork: An Approach to Comparative Art History', in *Circulations in the Global History of Art*, ed. Thomas DaCosta Kaufmann, Catherine Dossin, and Béatrice Joyeux-Prunel, Studies in Art Historiography (Farnham and Burlington, VT: Ashgate, 2015), 149–65. Though he does not mention creolization, his expanded approach to regional art histories is similar to my own. Piotrowski does not suggest that transregional art histories should replace the constructions of art histories that are more regionally bounded, but that they should be seen as intertwined or entangled with them. Unfortunately, Piotrowski passed away before being able to fully expand on the ideas he presents. I am thankful to him for giving a lecture on a version of this essay for me and my students who were studying 'Eastern European' art in the summer of 2014 as part of a study abroad trip I organized.
73 Édouard Glissant, *La cohée du Lamentin* (Paris: Gallimard, 2005), 15, as quoted in Jane Hiddleston, *Understanding Postcolonialism* (London; New York: Routledge, 2014), 146. First published in 2009.
74 I do not mean to elide the vertical, differential power dynamics among these categorical identifications that my horizontal listing of them might signify.
75 More than 2,600 people died at the World Trade Center in New York City and 125 died at the Pentagon in Washington, DC. An additional 256 died on the four hijacked planes. The death toll surpassed that of Pearl Harbor in December 1941, previously the largest loss of life suffered by the United States in a foreign attack on US soil. See National Commission on Terrorist Attacks Upon the United States, 'Executive Summary of "9/11 Commission Report: Final Report of the National Commission on Terrorist Attacks Upon the United States"', accessed 22 July 2004, www.9-11commission.gov/report/911Report_Exec.pdf.

2 Authorship: Anish Kapoor as British/Asian/artist

> I'm Indian. My sensibility is Indian. And I welcome that, rejoice in that, but the great battle nowadays is to occupy an aesthetic territory that isn't linked to nationality. (Anish Kapoor)[1]

> Being an artist is more than being an Indian artist. I feel supportive to that kind of endeavour … it needs to happen once; I hope it is never necessary again. (Anish Kapoor)[2]

Both the statements above are by India-born, England-based artist Anish Kapoor. The first was made during the opening ceremony of his first solo exhibition in India in 2010. He diplomatically notes that he is not ashamed of his Indian heritage while simultaneously indicating his desire for his work to have meaning outside of his Indianness. Of course, this is not very different from the well-known second statement that he made in 1989, when he declined to be a part of the seminal exhibition *The Other Story: Afro-Asian Artists in Post-War Britain*, organized in 1989 by artist, critic and curator Rasheed Araeen at the Hayward Gallery in London. In the context of the insistent focus of critics and historians on his genealogy in a way that does not happen for other superstar artists such as Damien Hirst or Jeff Koons, one can certainly understand Kapoor's anxieties and wishes.[3] The key difference between the two statements is that in the more recent one Kapoor is only partly on the defensive. He is in fact fashioning his identity as 'Indian' rather than responding to someone else's categorization of him as he did in 1989. This, in itself, indicates the plasticity of authorship and calls into question the coherency and legibility of the artist or 'author' that implicitly underpins a conventional history of artworks of artists of South Asian descent.

To reveal the slipperiness rather than the stability and knowability of the author, I hone in on the criticism of Anish Kapoor's artworks. Kapoor is one of the most critically and commercially successful artists of Asian descent in the West. His career has spanned nearly four decades and has spawned numerous reviews and critical essays; this archive provides an unprecedented opportunity to explore the shifting manner in which critics have identified him.

Unshackling the author's assumed stable stronghold allows for other kinds of art histories to be written, examples of which follow this chapter. Of course, this does not mean that we should no longer build histories based on genealogy or that those critics and historians who maintain more essentialized identifications as a means of productive political agency do not produce generative criticism and histories. Rather, the failure to locate Kapoor in any final or fixed way suggests a subtle but important shift in how art historians and critics might write the histories of works by artists with complex genealogies such as his. In particular, they can make their stakes clear in the framing of the work and thereby write always already contingent rather than fixed histories. I acknowledge this is not always possible – for instance in the context of a short review – but by doing so there is less a likelihood of fixing the author in the very ways that Kapoor above bemoans – rightly so – and even anticipates. In this way, I would reframe Kapoor's statements and direct them to art historians and critics as follows: the 'great battle' is not to ensure that his works occupy an aesthetic territory delinked from nationality – though the subtext that it be free of Orientalist overtones is right on target – but to make explicit that his works are always already and overtly linked to the complex web of national, faith-based, queer, gendered and other *provisional* identifications of those critics and historians who write about his works and who they believe Kapoor is.

I want to trace how Kapoor has been identified and the effects of these identifications on the purported meaning of his works before moving forward in the following chapters to implement different ways of writing art history. In particular, I focus on the constructions of Kapoor as 'Indian' in the early to mid-1980s period, 'British Asian' in the late 1980s to mid-1990s, just an artist – or effectively a 'white' or colourless one – in the late 1990s to mid-2000s period and 'Indian' (again) in the late 2000s, when he had his first exhibition in India. To theorize the copious writings on Kapoor's works, French philosopher Michel Foucault's elaboration of a 'discursive formation' as a '*general system of the formation and transformation of statements*' is appropriate to invoke.[4] Foucault notes that the 'statement' is a discrete unit of discourse that 'enters various networks and various fields of use and is integrated into operations and strategies in which its identification is maintained or effaced'.[5] I explore 'various networks' – composed of critics and academics – and their art criticism and art historical scholarship as 'fields of use'. (For the sake of polemics, I am leaving aside the fact that art criticism and art historical scholarship are governed by different expectations. The latter is often blind peer-reviewed, for instance, and includes citations. The former is often constrained by low word counts.) Together, I argue that these networks and fields of use create a complex web of 'operations and strategies' in which the signification, or identification, of Kapoor's artworks is 'maintained or effaced'.

Though perhaps old-fashioned, there is no better way to cut to the core of the issue – that there is no stable author – than invoking Foucault. At the same time, Foucault's discourse theory is incredibly useful in thinking through how Kapoor's works have been taken up in art criticism and art historical writing, but his theory is less useful for thinking about how we might practice art history and move beyond negative critique. The rest of the book increasingly becomes concerned with addressing this point. In the following, I explore the criticism of Kapoor's works chronologically from the early 1980s to the recent present.

Space of place: India

Kapoor first came to prominence in the early 1980s when he exhibited in the 40th Venice Biennale's Aperto in 1982, along with a group of other British sculptors to whose work the label New British Sculpture has often been applied.[6] In the early years of his career, Kapoor simultaneously drew on Arte Povera in his use of 'poor' materials, as well as Indian, or more specifically Hindu, cultural history. He indicated that a visit to India in 1979 during which he saw piles of raw pigment being sold for temple rituals was a source of inspiration for the use of pigments in his early brightly coloured, floor-based sculptures.[7] For instance, he arranged mounds of coloured, raw pigments in a series of artworks from 1979 to 1980, each one known as *1000 Names* – a tangential reference to the multi-named Hindu deity Krishna (Plate 1 and Figures 2.1–4).

These powder pieces were included in one of Kapoor's early exhibitions, *British Sculpture Now*, in 1982 at the Kunstmuseum Luzern in Switzerland. Organized by Martin Kunz, the exhibition also included fellow New British Sculpture artists Stephen Cox, Tony Cragg, Richard Deacon and Bill Woodrow. In Kunz's introductory essay for the accompanying catalogue, he enfolded the sculptural practice of Cragg and Woodrow into 'the method of the Nouveaux Réalistes in the '60s and all its variations in the '70s', placed Deacon in the 'formal world of the '50s' and associated Cox with 'the stonework that was still widespread in the '50s'. However, Kapoor's practice was not conceptually placed within broader Western art historical movements or styles as the other artists were. Instead, Kunz located Kapoor's artworks geographically outside of the West, citing 'Kapoor's references to Indian culture that enjoyed such popularity in the '70s among the occidental devotees of the orient with their "individual mythologies"'.[8]

This tendency to displace the artworks of Kapoor – and, indeed, those of other artists with complex genealogies – to the space of place, or effectively outside the West, did not abate anytime soon. Even in 1989 – seven years after the *British Sculpture Now* exhibition – this was effectively the curatorial

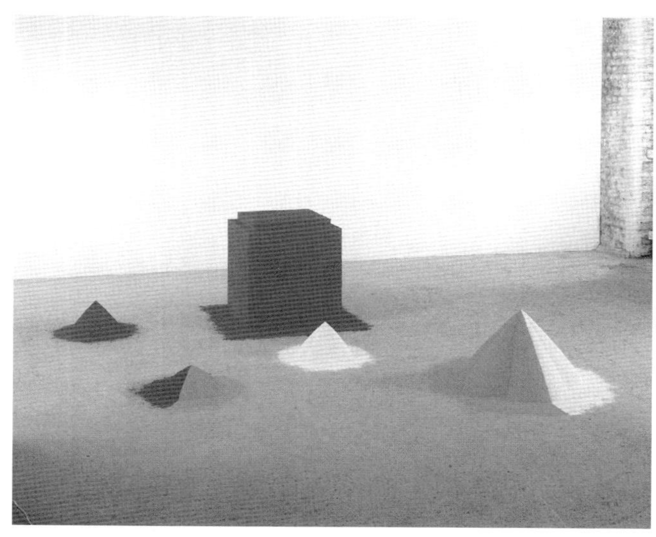

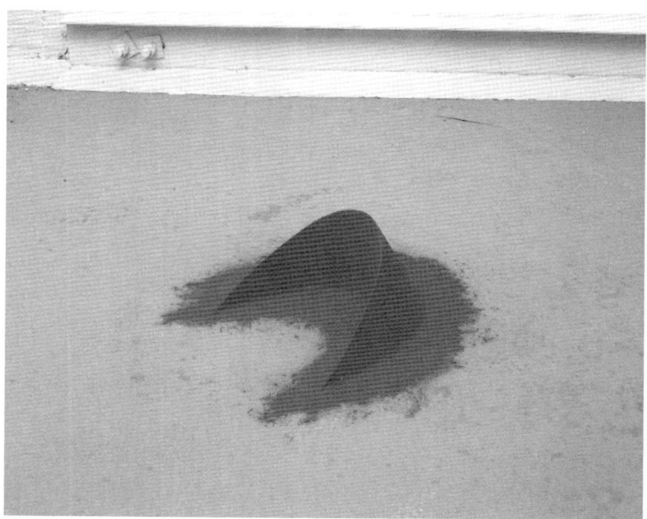

2.1–4 Anish Kapoor, *1000 Names*, 1979–80. Wood, gesso and pigment, dimensions variable.

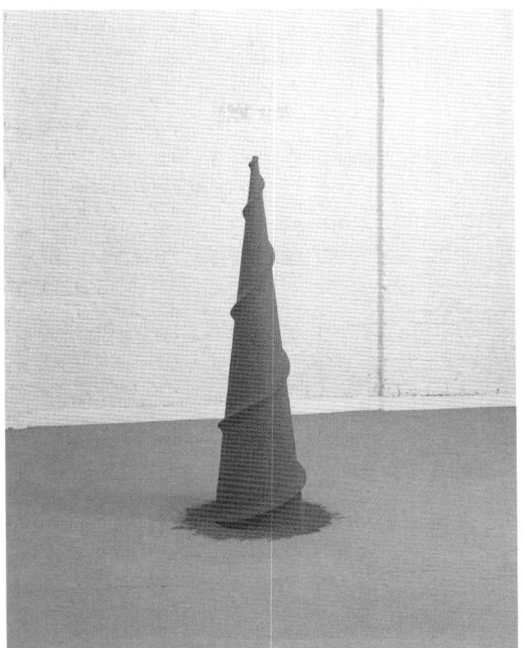

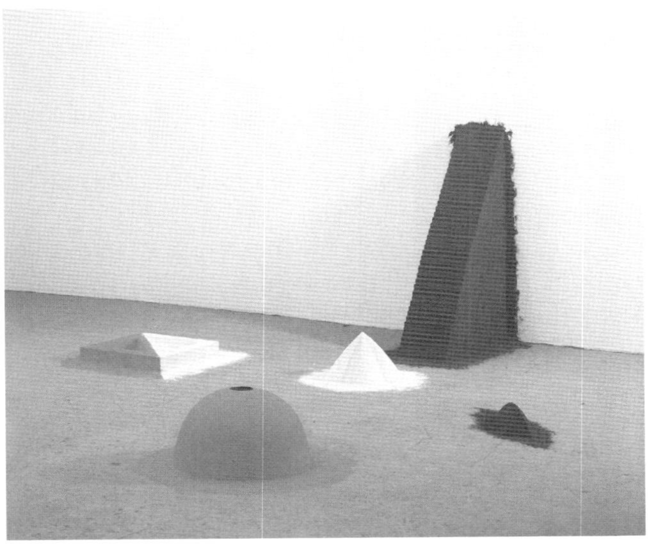

2.1–4

Continued

strategy of the exhibition *Magiciens de la terre* at the Musée National d'Art Moderne, Centre Georges Pompidou in Paris.[9] I briefly discuss this important but flawed exhibition before returning to examining the criticism of Kapoor's work. The exhibition included contemporary artworks produced by artists based in countries outside the 'developed' world in dialogue with Western artworks.[10] Signalling the promise the exhibition held, two of its catalogue authors were postcolonial theorist Homi Bhabha and critic Thomas McEvilley, who also wrote the catalogue's 'keynote statement'.[11] However, art critic Jeremy Lewison best sums up the reception of the exhibition when he notes that *Magiciens* was 'one of the most thought-provoking exhibitions of this decade [1980s] because it demonstrates the shallowness of our knowledge of art and our arrogant occidental attitudes'.[12] Lewison's statement reflects the sobering fact that not only was the Musée National d'Art Moderne the sole mainstream museum in the West attempting to address the xenophobia of the art world but also that the curators failed to effectively address the issues they set out to tackle. Indeed, after the exhibition opened, McEvilley amended his support for the exhibition by indicating that he believed in only the 'premises, not the details of the curation'.[13] More specifically, the inclusion of artworks by Western-based artists from diasporic communities in *Magiciens* was minimal. Of the five artists of South Asian descent in the exhibition, only one – Pakistan-born, UK-based artist Rasheed Araeen – did not live and work on the subcontinent. The design of the exhibition catalogue itself recalled the oversized format of an atlas, with the list of artists in the table of contents titled, tellingly, 'Atlas des 100 artistes exposés'.[14] Each artist's spread included a map situating them within one specific geographical location. The catalogue merely served to literally map out the differences between centre and margin, rather than collapse, or at least question, the divide.

Returning to critical writing on Kapoor's works in the early 1980s, it is worth noting that critics and historians did not completely eschew incorporating discussions of his formal concerns, which were otherwise not addressed in Kunz's essay in the *British Sculpture Now* catalogue. However, they were often subsumed, rather than expunged completely, and the critiques revealed a Western exceptionalism. For example, art historian and critical theorist Michael Newman's essay on Kapoor's artworks in the *British Sculpture Now* catalogue indicates that 'while there is an Indian source for the use of powder and the world view which informs these sculptures, they have also absorbed the principle of modern abstract painting and sculpture, that meaning can be created through immediate perceptual experience'.[15] However, Newman's insinuation that Kapoor's artworks absorbed 'the principle' that meaning created through 'immediate perceptual experience' is something of which 'modern abstract painting and sculpture' can claim sole ownership is suspect. Furthermore, though Newman places Kapoor's artworks in dialogue with

Western artistic traditions, he does so only by situating Kapoor's sculptures as being informed by an essential 'Indian source' and 'world view'. Newman's essay also contains numerous references to Hindu deities, such as Kali, Parvati, Siva and Krishna. For instance, he explains that Kapoor's use of the colour blue alludes to the Hindu deity Krishna. Newman does caution, though, that we should not interpret this 'in a one-to-one way'.[16] The comments by Newman, as well as those by Kunz cited previously, are representative of a broader tendency in the critical writing of the early to mid-1980s to hardly consider Kapoor's artworks outside of the artist's South Asianness.

In the 1980s, Kapoor's artworks were also frequently described as 'exotic' – a more explicit example of the troubling Orientalist overtones embedded in Newman's and Kunz's comments above. For instance, critic Richard Shone writes in a review of a contemporary British sculpture exhibition, in 1986, that 'Anish Kapoor, as might be expected, looked extraordinarily exotic.'[17] Shone's shorthand use of the artist's name for the artwork also has the unfortunate consequence of making it appear as if 'exotic' describes both the artwork and the artist.

Kapoor's biography reveals a much more complex cultural identity formation than 'South Asian' or 'Indian' implies. Kapoor was born in India in 1954 to an Iraqi mother who was Jewish and an Indian father who was 'anti-Hindu', according to Kapoor.[18] He grew up in a traditional Jewish household and was the only non-Hindu in school. After turning seventeen, he lived in Israel on a kibbutz for two years before finally arriving in the UK in 1973 to go to art school.[19] Kapoor has also indicated that he has an interest in a broad range of religions – such as Hinduism, Judaism, Christianity and Buddhism – and in spirituality more generally.[20] However, his mixed ethnic, faith-based and national background has remained largely unexplored in most critical writings about his artistic practice.

Rather than implying that the true meaning of Kapoor's art can be found in the details of his biography, I am more interested in fleshing out why his Indianness overwhelms other facets of his identity in the aforementioned criticism of his artworks. Sociologist Avery Gordon's theorization of 'diversity management' to describe a corporation's *attempt* towards racial and gender parity is instructive. Gordon indicates that diversity management could become nothing more than 'corporate multiculturalism'.[21] In other words, the company's larger interests would streamline the complex manner in which faith, sexuality, nationality, class, race and gender inform each other. In the early to mid-1980s, multiculturalism largely translated into difference as singular and homogeneous. The Euro-American art world could not synthesize Kapoor's complex artistic, national, ethnic and faith-based identity. Instead, it flattened the latter, ironically, in the name of 'diversity'. It is useful to invoke Foucault's author-function, which describes a 'complex operation whose purpose is to construct the rational entity we call an author.'[22] According to Foucault, Kapoor's 'Indianness' as an author-function maintains uniformity precisely through a process that 'neutralize[s] the contradictions' that may emerge from considering identity as heterogeneous.[23] Highlighting Kapoor's multiple identifications would have necessarily unravelled the arbitrariness of the structures that maintained the 'invisible [Western and white-dominated] center' of the art world.[24]

British Asian

An essay by Thomas McEvilley signalled an important shift in the critical writing about Kapoor's artworks during the early 1990s. McEvilley framed Kapoor's artworks as British, rather than Indian, and he did so without eliding their connection to British colonialism. Instead of his Indianness, Kapoor's British Asianness was emphasized. For instance, McEvilley notes that Kapoor reworks modernism – 'an ideology that incorporated India, and of course many other places, as fixtures of Empire' – as a source 'from which new expressions of cultural identity – *British* cultural identity! – might arise.'[25] McEvilley adds that 'the codes of the colonized and colonizing cultures' in Kapoor's artworks are blurred, creating a 'utopian glimpse' of the future.[26]

McEvilley also places Kapoor's use of powder in a dialectic with that of Western artists such as Yves Klein, but without implying that Kapoor's artworks merely 'absorbed the principle of modern abstract painting and sculpture', as Newman wrote in his essay.[27] The fact that McEvilley relegates information that connects the colour blue to the Hindu deity Krishna to a footnote is indicative of the shifting relative importance of Kapoor's Indianness in comparison to his British Asianness.[28] In fact, McEvilley avoids connecting Kapoor's artworks to any one specific faith at all, opting instead for language that is best described as metaphysical. For instance, he draws parallels with Yves Klein's belief that powdered colour represents spirit and suggests that blue is an indicator of 'transcendence and the absolute' and the 'vaporous mist of the sublime.'[29] In addition to broadening the reading of Kapoor's artworks by incorporating postcolonial theory, he also introduces psychoanalysis.[30]

It is worthwhile to point out that by the early 1990s, Kapoor's artistic practice had shifted from using pigment to primarily deploying stone. For instance, *Void Field* (1990) consisted of sixteen blocks of stone, purposefully left unfinished, with holes sunk about an inch or two into the stone and coated with black pigment (Figures 2.5–6). In other words, the bright colours and pigment – which Kapoor admitted 'on the face of it … looked more Indian than some of the things I'm doing now' – had given way to a rougher, more sombre aesthetic.[31] Nonetheless, as McEvilley's rereading of Kapoor's earlier powder artworks through a postcolonial lens above suggests, the shift in the reception

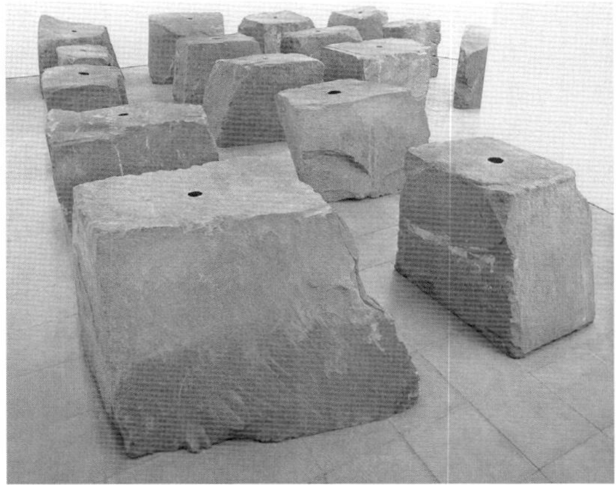
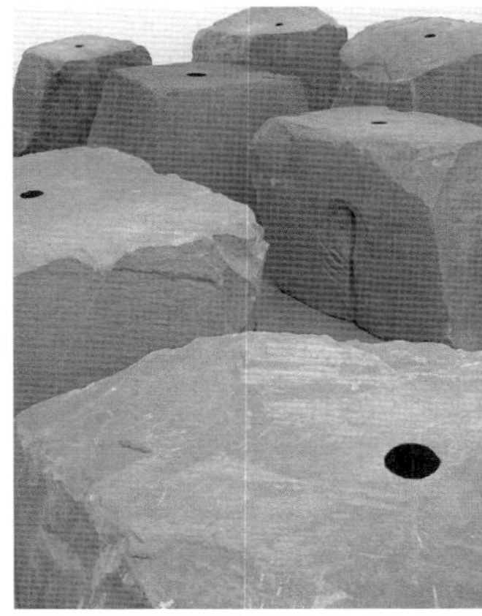

Anish Kapoor, *Void Field*, 1990. Sandstone and pigment, dimensions variable. **2.5–6**

of Kapoor's artworks in the 1990s had less to do with Kapoor's change of materials than the concomitant and increasing concerns of the art world with issues of hybridity. In 1990 the New Museum of Contemporary Art in New York City published *Out There: Marginalization and Contemporary Cultures*, which meditated on 'the process through which cultural margins are created, defined, and enforced'.[32] The seminal anthology featured contributions by a number of important postcolonialist theorists, such as Gayatri Chakravorty Spivak, Homi Bhabha and Edward Said, who interrogated the centre/margin dichotomy.

Throughout the 1990s, Kapoor's artworks were exhibited in roughly a dozen group exhibitions each year, as well as numerous international art biennials, all largely in Europe and North America. He was also given a series of solo exhibitions during this period.[33] By the early part of the twenty-first century, Kapoor had created a number of large site-specific artworks, including *Sky Mirror* at Rockefeller Plaza in New York City (2006), *Marsyas* at Tate Modern in London (2002) and *Taratantara* at the Baltic Centre for Contemporary Art in Gateshead, UK (2000). He had made some permanent public artworks, such as *Cloud Gate* at Millennium Park in Chicago (2004), as well. In addition, a number of high-profile museums began collecting Kapoor's artworks. For example, the Museum of Modern Art (MoMA) in New York City acquired a number of Kapoor's artworks in 1994 and 1998.[34]

Indian/artist/artwork

A critical essay by Anthony Vidler in the catalogue that accompanied Kapoor's 2004 solo exhibition, *Whiteout*, at Barbara Gladstone Gallery in New York

City, points to another crucial shift in the critical writing about Kapoor's artworks in the postmillennial period.[35] In sharp contrast to the criticism of Kapoor's early artworks, which seemed tethered to details of Kapoor's 'Indian' identity, Vidler expunges *all* references to Kapoor's ethnic, national, religious or other types of 'identity'. Vidler's invocation of theories of phenomenology to describe the relationship between the viewer and the artwork is particularly suggestive. Yet, he implies an abstracted viewing subject and his elision of references to postcolonial theory, which dominated much of the critical writing about Kapoor's art in the 1990s, remove any sense of historical specificity.

I consider the curtailing of discussions of identity and postcolonial theory in criticism of Kapoor's artworks in the context of the critical framing and display of Wifredo Lam's *Jungle* (1943) in the 1980s by MoMA per John Yau's cogent arguments.[36] Yau skilfully deconstructs the language used by William Rubin to describe Lam's artwork.[37] He shows how Rubin applies a formalist logic to describe Lam's painting that simultaneously negates any consideration of Lam's ethnic/racial identity. Lam, like Kapoor, had a mixed ethnic and national background; he was born in Cuba to a mother of African descent and a father of Chinese descent and spent significant amounts of time in Spain. Yau argues that Rubin erases Lam's hybrid identity altogether and constructs him as a 'colorless' or 'white' artist, thereby narrowing the scope of reading Lam's artworks.[38] In the same way, Vidler's traditional, Rubin-like, formal mode of analysis of Kapoor's artworks constructs the artist as colourless as well.

At the same time, criticism of Kapoor's artworks containing traces of the Orientalizing discourses of the 1980s did not disappear in the postmillennial period. Roberta Smith's 2008 *New York Times* review of Kapoor's exhibitions in Boston and New York City is instructive.[39] She writes that Kapoor's combination of 'many disparate strands of art, thought and culture' can be linked back to the fact that he 'did not begin life in a Western culture'. Smith further notes that his sculptures are 'in many ways one long ode to the modernist monochrome and its emphasis on purity', which he 'push[es] … back and forth between votive and technological, East and West'. Her reference to Kapoor's sculptures as veering between the East as 'votive' and the West as 'technological' is simplistic and Orientalist. The spatial metaphors are particularly ironic considering the rise of religious fundamentalism in the United States since 9/11 as well as the fact that the United States's claim to 'technological' ascendancy in the Cold War era was at least a partial result of an influx of advanced maths and science professionals from South Asia in the mid-1960s.[40] In fact, then President Lyndon B. Johnson's loosening of immigration laws can be directly linked to the dearth of maths and science professionals in the United States.[41]

Perhaps most surprising, though, is the poor word choice in the title of Smith's article, 'Sculptor as Magician'. Her use of the word 'magician' evokes the title of the *Magiciens de la terre* exhibition. Though she was referring to the illusory quality of Kapoor's artworks, which 'dispense multiple visual thrills and mysteries', it is unlikely that she would be unaware of the maligned history of the word 'magician'. Indeed, in 2005 – just three years before Smith's article – a special issue of *Art Journal* was dedicated to discussing identity politics in Western art exhibitions. Many of the articles focused on *Magiciens* at the very least as a point of reference.[42] In particular, Johanne Lamoureux's contribution delved into the politics of the word 'magician', which she argues has a number of uneasy implications, one of which is the return to the notion of the artist as a genius with special access to 'truth'.[43] In addition, she notes that though *Magiciens de la terre* has often been seen as a reference to Frantz Fanon's *Les Damnés de la terre* (1961), the exhibition catalogue indicates that the term 'magician' was borrowed from Sigmund Freud's essay 'Animism, Magic and the Omnipotence of Thought', which appeared in his book of collected essays exploring racial psychology, *Totem and Taboo: Resemblances between the Psychic Lives of Savages and Neurotics* (1913).[44] At worst, Smith's invocation of magician evokes uncomfortable associations with Freud's racist, xenophobic and Orientalist characterization of the 'magic of art' as a phenomenon that is non-Western and not contemporary.

Two years after Smith's article was published, Kapoor had his first major retrospective of his work in India in 2010.[45] The exhibition was spread across two locations, the National Gallery of Modern Art in New Delhi and Mehoob Film Studios in Mumbai, the only venue in the city large enough for Kapoor's work. The headlines announcing the exhibition are telling: 'Finally, the art world's most theatrical exponent is coming home – Return of the Prodigal', 'An artist returns to his roots' and 'Anish comes home'.[46] Even Kapoor, who had been averse to being tied down to any nationality, said, '[M]y India has found a voice in my art. It is very emotional for me coming back and to bring the works back',[47] and that his works 'have been, sub-consciously and consciously, inspired by India and now at last they get to be in the country that inspired them'.[48] Just as Smith's article indicates that Orientalist discourses are not historical but contemporary, these headlines suggest that neither is the notion that Kapoor and his works are 'Indian'. In comparison to the criticism of the early 1980s, of course, this discourse is not coming from the West – indeed, it is also coming from Kapoor himself – which radically shifts the ramifications of such statements.[49]

Arguably, though, by 2010, India was no longer on the periphery of the art world; cities such as New Delhi and Mumbai had come closer to occupying the position of a global art centre. Indeed, as Gerardo Mosquera and Jean Fisher remind us in their introduction to their seminal anthology *Over Here:*

International Perspectives on Art and Culture (2004), simplistic oppositional centre/margin paradigms are no longer useful as frames of reference given their increasing blurring in the postmillennial period.[50] Following on this point, it is worth noting that Kapoor's exhibitions in India were organized by the British Council in tandem with the Ministry of Culture, Government of India, National Gallery of Modern Art, New Delhi and the London-based Lisson Gallery, which represents Kapoor, and were sponsored by both the European fashion house Louis Vuitton and the Tata Group, a multinational conglomerate founded in India.[51] If by 2010 Kapoor and his works were Indian (again), then this construction is borne out of a syncretic cultural and financial transnational collaboration.

The conceit of this chapter is to definitively illustrate that the notion of a stable authorship or genealogy that is the bedrock of most racialized art histories is a fiction so as to begin to articulate art histories that were previously unthinkable. In so doing, I slowly move away from negative critique and towards generative art histories. The question remains, though: how does an art historian avoid writing about Kapoor without unintentionally reducing his work and career to simplistic notions of national style or identity? My own deconstruction of his art criticism has created a veritable impasse by maligning critics both for pointing out or obsessing about Kapoor's biographical details and for not highlighting them in the case of Vidler. At least one possible way out, I argue, is to make visible the critic's or art historian's own stakes in his or her writing. In my art historical practice, which is heavily invested in queer and South Asian as categories of identification, however flawed, I have therefore endeavoured to deploy them as complex and never fully knowable frameworks or points of departures *and* as highly contingent. That is, though I am advocating for a more ethical art criticism, I am just as invested in thinking through how the concerns and biases of critics or art historians can be acknowledged as part of the ways in which an artist's career is discussed and promoted, or not.

Notes

1 'Anish Kapoor, Interviewed by Shekhar Gupta', *Walk the Talk*, 3 December 2010, www.ndtv.com/video/player/walk-the-talk/walk-the-talk-with-anish-kapoor/175606.

2 As quoted in Sonya Dyer, 'Boxed in: How Cultural Diversity Policies Constrict Black Artists' (Manifesto Club Artistic Autonomy Hub, May 2007), 7, www.manifestoclub.com/files/BOXEDIN.pdf.

3 Of course, issues of 'class' still seep into discussion of Hirst's work. Indeed, as Jean Fisher notes, the Young British Art (YBA) movement of which Hirst was a part suddenly appropriated the identity debate from the British black arts movement and redefined Britishness as 'white, lower middle class, and

"laddish" and in a way palatable to an art hierarchy more comfortable with titillating sensation than with sober political realities'. See Jean Fisher, 'Dialogues', in *Shades of Black: Assembling Black Arts in 1980s Britain*, ed. David A. Bailey, Ian Baucom and Sonia Boyce (Durham, NC: Duke University Press in association with the Institute of International Visual Arts and the African and Asian Visual Artists' Archive, London, 2005), 191. Curator and writer Gilane Tawadros also notes that though the *The Other Story* exhibition – frequently cited as the tail end of the British black arts movement – and the *Freeze* exhibition – organized by Hirst and often cited as the beginning of the YBA movement – both appeared in the late 1980s, the artists of the former did not get launched into the lucrative international art market as the artists of the latter did. See Gilane Tawadros, 'A Case of Mistaken Identity', in *Shades of Black*, ed. Bailey, Baucom and Boyce, 123–32.

4 Emphasis in original. Michel Foucault, *The Archaeology of Knowledge and the Discourse of Language*, trans. A.M. Sheridan Smith (New York: Pantheon Books, 1972), 130.

5 Ibid., 41.

6 Thomas McEvilley, 'Darkness Inside a Stone', in *Anish Kapoor: British Pavilion, XLIV Venice Biennale, May–September, 1990* (London: Visual Arts Department of the British Council, 1990), 8.

7 Michael Newman, 'Anish Kapoor', in *Englische Plastik Heute = British Sculpture Now: Stephen Cox, Tony Cragg, Richard Deacon, Anish Kapoor, Bill Woodrow, Kunstmuseum Luzern, 11.7. – 12.9.1982*, ed. Martin Kunz (Luzern: Kunstmuseum Luzern, 1982), no pagination.

8 Martin Kunz, 'British Sculpture Now', in *Englische Plastik Heute*.

9 *Magiciens de la terre*, Musée National d'Art Moderne – Centre Georges Pompidou, and the Grande Halle, La Villette, Paris, 18 May–14 August 1989.

10 This was meant to remedy one of the chief complaints of the much-maligned *"Primitivism" in 20th Century Art: Affinity of the Tribal and the Modern (1984–85)* exhibition at the Museum of Modern Art (MoMA) in New York City. Curators William Rubin and Kirk Varnedoe structured their exhibition to highlight the formal similarities, or 'affinities', between primitive artworks and the artworks of modernist artists. Most disturbingly, as critic Thomas McEvilley notes in his scathing *Artforum* review – provocatively titled 'Doctor Lawyer Indian Chief: "'Primitivism' in 20th Century Art" at the Museum of Modern Art' – the curators expunged contextual information from the primitive artworks on display, including 'the dates of the works, their functions, their religious or mythological connections, [and] their environments'. See Thomas McEvilley, William Rubin and Kirk Varnedoe, 'Doctor Lawyer Indian Chief: "Primitivism" in 20th Century Art at the Museum of Modern Art', *Artforum* 23 (1984): 59. The provenance and identifying information of the European artworks, on the other hand, remained intact. In this way, the exhibition echoed postcolonial scholar Edward Said's observation of the manner in which Orientalist discourses operate – to temporally displace the non-West to the past in order to buttress the belief that the West is more advanced and culturally superior.

11 Homi Bhabha, 'Hybridité, identité et culture contemporaine', in *Magiciens de la terre*, ed. Jean Hubert Martin and Homi Bhabha (Paris: Editions du Centre Pompidou, 1989), 24–7. McEvilley's catalogue 'keynote statement' can also be found under the chapter titled 'Opening the Trap', in *Art & Otherness: Crisis in Cultural Identity*, ed. Thomas McEvilley (Kingston, NY: Documentext/McPherson, 1992), 57–72. It is also worth looking at McEvilley's post-exhibition reflections in an essay titled 'The Global Issue', in *Art & Otherness: Crisis in Cultural Identity*, ed. Thomas McEvilley (Kingston, NY: Documentext/McPherson, 1992), 153–8.

12 Jeremy Lewison, '"Bilderstreit" and "Magiciens de La Terre". Paris and Cologne', *The Burlington Magazine* 131, no. 1037 (August 1989): 587.

13 McEvilley, 'Global Issue', 155.

14 My own measurements of the catalogue: 36 × 29 × 2 cm.

15 Newman, 'Anish Kapoor', no pagination.

16 Ibid.

17 Richard Shone, 'Contemporary British Sculpture. Madrid (Review)', *The Burlington Magazine* 128, no. 997 (April 1986): 309.

18 'I'm used to being a foreigner', Kapoor says. 'Indians are very conscious of family background, so I grew up in an atmosphere of not being a run-of-the-mill, straightforward Indian boy. I grew up very conscious of [my] Jewishness since my father was positively anti-Hindu. An atmosphere of being different was just part of what life was for us.' See Louise Jury, 'Anish Kapoor: "The Government Doesn't Understand the Importance of Culture"', *The Independent*, 13 October 2002, http://news.independent.co.uk/people/profiles/article140025.ece.

19 Simon Hattenstone, 'Into the Deep', *Guardian*, 22 September 2006, www.theguardian.com/artanddesign/2006/sep/23/art.

20 Anish Kapoor, 'Mostly Hidden: An Interview with Marjorie Althorpe-Guyton', in *Anish Kapoor: British Pavilion: XLIV Venice Biennale: May–September 1990*, 46.

21 Emphasis in original. Avery Gordon, 'The Work of Corporate Culture: Diversity Management', *Social Text* 44 13, no. 3 (Fall/Winter 1995): 3. Kobena Mercer refers to 'multicultural managerialism', a variant of Gordon's term. Mercer writes that 'a managerial outlook' would 'say that in a culture of diversity, no one can play the minority card'. See Kobena Mercer, 'Iconography after Identity', in *Shades of Black*, ed. Bailey, Baucom and Boyce, 49–58.

22 Michel Foucault, 'What Is an Author?', in *Language, Counter-memory, Practice: Selected Essays and Interviews*, ed. Donald F. Bouchard, trans. Donald F. Bouchard and Sherry Simon (Ithaca, NY: Cornell University Press, 1977), 127. Essay originally published in French in 1969.

23 Ibid., 128.

24 Russell Ferguson, 'Introduction: Invisible Center', in *Out There: Marginalization and Contemporary Cultures*, ed. Russell Ferguson et al. (New York and Cambridge, MA: New Museum of Contemporary Art and MIT Press, 1990), 9–14.

25 Emphasis in original. McEvilley, 'Darkness Inside a Stone', 30.
26 Ibid.
27 Newman, 'Anish Kapoor', no pagination.
28 McEvilley, 'Darkness Inside a Stone', 40.
29 Ibid., 19.
30 McEvilley incorporated Carl Jung's scholarship. Kapoor read the latter as a postgraduate in the UK in the late 1970s. See Anish Kapoor, *Anish Kapoor* (London: Thames & Hudson, 1996), xv. Also, Jeremy Lewison discussed Kapoor's artworks through the work of Jung in more detail in his essay accompanying a 1990 exhibition of Kapoor's drawings at the Tate Gallery, London. See Jeremy Lewison, *Anish Kapoor: Drawings* (Millbank, London: Tate Gallery, 1990).
31 Anish Kapoor, Transcript of the John Tusa Interviews with the Sculptor Anish Kapoor, 6 July 2003, www.bbc.co.uk/programmes/pooncbc1.
32 Ferguson, 'Introduction: Invisible Center', 14.
33 'Anish Kapoor's Biography', *Gladstone Gallery*, accessed 2 January 2016, www.gladstonegallery.com/artist/anish-kapoor/biography.
34 Most of Kapoor's artworks were accessioned by the Museum of Modern Art, New York, in the 1990s: specifically, three in 1994 and ten in 1998. However, one Kapoor artwork was bought as early as 1987. In 2003 the New York-based Judith Rothschild Foundation also donated a large number of drawings. I thank Kathleen Curry, assistant curator, Research and Collections, Department of Drawings and Print at MoMA, for supplying this information.
35 Anthony Vidler, 'Reflections on Whiteout: Anish Kapoor at Barbara Gladstone', in *Anish Kapoor: Whiteout* (Milan: Charta, 2004).
36 John Yau, 'Please Wait By the Coatroom', in *Out There: Marginalization and Contemporary Cultures*, ed. Ferguson et al., 133–41.
37 Rubin had curated the maligned *"Primitivism"* exhibition discussed in note 10.
38 Yau, 'Please Wait By the Coatroom', 138.
39 Roberta Smith, 'Sculptor as Magician', *The New York Times*, 30 May 2008, www.nytimes.com/2008/05/30/arts/design/30kapo.html.
40 For more on the rise of fundamentalism in the United States after 9/11, see Kevin Phillips, *American Theocracy: The Peril and Politics of Radical Religion, Oil, and Borrowed Money in the 21st Century* (New York: Viking, 2006).
41 Vijay Prashad, *The Karma of Brown Folk* (Minneapolis: University of Minnesota Press, 2000), 74.
42 The essays in the special issue of *Art Journal* 62, no. 1 (Spring 2005) include Norman L. Kleeblatt, 'Identity Roller Coaster', 61–3; Johanne Lamoureux, 'From Form to Platform: The Politics of Representation and the Representation of Politics', 64–73; Elisabeth Sussman, 'Then and Now: Whitney Biennial 1993', 74–9; Sylvester Okwunodu Ogbechie, 'Ordering the Universe: Documenta II and the Apotheosis of the Occidental Gaze', 80–9; and Reesa Greenberg, 'Identity Exhibitions: From *Magiciens de la terre* to Documenta II', 90–4.

43 Johanne Lamoureux, 'From Form to Platform: The Politics of Representation and the Representation of Politics', *Art Journal* (2005), 64–73. The artist as a special subject (in the extreme case as conflated with god) can be traced back at least to Giorgio Vasari's 1568 book, *The Lives of the Artists*, a biographically based art history, the contemporary incarnation of which is the artist monograph that many museums still use as a model.

44 See Frantz Fanon, *The Wretched of the Earth*, trans. Constance Farrington (New York: Grove Press, 1965). Originally published in French in 1961. Sigmund Freud, *Totem and Taboo: Resemblances between the Psychic Lives of Savages and Neurotics*, trans. Abraham A. Brill (Harmondsworth: Penguin Books, 1938). Originally published in German in 1913.

45 Kapoor notes that the delay in exhibiting in India is at least partially a practical one: 'I have wanted to put on a show in India for decades, but I have struggled to find the right space. My works are enormous and also very fragile, so they do not travel easily from my studio in London.' See Florence Waters, 'Anish Kapoor Saves His Best for India', *The Telegraph*, 3 November 2010, www.telegraph.co.uk/culture/art/art-news/8108384/Anish-Kapoor-saves-his-best-for-India.html. Many bloggers speculated that the sudden presence of Kapoor in India was not just because of the availability of adequate space to install his work, though. For instance, blogger Very Deadly Kali in her 30 November 2010 entry titled 'Look Out India! Anish Kapoor Is Here!!!' wrote this: 'So why did Anish Kapoor come to India? … This is not about Indian-ness or British-ness. This is a simple business proposition. Can he get a commission for a mega public sculpture? He knows that with the Indian economy booming, India CAN. All he needs is a simple invitation and a pay cheque' (capitalisation in original). See Very Deadly Kali, 'Deadly Kali: Look Out India! Anish Kapoor Is Here!!!', blog, *Deadly Kali* (30 November 2010), http://deadlykali.blogspot.com/2010/11/look-out-india-anish-kapoor-is-here.html.

46 John Elliott, 'Anish Kapoor on Show in India – a Permanent Public Sculpture Is Planned', blog, *Riding the Elephant* (29 November 2010), https://ridingtheelephant.wordpress.com/2010/11/29/anish-kapoor-on-show-in-india-%e2%80%93-a-permanent-public-sculpture-is-planned/.

47 'Sonia Gandhi Inaugurates Anish Kapoor Retrospective at NGMA', Indo-Asian News Service (IANS), *Sify News* (27 November 2010), www.sify.com/news/sonia-gandhi-inaugurates-anish-kapoor-retrospective-at-ngma-news-national-kl1uOlehaaj.html.

48 Georgina Maddox, '"Inspiring, Even Daring" Anish Kapoor in Delhi', *The Indian Express*, 28 November 2010, http://archive.indianexpress.com/news/inspiring-even-daring-anish-kapoor-in-delhi/717199/2.

An early version of this essay was given as a conference paper, titled 'Queer Desi Art Criticism', at the 'Queer Diasporas' conference at the University of Manchester in May 2007.

49 For a fascinating discussion of Kapoor's work through the lens of the artist's words, see Denis Vidal, 'The Return of the Aura: Anish Kapoor, the Studio and the World', in *Arts and Aesthetics in a Globalizing World*, ed.

Raminder Kaur and Parul Dave-Mukherji (London: Bloomsbury Academic, 2015), 39–60.

50 Gerardo Mosquera and Jean Fisher, 'Introduction', in *Over Here: International Perspectives on Art and Culture*, ed. Jean Fisher and Gerardo Mosquera (New York; Cambridge, MA: New Museum of Contemporary Art; MIT Press, 2004), 6.

51 'Anish Kapoor: Delhi Mumbai', press release, British Council Visual Arts (2010), http://visualarts.britishcouncil.org/exhibitions/exhibition/anish-kapoor-delhi-mumbai-2010.

Form: queer zen 3

In the summer of 2012 I participated in the National Endowment for the Humanities (NEH) Summer Institute programme titled 'Re-envisioning American Art History: Asian American Art, Research, and Teaching'.[1] Margo Machida, one of the pioneers of exploring artworks by artists of Asian descent through a transnational lens, and Alexandra Chang, curator of special projects and the director of global arts programs at the Asian/Pacific/American Institute research centre at New York University (NYU), organized the intensive three-week programme and brought together an interdisciplinary mix of curators, art historians, scholars, artists and museum administrators.[2] The programme consisted of visits to artist studios and galleries as well as presentations by participants and guest lecturers, such as curator Jeffrey Wechsler, who discussed his important exhibition *Asian Traditions/Modern Expressions: Asian American Artists and Abstraction, 1945–1970*. Held at the Jane Voorhees Zimmerli Art Museum, Rutgers, the State University of New Jersey, in 1997, Wechsler's exhibition focused on 'art by Asian Americans produced during the era of Abstract Expressionism that incorporates the technical and philosophical precedents and parallels to abstraction found in traditional Eastern art'.[3] He showed some of the more than 150 works in the exhibition by 57 artists, including Win Ng, Chen Chi, Genichiro Inokuma, Seong Moy, Kenzo Okada and Ansei Uchima.[4]

I realized at that time that my own focus on identity was (and to a large degree still is) skewed towards the post-1980s period, and therefore the contributions of these artists were largely unknown to me.[5] One aim of this chapter is to focus on the 1960s and 1970s rather than the contemporary, which is often the focus of scholarship that explores identity. Another is to hone in on form – and specifically abstraction – as a point of departure to rethink everything from Asian American and lesbian, gay, bisexual, trans*, queer, questioning and intersex (LGBTQI) art histories to movements such as Abstract Expressionism.[6] Discussing the importance of explorations of form in works by artists who are often identified by their biographical details, art historian Joan Kee points out: 'Humanist as it [inclusion] seems, it denies that which its presumptive beneficiaries want most – serious consideration of the artwork – in favour of reifying the artist through her biography.'[7] In other words, while quiet exclusion of the works of artists of colour (as well as most women) in the post-Second World War context is being somewhat corrected, even a welcome inclusiveness has not always meant a 'serious consideration of the artwork' of this group of marginalized artists.[8]

At the same time, I do not want to set up a binary between the formal properties of the work and the author as completely distinct entities. Perhaps it is more accurate to write that I explore *queer* form as loosely articulated by a conversation between visual theorist Jennifer Doyle and art historian David Getsy, an edited transcript of which was published under the title 'Queer Formalisms' in *Art Journal* in 2013.[9] Form is not just colours, lines and shapes. Doyle gives the example of Andy Warhol's seemingly simple gesture of turning all the books in his home so that their spines face the wall rather than facing out at the viewer. By doing so the book becomes an 'object … a block shaped by one formal logic and deployed in another'. They are no longer cultural capital but decoration.[10] Getsy provocatively notes, 'It also produces a kind of anonymous cruising in that the relation with the object occurs in willful ignorance of the book's title, author, and cultural positioning.'[11] For both Doyle and Getsy, form is not disembodied; it can be a mode through which the relations between the viewer and artwork are, as Doyle puts it, 'deployed into another formal logic'. She further writes that 'to see a material or an object in a different way – against or to the side of its intended use – is a queer tactic'.[12]

David Getsy writes that 'though there seemed to be little queer politics in Minimalism, I realized I could draw queer politics out of Minimalism, according to its own logic'.[13] He notes that many of the artists associated with Minimalism were deeply concerned with the body of the viewer, but it was strangely a disembodied, even clinical, relationship. In a similar way, I focus on abstract works produced in the post-Second World War period from which I draw a queer politics. I also explore writing by art critics (as in Chapter 2) as well as interviews with artists in order to recast this work through a queer formalist lens.

While I am referring to 'queer' as more expansive than simply non-normative sexuality, it is important to foreground that the latter has been largely ignored in scholarship on Abstract Expressionism and Asian American art historical scholarship. In terms of the former, art historian and queer studies scholar Jonathan Katz has done much of the work of reimagining the works of John Cage, Jasper Johns, Robert Rauschenberg and, more recently, Agnes Martin through a queer framework.[14] The 2008 publication *Asian American Art: A History, 1850–1970* was a watershed moment for making visible the contributions of a broad range of artists of Asian descent; the volume includes 150 artist biographies and 400 reproductions.[15] However, a quick glance at the book's index reveals that words such as gay, lesbian, queer, bisexual, transgender, gender and sexuality are missing.[16] In the NEH summer institute, one of the subgroups formed tackled these exclusions. Many involved (including myself) contributed to the volume that resulted from these discussions, *Queering Contemporary Asian American Art* (University of Washington Press, 2017), coedited by artist Laura Kina and independent curator Jan Christian Bernabe.

In a brochure accompanying an exhibition that addressed why emerging contemporary queer and transgender artists were moving towards abstraction, Getsy's thoughts on it and its supposed opposite – representation – are useful in understanding why abstraction might be a powerful mode through which to explore identity:

> Abstraction has capacity. It is productive and proliferative. Rather than as an avoidance of representation, it must be considered an embrace of potentiality and a positing of the unforeclosed. It makes room … Rather than seeing abstraction as erasure, it appears to many as plenitude. Increasingly, what is called for are more accounts of abstraction that are positively-defined, not negatively cast – accounts that ask how abstraction can perform and what it produces.[17]

Abstraction's 'capacity', 'potentiality', 'plenitude' and 'positing of the unforeclosed' do not so much eschew representation as invoke a body that is not culturally marked. Abstraction, as Getsy writes, can 'resist bodies' readability and the assumptions made about gender from visual clues'.[18] I would expand the latter to refer to other kinds of clues, or identifications, such as race, ethnicity and nationality.

In addition to queer form, Asian American studies and literature scholar Kandice Chuh's suggestion that we approach 'Asian American' in Asian American studies as a category of discursive knowledge that may or may not necessarily involve artists of Asian descent is particularly useful as an overarching frame for my investigation in this chapter.[19] Chuh is concerned with literature rather than visual art, but her point is transferable to art history. She writes that rather than a 'desire for subjectivity', the field of Asian American studies should be 'subjectless'.[20] It should 'prioritize difference by foregrounding the discursive constructedness of subjectivity' rather than the certitude of subjectivity.[21] Chuh is careful to note that this 'does not occlude the possibility of political action'.[22] She further writes that a 'strategic *anti*-essentialism' is what coheres Asian American studies rather than bounded notions of identity.[23] In a similar way, LGBTQI studies is cohered through an '*anti*-essentialism'; it is important to approach Asian American and LGBTQI as subjectless – in other words, not cohered around fixed but contingent notions of subjects. To do so means that this chapter also reimagines a different kind of LGBTQI art history in addition to Asian American art history and a history of Abstract Expressionism.

What might comprise an Asian American art history, LGBTQI art history, or history of Abstract Expressionism if we focused on queer form and the 'subjectless'?[24] Answering this question has led me (somewhat surprisingly) to the abstract works from the 1960s and 1970s of Cy Twombly (1928–2011) and Natvar Bhavsar (b. 1934) and their interlocutors. At first glance, I admit they are curious bedfellows. While Bhavsar's works could be enfolded into a history of artworks of artists of Asian descent since he was born in India and lives in New York City, Twombly's works could not. Moreover, neither of these individuals is queer-identified nor explicitly explores sexuality in his work. It is worth belabouring again that rather than focus on authorship ('roots' and 'routes' as well as sexual identification), I explore queer form and the subjectless to recast categories such as Asian American and LGBTQI as more malleable.[25] Getsy writes that abstraction offers 'a position from which to imagine, recognize, or realize new possibilities'.[26] I argue that the works of Twombly and Bhavsar offer such new possibilities by prefiguring contemporary queer and transnational theories, though not through figuration. To that end, I explore first the works of Twombly and then those of Bhavsar through the frame of what I describe as 'queer Zen Buddhism' or 'queer Zen'.[27]

Before turning to the artworks of Twombly and Bhavsar, I further characterize 'queer Zen' by discussing the inspiration for it, Jonathan Katz's groundbreaking work in which he theorizes that the abstract works of Agnes Martin (1912–2004) from the 1960s can be read as expressions of a queer-inflected Zen Buddhism.[28] Martin's now canonical oeuvre of paintings and drawings of all-over finely hand-drawn grids belie a trace of the artist in contrast to classical minimalist works invoking the grid as mechanical and disembodied.[29] She lived most of her life in New Mexico and though she did have same-sex relationships with women, she did not publicly identify as a lesbian.[30]

I was first introduced to Katz's work on Martin through a video of a lecture he gave as part of a symposium connected to an exhibition he co-curated with David C. Ward at the National Portrait Gallery in Washington, DC, in 2010, *Hide/Seek: Difference and Desire in American Portraiture*.[31] I think highly of Katz's scholarship; however, my immediate reaction was scepticism. I thought it might be a stretch to discuss sexuality in the context of Martin and her work given that I noted she never self-identified as a lesbian, and also because of the non-representational character of her artistic practice. Katz, though, was careful not to focus on authorial details as 'truths'. As Katz notes in his article on Martin, sexuality does not necessarily come in forms that are legible: 'where would we be if we made acknowledgement the truth test of art-historical knowledge?'[32] Moreover, Martin's works have been often linked to Zen Buddhism.

The artist was not a practising Buddhist herself, but as Katz writes, she 'often looked and sounded like one'.[33] Martin presumably encountered Zen Buddhism at one of the lectures of Buddhist monk Daisetz Teitaro Suzuki (1870–1966) at Columbia University, New York City, where he lectured from 1951 to 1957.[34] This time overlaps with the period when Martin was pursuing a master's degree at Columbia (1951–52 and 1954).[35] Indeed, Zen was important to a number of American artists who were not of Asian descent whose works emerged in the 1950s and 1960s.[36] Through Martin's work, Katz radically reworks her negation of identification as a lesbian into an expression of identity that uncannily prefigures queer understandings of sexual identity. Katz makes convincing parallels between the non-dualistic conception of identity often associated with Zen and queer as an unstable signifier of sexual identity.[37]

Cy Twombly's *Ferragosto* series and Queer Zen

Expanding on Katz's work, if sexuality is a referent for queer, then I suggest that Asia (both East and South) could be one for Zen Buddhism, since the entire region is frequently associated or conflated with the religious practice. In the same way that Martin's abstract yet embodied artworks prefigure theories of sexuality as queer or unstable, can the latter foreshadow contemporary theories of Asian American identity as transnational, or blurred across regions or nations?

In my search for an answer to this query, I came across the writings of French philosopher Roland Barthes that use Zen to examine the works of Cy Twombly.[38] Maybe it is more accurate to write that I was 'cruising' for information. Instead of trying to foreclose the 'irregular connections and disorderly encounters' that art historian Simon Ofield-Kerr theorizes 'cruising' brings about, I attempt here to engage (wrestle?) with Barthes's writing.[39] Of course, it is fitting that Ofield-Kerr's theory is based on Barthes's own writing on cruising. Barthes's writings on Twombly were intriguing for two reasons. First, Barthes is not known for his writing on artworks, so why did Twombly seek him out as he did to write about his?[40] What did Twombly's work *do* that compelled Barthes to accept his invitation? Second, Twombly had attended lectures of the Suzuki at Columbia University in 1951 and a number of John Cage's legendary performances in the summer of 1952 at Black Mountain College.[41] In contradistinction to Cage, whose indebtedness to Zen Buddhism and Suzuki is explicit, however, how these lectures affected Twombly's artistic practice is unclear.[42] So, why did Barthes turn to Zen when writing about his artworks?

I argue first that Barthes's writing and Twombly's artworks suggest a queer understanding of sexuality that is integral to answering these questions I have posed. I am not interested in 'outing' Twombly and Barthes or gauging intentionality (which of course is mediated, too). What I am interested in is how Barthes's writing and Twombly's work might suggest a queer approach to sexuality as Katz argued that Martin's work did. I then reread Barthes's writing to suggest that it prefigures (if implicitly) Katz's writings on queer Zen in ways that move beyond just discussions of sexuality as unfixed. That is, I illustrate that Barthes's writings indicate that Twombly's works gesture towards the notion of regionality and nationality as always already queer, or unstable. Twombly, of course, is technically a transnational artist. He lived primarily in Italy after 1957. However, moving within the Euro-American art world is not the same as the shift that Natvar Bhavsar made from the marginalized Global South to the United States.[43] Overall, Twombly's work and Barthes's writing can help think through queer notions of nationality as well as sexuality.

To further animate my points above, I begin by exploring the five works that comprise Cy Twombly's *Ferragosto* series from 1961; and then filter my findings through Barthes's writing as well as other interlocutors of Twombly's larger body of work. Each canvas of the *Ferragosto* series is roughly the same size (5½ × 6½ ft) and constructed of the same materials – oil paint, lead pencil and wax crayon. The corporeal body is evoked in several ways. Body parts – penises, buttocks and breasts – hover somewhere between representation and abstraction throughout the entire series. Twombly's handprints are visible – especially in *Ferragosto IV* – indexing a trace of the artist's body on the canvas (Figure 3.1). By *Ferragosto V*, Twombly has worked over the entire canvas with smears of paint, and more evidence of the artist using his fingers – rather than brushes – to paint is visible. Intense colours such as pink, red and brown are also suggestive of flesh, blood and excrement, respectively.[44] Art historian Elizabeth J. Trapp even suggests that 'one can smell the decay' of trash rotting in the summer months of August during which Twombly made these works.[45] Finally, while there is an economy of paint early in the series, such as in *Ferragosto II* (Plate 2), by *Ferragosto V*, the generous amounts of thickly applied paint gives the work a tactile quality. Art historian Claire Daigle's description of *Ferragosto V* captures the work's dynamism and corporeality: 'A thickly encrusted palette of brown, pink and red takes on a viscerality paired in the work with a body parcelled into pictograms: pendulous breasts, erupting penises, scatological posteriors.'[46] These colours, textures and representations coupled with his complex smudging, smearing and scratching on his large canvases beckon the viewer.

The artworks' size and materiality coupled with the semi-abstracted body parts rendered in colours evoking the body blur the boundaries between viewer and artwork. Given that male and female sexual organs (albeit abstracted) populate each of the canvases of the series in varying degrees, this intertwining can be considered erotically charged, even if ambiguously so.

Cy Twombly, *Ferragosto IV*, 1961. Oil paint, wax crayon and lead pencil on canvas, 65¼ × 78⅞ in. Image courtesy Gagosian Gallery. 3.1

Both David Batchelor, artist and writer, and Charles A. Riley II, former editor of various art magazines and currently professor of English, have interpreted Barthes's description of Twombly's use of colour (or lack thereof) as a synonym for ecstasy.[47]

Moreover, Barthes has referred to Twombly's use of colour as 'A kind of bliss' and 'like a closing eyelid, a tiny fainting spell'.[48] Riley writes that the latter 'has an obvious association with the orgasm'.[49] At the same time, Barthes wrote more generally about Twombly's works that 'it is not necessary that color be intense, violent, rich, or even delicate, refined, rare, or again, thick-spread, crusty, fluid'.[50] As a way to describe Twombly's typical approach, he writes that 'color is *also* an idea (a *sensual* idea)'.[51] In the *Ferragosto* series, colour does become many of the adjectives Barthes uses that do not typically describe Twombly's work. We might extrapolate that if Twombly's more typical works – largely colourless – could provoke ecstasy, then the *Ferragosto* series is orgiastic. Of course, the latter works cannot be easily coded as heteroerotic or homoerotic, especially given that, as I am arguing, the works elicit an embodied relationship with a contingent viewer. Moreover, David Getsy has noted that 'a staging of relations between bodies establishes sexuality's potential to emerge within those relations. This can even be seen in the evidence of a past gesture or act, where the viewer must reconstruct the scene that left its trace, inhabiting the place of the agent that made it'.[52] In this way, Twombly's traces bring into play the viewer who, through his or her act of reconstruction, activates the potential for desire alluded to on the canvas.

Barthes writes that 'whatever is scribbled it [the work] comes as an enigmatic supplement'.[53] At least implicitly, Barthes is invoking Jacques Derrida's aforementioned supplement: Twombly's works in his estimation effectively act as supplements – meaning is never complete.[54] For Barthes, Twombly's works produce a gap between sign and signified – and this space is one in which connections can be made and unmade. Following Barthes's description of Twombly's painting as producing gaps, the *Ferragosto* works could be said to engender a productive space of possibility for reworking norms of sexual identity as queer.

This reading gains more traction when Barthes writes the titles of Twombly's paintings and when the often semi-legible inscriptions found on them function as citations. That is, their meanings are identified through the very act of naming. Art historian Rosalind Krauss expands upon Barthes's thinking by invoking J. L. Austin's 'performative', which articulates the idea that to say something is also to do something.[55] The classic example of the performative is the utterance of 'I now pronounce you husband and wife' within a marriage ceremony, which 'hails or interpellates' the two individuals as a married couple.[56] In other words, speech acts simultaneously to do what one is saying. Krauss writes, 'It is thus a linguistic operation in which reference is suspended in favor of action: not meaning something, but saying something.'[57] Barthes, too, notes that Twombly's work 'does not derive from a concept (*mark*) but from an activity (*marking*)'.[58] Trace is the record of a gesture and 'line is a visible action'.[59] Thus, the title '*Ferragosto*' does not illustrate the content of the work but refers to the action of naming it as such. Interestingly, embedded within the genealogy of the word '*Ferragosto*' is an illustration of how performativity as well as history and power operate. Originally referring to a day to honour Diana, the goddess of fertility, it has become transformed ironically to honour the Assumption of the Virgin Mary.[60] Krauss's essay appeared in the September 1994 issue of *Artforum*, a little less than a year after Judith Butler's 'Critically Queer' appeared in *GLQ: A Journal of Lesbian and Gay Studies*, one of the early essays formulating queer theory, which was in its infancy in the early 1990s.[61] Whether or not Krauss was aware of Butler's article is unclear, but given that performativity – and its productive misfires – is the bedrock of queer theory it seems extending the discussion above to gender and sexuality is appropriate.

For Barthes, though, deconstruction was not enough to describe Twombly's works. He turned to Zen. He observes, for instance, that Twombly's mark-making is similar to the Japanese Zen notion of *satori* – '[a] sudden (and sometimes very tenuous) break in our causal logic'.[62] Interestingly, this has parallels with Butler's theorization of the break in a performative that can redirect norms. For Barthes, the works engendered an affect in the West that he felt was otherwise only possible in the East: 'if we required some reference for this [Twombly's] art, we could go looking for it only very far away … outside the West'.[63] Following this point, Twombly's works effectively detach Zen from Asia in Barthes's estimation. Of more importance for the discussion here, Barthes stages the possibility of Zen as a transregional phenomenon. His essay not only suggests a queer relation to sexuality but also to regionality.

Brief notes on queer methods

As intimated earlier, a queer exploration of sexuality and regionality would necessarily also involve exploring silences – literally what is not said. It is important to note that my investigation requires methods beyond a traditional formal analysis of Twombly's works or a recontextualizing of the writing about them. These methods can only be described as queer or unusual for art history. Evidence I utilize is often anecdotal or what is not written, said or known. For instance, when Barthes had the perfect moment to 'out' himself when he wrote the preface to Renaud Camus's sexually explicit *Tricks*, he refuses the call to do so. In his preface he wrote: 'Ultimately, the attribute is of no importance; what society will not tolerate is that I should be … *nothing*, or more precisely, that the *something* that I am should be openly expressed as provisional, revocable, insignificant, inessential, in a word: irrelevant.'[64] I will return to Barthes's poignant entreaty to a specifically activist 'society', but for the moment what is of interest is the refusal to identify as anything but '*nothing*'.

In a related manner, hardly any information exists regarding Twombly's same-sex relationships. What does exist is innuendo or gossip, especially regarding a romantic relationship with the artist Robert Rauschenberg.[65] Irit Rogoff notes how exploring gossip in visual studies can be productive: 'in Foucauldian terms it [gossip] serves the purpose through negative differentiation, of constituting a category of respectable knowledge … In Derridean terms gossip allows for the constitution of the formal boundaries of the genre and its outlawed, excessive and uncontainable narratives.'[66] Rogoff compellingly argues that a consideration of gossip can be useful in reassessing the mechanisms that bound and define certain knowledge as 'true' or 'acceptable'. Building on Rogoff's scholarship, Gavin Butt uses gossip to reexamine art world practices in the 1950s and 1960s, especially in relation to homosexuality.[67]

Innuendo is all the evidence that may be available regarding any discussion of Twombly's sexuality, as this was a topic that would have understandably fallen outside Cold War-era America as a (drawing on Rogoff) 'category of respectable knowledge'. The intellectual history regarding the links among the Cold War, sexuality and artistic practice can be traced back to a prescient article written by art historian Moira Roth in 1977.[68] It is important to note that this category of respectable knowledge was consolidated not only through an active homophobia but also xenophobia. Indeed, '[h]omosexuals and [c]ommunism were quickly conflated' by McCarthyism, as the US State Department's own archives now readily admit.[69] Moreover, the Japanese internment camps were still fresh in the minds of many Americans of Asian descent.

Cy Twombly's double gestures: towards Barthes's transnational Zen

Jonathan Katz has expanded on Moira Roth's brilliant work to explore the activist potential of silence.[70] Bearing in mind this point, this section is devoted not only to exploring what Twombly did say about his artworks, but also what he did not. That is to say, Twombly was largely reticent about his work. Katz writes that silence can be performative. He further explains that performatives effectively remove 'claims to meaning which are usually recognised and solidified through language and speech acts. Silence therefore allows us to reflect upon the ways in which we create and construct meanings and possibilities, and this reflective process involves the recognition that our socio-cultural constructions are always situated, conditional and partial.'[71] In this way, I consider what Twombly refers to as 'partial' and consider his performative silence an opportunity for me to extrapolate a range of different possible meanings.

Twombly gave only two interviews during his lifetime: one conducted by David Sylvester in 2000 and the other by Nicholas Serota in 2007.[72] Indeed, when Serota writes about the 'rare opportunity' he had to interview Twombly, he is referring to Twombly's long-standing refusal to speak about his work.[73] Serota's interview with Twombly took place in advance of the 2007 exhibition, *Cy Twombly: Cycles and Seasons*, which Serota was organizing at Tate Modern. Monographic exhibitions by definition are going to lean towards connecting biographical details to artistic meaning. In the special case of exhibitions of well-known living artists' artworks, an artist's spoken or written explanations of their work sometimes even take on stable meanings. It is important to keep in mind the unreliability of the author as I discuss the end of Serota's interview with Twombly when Serota says, 'Cy, I think we've got plenty' to which Twombly replies, 'You've got enough. And if there's something I didn't say, you could make it up.'[74] Twombly's response could be read as indifference to, cynicism towards or a defensive posture against art historical writing and criticism in general. Given the manner in which his works had been excoriated both within the art world (consider the vitriolic response to his 1964 Leo Castelli Gallery exhibition)[75] and outside of it (the characterization of his artistic practice as akin to the scribbles of a child),[76] this is certainly reasonable. However, his statement could also be considered evidence of the artist downplaying the weight of his spoken words in his works' meaning. Then again, he does not explicitly negate the importance of his words at any point, either, which could just as well signal to Serota that he should not 'make it up'.

More to the point, Twombly's response produces a chain of meanings, which mirrors how I argue his *Ferragosto* works function, as I explore in the next section. Twombly manages to deflect attention from him and his work to his interviewer. That is, though he literally gets the last word, he does so in a manner that delays it from ever arriving. This double gesture of the artist – providing insight into his practice and simultaneously erasing its potential import on the meaning of his works – produces a Derridean supplement that 'is in reality *différance*', the simultaneous process of difference and deferral, which prevents the definitive closure of the meaning of Twombly's work.[77]

Again, it is important to underscore that for Barthes, deconstruction was not enough to characterize Twombly's works. He turned to Zen. For instance, Barthes ends both of his essays on Twombly's work with the following from the Tao Te Ching that seems to resonate with the double gesture I have just outlined:

> He produces without taking for himself;
> He acts without expectation,
> His work is done, he is not attached to it,
> and since he is not attached to it,
> his work will remain.[78]

In so doing, the potential for a queer relation not only to sexuality but also to the region – specifically the East or Asia, the referents for Zen – becomes possible. To be sure, Barthes's writings on Zen do at first glance veer towards being Orientalist, the most egregious example of which is as follows (previously cited): 'if we required some reference for this [Twombly's] art, we could go looking for it only very far away, outside painting, outside the West, outside the historical period, at the very limit of meaning'.[79] The West/non-West dualism is simplistic and reductive, as is the implicit signification of the non-West as geographically ('very far away'), temporally ('outside the historical period') and discursively ('outside painting' and therefore art history) distinct from the West. The characterization of the non-West as being outside of 'meaning' suggests the non-West is where rationality dissolves. The West is rational and the non-West is not.

Rather than Orientalist, it is perhaps more appropriate to write that his xenophilia is what is problematic. At the same time, viewing the above through the lens of the preface he wrote for Camus's *Tricks* could yield a more sympathetic, nuanced reading. Barthes was often seen as a traitor to the gay rights movement because he refused to identify as gay; in this way, this text can be seen as a defence against activists who wanted him to identify as something (rather than nothing). Meanwhile, academia often undercut the seriousness of his scholarship because he was nonetheless coded as gay anyway. Harvard scholar and poet Helen Vendler, for instance, notes that she was once chastised for liking Barthes, whom she writes was referred to as 'that silly homosexual' by an otherwise esteemed colleague of hers.[80] In this way, it is not surprising that he would not want to be in the Occident with its overdetermined systems of signification. Indeed, Nicholas de Villiers provocatively argues that Barthes has been closeted as opposed to closeting himself. He recasts Barthes's silence as a queer tactic of 'opacity' in which his relationship to the closet is a productive inscrutability.[81]

According to de Villiers, Barthes's philosophy of identity was effectively queer and at odds with his lived reality. When Twombly invited him to write an essay for the catalogue accompanying his retrospective at the Whitney Museum of American Art in New York City in 1979, it seems that Barthes might have found an analogue for his more nuanced approach to identity in Twombly's work. One imagines his artwork evoked an affect that resonated with the queer way in which Barthes lived and that he could describe only through Zen. His mention of Zen as being 'at the very limit of meaning' might not be where rationality dissolves – as I previously suggested – but perhaps where meanings do not cohere into recognizable entities.[82] The works effectively brought a Zen-like affect to the West thereby decoupling Zen from a stable, regional referent.

It is worth noting that the majority of Twombly's works do not reference the East. However, Claire Daigle suggests that his references to classic polytheistic tradition can be linked to the East through what Barthes says about the signifiers of Japan: 'they are empty because they do not refer to an ultimate signified, as our [the West's] signs do, hypostatized in the name of the God, science, reason, law, and so forth'.[83] However, given that Twombly drew on the polytheistic tradition of the West that also had no singular 'ultimate signified', his works could be said to exemplify the empty signs Barthes refers to as being the province of the East.

Twombly's work can be read as explicating a mode of identity that is effectively queer, and his interlocutors' reliance on performativity and Zen add a specific traction by gesturing towards a queering of both sexuality and the region or nation. This, of course, only became possible by shifting attention away from an essentialized understanding of what is 'Asian American'. Perhaps more provocatively, by recalibrating the lens through which one views the hegemonic canon or archive of art history – the one that includes Twombly and Barthes and Krauss – it becomes clear that, retrospectively, art history has always been concerned with queer notions of sexuality and the region.

Natvar Bhavsar/Cy Twombly

Before I go on to explore the abstract works of Natvar Bhavsar, it is useful to map out similarities and important differences between his and Cy Twombly's careers to delineate what is at stake in my inclusion of his work here. Bhavsar was born in Gothava in the state of Gujarat in India in 1934, six years after Twombly.[84] Bhavsar would not arrive in the United States until 1962; Twombly had left for Europe several years prior to this, in 1957.[85] The works of both were in the 1969 Whitney Museum of American Art's annual exhibition that surveyed trends in recent American art.[86] That is to say, both Bhavsar and Twombly were at the forefront of *American* art in 1969 at least.[87] In general, though, the works of both Twombly and Bhavsar were constructed as troublesome for they did not fit into dominant art movements in the postwar period. Though much is made of the lukewarm to vitriolic responses to Twombly's work in the United States – such as the disastrous reception of his 1964 exhibition at Leo Castelli Gallery in New York City – his work was on the cover of the 1969 Whitney annual exhibition catalogue.[88] While Twombly's work has now been safely incorporated into the canon of American art history, Bhavsar's has not.

To be clear, Bhavsar has been commercially successful. There also have been influential critics who have championed his work, such as Irving Sandler and Carter Ratcliff.[89] He has had some attention from museums, too: Jeffrey Wechsler, for instance, organized a solo exhibition of Bhavsar's works in 2007 at the Jane Voorhees Zimmerli Art Museum, Rutgers, the State University of New Jersey.[90] However, he has not had critical attention by art historians commensurate with any of these successes. He has been absent from discussions of Abstract Expressionism in art history as well as from Asian American art history. He does not appear in the important 2008 publication *Asian American Art: A History, 1850–1970*.[91] However, Asian American art history is a nascent field just beginning to cohere; what is of more concern is his elision from hegemonic art history.[92] Later in this chapter, I discuss in more detail how his work gets edited out of critical discussions in the 1960s and 1970s in the US context *and* the context of India, which up to this point I have left undiscussed. The latter remains important in underscoring why using a frame such as queer Zen is crucial in thinking about work beyond the national. In the next section, I suggest that the way out of this aporia is embedded in Bhavsar's artworks from the 1960s and 1970s.

Natvar Bhavsar's colour: beyond beauty

In 1957 Bhavsar had the opportunity to see the work of Mark Rothko in his, then, home town Ahmedabad, the capital city of Gujarat, India. Organized by the Museum of Modern Art (MoMA) in New York City, the travelling exhibition was meant to bring the latest trends in art to audiences in what the press release referred to as the 'Orient'.[93] Bhavsar's encounter with the work was a watershed moment that eventually resulted in him moving away from his training in figuration in art school in India and towards what would become his lifelong subject matter of exploration: colour.

Natvar Bhavsar moved to the United States (where he continues to live) in June 1962 to go to graduate art school in Philadelphia.[94] His interest in colour has deeper roots than his encounter with Rothko's work, though. He counts *rangoli*, the tradition of constructing colourful floor designs from dry pigments and *Holi*, or spring, festivals in India in which coloured pigments are thrown around onto bodies, as two important influences.[95] In terms of the *Holi* festival, water is often sprayed or thrown onto the revellers, too, so that the pigment adheres to the clothes, which become richly coloured over time. He also cites as an influence the dyed and sewn textiles he saw lying on the grass in his grandfather's village.[96]

Bhavsar does not preplan his works nor is there any kind of trace of a subject (at least a figural one) or clearly defined forms. His process usually involves working on the floor or on a horizontal screen. He typically soaks his canvas in acrylics or acryloids and using varied mesh screens he 'brushes' raw coloured pigment onto the canvas. To create a large 'stroke' he usually raises the screen to disperse the pigment over a larger surface area. Similarly, working close to the canvas allows for fine detail. He has developed a number of sieves and funnels over the years that allow for a variety of different dispersions of pigment.[97] The canvas being wet with binder allows the raw pigment to adhere. This process is repeated a number of times (perhaps even up to two hundred, according to the artist) to create a depth of colour.[98]

Like Twombly, Bhavsar has neither an explicit interest in Zen nor is he queer identified. While Twombly's work contains faint representations of genitalia that seemed to direct one towards a queer reading, in Bhavsar's work there is nothing even remotely representational. Nonetheless, his works, as I argue, are bound up with desire, much like Twombly's. I invoke David Getsy regarding abstraction, iconography and sexuality to contextualize my approach. He writes:

> Too often, the study of sexuality in art is dismissed if it departs from the iconographic depiction of sexual acts or bodies that are deemed to be erotically appealing. It's one of the ways that those suspicious of or uncomfortable with queer theory, for instance, attempt to domesticate its critique – by claiming that anything other than the obvious is 'reading into' or hopeful projective fantasy.[99]

Lack of representation does not equal lack of the possibility of discussing sexuality, as Getsy writes.

As mentioned, Getsy re-fashions abstraction as 'capacity', 'potentiality', 'plenitude' and the 'positing of the unforeclosed'.[100] To this list, I would also add 'queer Zen'. Getsy further writes: 'A capacity manifests its powers as potentiality incipience, and imminence. Only when exercised do capacities become fully apparent, and they may lie in wait to be activated.'[101] In this way, I argue that viewers activate the 'queer Zen' of Bhavsar's abstractions and thereby instantiate new conceptions of the transnational and queer. To explore *how* this manifests, I hone in on Bhavsar's works that were included in the 1970 group exhibition *Beautiful Painting and Sculpture* at the Jewish Museum in New York City. In addition to his works, the exhibition included the work of three other relatively young artists who had not yet exhibited much: sculptor Anthony Sorce and painters Jake Berthot and Harvey Quaytman.

Seven of Bhavsar's large-scale works were hung in one room. They had all been completed either in the year of the exhibition or the year before, roughly eight to nine years after Twombly completed his *Ferragosto* series. Five of Bhavsar's works are a little over 2 metres tall while the largest two measure just under 3 metres in height. The widths of the works vary from 5 metres to a staggering 9 metres.[102] Colour photographs of the installation are not available though one black-and-white photograph suggests the vastness of the room that must have created an immersive experience for the viewer.[103] The Jewish Museum during this period was known for its cutting-edge, even progressive – in this case seeing beyond nationality – contemporary art exhibitions. However, this show was probably the last of its kind. In 1971 the museum decided to forgo all contemporary exhibitions (deemed too expensive) that ostensibly had nothing to do with Jewishness.[104]

Curator Tejas Englesmith described the genesis of his exhibition as follows in his press release: 'The exhibition came about, more or less, as a reaction to some of the negative feeling which seems to pervade so much of today's thought and action. It is a stand for a return to the positive.'[105] As also noted in the press release, Englesmith writes that the exhibition included works by artists that in his estimation were not concerned with 'anti-establishment' attitudes '(i.e. anti-art, conceptual art, earthworks, etc.)'. He further notes, 'Hence the use of the word beautiful which conjures up a positive approach and a timeless quality.'[106] The theme is suspect as several critics note in their reviews of the exhibition. For instance, John Gruen writes in his review tellingly titled 'A Thing of No Beauty': 'Any claim to "beauty" is moot and surely a matter of minor concern for these artists.'[107] Gruen was also most likely referring to the baggage that surrounds such a term in Western aesthetics and art history.[108] At the same time, Gruen himself uses the word 'beautiful' to describe his experience of viewing Bhavsar's paintings:

> [T]hese … arresting paintings contain myriad constellations of both dry and luminous pigments, and produce a remarkable atmospheric blending of color,

> space, and light. These vast canvases are *beautiful*, and provide the only moments of genuine serenity in what is an otherwise unmemorable show.[109]

Almost four decades later, critic Benjamin Genocchio uses a variant of the word to title his review of a survey of Bhavsar's work curated by Jeffrey Wechsler in 2007 as 'The Details Are in the Beauty'.[110] Ratcliff sums it up best when he ends his 1972 review of Bhavsar's exhibition with the following: 'His paintings are beautiful and beyond the ordinary definitions of beauty as well.'[111] In fact, Gruen's conflict with the use of the word, I would argue, is his understanding that Bhavsar's paintings went 'beyond the ordinary definitions of beauty' while not being able to pinpoint another word or phrase to describe his experience. I consider how queer Zen might be more useful to describe the experience of viewing Bhavsar's work. In so doing, I circumvent the troubled history of the 'beautiful' or 'beauty' that Englesmith, Gruen, Genocchio and Ratcliff all use while steering the discussion to explore the transnational and sexuality.

I focus on Bhavsar's work *VAATRI* (1969) which was in the Jewish Museum exhibition (Plate 3). I had an opportunity to see the work when it was exhibited at Cara Gallery in New York City in 2015.[112] From a distance, two distinct energetic showers of colour dominate the picture plane of the painting: one is composed of pigments of fiery red and bright orange while the other is of electric blue and royal purple. As one walks closer, what looked like cascading showers begin to look more like clouds of colour that are dynamic in a different way: they begin to sparkle, especially as one moves closer to the canvas. Art historian Santhi Kavuri-Bauer describes the latter as resembling a field of fireflies.[113] Also, a multitude of other streaks of various coloured pigments come into focus if only for a moment: these include not only different hues of the colours mentioned, but also vibrant yellows, magentas and greens. Oddly enough, much of Barthes's description of Twombly's use of colour could be said of this work, too. Colour here is always on the verge of vanishing: 'like a closing eyelid, a tiny fainting spell'.[114] It does not, however, disappear and leave a bare canvas in its wake; here, colour vanishes and re-emerges as yet another colour ad infinitum. While this is most dramatic when looking at a painting of Bhavsar's over time in a room with daylight, it is discernible even in the white cube. Rather than fields of the same colour, Bhavsar has opted for fields of gradations of multiple colours at varying depths that blur into each other in space. This distinction keeps the works ever changing even from a fixed vantage point.

This also makes describing the colours somewhat moot. Rather, it might be more useful to consider these colours as vectors with various speeds and directions infinitely colliding – paraphrasing Barthes, blink and you will miss it. Moreover, given Bhavsar uses raw pigment, often the materiality of colour is palpable. Indeed, as one moves closer, the work shifts from being about surface to depth or from optical to tactile. Upon close inspection of the canvas it is possible to discern some of Bhavsar's layering process. It becomes clear that the intensity of the sparkling is a function of not only colour but how deep the pigment is embedded in the canvas. Because of its size, *VAATRI* is at first a bit overwhelming, though this initial feeling quickly dissipates as one gets lost in the seemingly unending and fascinating details of the work.

Visible in the photographic documentation of the installation at the Jewish Museum are at least two rectangular cushioned benches, where one might imagine visitors sitting to contemplate the work over a longer period. However, one could just as easily stand at varying distances and get a similar effect. In the earlier quote, Gruen notes that the works provide 'serenity' and Genocchio that they 'focus the eyes and mind so intensely that looking ultimately becomes an act of meditation.'[115] At any rate, the 'act of meditation' – that Genocchio referred to – is akin to a state of Zen. Given that I mobilized Zen through a largely Eastern context in my analysis of Twombly's work and Barthes's writing, it is worth noting that Zen has deep roots in South Asia even as it has morphed and changed through time and through various cultures (not the least of which is the United States in the art world in the 1960s). Indeed, 'Zen' is the Japanese mispronunciation of the Chinese term 'Ch'an', which is an abbreviated version of the longer 'Ch'an-Na', itself a Chinese mispronunciation of the Sanskrit word 'Dhayana' meaning meditation.[116]

It is counterintuitive that colour could produce what is effectively a state of Zen. That is, colour is often only associated with the emotional, the embodied and the 'other'. This is a case, though, where the artist manages to mine the materiality of colour to produce – as art critic Christopher Andreae in his review of the *Beautiful Painting and Sculpture* exhibition writes – 'A visual equivalent, perhaps, of "eloquent silence"'.[117] The latter, of course, is an oxymoron that points out that if the work enacted a state of Zen it was decidedly a queer, or strange, one. That is, the moments of serenity and meditation in viewing Bhavsar's works are cut through with a seemingly irreconcilable desire, both of which emerge from the colour fields of his paintings. Indeed, the Hindi word '*rang*' for colour also means ecstasy.[118] In an interview Bhavsar directly addresses the latter when he says that *rang* 'evokes physical, emotional and sexual connotations.'[119] Andreae perfectly describes the 'paradox' of viewing Bhavsar's work: 'What is easily missed by people looking at these paintings in their usual hurry is that their expressiveness is not of the hit-you-between-the-eyes variety. It is an expressiveness which arises in a strange paradox somewhere between extremely felt sensuousness and extremely felt contemplation.'[120] One's experience is somewhere in between 'felt sensuousness' to 'felt contemplation' as Andreae points out; these affects intermingle and become increasingly unable to separate over time.

In the context of another exhibition in 1972, Ratcliff describes Bhavsar's works as effectively avoiding 'all separation of thought, emotion, and perception.'[121] He even goes as far as to suggest that 'the value of Bhavsar's painting is prior to such projections [of meaning]'.[122] If queer is a state of in-betweenness – between more stable and fixed categories of identity – then it is one prior to projections of fixed meanings. Bhavsar's works straddle the productive space between the mind and body; optical and haptic; meditation and sensuality and the universal and the particular.

If on the level of materiality (his pigments) and his titling of works (neologisms based on Sanskrit) Bhavsar's work can be connected to the subcontinent, then in the experience of the work the notion of bounded space (national or otherwise) disappears.[123] Over time his abstractions begin to resemble recognizable forms that veer between the macro- and microscopic. For instance, the widest work in the Jewish Museum exhibition *THEER-A-THEER-A* (1969) is a field of softer clouds of orange, red and purple pigment all commingling and bleeding into one another (Plate 4). On the one hand, it looks like it could resemble the beginnings of the universe and on the other hand, it could be a depiction of fields of sub-atomic particles. Of course, it is neither/nor but both/and. Within this context, discussing the national and transnational – even 'here' and 'there' – seems obsolete. The reality, though, is that the politics of nationality played a big part in the lack of historicization of Bhavsar's work in the Indian and American contexts. In the next section I elaborate on this point to underscore why frames such as queer Zen are necessary to see his works anew.[124]

Nationalist rhetoric in the art world

If Natvar Bhavsar is one of a number of artists of Asian descent whose works have been largely ignored as part of post-Second World War art history, then this was at least partly due to the fact that critics such as American Clement Greenberg downplayed the influence of Zen and Asian philosophy on Western art. Greenberg, for instance, wrote:

> Actually, not one of the original 'abstract expressionists' … has felt more than a cursory interest in Oriental art. The sources of their art lie entirely in the West; what resemblances to Oriental modes may be found in it are an effect of convergence at the most, and of accident at the least.[125]

The title of the famous essay in which this was written, 'American-Type Painting', suggests what was at stake here. Greenberg was outlining characteristics of a national category and this meant ensuring that the country's output could not be confused with that of any other country or region. Art historian

Bert Winther-Tamaki outlines that artists such as Mark Rothko, Robert Motherwell and especially Franz Kline all disavowed any connection to the influence of Asia.[126] The essay in which Winther-Tamaki discusses the latter is part of a catalogue accompanying the important 2009 exhibition, *The Third Mind: American Artists Contemplate Asia, 1860–1989*, at the Guggenheim Museum in New York City. Organized by curator Alexandra Munroe, the exhibition began reimagining productive connections between post-Second World War artists and the East.[127] At the same time, enfolding the production of artists of Asian descent living in the West into American art history had just begun.[128]

To expand on discourses of modernist art history in the United States, it is productive to bring up Greenberg's only visit to India in 1967. Greenberg was there to accompany the exhibition *Two Decades of American Painting: 1945–1965*, organized by Waldo Rasmussen for the Museum of Modern Art (under the auspices of the museum's International Program).[129] The exhibition included a number of Abstract Expressionist, Color Field and Pop Art works: in total, about a hundred works by thirty-five artists were on display at the Lalit Kala Akademi in New Delhi. Included, too, was the 1961 painting *The Italians* by Cy Twombly. The participants of the seminar on contemporary American and Indian art connected to the exhibition asked Greenberg to give a walk-through of the exhibition before the discussion began.[130] During this tour, according to artist Gieve Patel, Greenberg openly disagreed with many of Rasmussen's selections:

> Barring a polite nod at [Kenneth] Noland and [Morris] Louis he dismissed the second-generation Abstract and Pop [art] as 'tasteful', carrying the dead remains of Cubism … Greenberg bulldozered through [Larry] Rivers, [Philip] Guston, [Joan] Mitchell, [Robert] Rauschenberg, [James] Rosenquist.[131]

It is not surprising that Greenberg 'bulldozered' over the works mentioned by Patel and favoured those of Noland and Louis, whom Greenberg singled out as 'serious candidates for major status' in 1964 several years prior to his trip to India.[132] Their methods included pouring paint directly onto unprimed cotton canvas that effectively soaked it: colour and canvas were deeply intertwined. Paint was not just on top of but in the canvas itself.[133] Greenberg would refer to their method of painting as Post-Painterly Abstraction, or what is more generally known now as Color Field.[134] Louis and Noland fit neatly into Greenberg's belief that modernist painting was continuing the evolution of Western art towards the suppression of sculptural, three-dimensional tendencies, in favour of 'the ineluctable flatness of the surface [of the canvas]'.[135] More specifically, he wrote that to experience painting 'only with the eye' is the end result of 'the last four centuries' of Western painting, the concerns of which

Modernism continues 'without gap or break'.[136] In this way, modernist painting was the teleological heir to 'some of the greatest feats of Western painting'.[137] Referring to Louis's works, he wrote: 'The more closely color could be identified with its ground, the freer would it be from the interference of tactile associations; the way to achieve this closer identification was by adapting watercolor technique to oil and using thin paint on an absorbent surface.'[138] However, Wechsler has pointed out that the United States cannot so easily claim that stain paintings are its invention 'given the millennial-old Eastern tradition of water-based inks and colorants soaked into paper or silk'.[139]

Greenberg was aware of Bhavsar's work. By sifting pigments and using a binder so that they would adhere to the canvas, Bhavsar's work partially adheres to Greenberg's ideology. However, his work is less optical than haptic. Moreover, Greenberg was as much a formalist as he was a nationalist, and Bhavsar did not fit into the mould of a prototypical American subject. The issue is not his transnational roots, given that many of the most celebrated artists of that time were European émigrés, but that he was from South Asia, work from which was not considered part of the contemporary conversation of serious art as far as Greenberg was concerned. With the exception of the brief period when the Whitney Museum of American Art included his work in their annual exhibition in 1969, Bhavsar has been shut out of histories of American art. Bhavsar spent time at the Cedar Tavern, the legendary hangout in New York City for many artists whose works are defined as Abstract Expressionist. Though he was not perhaps a frequent visitor, that his presence in such social settings is invisible in critical writing is stunning.[140]

Bhavsar's work does not sit so easily in discourses of Indian art history, either. After independence from British rule in 1947, there was a strong interest in nation-building in India; artists responded by drawing on South Asia's rich culture and history, but this largely meant abstraction was *not* favoured.[141] By the mid-1960s, when Greenberg visited India, this was less the case. Art historian Devika Singh writes, 'At a time when Indian artists were experimenting with abstraction, pitching his conception of American modernism should not have been that difficult.'[142] Of course, for Greenberg to admit abstraction was not singularly American in character would be to undermine his positioning. Therefore, he was not interested in winning over his audience. Moreover, despite the rise of abstraction in India, nationalist rhetoric continued. Art historian Sonal Khullar explains that 'indigenism' and 'internationalism' emerged as prevailing and binary discourses in the 1970s.[143] These two terms are invoked and explicated by important Indian art historian Geeta Kapur in her 1970 master's thesis titled 'In Quest of Identity: Art & Indigenism in Post-Colonial Culture with Special Reference to Contemporary Indian Painting' – subsequently published in the monthly English language-magazine *Vrishchik*, published in Baroda, India). As Kapur notes, 'the language of postcolonial art could not be the same as that of Western art'.[144] Such rhetoric left little room for the work of Bhavsar who was living in the West and whose work very much grew out of the conversations regarding abstraction in the United States.

It is worth considering the reaction of artists and critics to MoMA's travelling exhibition. The art critic for the Indian English-language daily newspaper the *Statesman* wrote that it was '[a]n exhibition for which we feel grateful to the USA, and which gives ample evidence of the vitality and liveness of art now in America … We have many Abstract Expressionists in India, and some of them do not know how much they have been influenced by this vital American movement.'[145] This critic illustrates the presence of abstraction in India, though, as being in direct debt to the West. Artists, however, were quick to divorce themselves from what they described as the 'local scene of the West'. For instance, Krishen Khanna, an artist who had painted and exhibited in New York City, said: 'American painting is not universal … A lot of it is terribly local. The painting's [*sic*] of Frank Stella, for instance, are only important in the New York situation, as a reaction to other paintings. They're part of a little "in" joke. They're not important here.'[146] The title of an article in the *Times of Delhi*, 'New York Centre of World Art, Feels U.S. Critic', points to what Khanna was reacting against: the cavalier self-appointed supremacy of American art.[147] Khanna's point that American painting is 'local' is well taken. Bhavsar's works, which were not part of the exhibition that MoMA brought over, were very much a product of the debates in the New York art world. Ironically, he was neither American enough for American art history nor Indian enough for Indian art history.

As adamant as Greenberg was in policing the borders of American modernist painting, the artists, critics and general public of India seemed similarly to want to disengage themselves from any connection to American abstraction. Overall, the reviews of the exhibition in the Indian press were generally less charitable in their assessments of the exhibition than that of the *Statesman*. One critic wrote, 'In this brave new world of ideas that almost cancel out one another, that demand attention, create sensation, provide visual stimuli but offer little or no satisfaction.'[148] The art critic for the (now defunct) independent left-wing newspaper *Patriot* wrote, 'A sufficient number of good works mixed with lots of chaff which can only be termed as "gimmicks".'[149] In terms of visitors to the exhibition, comments in the guest book were more varied. They ranged from 'extremely exciting', 'delicious' and 'mystifying in a nice way' to 'inexplicable', 'decadent and boring', 'tragic!', 'degenerate' and 'American artists are mad'.[150]

Bhavsar, therefore, did not fit neatly into what were effectively nationalist discourses of art in the United States and India. In the context of a global modernist frame, art historians Sonal Khullar and Atreyee Gupta have suggested the way out of such unresolvable positions. Khullar writes about 'cosmopolitan belonging' and 'worldly affiliations' as always already part of modernism in India.[151] She writes that 'the idea of modernism as affiliation holds matters of identity and difference in tension and allows for spatial, temporal, conceptual, and material divergences between artistic practices and movements across the globe'.[152] Gupta notes that one way out of the 'epistemological tensions' that non-Western contexts posed for the modernist canon is through 'a dialectic between modernism and modernization'.[153] In a similar way, my focus on queer Zen similarly attempts to move beyond the aporia created by the discourses of both modernism in post-partition India and post-Second World War United States and to consider Bhavsar's work through other frames.

My approach to reading the archives of art history is a mode of what media theorist Alex (Alexandra) Juhasz has conceptualized as 'queer archive activism'.[154] She coined the term to describe her practice of editing her repository of an AIDS video archive so that it maintains 'an indexical trace of the past but creates the possibility for an anticipated trace of the future'.[155] The works of both Bhavsar and Twombly (and their interlocutors) from the 1960s and 1970s function as 'trace[s] of the past' that contain the seeds of the 'trace[s] of the [queer and transnational] future'. Embedded in both artists' abstractions are the limits of conventional identity politics; and suggest that it remains even more important than ever for art historians interested in identity to look at artistic practices in the past – prior to 1980 – to better understand the present.

Drawing on Juhasz, women's and gender studies scholar Ann Cvetkovich notes that the 'radical potential' of LGBT archives can be activated by taking 'an activist relation to the archive that remains alert to its absences and that uses it to create new kinds of knowledge and new forms of collectivity'.[156] Cvetkovich is referring to the absence of lesbian paraphernalia in archives dedicated to LGBTQI subjects whereas I am referring to a very different kind of archive. Through my reading I am connecting the works of artists that perhaps would never be seen in the same frame and in this way I have aimed 'to create new kinds of knowledge' and art histories outside of conventional identity politics.

The following by Barthes on the work of Twombly (whom he refers to as 'TW') – and which I think can be extended to that of Bhavsar – is instructive: 'Of writing TW retains the gesture, not the product … even if TW's productions link up with (they cannot escape) a History and a Theory of Art, what is *shown* is a gesture. What is a gesture? … it seeks only to provoke an object, a result.'[157] My hope is that my own writing acts as a gesture 'to provoke' the production of art histories even as I am aware that '(they cannot escape) a History and Theory of Art'.

Notes

1 Historian and curator Jack (John Kuo Wei) Tchen managed the institute. The legacy website can be found here: 'Re-envisioning American Art History: Asian American Art, Research, and Teaching', accessed 7 November 2015, www.nyu-apastudies.org/research/NEH/?page_id=9.

2 I am referring to Machida's 1994 seminal exhibition: see Margo Machida et al., *Asia/America: Identities in Contemporary Asian American Art* (New York: Asia Society Galleries; New Press, 1994). Also see Margo Machida, 'Reframing Asian America', in *One Way or Another: Asian American Art Now*, ed. Melissa Chiu, Karin M. Higa and Susette S. Min (New Haven, CT: Asia Society with Yale University Press, 2006), 15–20.

3 Jeffrey Wechsler, 'From Asian Traditions to Modern Expressions: Abstract Art by Asian Americans, 1945–1970', in *Asian Traditions/Modern Expressions: Asian American Artists and Abstraction, 1945–1970* (New York: Harry N. Abrams in association with the Jane Voorhees Zimmerli Art Museum, Rutgers, the State University of New Jersey, 1997), 136.

4 I culled this information from a press release from one of the venues to which the exhibition travelled: 'Japanese American National Museum And Fisher Gallery, USC Present "Asian Traditions/Modern Expressions: Asian American Artists And Abstractions, 1945–1970"', press release, *Japanese American National Museum* (1997), www.janm.org/press/release/69/. The exhibition travelled to one more location in the United States, the Chicago Culture Center. Abroad, it travelled to Taiwan (Taipei Fine Arts Museum; Kaohsiung Museum of Fine Arts) and Japan (Marugame Genichiro Inokuma Museum; Fukuoka Asian Art Museum; Akita Senshu Museum). Although it falls outside of the scope of this book, it would be interesting to explore the reception of the exhibition in Asia.

5 That fall, I adjusted my syllabus for the contemporary art course I teach to include some of the abstract works by artists of Asian descent alongside Jackson Pollock's drip paintings and Franz Kline's gesture artworks. When I teach Pollock alongside Kenzo Okada, for instance, I first focus on formal connections – often showing works without including the authors' names. Later on, I discuss the politics of authorship and the canon. In a similar way here, I explore form first to allow for juxtapositions that might not be possible while not eschewing the politics of authorship.

6 The asterisk refers to all transgender, non-binary and gender non-conforming identities.

7 Joan Kee, 'The World in Plain View: Form in the Service of the Global', in *Contemporary Art: 1989 to the Present*, ed. Alexander Blair Dumbadze and Suzanne Perling Hudson (Chichester, West Sussex: Wiley-Blackwell, 2013), 98.

8 Critic Lowery Sims's review of Natvar Bhavsar's work in 1984 is an exception. It is an example of how inclusiveness can result in a serious consideration of the artwork. That is, the review begins with a discussion of exclusion of artists of colour and woman artists but her review shows a careful attention to the

work of Bhavsar that moves beyond the author and artwork dipole. See Lowery S. Sims, 'The Paintings of Natvar Bhavsar', *Arts Magazine* (December 1984): 122.

9 Jennifer Doyle and David Getsy, 'Queer Formalisms: Jennifer Doyle and David Getsy in Conversation', *The Art Journal* 72 (2013): 58–71.

10 Ibid., 60. According to Doyle, Warhol reoriented the books that came with the home when he bought it because he had no personal connection to them.

11 Ibid., 61.

12 Ibid., 63. Doyle notes that criticism by art historians of this approach that 'carve[s] out semantic space for differently identified individuals' often masks 'a defensive and pernicious desire to uphold the normative'. Unfortunately, the latter is what has led many scholars to move away from art history to other disciplines such as performance studies, which has produced some of the most forward-thinking scholarship related to the visual in the last fifteen years. Having said that, moving beyond these polarizing debates is important to avoid trapping knowledge into silos. This is an important aim of this book.

13 Ibid., 62.

14 For instance, see Jonathan D. Katz, 'Agnes Martin: Sexuality of Abstraction', in *Agnes Martin*, ed. Lynne Cooke, Karen J. Kelly and Barbara Schröder (New Haven, CT: Yale University Press and Dia Art Foundation, 2011), 170–97. Also, see the following: Jonathan D. Katz, 'John Cage's Queer Silence; Or, How to Avoid Making Matters Worse', *GLQ: A Journal of Lesbian and Gay Studies* 5 (1999): 231–52. The latter is reprinted alongside many of his other essays that are germane to this topic here: *Queer Cultural Center*, accessed 8 May 2015, www.queerculturalcenter.org/Pages/KatzPages/KatzIntro.html.

15 'Asian American Art: A History, 1850–1970', *Stanford University Press*, accessed 8 May 2015, www.sup.org/books/title/?id=9403.

16 Gordon H. Chang et al. (eds), *Asian American Art: A History, 1850–1970* (Stanford, CA: Stanford University Press, 2008).

17 David J. Getsy, 'The Unforeclosed', in *FLEX*, Brochure for Exhibition of Same Name (New York: Kent Fine Art, 2014), www.kentfineart.net/attachment/en/5374fae0a9aa2cd3748b4568/TextOneColumnWithFile/53d287e252d850f22a6f02eb.

18 Ibid.

19 Kandice Chuh, *Imagine Otherwise: On Asian Americanist Critique* (Durham, NC: Duke University Press, 2003).

20 Ibid., 151.

21 Ibid., 9.

22 Ibid., 11.

23 Emphasis in original. Ibid., 10.

24 I do not mean to minimize the importance of other identifications, such as pansexual and two-spirit identity, when I use LGBTQI. Indeed, this is the endgame from which I am trying to move away in this chapter. I explore identity as moving beyond yet still referencing these categories.

25 I am invoking British sociologist Paul Gilroy's alternative to diaspora, which privileges both 'roots' (where one is from) and 'routes' (where one has been). Paul Gilroy, *The Black Atlantic: Modernity and Double Consciousness* (Cambridge, MA: Harvard University Press, 1993), 133.
26 Getsy, 'The Unforeclosed'.
27 Recently, art historian Majella Munroe explored how Zen can be a useful intellectual framework to explore transnationalism in her analysis of the work of Mira Schendel. See Majella Munroe, 'Zen as a Transnational Current in Post-War Art: The Case of Mira Schendel', *Tate Papers*, no. 23 (Spring 2005), www.tate.org.uk/research/publications/tate-papers/zen-transnational-current-post-war-art-mira-schendel.
28 Katz, 'Agnes Martin: Sexuality of Abstraction'.
29 Martin's works are notoriously difficult to photograph. For the book with the most high-quality images, see Arne Glimcher, *Agnes Martin: Paintings, Writings, Remembrances by Arne Glimcher* (London; New York: Phaidon Press, 2012).
30 As summarized in the following review of Nancy Princenthal's 2015 biography of Agnes Martin, Martin had relationships with several women in the 1950s, including Greek sculptor Chryssa, gallerist Betty Parsons and fibre artist Lenore Tawney: Ann Landi, 'Living On and Off the Grid', *The Wall Street Journal* (Online), 24 July 2015, www.wsj.com/articles/living-on-and-off-the-grid-1437768845; Nancy Princenthal, *Agnes Martin: Her Life and Art* (New York: Thames & Hudson, 2015). Landi also notes that a documentary by Jina and Kathleen Brennan titled 'Agnes Martin: Before the Grid' suggests she also had a 'lengthy relationship' with Mildred Kane, who Martin met at Columbia University. www.taosnews.com/entertainment/agnes-martin-before-the-grid-set-to-premier/article_5f0e9568-7a7d-11e6-bb2f-cb3c957230cd.html.
31 The lecture was part of a symposium connected to the National Portrait Gallery's 2010–11 exhibition *Hide/Seek: Difference and Desire in American Portraiture*, which Katz co-curated. See *Katz, Jonathan D., Presentation on Agnes Martin for 'Hide/Seek' Exhibition Symposium*, 2011, *YouTube*, accessed 7 May 2015, www.youtube.com/watch?v=BbFLur5zdAI&feature=youtube_gdata_player.
32 Katz, 'Agnes Martin: Sexuality of Abstraction', 173.
33 Ibid., 177. Katz does not explain what he means by this but he does cite several sources. See ibid., 195–6 (note 15).
34 Katz, 'Agnes Martin: Sexuality of Abstraction', 177.
35 Ibid.
36 Alexandra Munroe's 2009 important exhibition *The Third Mind: American Artists Contemplate Asia, 1860–1989* at the Guggenheim Museum in New York City explores this topic in some detail. See Alexandra Munroe, 'Buddhism and the Neo-Avant-Garde: Cage Zen, Beat Zen, and Zen', in *The Third Mind: American Artists Contemplate Asia, 1860–1989*, ed. Alexandra Munroe (New York: Guggenheim Museum, 2009), 199–216. Also, see Ellen Pearlman, *Nothing & Everything: The Influence of Buddhism on the American Avant*

Garde 1942–1962 (Berkeley, CA: Evolver Editions, 2014). I thank Hrag Vartanian for pointing the latter reference out to me.

37 Rather than suggesting that Zen has any kind of fixed meaning, I aim to productively mobilize the interpretation of Zen by Katz and reinterpret that of Roland Barthes later in this chapter.

38 I am referring to two of Barthes's essays: Roland Barthes, 'Cy Twombly: Works on Paper', in *The Responsibility of Forms: Critical Essays on Music, Art, and Representation*, trans. Richard Howard (New York: Hill & Wang, 1985), 157–76. [Originally written in 1976 and titled '*Non Multa Sed Multum*', the preface to volume 6 of Yvon Lambert's *Cy Twombly: Catalogue Raisonné of Works on Paper* (Milan: Multhipla, 1979): 7–13.]; and Roland Barthes, 'The Wisdom of Art', in *The Responsibility of Forms: Critical Essays on Music, Art, and Representation*, trans. Richard Howard (New York: Hill & Wang, 1985), 177–94. [Originally published in *Cy Twombly: Paintings and Drawings, 1954–1977: Whitney Museum of American Art, April 10–June 10, 1979* (New York: Whitney Museum of American Art, 1979), 9–22.]

39 Simon Ofield-Kerr, 'Cruising the Archive', *Journal of Visual Culture* 4, no. 3 (1 December 2005): 357.

40 This is noted in Claire Daigle, 'Cy Twombly: Lingering at the Threshold Between Word and Image', *TATE ETC*, no. 13 (2008): 62–69, www.tate.org.uk/context-comment/articles/lingering-threshold-between-word-and-image. (An interesting bit of trivia is that Yvon Lambert approached Barthes after having been turned down by Michel Foucault; see Richard Leeman, 'Roland Barthes et Cy Twombly: Le "Champ Allusif de L'écriture"', *Rue Descartes* 34, no. 4 (2001): 61 (note 1).) See also Daigle's doctoral dissertation in which she focuses on Barthes and Twombly: Claire Daigle, 'Reading Barthes/Writing Twombly' (PhD dissertation, City University of New York, 2004). She connects the two through a sustained interest in the slipperiness of signifiers, though she does not extend her analysis to sexuality.

41 This information is based on information provided by Twombly to Achim Hochdörfer. See Achim Hochdörfer, '"Blue Goes Out, B Comes In": Cy Twombly's Narration of Interminacy', in *Cy Twombly: States of Mind. Painting, Sculpture, Photography, Drawing* (Munich and Vienna: Schirmer/Mosel Verlag; Museum Moderner Kunst Stiftung Ludwig Wien, 2009), 22, 39 (note 13).

42 This is perhaps why Twombly's works were not included in Alexandra Munroe's important 2009 exhibition exploring the influence of Zen on American artists who were not of Asian descent and whose works emerged in the 1950s and 1960s. See Alexandra Munroe (ed.), *The Third Mind: American Artists Contemplate Asia, 1860–1989* (New York: Guggenheim Museum, 2009).

43 Claire Daigle, 'Biography', *Cy Twombly*, accessed 7 May 2015, www.cytwombly.info.

44 Under the biography section of Cy Twombly's official website, Claire Daigle notes that in the upper third portion of *Untitled*, 1962 (not illustrated, unfortunately), there is a veritable legend of sorts for Twombly's colour scheme/graphite marks: a white circle swirled with pink is labelled 'blood' and an

aggressive red 'x' reads as 'flesh', for instance. The fixity of these meanings seems so discordant with how I describe Twombly's work in this chapter that I offer this information merely as an interesting counterpoint to my argument. See ibid.

45 Elizabeth J. Trapp, 'Cy Twombly's Ferragosto Series' (Master's thesis, Ohio University, 2010), 39, www.ohiolink.edu/etd/view.cgi?ohiou1276609006.

46 Daigle, 'Cy Twombly: Lingering at the Threshold Between Word and Image', www.tate.org.uk/context-comment/articles/lingering-threshold-between-word-and-image.

47 David Batchelor, *Chromophobia* (London: Reaktion, 2000), 32; Charles A. Riley II, *Color Codes: Modern Theories of Color in Philosophy, Painting and Architecture, Literature, Music, and Psychology* (Lebanon, NH: University Press of New England, 1995), 60. It is worth noting that Twombly says that 'I'm not too sensitive to colour, not really. I don't use it with any nuance, that I know of. The form of the thing is more interesting to me than colour … I take the colour as primary … like, if it's the woods, it's green; if it's blood, it's red; if it's earth, it's brown.' At the same time, he says that he is interested, 'in creating … emotional form'. This latter statement makes clear that he was not attempting to rid the canvas of colour because of its potential affective qualities. Nicholas Serota, 'History behind the Thought (interview with Twombly)', in *Cy Twombly: Cycles and Seasons*, ed. Nicholas Serota (London: Tate Publishing, 2008), 52.

48 Barthes, 'Cy Twombly: Works on Paper', 166.

49 Riley, *Color Codes*, 60.

50 Barthes, 'Cy Twombly: Works on Paper', 166.

51 Emphasis in original. Ibid.

52 Doyle and Getsy, 'Queer Formalisms: Jennifer Doyle and David Getsy in Conversation', 59. Getsy also notes, 'I think it's crucial to remember that bodily relations immediately and inescapably activate questions about gender and sexuality. Historically, sculpture and performance art have shared this as a fundamental issue. Both rely on the viewer's proprioceptive assessment of their copresence with the sculpture or performer.'

53 Roland Barthes, 'Non Multa Sed Multum', in *Cy Twombly: Fifty Years of Works on Paper*, trans. Henry Martin (Munich: Schirmer/Mosel, 2004), 32. This is the only place where I do not draw on Richard Howard's translation of the original essay. Instead of 'enigmatic supplement', Howard refers to an 'enigmatic surplus'. See Barthes, 'Cy Twombly: Works on Paper', 167.

54 Jacques Derrida, *Of Grammatology* (Baltimore: Johns Hopkins University Press, 1976), 144–5.

55 J. L. (John Langshaw) Austin, *How to Do Things with Words*, 2nd edn, The William James Lectures 1955 (Cambridge, MA: Harvard University Press, 1975); Rosalind Krauss, 'Cy Was Here: Cy's Up', *Artforum* 33, no. 1 (1994): 70 5, 188.

56 Louis Althusser, 'Ideology and Ideological State Apparatuses', in *Lenin and Philosophy, and Other Essays*, trans. Ben Brewster (New York: Monthly Review Press, 1972), 127–86.

57 Krauss, 'Cy Was Here', 74.
58 Emphasis in original. Barthes, 'Cy Twombly: Works on Paper', 173.
59 Ibid., 170.
60 The pagan turned Roman Catholic holiday illustrates how (as Krauss notes via Michel Foucault) 'sequestered within every seemingly neutral historical narrative was the discursive axis of the performative's relations of authority'. Moreover, Krauss's reading of Barthes via Twombly's works differs in that Krauss argues that the present tense of the performative gives way to the unequivocal 'past tense of the index'. Krauss, 'Cy Was Here'. Barthes, however, suggests that the '*past tense* of the stroke can also be defined as its *future*'. He further notes that 'TW's work seems to be conjugated in the past tense or in the future, never really in the present'. Emphasis in original. Barthes, 'Cy Twombly: Works on Paper', 167.
61 Judith Butler, 'Critically Queer', *GLQ: A Journal of Lesbian and Gay Studies* 1, no. 1 (1 November 1993): 17–32, doi:10.1215/10642684-1-1-17. Along with Butler, Teresa de Laurentis and Eve Kososfky Sedgwick are credited with founding the main concerns of queer theory as it has developed since. See William B. Turner, *A Genealogy of Queer Theory* (Philadelphia: Temple University Press, 2000), 107.
62 Barthes, 'Cy Twombly: Works on Paper', 161.
63 Ibid., 175.
64 Roland Barthes, 'Preface to Renauld Camus's *Tricks*', in *The Rustle of Language*, trans. Richard Howard (Berkeley: University of California Press, 1989), 291–2. Emphasis in original.
65 See Jonathan D. Katz, '"Committing the Perfect Crime": Sexuality, Assemblage, and the Postmodern Turn in American Art', *Art Journal* 67, no. 1 (March 2008): 39 (note 1), doi:10.1080/00043249.2008.10791293. Also available from www.queerculturalcenter.org/Pages/KatzPages/KatzIntro.html. Katz 'recovers' via poet and art critic John Yau a series of letters between poets Charles Olson and Robert Creeley that indicate 'matter of factly' that Twombly was in a romantic relationship with Robert Rauschenberg. Twombly and Rauschenberg attended Black Mountain College when Olson was the director.
66 Irit Rogoff, 'Gossip as Testimony: A Postmodern Signature', in *The Feminism and Visual Culture Reader*, ed. Amelia Jones (London and New York: Routledge, 2003), 272.
67 Gavin Butt, *Between You and Me: Queer Disclosures in the New York Art World, 1948–1963* (Durham, NC: Duke University Press, 2005).
68 See Moira Roth, 'The Aesthetic of Indifference', *Artforum*, November 1977. This has been reprinted in Moira Roth and Jonathan D. Katz, *Difference/Indifference: Musings on Postmodernism, Marcel Duchamp and John Cage* (Amsterdam: G+B Arts International, 1998).
69 Department of the Bureau of Diplomatic Security of the United States Department of State, *History of the Bureau of Diplomatic Security of the United States Department of State*, 7 December 2011, www.state.gov/m/ds/rls/rpt/c47602.htm. See chapter 4, 'McCarthyism and Cold War'.

70 See Jonathan D. Katz, 'Passive Resistance: On the Critical and Commercial Success of Queer Artists in Cold War American Art', *Queer Cultural Center*, accessed 7 May 2015, www.queerculturalcenter.org/Pages/KatzPages/KatzLimage.html. Originally published in *L'image*, Paris, no. 3 (Winter 1996).

71 Katz, as cited in Tui Nicola Clery, 'The F-word: Challenging Gender Norms, Performing Possibilities and Celebrating Lesbian Relationships in Contemporary Fiji, *Intersections: Gender and Sexuality in Asia and the Pacific* 35 (July 2014) http://intersections.anu.edu.au/issue35/clery.htm.

72 David Sylvester, 'Cy Twombly (2000)', in *Interviews with American Artists* (New Haven, CT: Yale University Press, 2001), 171–81; Serota, 'History behind the Thought (interview with Twombly)'.

73 Nicholas Serota, 'Interview: US Artist Cy Twombly Talks to Tate Director Nicholas Serota', *Guardian*, accessed 27 May 2015, www.theguardian.com/artanddesign/2008/jun/03/art1.

74 Serota, 'History behind the Thought (interview with Twombly)', 53.

75 Randy Kennedy, 'Cy Twombly, Idiosyncratic Painter, Dies at 83', *The New York Times*, 5 July 2011, http://artsbeat.blogs.nytimes.com/2011/07/05/cy-twombly-idiosyncratic-painter-dies-at-83/?_r=0. Kennedy notes that even 'artist and writer Donald Judd, who was hostile toward painting in general, was especially damning even so, calling the show a fiasco.' 'There are a few drips and splatters and an occasional pencil line', he wrote in a review. 'There isn't anything to these paintings.' Full quote reads: 'Twombly has not shown for some time, and this adds to the fiasco. In these paintings there are a couple of swirls of red paint mixed with a little yellow and white and placed high on a medium-gray surface. There are a few drips and splatters and an occasional pencil line: There isn't anything to the paintings. The poster for the show is an example of Twombly's earlier work and is easily the best thing present. Twombly usually scribbles on a white ground, using color infrequently.' See Donald Judd, 'Cy Twombly', *Arts Magazine* 38, nos 8–9 (May–June 1964): 38.

76 By the time Twombly had his retrospective at the Museum of Modern Art in New York City his reputation had certainly been cemented. Even so, the curator of the exhibition's title of an article for the museum's bulletin is telling: see Kirk Varnedoe, 'Your Kid Could Not Do This, and Other Reflections on Cy Twombly', *MoMA*, no. 18 (Autumn–Winter 1994): 18–23. Art historian Jon Bird notes that Twombly's work turned Barthes the critic into an artist – well, at least for a brief moment – in which he discovers that mark-making is less straightforward than he might have thought. See Jon Bird, 'Indeterminacy and (Dis)order in the Work of Cy Twombly', *Oxford Art Journal* 30, no. 3 (1 October 2007): 484–504, doi:10.1093/oxartj/kcm024. He further writes, 'The critic turns artist in the forelorn attempt to comprehend what his critical tools have failed to provide – an interpretation adequate to its object' (page 487).

77 Jacques Derrida, *Speech and Phenomena: And Other Essays on Husserl's Theory of Signs*, trans. David B. Allison (Evanston, IL: Northwestern University Press, 1973), 88. See also xliii in the 'Preface'.

78 Barthes, 'Cy Twombly: Works on Paper', 176. See also Barthes, 'The Wisdom of Art', 194.
79 Barthes, 'Cy Twombly: Works on Paper', 175.
80 Helen Vendler, 'The Medley Is the Message', *The New York Review of Books*, 8 May 1986, www.nybooks.com/articles/archives/1986/may/08/the-medley-is-the-message/.
81 Nicholas de Villiers, *Opacity and the Closet: Queer Tactics in Foucault, Barthes, and Warhol* (Minneapolis: University of Minnesota Press, 2012), 118. See especially chapter 4, 'Unseen Warhol/Seeing Barthes'.
82 Barthes, 'Cy Twombly: Works on Paper', 175.
83 Roland Barthes, '"L'Express" Talks with Roland Barthes', in *The Grain of the Voice: Interviews 1962–1980*, trans. Linda Coverdale (New York: Hill & Wang, 1985), 98, as quoted in Daigle, 'Reading Barthes/Writing Twombly', 225.
84 Irving Sandler, *Natvar Bhavsar: Painting and the Reality of Color* (Sydney: Craftsman House; G+B Arts International, 1998), 8.
85 Ibid., 14.
86 Whitney Museum of American Art, *1969 Annual Exhibition: Contemporary American Painting. December 16, 1969–February 1, 1970, Whitney Museum of American Art* (New York: Whitney Museum of American Art, 1969). The annuals had alternated between a focus on painting and sculpture since 1932. However, in 1973 the museum switched to a biennial structure. John I. H. Baur, director of the Whitney Museum, wrote in the foreword of the 1973 catalogue that since there was a 'growing tendency of both painting and sculpture to escape their traditionally self-contained limits and become events in the environment', it no longer made sense to have medium-specific exhibitions. The square footage the biennials took up was correspondingly doubled given the broader remit. Whitney Museum of American Art, *1973 Biennial Exhibition: Contemporary American Art. Whitney Museum of American Art, New York, January 10–March 18, 1973* (New York: Whitney Museum of American Art, 1973), no pagination.
87 Jeffrey Wechsler notes that some parts of the art world were exceptional in their embrace of artists of Asian descent during the postwar period in the United States and often claimed them as simply 'American': 'Survey exhibitions of American art, of which there were many more in the 1950s and 1960s than the present, seemed anxious not just to include Asian Americans but to claim them simply as American, even if they had been in the country only a few years.' See Wechsler, 'From Asian Traditions to Modern Expressions', 71.
88 Whitney Museum of American Art, *1969 Annual Exhibition*, cover.
89 Sandler, *Natvar Bhavsar*; Carter Ratcliff, 'Natvar Bhavsar: The Purpose of Looking', *Art International* 16, no. 8 (October 1972): 17–20.
90 See Jeffrey Wechsler and Marius Kwint, *Natvar Bhavsar: Dimensions of Color*, ed. Jeffrey Wechsler (New Brunswick, NJ: Jane Voorhees Zimmerli Art Museum, Rutgers, the State University of New Jersey, 2007).
91 Chang et al., *Asian American Art: A History, 1850–1970*.

92 Even when cultural production became more prominent as an object of study in the 1980s in Asian American studies, literary works received most of the attention by critics. The discipline has downplayed cultural production, more generally, in favour of focusing on history and sociology – largely because these were the main disciplines of the scholars who created the field. See Inderpal Grewal, *Transnational America: Feminisms, Diasporas, Neoliberalisms* (Durham, NC: Duke University Press, 2005), 61. In addition, the differences between the formation of South Asian and other Asian American subjects led to the former being excluded from academic Asian American studies until only recently. See Shilpa Davé et al., 'De-Privileging Positions: Indian Americans, South Asian Americans, and the Politics of Asian American Studies', *Journal of Asian American Studies* 3, no. 1 (2000): 67–100. This was primarily because the first migrants from South Asia, largely Punjabi farmers, remained few in number since they could not bring their families to the United States. By 1950, only 815 'East Indians' resided in California, where most immigrants worked as farmers – a sharp decline from a high of 1,948 in 1910. See Grewal, *Transnational America*, 61.

93 A small group exhibition by MoMA was put together by Sam Hunter to represent the United States at the larger 3rd International Contemporary Art Exhibition that included work by 35 other countries. It was held at the All-India Arts and Crafts Society in New Delhi, India, from 23 February to 7 March 1957. The MoMA exhibition later travelled to a number of other cities in India such as Calcutta, Hyderabad, Mumbai (then Bombay), Amritsar and Ahmedabad, where Bhavsar encountered the work. The exhibition was meant to introduce the styles of artworks from the last fifteen years and (in addition to the work of Rothko) included those of Stuart Davis, Arshile Gorky, Adolph Gottlieb, Grace Hartigan, Willem de Kooning, Jackson Pollock, Niles Spencer and Mark Tobey. See 'U.S. Representation in 3rd International Contemporary Art Exhibition, India', press release, *The Museum of Modern Art* (18 February 1957), www.moma.org/momaorg/shared/pdfs/docs/press_archives/2156/releases/MOMA_1957_0014.pdf?2010.

94 Sandler, *Natvar Bhavsar*, 14. Visas at that time were only being given out to study a technical field. So, Bhavsar initially enrolled at Philadelphia College of Art (then Museum College) to study industrial design. However, he was there for only a semester. See Natvar Bhavsar, 'Interview with Abeed Hossain. "The Metaphysics of Expression: A Conversation with Natvar Bhavsar"', *South Asia Journal* no. 4 (21 March 2012), http://southasiajournal.net/the-metaphysics-of-expression-a-conversation-with-natvar-bhavsar/. He transferred to study art at Tyler School of Art and eventually graduated with an MFA from the University of Pennsylvania. He had already obtained a master's degree in art from C.N. School of Art in Ahmedabad in 1958. The following year he received a government diploma in art and then in 1960 a bachelor's degree in English literature from Gujarat University.

95 Natvar Bhavsar, interview by Alpesh Kantilal Patel, 6 August 2015. It is worth noting that Po Kim, Chao Chun-Hsiang and other artists of East Asian

descent used bright colours, too. Chao even incorporated phosphorescent pigments into his ink and acrylic media. Wechsler surmises that this colourful body of work has largely gone unnoticed 'because it reversed the stereotypical cultural association' of these artists using muted tonalities. See Wechsler, 'From Asian Traditions to Modern Expressions', 74. Exploring colour among artists of South Asian and East Asian descent during the 1960s and 1970s would be an interesting investigation that not only challenges the latter point but also allows for the work of artists descended from various sectors of Asia to be considered in one frame.

96 Robert C. Morgan, 'Natvar Bhavsar's Threshold of Purity', in *Natvar Bhavsar: Five Decades*, ed. Irene Cassina, Marco Cassina and Akaash Mehta (New York: Cara Gallery, 2015), 6.

97 Marius Kwint, 'Color Immersion: Natvar Bhavsar in Conversation', in *Natvar Bhavsar: Poetics of Color* (Milan: Skira Editore S.p.A., 2008), 10.

98 Vibhuti Patel, 'New Explorations in a Universe of Color; Natvar Bhavsar Talks About a New Show of His Dry-Pigment Canvases', *Wall Street Journal* (Online), 28 May 2013.

99 Doyle and Getsy, 'Queer Formalisms: Jennifer Doyle and David Getsy in Conversation', 59.

100 Getsy, 'The Unforeclosed'.

101 David Getsy, *Abstract Bodies: Sixties Sculpture in the Expanded Field of Gender* (New Haven, CT: Yale University Press, 2015), 34.

102 The exhibition included the following works (all pigment and acrylic on canvas): *SHRAAVANAA*, 1969, 81½ × 192 in.; *VARSAA*, 1969, 81½ × 192 in.; *VANA-RAA*, 1970, 108 × 168 in.; *THEER-A-THEER-A*, 1969, 81½ × 360 in.; *SAMA-LAA*, 1969, 81½ × 240 in.; *KALA-RAA*, 1969, 108 × 192 in.; *VAATRI*, 1969, 108 × 192 in.; and *SULA-DHA*, 1970, 81½ × 240 in. Many thanks to the Jewish Museum's Leon Levy, former Assistant Curator Daniel S. Palmer and archivist Barbara Packer for providing me with this information; and to Janet Brosious Bhavsar for help in identifying details of works in the exhibition.

103 Sandler, *Natvar Bhavsar*, 20.

104 For a thorough account of the history of the museum, see Matthew Israel, 'A Magnet for the With-It Kids: The Jewish Museum, New York, of the 1960s', *Art in America*, October 2007, 72–83. I thank Daniel S. Palmer for pointing me to this engaging article. Although it falls outside the parameters of this chapter, it would be fascinating to consider what art history would look like if it were a reflection of the curatorial practices of that time.

105 'Three Exhibitions Opening at the Museum' (The Jewish Museum, n.d.), press release. A critic of the exhibition questioned exactly what was anti-art about conceptual art and earthworks.

106 Emphasis in original. Ibid.

107 John Gruen, 'A Thing of No Beauty', *New York Magazine*, 6 April 1970.

108 William Pietz has noted that Kant in his *Observations on the Feeling of the Beautiful and the Sublime* (1764) described the quasi-religious fetishes that supposedly characterized African culture as products of a debased aesthetic sensibility whose degraded sense of the beautiful lacked all sense of the

sublime. Desire was shifted on to the non-West. He goes on to write that aesthetics and religious fetishism were both coined not only in relative historical contiguity by Alexander Baumgarten in his *Aesthetica* (1750) and Charles de Brosses in his *Du culte des dieux fétiches, ou Parallèle de l'ancienne Religion de l'Egypte avec la Religion actuelle de Nigritie* (1760), respectively, but also in 'theoretical proximity'. See William Pietz, 'Fetish', in *Critical Terms for Art History*, ed. Robert S. Nelson and Richard Shiff, 2nd edn (Chicago: University of Chicago Press, 2010), 307.

109 Emphasis mine. Gruen, 'A Thing of No Beauty'.

110 The word 'beauty' only appears in the title of the review. Benjamin Genocchio, 'The Details Are in the Beauty', *The New York Times*, 6 May 2007, sec. New York/Region / New York/Region Special, www.nytimes.com/2007/05/06/nyregion/nyregionspecial2/06artsnj.html.

111 Ratcliff, 'Natvar Bhavsar: The Purpose of Looking', 20.

112 Cf. Irene Cassina, Marco Cassina and Akaash Mehta (eds), *Natvar Bhavsar: Five Decades* (New York: Cara Gallery, 2015).

113 Natvar Bhavsar, interview by Alpesh Kantilal Patel and Santhi Kavuri-Bauer, 17 July 2012.

114 Barthes, 'Cy Twombly: Works on Paper', 166.

115 Genocchio, 'The Details Are in the Beauty'.

116 Herbert Sullivan, 'Zen Buddhism: An Ancient Eastern Religion, It Is Gaining Popularity as a Philosophy in the Western World', *Duke Alumni Register*, April 1961, 8, https://ia800307.us.archive.org/5/items/dukealumniregist471961/dukealumniregist471961.pdf.

117 Christopher Andreae, 'Beautiful Painting and Sculpture at the Jewish Museum', *Christian Science Monitor*, 20 April 1970.

118 Bhavsar, interview, 17 July 2012.

119 Patel, 'New Explorations in a Universe of Color'.

120 Andreae, 'Beautiful Painting and Sculpture at the Jewish Museum'.

121 Ratcliff, 'Natvar Bhavsar: The Purpose of Looking', 17.

122 Ibid., 20. In the 2009 exhibition *The Third Mind: American Artists Contemplate Asia, 1860–1989*, organized by Alexandra Munroe, Bhavsar's work was curated into the section titled 'Abstract Art, Calligraphy, and Metaphysics'. Though Bert Winther-Tamaki does not reference Bhavsar's work directly when he discusses the metaphysical (or his work at all actually), see his exhibition catalogue chapter that is ostensibly connected to this particular curated section. Bert Winther-Tamaki, 'The Asian Dimensions of Postwar Abstract Art: Calligraphy and Metaphysics', in *The Third Mind: American Artists Contemplate Asia, 1860–1989*, ed. Alexandra Munroe (New York: Guggenheim Museum, 2009), 145–98.

123 The titles are all loosely derived from words in Sanskrit meaning: 'slowly slowly' (in the case of *THEER-A-THEER-A*) and 'rain, cloud, and forest' (in the case of *VARSAA* and *VANA-RAA*). As Janet Brosious Bhavsar writes, however, 'As for the meaning of the titles – it is not about meaning; it is Natvar's linguistic romance for the language, mostly in Sanskrit, and the sound and rhythm of words that relate to music, places, literature, people, etc, and

the rhythms of nature.' Email communication with author, 16 November 2015.

124 This point has been brought up by Santhi Kavuri-Bauer in the context of Bhavsar's work. See Santhi Kavuri-Bauer, 'Colors in Motion: The New York Paintings of Natvar Bhavsar' (unpublished manuscript, San Francisco State University, 2015). My engagement of Bhavsar's work is a direct result of Kavuri-Bauer's generous invitation to accompany her on a visit to Bhavsar's studio during the summer we both attended the NEH Summer Institute 'Re-envisioning American Art History: Asian American Art, Research, and Teaching'. It is worth noting that she and I were the only participants primarily interested in Asian American art history from the perspectives of the South Asian diaspora at the Institute. It is also worth noting that curator and artist Jaishri Abichandani, who was the only invited lecturer to focus on this subject, has been an important force in making visible the contributions of women artists of South Asian descent based in the United States. She founded the influential South Asian Women's Creative Collective (SAWCC), which she directed from 1997 to 2013 and which has chapters in New York City and London. See chapter 2 of my doctoral dissertation for a provisional South Asian American art history that is largely based on the curatorial practices of those like Abichandani: Alpesh Kantilal Patel, 'Queer Desi Visual Culture Across the "Brown Atlantic"' (PhD dissertation, Manchester University, 2009).

125 Clement Greenberg, 'American-Type Painting', in *Art & Culture: Critical Essays* (Boston: Beacon Press, 1961), 220. This is the 1958 version of the essay. It originally appeared in a slightly different form in *Partisan Review* 22 (1955): 170–80, 196.

126 See the section titled 'Denial' in Winther-Tamaki, 'The Asian Dimensions of Postwar Abstract Art: Calligraphy and Metaphysics', 151–3. It is worth noting that Kline did not initially disavow his influence of Asia. See Bert Winther-Tamaki, 'Japanese Margins of American Abstract Expressionism', in *Art in the Encounter of Nations: Japanese and American Artists in the Early Postwar Years* (Honolulu: University of Hawaii Press, 2001), 57–8.

127 See Munroe, 'Buddhism and the Neo-Avant-Garde: Cage Zen, Beat Zen, and Zen'.

128 Bert Winther-Tamaki outlines several sources. See Winther-Tamaki, 'The Asian Dimensions of Postwar Abstract Art: Calligraphy and Metaphysics', 157 (note 48).

129 The exhibition travelled from Japan (Tokyo: 15 October–27 November 1966; Kyoto: 10 December 1966–22 January 1967) to New Delhi, India (27 March–16 April 1967) and to Australia (Melbourne: 6 June–8 July 1967; Sydney: 17 July–20 August 1967). See 'International Program: Timeline and Map', *The Museum of Modern Art*, accessed 19 October 2015, www.moma.org/learn/intnlprograms/timeline. The latter also includes images of Greenberg and Rasmussen giving talks in New Delhi as well as other archival photos. For a detailed discussion of the proliferation of international exhibitions in India

in the postwar period, see Devika Singh, 'A Modern Formation?: Circulating International Art in India, 1950s–1970s', in *Western Artists and India: Creative Inspirations in Art and Design*, ed. Shanay Jhaveri (Mumbai: Shoestring Publisher, 2013), 46–57. There has been a lot of speculation regarding whether or not the CIA was involved in MoMA's International Program – effectively leveraging it to promote the United States. The International Program's current director downplays the latter in a recent interview on MoMA's blog: Amy Horschak, 'MoMA and the World: The International Program: An Interview with Jay Levenson, Director, International Program, The Museum of Modern Art', blog, *Inside/Out: A MoMA/MoMA PS1 Blog* (30 August 2010), www.moma.org/explore/inside_out/2010/08/30/what-is-momas-international-program/. Finally, for an interesting discussion of the Australia leg of the exhibition and hi-res colour photos of the installed works of this touring exhibition, see Charles Green and Heather Barker, 'The Watershed: Two Decades of American Painting at the National Gallery of Victoria | NGV', *National Gallery of Victoria*, accessed 19 October 2015, www.ngv.vic.gov.au/essay/the-watershed-two-decades-of-american-painting-at-the-national-gallery-of-victoria/.

130 Gieve Patel, 'The Decades and the Seminar', *CONTRA'66*, nos 5–6 (June 1967): 5. See Asia Art Archive, accessed 25 November 2016, www.aaa.org.hk/Collection/CollectionOnline/SpecialCollectionItem/16430.

131 Ibid.

132 Clement Greenberg, 'Louis and Noland', in *The Collected Essays and Criticism, Volume 4, Modernism with a Vengeance, 1957–1969*, ed. John O'Brian (Chicago; London: University of Chicago Press, 1993), 95. Originally appeared in *Art International* 4, no. 5 (May 1960): 26–9.

133 Ibid., 97.

134 Clement Greenberg, 'Post-Painterly Abstraction', in *The Collected Essays and Criticism, Volume 4, Modernism with a Vengeance, 1957–1969*, ed. John O'Brian (Chicago; London: University of Chicago Press, 1993), 192–6. Greenberg invoked Swiss art historian Heinrich Wölfflin to help define 'post-painterly abstraction'. He writes that 'Wölfflin used the German word, *malerisch*, which his English translators render as "painterly," to designate the formal qualities of Baroque art that separate it from High Renaissance or Classical art. Painterly means, among other things, the blurred, broken, loose definition of color and contour. The opposite of painterly is clear, unbroken, and sharp definition, which Wölfflin called the "linear".' See ibid., 192.

135 Clement Greenberg, 'Modernist Painting', in *The Collected Essays and Criticism, Volume 4, Modernism with a Vengeance, 1957–1969*, ed. John O'Brian (Chicago; London: University of Chicago Press, 1993), 87.

136 Ibid., 90, 88, 92.

137 Ibid., 88. Recorded in 1960 and broadcast in 1961. See also the following for a detailed analysis of the evolution of Greenberg's thinking in the various versions of the essay: Francis Frascina, 'Institutions, Culture, and America's

"Cold War Years": The Making of Greenberg's "Modernist Painting"', *Oxford Art Journal* 26, no. 1 (1 January 2003): 69–97, doi:10.1093/oxartj/26.1.69.

138 Greenberg, 'Modernist Painting', 97.

139 Wechsler, 'From Asian Traditions to Modern Expressions', 78.

140 Bhavsar, interview, 6 August 2015.

141 Beth Citron, 'Modernist Art from India' (Rubin Museum of Art, New York, 2012), exhibition brochure. The exhibition was rolled out in three parts, 'The Body Unbound', 'Approaching Abstraction' and 'Radical Terrain'.

142 Singh, 'A Modern Formation?: Circulating International Art in India, 1950s–1970s', 52.

143 Sonal Khullar, *Worldly Affiliations: Artistic Practice, National Identity, and Modernism in India, 1930–1990* (Berkeley: University of California Press, 2015), 194–200. See section titled: 'Indigenism versus internationalism'.

144 Geeta Kapur, 'In Quest of Identity: Art & Indigenism in Post-Colonial Culture with Special Reference to Contemporary Indian Painting', *Asia Art Archive*, 1973, www.aaa.org.hk/Collection/CollectionOnline/SpecialCollectionItem/15579. This essay was developed out of the author's MA thesis submitted to Royal College of Art (London) in 1970. The title was first published as a series of articles in *Vrishchik* magazine in 1971 beginning with its Year 2, Nos 10–11 issue. *Vrishchik*, which means scorpion, was founded by artist Gulammohammed Sheikh in 1969 and ran until 1973. Published from Baroda, the magazine was edited by Sheikh and artist Bhupen Khakhar. According to the Asia Art Archive, 'The magazine became an active forum for contemporary artistic and literary expressions, and also a catalyst for artists' views on the art field, art institutions, and social concerns. The magazine featured an array of content that included poems, stories, critical essays, and folios of printed artworks.' See 'Vrishchik', Asia Art Archive, accessed 2 March 2016, www.aaa.org.hk/Collection/CollectionOnline/SpecialCollectionFolder/2133.

145 'A Grand Exhibition of U.S. Painting Comes to India', *Statesman*, 26 March 1967. Other positive reviews include an earlier article by the same newspaper and one in *Hindustan Times Sunday Magazine*: 'Two Decades of U.S. Painting: Rabindra Bhavan Gets Ready for Exhibition', *Statesman*, 8 March 1967; 'Two Decades of American Painting 1946–66', *Hindustan Times Sunday Magazine*, 26 March 1967.

146 As quoted in Joseph Leylveld, 'Modern U.S. Art Stirs New Delhi', *The New York Times*, 10 April 1967.

147 'New York Centre of World Art, Feels U.S. Critic', *Times of Delhi*, 28 March 1967, as cited in Khullar, *Worldly Affiliations*, 312.

148 'The Art of Negative Sensation: Modernism In American Painting On View', *Times of India*, 28 March 1967. This reviewer also wrote: 'The endeavour is apparent. About the achievement I have some reservation … particularly of the younger generation … The canvases are large; the American painter relies on shock tactics; his approach to painting is often unorthodox; his methods of eliciting attention and evoking feeling are sensational … There is a touch of anti-art in the endeavour to shock the philistines with a new form of

philistinism.' The last sentence I find especially illuminating. The critic understood the audiences of the exhibition were being treated as 'philistines' so he uses this against them by suggesting the work produced its own kind of 'philistinism'.

149 *Patriot*, 26 March 1967.

150 Leylveld, 'Modern U.S. Art Stirs New Delhi'. According to the article, the 'galleries were not crowded': there were 123 to 475 visitors a day. In regards to the negative comments, Leylveld reported that Clement Greenberg reasoned that 'the range of popular comments in any American city to the same show might well be more hostile'. Greenberg then said: 'The lay public doesn't matter any more.'

151 Khullar, *Worldly Affiliations*, 14.

152 Ibid., 15.

153 Atreyee Gupta, 'In a Postcolonial Diction: Postwar Abstraction and the Aesthetics of Modernization', *Art Journal* 73, no. 3 (Fall 2013): 45–6.

154 Alexandra Juhasz, 'Video Remains: Nostalgia, Technology, and Queer Archive Activism', *GLQ: A Journal of Lesbian and Gay Studies* 12, no. 2 (2006): 319–28.

155 Ibid., 326.

156 Ann Cvetkovich, 'Queer Art of the Counterarchive', in *Cruising the Archive: Queer Art and Culture in Los Angeles, 1945–1980*, ed. Sarah Kessler and Mia Locks (Los Angeles: ONE National Gay & Lesbian Archives, 2011), 32.

157 Emphasis in original. Barthes, 'Cy Twombly: Works on Paper', 160.

4 Subject matter: writing as a racial *pharmakon*

In this chapter, I explore 'subject matter' – often characterized as the polar opposite of form – and turn my attention to works of authors who deploy signifiers that connect broadly to South Asia.[1] My central aim is to provincialize whiteness – the ground for all racialized art histories – or as British film and queer theorist Richard Dyer puts it in his important book *White: Essays on Race and Culture* (1997): make it 'strange'.[2] This will also demand that I explore how blackness fits into writing transnational South Asian art histories. That is, I cannot explore whiteness in relation to what I provisionally refer to as brownness without acknowledging whiteness's other: blackness. Dyer writes that no other colour but white has a complete opposite.[3] More specifically, I explore artworks, their consumption by critics and curators as well as my own experience viewing them, in person where possible, by four artists: Stephen Dean (b. 1968), Mario Pfeifer (b. 1981), Adrian Margaret Smith Piper (b. 1948) and Kehinde Wiley (b. 1977). With the exception of Piper, who is one-eighth East Indian (as she notes on her website), none of these artists are of South Asian decent. However, at some point in their careers they incorporated sites in South Asia and/or signifiers connected to that part of the world as part of their artistic practices.

Art historian Donald Preziosi's invocation of Jacques Derrida's *pharmakon* – the Greek word for both 'remedy' and 'poison' – is instructive in theorizing further how I approach whiteness.[4] In his groundbreaking book *Rethinking Art History: Meditations on a Coy Science*, Preziosi provocatively writes that the 'historian-critic possesses a measure that can be used both to remedy and to poison – a true *pharmakon*'.[5] I consider Preziosi's point in the context of the writing of transnational South Asian art histories. On the one hand, when based on genealogy, these histories 'remedy' art history of what could be described as its racist and Eurocentric 'ills'; on the other hand, they leave intact binaries such as South Asian/non-South Asian and non-white/white. Rather than providing yet another remedy (to the cure, if you will), I present case studies in this chapter, each of which functions as a racial *pharmakon* that disrupts these dipoles and keeps them in play.[6]

Derrida notes that in Greek *pharmakon* 'also means paint, not a natural color but an artificial tint, a chemical dye that imitates the chromatic scale given in nature'.[7] He further writes that the *pharmakon* is 'that dangerous supplement'.[8] In French *supplément* means both 'an addition' and 'a substitute'.[9] It refers to replacing something that is not present and therefore necessary as well as to adding something that is already there and therefore superfluous. Derrida explains that the supplement 'is not, so to speak, dangerous in itself, [but] … Its slidings slip it out of the simple alternative presence/absence. *That* is the danger.'[10] In other words it is both artificial and natural; presence and absence. Colour, then, is dangerous for being unstable and unfixable – qualities of colour I explore throughout this chapter.

It is therefore not surprising that Immanuel Kant's aesthetic disinterestedness described in his *Critique of Judgement* (1790) subordinates colour to line and form. He writes:

> The colours which give brilliancy to the sketch are part of the charm. They may no doubt, in their own way, enliven the object for sensation, but make it really worth looking at and beautiful they cannot … The charm of colours … may be added … but the design … constitute[s] the proper object of the pure judgement of taste.[11]

To shore up the disinterestedness that is requisite in Kant's model, colour, which 'enliven[s] the object for sensation', had to be subsumed by 'the design', which 'constitute[s] the proper object of the pure judgement'. Contemporary artist David Batchelor has written that in the West colour is not only 'relegated to the realm of the superficial, the supplementary, the inessential or the cosmetic … and thus unworthy of serious consideration' but also 'is made out to be the property of some "foreign" body – usually the feminine, the oriental, the primitive … the queer … [and thus] is regarded as alien and therefore dangerous'.[12] Moreover, even Johann Wolfgang von Goethe's theories of colour that were in opposition to those of French philosopher René Descartes were ultimately prey to the same xenophobia that characterized Descartes's writing. For instance, Goethe writes: 'Lastly it is also worthy of remark, that savage nations, uneducated people, and children have a great predilection for vivid colours.'[13] Indeed, colour was conflated with the people of the non-West who were incapable of supposedly higher order of thought. It is no surprise that Derrida notes that aesthetics is ultimately an 'ethnology' and that 'the effects of aesthetic signs are determined only within a cultural system'.[14]

The slippage between colour as hue, skin colour and symbol is key in all the works I discuss in this chapter as is making clear that this point extends to the special case of 'white' that, Dyer writes, is often not characterized as a colour at all.[15] He writes that the slippage between white being a colour and colourless is what makes white people 'both particular and nothing in particular … both something and non-existent'.[16]

Stephen Dean's *Pulse* (2001)

Colour is particularly relevant when discussing Stephen Dean's *Pulse* (2001), a 7-minute, single-channel video installation that captures the metaphysical 'pulse' of *Holi* – the Indian festival that marks the arrival of spring through the throwing of colourful pigment and water in the air and often onto bodies themselves (Plate 5).[17] Dean went to an area known for its overzealous engagement with the *Holi* tradition in Uttar Pradesh, a state in the north of India. He projected his team's footage of the pigment-saturated air onto the walls of an enclosed space, immersing the viewer within a whirl of large washes of colour (magenta, cyan, yellow, orange and green). His video cuts in quick succession from one close-up shot of saturated colour to another in a dizzying, hypnotic psychedelic manner, and includes alternating passages of frenetic sound and silence, simulating the heightened emotion and sensuousness of the *Holi* festival. Brown bodies are certainly visible but they often cannot be separated from the world around them; the former and latter are intertwined. In fact, Dean's video becomes so abstract that it often seems painterly, with the installation a veritable temporo-spatial version of a Color Field painting.

Pulse represents Dean's long-standing interest in the formal, emotive qualities of colour, although prior to this he had never used time-based media. As early as 1995, when he began to exhibit his art publicly, he presented newspapers painted with coloured rectangular blocks at the Drawing Center in New York City. In *Account* (2001), which Dean made in the same year as *Pulse*, he created a subtle colour gradation through the discoloured edges of the pages of jettisoned paperback books, which he stacked together into a sculptural column. In a more recent example, *Ladder* (2006), Dean replaced the spaces between each step of aluminium ladders with glass that was vacuum-coated with metallic oxides so that the colour produced by light passing through the glass was different from the light that merely reflected off it, recalling artist Larry Bell's use of dichroic glass in the 1960s.

Critics have often alluded to the politics of Dean's use of his source material in *Pulse*, despite the overwhelming abstraction of his work. I suspect this is because Dean is not of South Asian descent – he was born in Paris and lives in Brooklyn, New York. Curator Lawrence Rinder almost did not include *Pulse* in the 2002 Biennial exhibition he organized at the Whitney Museum of American Art in New York City because he wondered if it was too 'anthropological' or 'journalistic' to be art.[18] *Artforum*'s George Baker in his exhibition review describes Dean's artwork as turning 'the Third World other into fodder for the revitalization of mythic aesthetic modes (e.g., painting, by which it was surrounded in Rinder's installation)'.[19] Baker's language implies that Dean has appropriated another culture to revitalize 'mythic aesthetic modes' – one assumes he means the painterly abstraction of American Mark Rothko's paintings. His criticism also eerily echoes art critic Thomas McEvilley's diatribe against the curators (William Rubin being one) of the Museum of Modern Art's exhibition *"Primitivism" in 20th Century Art: Affinity of the Tribal and the Modern (1984–85)*. McEvilley argued that the organizers of that show used 'primitive art' paradoxically to buttress MoMA's modernist formalist claims rather than to seriously engage with the Western art world's xenophobia and self-proclaimed cultural supremacy.[20]

In contrast to the above, I contend that Dean's artwork is neither concerned with the literal facts nor with the documentation of cultures and people typically associated with the fields of journalism and anthropology, respectively. His camera does not linger on any of the bodies – which often become subsumed by thick clouds of coloured pigments when visible, precluding any sense of geographical specificity for the viewer. Festival participants remain anonymous, and therefore Baker's collective description of them as the 'Third World other' is presumptive. Even when someone's gaze briefly meets the camera's lens, the subject's 'wildly colored skin' and 'owl like stare' hardly makes him or her look human, as noted by critic Elisabeth Kley in her review of *Pulse*.[21] *The New Yorker* magazine art critic Peter Schjeldahl was 'startled to read' that Dean, whose work 'most moved' him in the Biennial, 'almost didn't make the cut'.[22] He noted: 'Are these things art? The question lacks traction in a show in which "art" is moot except as a catchall for objects and activities that aren't clearly something else.'[23] Whether or not the work was art, it can be said that the reactions to Dean's work were starkly different but all passionate.

I speculate that Rinder's assessment of Dean's artwork as potentially not art and Baker's facile criticisms of *Pulse* as resonant with those of the exhibition *"Primitivism" in 20th Century Art* reflect a certain anxiety about the artist's apparent whiteness. That is, Dean's artistic practice becomes conflated with issues of the perceived identity of the author, while his subject matter – abstracted colour – becomes enmeshed with and overwhelmed by the politics of who should or can appropriate this particular source material – the *Holi* festival.[24] Also, though most of the curatorial organization had been well underway prior to 9/11, the experience of viewing the exhibition which opened in March 2002 in New York City cannot be divorced from them. It was at this time that South Asian subjects in the United States – especially turban-wearing Sikhs and Muslims – were being misread as 'Arab' and re-coded as potential 'terrorists' in contradistinction to the status of at least some of these subjects as 'model minorities'.[25] In this context, the abstract elements of Dean's work can become political.

It is useful to describe my own experience of viewing Dean's artwork at the Whitney Museum of American Art and to further tease out the complex manner in which artistic meaning manifests itself. When I first entered the installation space, I was washed up in a sea of colours, which reflected off me and the other viewers. I felt that I was less a viewer of than a participant in Dean's *Pulse*. It is easy to see why Schjeldahl was moved and swept up by the artwork. The colours, sound and what appeared to be people throwing coloured pigments and water was quickly reminiscent of the *Holi* festival, and I (at least subconsciously) assumed the artist of the work was of South Asian descent.

It was not until I read the object label indicating the name of the artist, who was listed as being born in France and currently living in New York City, that it occurred to me that the author of the work might *not* be South Asian identified. Rather than imply that Stephen Dean could not be a name for a person of South Asian descent, I posit that my response to Dean's artwork reflects a deeply embedded and socially constructed visual response that gave me, as well as Rinder and Baker, reason to pause.

Mario Pfeifer's *A Formal Film in Nine Episodes, Prologue & Epilogue* (2010)

Stephen Dean's work extracts the physicality of colour from the repetitive structure of cultural rituals. He foregoes the linear nature of a narrative and focuses on the excess of colour as a highly unstable signifier of an event. Peripatetic artist Mario Pfeifer's work *A Formal Film in Nine Episodes, Prologue & Epilogue* (2010) also forgoes linearity in favour of the materiality of colour, but relies less on abstraction. While Dean's intent is not to bring up the politics of framing into which critics and I have enfolded his work, Pfeifer seems concerned with what I have described as the 'anxiety of whiteness'. While Pfeifer had travelled to Southeast Asia, he had never been to South Asia. He was given the opportunity to do so when artists Shumona Goel and Shae Heredia hired him to edit their 16 mm film for the Guggenheim Museum's 2010 exhibition *Being Singular Plural*.[26] When Pfeifer accepted the invitation he had less than a month to move to Mumbai, so instead of doing some background research (watching films or reading books) on the city he 'was more interested in generating all my knowledge locally'.[27] By this he meant his multi-sensory engagement with the site over time.

After his work on the film had concluded, he decided to stay an additional three months to do research for his own film project. He wanted to convey his various embodied experiences in the city while also thinking through his position as a relative outsider, describing his approach as 'a formal consideration of a complex situation'.[28] For instance, Pfeifer was intrigued by the forms of blocks of ice that he saw being hauled through the hot and humid city – a visual that would become the inspiration for one of the episodes of his film. Eventually, he employed two research assistants who lived and worked in Mumbai to contextualize and deepen his understanding of his observations and experiences.[29] A key point here is that for Pfeifer, form functions as a point of departure rather than a rigid delineation of structure or detachment from content.

Pfeifer uses various sites throughout his film, including national landmarks, markets, interior spaces, factories, businesses and even an auto rickshaw.[30] However, he is less interested in representing the city than 'specific situations in an urban environment and its specific culture'.[31] The word 'Mumbai' in any language does not appear in either the title of the film or in the work's various English-language subtitles or Hindi title slides for each episode.

The diverse scenes found in *A Formal Film in Nine Episodes, Prologue & Epilogue* are short in duration. Most are approximately five minutes; the shortest is two minutes and the longest is nine minutes. The scenes include a young man (Gopal) having his head shaved; a family living in makeshift shelters around the area known as Belapur, an area just on the outskirts of Navi Mumbai, a satellite city on the mainland; a young woman (Nandini) getting her eyes checked for potential Lasik surgery; the production and maintenance of ice at an ice-producing factory; and a *hijra* requesting money from passengers in a taxi stopped at a traffic light in exchange for blessings for love, marriage and a prosperous life. (A *hijra* can refer to eunuchs, intersex or transgender subjects.) There is a loose narrative of the budding relationship between Gopal and Nandini.

Pfeifer shot his film in what could be described as a documentary style, but there is a tension between truth and fiction, the authentic and inauthentic. He did not use professional actors, and the first names of the actors are also their characters' names. In addition, each scene was shot only once.[32] While this was partly because of budget constraints, it became a conceptual conceit for Pfeifer: he was comfortable with the scenes not going as planned and used 95 per cent of the footage he took.[33] He says: 'I was not interested in whether what happened on camera was perfect or not, seeing it rather as something real in the moment of filming.'[34] The light editing and the use of non-actors suggests a kind of realism or authenticity, yet Pfeifer also challenged this in other ways. For instance, the subtitles are largely summaries of the action depicted and they are written in the third person: this Brechtian distancing effect is one way in which the viewer is made aware that what is depicted is a representation.

Pfeifer exhibited his film at several different institutions in Germany: Frankfurter Kunstverein and MMK 3, Frankfurt am Main (2010–11); KOW, Berlin (2011); and MMK Museum für Moderne Kunst, Frankfurt am Main

(2012–13). He felt the project would not be complete until 'it is properly shown and discussed in India' to an audience that would have potentially a different relationship to the source material.[35] In 2013 he installed the work at KHOJ International Artists' Association, New Delhi, where I experienced it, and Project 88, Mumbai – the city that provided Pfeifer's source material. At each location, the work was adapted to the architecture of the space in which it was installed. That is, there was no prescribed sequence for the episodes, and the size of the screens and the sound levels were variable, too.[36] Each episode did not necessarily have its own screen. For instance, the installation at KHOJ included three channels, each playing several episodes and projected onto its own wall.

At MMK 3 in Frankfurt, the multi-channel installation included projections opposite large windows overlooking the city. In this way, as noted by curator Amira Gad in her 2010 essay 'Blurring the Boundaries', Pfeifer juxtaposed depictions of the skyline and the mundane everyday goings-on of Mumbai with that of Frankfurt (Figure 4.1).[37] The episodes of the film were distributed in different rooms as well as across different art spaces, separated by a short three-minute walk. One had to walk outside of MMK 3, through a public space and to the Frankfurter Kunstverein (or vice versa) to see more episodes.[38] This further ensured that viewers could not completely enter the space of the film without being reminded of what was outside of the frame. Overall, there was productive disruption in linearity and flow that, as Gad argues, prevented any totalizing view of the work to emerge. This fracturing

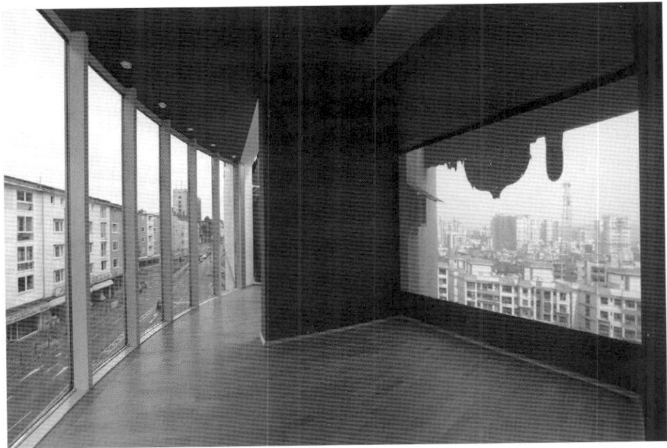

Mario Pfeifer, *A Formal Film in Nine Episodes, Prologue & Epilogue*, 2010. 35 mm film transferred to HD video; stereo, 52 min; multiple projections for exhibition space (variable). Hindi, Tamil with English subtitles. Installation view: Frankfurter Kunstverein, 2010. **4.1**

of the work was reinforced in other ways: as mentioned, there was only a slight narrative to hold on to, and in contradistinction to what the installation's title might indicate, there were not eleven but ten distinct film episodes in total as the prologue and epilogue were one and the same. Gad draws on French anthropologist Marc Augé's discussion of the 'non-place' as a way to describe Pfeifer's overall approach to space, in which he complicated 'the binary of continuity and discontinuity in our globalized world'.[39]

Also contributing to the disruption of a totalizing view is Pfeifer's use of colour throughout the film.[40] He used 35 mm film specifically because of its 'materiality and colour depth'.[41] In almost every episode there are moments when a field of colour dominates. I am referring to the golden sandalwood powder that is smeared and rubbed onto Gopal's recently shaved head; the hues of blue of the equipment and decor of the doctor's office that Nandini visits and of the saris and shirts of those in the waiting room; the greys and blues of the wet floors and ceiling of the 24-hour ice-production facility (Plate 6); the commingling of blues and the grey of the sky outside of the window through which Nandini stares as she gets her henna applied; the literally electric yellow colour of the single lightbulb preceding the scene with the fisherman; the rich golden colour of the jewellery hung in a shop through which we spy Gopal and Nandini and the multicoloured lights which flash in sync with the music playing in a moving taxi. It is instructive to invoke historian of South Asian art Natasha Eaton who articulates 'nomadism' in the 'nomadism of colour' as follows:

> To be nomadic is to ride difference and to do away with the artificial divisions between representation, subject, concept, human and thing. To be nomadic is not merely to reflect on the world but also to be immersed in a changing state of things – it is to take/make method as *flux*.[42]

In each of these situations, colour detaches itself from the objects to which it is initially experienced by the eye – and from narrative – and at this moment 'the divisions between representation, subject, concept, human and thing' dissolve. Pfeifer achieves this effect by letting the camera linger.

At KHOJ, where I experienced the work, Pfeifer's film was projected onto three walls of one room. The inclusion of all screens into one room heightened the 'inherently fugitive nature of colour', especially when there was a chance moment when two or three scenes of colour were playing simultaneously.[43] Colour is often considered 'fugitive' because it changes in intensity over time. The editors of *PANTONE®: The 20th Century in Color* assert that the concept of 'fugitive' also applies to how colour changes when photographed or digitally manipulated.[44] To this, I would add that it could just as easily be applied to colour's inability to stay fixed to the object with which it appears to be associated. In one instance, the medical office was depicted on one screen and opposite it was the ice-production facility. The space was hypersaturated with greys and blues, and this commingling – in addition to collapsing boundaries between the two scenes as well as the viewer and artwork – seemingly hastened the ability of colour to disentangle itself from its sources.[45]

Eaton, however, reminds us, 'The paths taken by the nomad are curvilinear, spiral and transversal, and they create a space in which things are distributed as a rhythm without measure which relates to the upswell of a flow. Power then is dispersed in unpredictable ways …'.[46] Indeed, colour swings the viewer from moments in which subject and object are productively intertwined, as described above, to other lines of thought in which colours stratify or more clearly demarcate hierarchies. In this way, colour behaves like a *pharmakon*. For instance, when Pfeifer's camera lingers on the labourers of the ice-producing facility instead of the floors and ceilings, the grey-blue colour transforms the space from being haptic and 'a changing state' into a more optical and oppressive space. That is, one becomes aware of distinct class/caste differences among the workers – there is a presumption that those talking are supervisors and those who are not are labourers. Also, immediately after the scene of the close-up of the dangling bulb in a nondescript enclosure, we switch to one of fishermen on the water. We never quite see the larger space in which the light is installed but one's thoughts drift to wonder if this is their home and the bulb the only source of light. Finally, when the focus shifts from bright colours, which change according to the tempo of the song playing on the radio inside a moving taxi, to the harsh fluorescent light of the interior falling on the face of the *hijra* the mood shifts from the convivial to thoughts of the dual paradoxical position *hijras* have in society as both 'marginalized and sanctified'.[47]

Another scene in which colour goes back and forth between abstraction and narrative includes a shot of Gopal – recognizable from the golden yellow sandalwood paste on his freshly shaved head from another episode – from a fixed point, showing him walking down a dirt road. He becomes smaller as he walks further down the road. Just before he completely disappears from view he is no longer recognizable and becomes closer to being *just* the colour yellow, if even moving. At this point, however, Pfeifer had Gopal stop at an indistinct dwelling and turn to his immediate right to ask someone who is obstructed from our view for water. In the scene that follows, Gopal asks this person for tips on finding employment. In this way, just as quickly as colour can be detached from narrative, it can return. The viewer can infer further meaning by understanding that the shaving of one's head is a ritual that young men go through when they lose their father – or mother, depending on the caste – and therefore Gopal's journey can also be seen as one growing from a boy to a man. He will now take on additional familial duties, which often includes finding employment to support the family. Pfeifer never gives us this full context, though. It is only intimated. For anyone unfamiliar with the ritual – as Pfeifer was – the golden yellow sandalwood paste associated with it would not have a specific signified. I would argue that in this gap between signifier and signified, colour eludes fixity of meaning.

Upon first viewing Pfeifer's work, it was difficult for the colours to detach from objects and narratives in the way I have described. In this way, Pfeifer's vignettes began to feel like a stock portrait of India, including what seemed like the perfunctory inclusion of a *hijra*, a love story without the Bollywood fanfare and images of the destitute. Interestingly, a colleague who had accompanied me to New Delhi and saw the work with me had a different reaction – he spoke more about the colours, lines and shapes which he felt Pfeifer had handled brilliantly. It turns out that Pfeifer had anticipated both my and my colleague's responses to the work. In the almost two-year gap between having finished the work and installing it in India, he had been working on a 'critical reader' that explored a variety of reactions, including those of my colleague and mine in which subject matter and form are effectively cleaved.

The reader is 300 pages long and is written in both English and Hindi.[48] In addition to Gad's essay and an overview from the artist, it includes transcriptions of two informative conversations, one between Pfeifer and the director of MMK Museum für Moderne Kunst Frankfurt am Main; and another among Pfeifer and Shuddhabrata Sengupta, co-founder of Raqs Media Collective, and Nikolaus Hirsch, architect, curator and writer. In an essay provocatively titled '"Inside" and "Outside" a Frame of Historical and Cultural Referentiality?', curator and writer Shanay Jhaveri considers Pfeifer's work in the context of the history of Western depictions of India on film as well as the long-standing connection that the film industries of Germany and India share.[49] There are also essays by cultural theorist, curator and poet Ranjit Hoskote and film historian Kaushik Bhaumik.

Pfeifer assembled a diverse range of leading and emerging thinkers primarily based in India to expand the conversation that his multi-channel installations began. You might even say that he does this not so much to control the conversation but to further his investigation. This is not to imply that the installation is somehow not important on its own, but that when dealing with signifiers that have strong meanings, Pfeifer seemed aware that it was important to think about the diverse ways one might address them. It became clear that the artist openly interrogates what it meant for him to be a 'white' artist sourcing South Asian imagery in the supposedly postmillennial 'globalized' world. The critical reader tackles this question without coming up with any answers. It fulfils part of art historian Joan Kee's call not only for works by racialized subjects to be seen outside of 'cultural difference' but also for the 'need to approach contemporary art made by white artists with an eye to their own possession of ethnicity'.[50]

Now convinced that Pfeifer had been quite thoughtful about his positionality, I was ready to look at the work again. That is, what became clear in the conversation with my colleague was that if he had been focused on form, I had been focused on subject matter; and I wanted to go back to think about form in a way I was unable to prior to engaging with the critical reader, when I had been blocked by anxiety regarding authorship. The reader does not engage with colour, but the manner in which Pfeifer mobilizes it is absolutely crucial to the work's significance.

More broadly, what Pfeifer's work and the critical texts about it do is blur the often rigid delineation between art-making and its eventual 'consumption' by viewers, including art historians and critics. His reader suggests how writing, discussing and curating (Pfeifer has carefully selected his interlocutors) can be powerful modes of art-making. I return to this point in the second half of the book in which my art historical practice meshes with the curatorial.

Adrian Margaret Smith Piper's portraits: *The Color Wheel Series* (2000–4)

Adrian Margaret Smith Piper tackles the slippage between colour as a hue and skin colour in *The Color Wheel Series*. She is perhaps best known for her work in the 1980s, such as her performance work *Calling Card* (1986) and drawing *Self-Portrait Exaggerating My Negroid Features* (1981). The former refers to cards that Piper would give out to those she perceived were white to admonish them for having made racist remarks in social settings as they happened. In the latter she depicts herself, as the title suggests, with Negroid features that we are to assume her face otherwise does not have. As art historian Amelia Jones notes, both these early works pivot around a notion that identity is visible and that there exists a white/black binary.[51]

Piper does begin to trouble the binary in her lesser-known and relatively more recent *The Color Wheel Series*, artworks from which appeared in the December 2001 issue of the College Art Association *Art Journal*. Digital prints accompanied the articles, all published under the rubric 'Blinded by the White: Art and History at the Limits of Whiteness'. Organized by art historian John P. Bowles, the forum included short texts by Piper as well as artist and scholar Olu Oguibe, art historian Ellen Fernandez-Sacco and art historian, curator and critic Maurice Berger.[52] Interestingly, much like Mario Pfeifer's work, this particular variant of the series is bound up with language and with interlocutors who are deeply enmeshed in the art world. In Piper's essay titled 'Whiteless', she notes that most cultures do not refer to Euroethnics as 'white' but as 'pale', 'colorless' or 'light', and that one way to combat racism is by getting them 'to stop thinking they're white. No one else thinks they are white.'[53]

In her notes on *The Color Wheel Series*, Piper writes that for her 'white is not really a color but rather the miscegenation of all colors'.[54] The series serves as an allegory for this line of thinking that strips whiteness of its power without displacing or conferring that power on to its Other (an Other which becomes increasingly unclear and unfixable). In this way, as art critic Holland Cotter notes in his reference to an exhibition that contained variants of these works, 'as weird as it looks with its garish colors and glossy surfaces' the series is not as anomalous in Piper's oeuvre as it might at first seem.[55]

Piper's 'Removed and Reconstructed en.Wikipedia Biography' provides more information about her racial background and suggests a subtle but important shift in how a viewer might perceive Piper's identity. In the third person she writes: 'Like all Americans, Piper is racially mixed. She is 1/32 Malagasy (Madagascar), 1/32 African of unknown origin, 1/16 Ibo (Nigeria), and 1/8 East Indian (Chittagong, India [now Bangladesh]).'[56] In contradistinction to the other artists discussed in this chapter, Piper is partly of South Asian descent and so her works might be a more 'proper' subject for inclusion in a more traditional transnational South Asian identity that pivots around the genealogy of authorship. Yet this biographical detail (though interesting) is not why her work is being included here. The understanding of self that the viewer might find in her self-portrait *Thwarted Projects, Dashed Hopes, A Moment of Embarrassment*, which she produced for her 64th birthday in September 2012, blasts the binary around which critical writing of her earlier work often pivoted (Figure 4.2). The digital image depicts Piper in blackface. At the bottom of the image she clarifies:

> Dear Friends, For my 64th birthday, I have decided to change my racial and nationality designations. Henceforth, my new racial designation will be neither black nor white but rather 6.25% grey, honoring my 1/16th African heritage. And my new nationality designation will be not African American but rather Anglo-German American, reflecting my preponderantly English and German ancestry. Please join me in celebrating this exciting new adventure in pointless administrative precision and futile institutional control! Adrian M. S. Piper/20 September 2012.

On her website, next to the self-portrait she further writes: 'Adrian Piper has decided to retire from being black. In the future, for professional utility, you may wish to refer to her as The Artist Formerly Known as African-American.'[57]

In the *Art Journal* issue that featured *The Color Wheel Series*, each writer's spread is accompanied by a portrait of the writer flanked by two figures, both of which wear theatrical masks with perforations for the mouth and eyes (Plate 7). The mouth of the left figure is covered, as are the ears of the right figure. These figures, which Piper refers to as 'Acting Heads', evoke the three wise

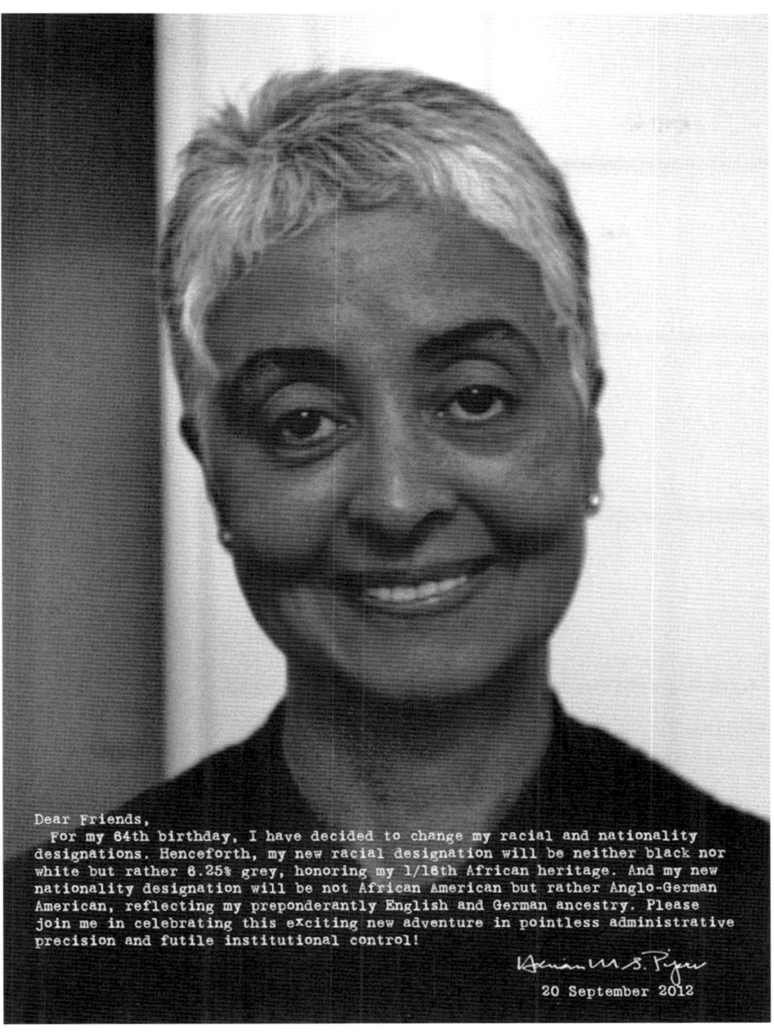

Adrian Piper, *Thwarted Projects, Dashed Hopes, A Moment of Embarrassment*, 2012. Digital self-portrait, 6 × 7.83 in. **4.2**

monkeys that hear no evil, see no evil and say no evil, with the important exception that the writer's eyes are *not* covered. The meaning of the three-monkey theme is anything but singular. It is found in many cultures, including those of Japan, India, China and Egypt. Even within each culture, the meaning attached to the three monkeys has been unstable over time. Two in particular are worth noting given Piper's focus on non-dualistic Vedantic philosophy. As historian Emiko Ohnuki-Tierney summarizes in the context of the three-monkey theme in Japan, one is the belief that the monkeys 'called upon the person to examine closely or identify objects and phenomena in life through the use of three senses'.[58] Another more abstract interpretation is that the monkeys represent the state of 'undifferentiatedness' in which the senses are yet to be even activated – that is, the 'ineffable undifferentiatedness of the primeval chaos'.[59] Both of these suggest the slipperiness of identity as being neither stable nor separable into the kinds of intractable categories to which the West subscribes. In its lack of fixity, there is a hint of the notion of the multiple/shifting meaning of the *pharmakon*.

It is worthwhile to note the characterization of the monkey in Hindu and Buddhist mythology as a 'trickster' that seems to typify the nature of the *pharmakon* more closely. In the context of African American literature, Henry Louis Gates, Jr, extensively explores the trickster figure in his essay 'Signifying Monkey'. He uses the term 'Signifyin(g)' as a means of differentiating between the traditional black American rhetorical device of 'signifying' from the academic term of the same name. He writes that 'to revise the received sign (quotient) literally accounted for in the relation represented by *signified/signifier* at its most apparently denotative level is to critique the nature of (white) meaning, itself, to challenge through a literal critique of the sign the meaning of meaning'.[60]

Piper explicitly connects her use of colour to skin colour, and thereby connects to the notion of the *pharmakon* as both skin and paint (here digital ink). In her description of *The Color Wheel Series*, she briefly reviews Western philosophy's positioning of colour as a secondary quality because: 'Like sounds, textures, odors, and tastes, colors are subjective modes of perception that can vary from one perceiver to the next, and so do not supply objective knowledge of objects.'[61] Piper has a formula for how colour is employed in her work. First, two colours are repeated throughout the series of digital prints: blue for the grid and red for the Target Wheel, which is aimed at the central Acting Head, in this case of the *Art Journal* writer. Importantly, she refers to these as the only 'two genuine color constants across the skin color of all individual Acting Heads in the series'.[62] Piper does use white throughout the series for the gloves and mask, but in keeping with her logic this is not a colour. In addition, the mesh-like pattern that appears on top of most of the image and the use of colours that are 'garish' per Cotter – even if accidental – puts in tension the colour as flesh and as artificial.

Piper randomly assigns the remaining colours to the three Acting Heads in each work of the series based on a colour wheel, a device constructed for the display of the PANTONE MATCHING SYSTEM®, an international 'colour language' employed in printing and publishing.[63] More specifically, Piper uses the PANTONE® Color Formula Guide 1000, which at that time contained 1,012 different colours, to determine the colours of each of the three 'Acting

Heads' per work.[64] There are, in total, 335 works in print, reproduction and website forms that are further divided into five groups of 67 works each.[65] Each group represents a layer, or *adhyasa* – a Sanskrit word meaning 'superimposition' or the mistaken attribution on to something of an essential nature not belonging to it. This layer effectively conceals one's true self according to the foundational philosophy of Hinduism, Vedanta. As the artist explains:

> These [layers] progress from the most material and condensed to the most subtle, pervasive and diffuse. The *annomayakosha* or physical sheath is composed of nutrients. The *pranamayakosha* or energy sheath is composed of breath. The *manomayakosha* or mental sheath is composed of cognition. The *vijnanamayakosha* or intellectual sheath is composed of reason. And the *anandamayakosha* or bliss sheath is composed of intelligence. Beneath all of these layers of illusion is the true self, i.e. ultimate reality beyond the laws of psychology or physics.[66]

As Piper further notes, the ego projects the first three layers on to 'ultimate reality', per the first-century BCE Vedantic philosopher Shankara. Thereby, 'The work of self-knowledge then consists in training consciousness – through meditation, self-inquiry, analysis, reasoning, close observation, etc. – to gradually peel away these *adhyasas* … until the true self is uncovered.'[67] According to Piper, each individual work in *The Color Wheel Series* is a tool for this practice. The photographed statue of Shiva, the ascetic Hindu god of yoga and dance known as the Destroyer of Illusion, positioned above the 'Acting Heads' functions as a signifier connected to these activities. He manifests here as Lord Nataraja, the dancer, encircled by a Fire Wheel and dancing on the back of the demon Apasmarapurusha.

Of course new colours are added to the PANTONE® Color Formula Guide 1000 every year so presumably the series could continue. Indeed, even within the system Piper describes she does not exhaust all colours as she claims she does; three colours end up not being used. To explain, she needed to use 202 colours per each of the five layers to equal 1,010 (the number of colours left after red and blue are subtracted). However, since there are three heads/works, each layer would need 67.33 works. Piper had to round this down to 67. More to the point, there is always already a remainder, or a supplement – indeed, a dangerous supplement given that skin colours come in complex gradations that defy compartmentalization into discrete categories. Mantra #11, the Sanskrit text bisecting the intersection of the Fire Wheel and Target Wheel in each work, alludes to this point. From Shankara's *Atma-Bodha* (Self-Knowledge), the mantra can be translated roughly as follows: 'Because we associate the true self with various limiting aspects, we superimpose such ideas as caste, color, and status upon it just as we superimpose flavor, color, etc. on water.'[68]

Kehinde Wiley: *The World Stage: India, Sri Lanka* (2010)

Kehinde Wiley is well known for incorporating black males into – as *The New York Times* art critic Roberta Smith succinctly puts it – the 'lily-white history of Western portraiture'.[69] He does this by casting his subjects as saints, kings, emperors, burghers, military leaders and prophets from largely Old Master and Renaissance paintings.[70] However, in 2010 he exhibited a series of portraits based on his travels to India as well as Sri Lanka at Rhona Hoffman Gallery in Chicago. This series is the focus of this final section.

These works are part of Wiley's ambitious series *The World Stage*. Begun in 2006, the series continues the artist's project of elevating the marginalized or the invisible across a broad range of cities and nations outside of the United States. In addition to India and Sri Lanka (2010), these include China (2006), Lagos and Dakar (2008), Brazil (2008–9), Israel (2011), France (2012), Jamaica (2013) and Haiti (2014). All these countries have been impacted by colonialism of some form or have variegated populations. On his website Wiley explains that his location choices 'have to do with a level of curiosity, but it also has to do with their broader, global, political importance – strategically for America, and the world community at large'.[71] Indeed, Wiley came across a 2001 Goldman Sachs global economics paper titled 'Building Better Global Economic BRICs' that art historian Robert Hobbs notes was a partial catalyst for the series. BRIC is an acronym that refers to the countries Brazil, Russia, India and China, all of which were forecasted by Goldman Sachs in this report to have prodigious development over the next fifty years.[72] With the exception of Russia, each of these countries have become part of Wiley's series.

Regarding his choice to foreground his work in the context of the history of painting specific to each country, Wiley notes:

> If I am finding completely unknown guys on the streets of America, what does that look like when it happens in West Africa, in India? And when I started to do that, I had to ask myself some questions. Am I going to base this project on Western painting? Increasingly the answer was no because there was a wealth of history in each of these countries.[73]

Each exhibition was accompanied by a catalogue with essays further describing the historical relevance of the sources from which he drew.[74] The publications were identical in size and of roughly the same length: together they formed a sort of encyclopaedic set. Interestingly, in the spring of 2001, while a graduate student at the Yale School of Art, Wiley enrolled in Molly Nesbit's class titled 'The World Picture'.[75] The title of the class is most certainly a partial reference to Martin Heidegger's essay 'The Age of the World Picture'.[76] Heidegger writes that the 'world picture … does not mean a picture of the world but the world conceived and grasped as picture'.[77] Feminist postcolonial literary scholar Gayatri Chakravorty Spivak famously reworks Heidegger's 'world picture' but via another of Heidegger's texts, 'The Origin of the Work of Art'.[78] In the latter, Heidegger describes how an artwork such as Vincent van Gogh's painting of peasant shoes functions not only to represent an image, but also to bring into being what he calls 'a world', heretofore invisible but always present. For Heidegger, an artwork is 'the disclosure of [...] truth [...] This entity [the shoes] emerges into the unconcealment of its being.'[79] Spivak filters Heidegger's largely abstracted term through the specific context of imperialism, which she writes 'had to assume that the earth that it territorialized was in fact previously uninscribed ... this worlding is actually also a texting, textualising, a making into art, a making into an object to be understood'.[80] Wiley's set of books can be viewed as operating through Spivak's understanding of worlding as deeply informed by power rather than a multiculturalist approach to depicting the world as 'an object to be understood'.

Wiley's series could be seen as a critique of the 'Grand Tour' of cities – such as Paris, Venice, Florence and Rome – that young and monied European (and some American) upper-class men would take to complete their classical education from roughly the 1500s to the 1800s.[81] Wiley's 'tour' (if you will) illustrates that the West is just another region of study. At the same time, he could also be perceived as a contemporary variant of his predecessors – another dilettante – sampling the offerings of different countries. At a lecture he gave at the Brooklyn Museum in New York City on 16 April 2015, Wiley described his awareness of the potential pitfalls of working with other cultures. Critic Alissa Guzman summarizes, using Wiley's own words:

> 'It's a rich opportunity to say, fuck it, I don't know what I'm doing,' he candidly elaborated. Kehinde was adamant about remaining fearless of 'getting it wrong' when portraying other cultures, and as reactions to his own work suggest, understanding begins with a great deal of misunderstanding. Aware of the responsibility he takes on as an artist representing others, Kehinde asks his viewers to be equally aware.[82]

As I argue, through the *The World Stage: India, Sri Lanka* (2010) series Wiley keeps in play rather than resolves this dilemma. For instance, true to Wiley's larger practice, the titles of the works in this series reference the artworks that he re-works rather than the depicted subject(s). In this way, he neither fully adopts any kind of revisionist mode nor rejects the possibility that his approach could indeed be construed as problematic. Moreover, it is not clear whether the depicted subjects are from India or Sri Lanka. While this could be seen as a problematic conflation, by not participating in defining his subjects as Indian or Sri Lankan he also sidesteps these politicized, highly fraught and ever-changing constructions.

In her essay accompanying the catalogue for *The World Stage: India, Sri Lanka*, art historian Gayatri Sinha notes that the young men Wiley depicts are representative of the 'chromatic colours of the south'.[83] Sinha is referring to the darker tones of the men depicted. Given the ongoing emphasis and preference for light skin in India, these paintings are a welcome intervention. Indeed, one has to imagine that Wiley's own awareness of the politics of skin colour led to this decision. To be sure, Wiley is a (very) successful artist from the West and so there are discrepancies in class to consider, between him and his subjects, but his blackness puts him in a different position from Mario Pfeifer. To clarify, both Wiley and his subjects have dark skin. They are marked not necessarily as equivalent but certainly as 'Other' to whiteness.

For his painting *Femme Fellah* (2010), Wiley mobilizes a broad array of medium to dark browns with hints of red and blue (and perhaps green) to enflesh or transform paint into the veritable skin of his subject (Plate 8). Jacques Derrida notes that 'the painter who wants to depict anything … sometimes mixes up several colors, as his method is when he has to paint flesh'.[84] As discussed earlier, paint is a *pharmakon* flitting between artificiality and nature – this is equally so in Wiley's works.[85] Roberta Smith's adulation of Wiley's ability to strike 'a wonderful balance between skin as flesh and as paint' in reference to a completely different set of works – those resulting from his trip to Lagos and Dakar – is appropriate to invoke here, too. She even writes, 'He is beginning to paint skin in ways you can't stop looking at.'[86] Wiley's painting process hovers between naturalizing these subjects and denaturalizing them.

Wiley has said that 'there's no model that exists in art education for painting black skin'.[87] He also notes that he learned how to paint black skin from his white high school teacher. In an interview with curator Christine Y. Kim, he said: 'Ironically, it's from him that I learned how to mix colors and manipulate paint for black skin and bodies. It was a very bizarre thing.'[88] Art historian Krista Thompson has elegantly argued the importance of light in understanding Wiley's formal choices. Both she and Robert Hobbs have pointed out that Wiley was influenced by Richard Dyer's *White*, in particular a chapter titled 'Lighting for Whiteness',[89] where Dyer explores the technology of light and lighting as well as the reflective properties of skin. He writes that 'photographic media and, *a fortiori*, movie lighting assume, privilege, and construct whiteness'.[90] Based on what Wiley said, we can extend this to the technology of painting as privileging the depiction of white skin. Dyer further writes that as a white face reflects more light than a black face, 'This creates problems if shooting very light and very dark people in frame.'[91] He gives the example of school photographs in which either the faces of black subjects look like 'blobs' or those of white subjects look 'bleached out'.[92]

Ironically, Dyer's discussion of lighting in Western cinema could just as well apply to that of Bollywood films. Given the preference of casting light-skinned actors in the latter, it stands to reason that lighting in Bollywood would similarly be focused on constructing its actors as light if not white. Wiley, by depicting his South Asian subjects as glowing, reverses this logic. As Dyer writes, whiteness operates through the dual and paradoxical movement of transcending the corporeal body while also being of it.[93] Wiley has given brownness this quality; and this is underscored by the yogic poses and the subtle and sacred hand gestures, or mudra – commonly seen on Hindu and Buddhist sculptures – found in works such as *The White Slave* that effectively deify the young men.

Art critic Martha Schwendener has written in the context of other paintings by Wiley that 'the paintings themselves … look particularly bland and factory-produced when viewed up close'.[94] This is often a complaint of Wiley's work. At least in this series, I would argue that the bland background in comparison to the foreground heightens the tension between the empowered subject and the fading – if still looming – spectre of Orientalism. For example, consider his *Bonaparte in the Great Mosque of Cairo* (2010) (Plate 9), based on the eponymously titled 1890 work by Henri-Léopold Lévy, which depicts the defiling of the Azhar mosque by French troops and the repression of the popular revolt of Cairo on 21 October 1798. Napoleon functions as a symbolic figure since apparently he was not even there. In Wiley's appropriation of the work, the figure of Napoleon and the defeated revolters who are all gazing at him form the backdrop for two young dark-skinned men in everyday dress who are depicted in poses of benediction, gazing out at the viewer. Napoleon ignores the gaze of his revolters whom he has subjugated, and these young men ignore the depiction of the Orientalist fantasy of his superiority. Though the colours in the background are flat, they are bolder and brighter than in Lévy's; they are the kind you might expect to see in South Indian poster art. Wiley is using the formal language of the pedestrian and supposedly low status of popular poster art in the subcontinent to further unsettle Napoleon's victory. Moreover, as Sinha notes, the entire tableau in the background is oddly reminiscent of what one would expect to find in local photography studios throughout the subcontinent.[95] Critic and curator Murtaza Vali makes a similar point regarding another aforementioned *The White Slave*, based on nineteenth-century painter Jean Lecomte du Nouÿ's painting of the same name of a concubine luxuriating in a harem. Vali writes that the Orientalist backdrop in this work functions 'not as a model of power to be emulated, but as one more hand-painted backdrop, like those commonly used in local photography studios throughout the subcontinent'.[96]

Art historian Derek Conrad Murray has posited that Wiley's works more generally are 'representative of a sophisticated artist entering into a dialogue with kitsch'.[97] That is, 'The fact that they look like good illustration, but not good painting, is arguably neither the result of a deficient taste level, nor the failure of a less studied vision.'[98] I would agree with Murray here and wonder if Schwendener's review reflects the superciliousness that Wiley's work attempts to debunk. Murray also makes the interesting claim that Wiley's work is better in reproduction than in the original.[99] Indeed, in reproduction much of what Schwendener bemoans is less apparent. If we follow this argument, then how the original looks in person seems immaterial. I want to extend Murray's argument by circling back to my earlier point about how the painting of flesh hovers between the corporeal and imitation. This quality of the work seems to be heightened in reproduction.

The blandness of the background in these works is a ruse, especially if we consider the openwork, intricately hand-carved wood frame of *Bonaparte in the Great Mosque of Cairo*. As with many of Wiley's works, frames serve to legitimize those depicted on the canvas within it; and given Bollywood's predilection for light-skinned actors and actresses, Wiley's attention to the frame ennobles the subjects depicted even if not as individuals but as types – darker-skinned subjects.

Orientalism is about a complicated desire for the other and it is worth exploring the complex vectors of desire operating in Wiley's works. First, he has openly admitted there is a homoeroticism in the relationship he has with his subjects:

> 'My work is political and it is religious, but it's also decidedly homoerotic,' Wiley explains. 'When I'm approaching these guys, there's a presupposed engagement. I don't ask people what their sexualities are, but there's a sense in which male beauty is being negotiated in each of these works.'[100]

I would be remiss if I did not add my own desire as a queer man for these men. The subject in *Femme Fellah*, for instance, peers out at the viewer with quiet, assured confidence. He is depicted as having agency and can short-circuit the twisted desire that is the nefarious origin of Orientalism as well as the perhaps relatively tame desire of mine and Wiley's.

Femme Fellah is a reworking of the eponymously titled 1866 painting by Charles Zacharie Landelle (Figure 4.3). Fellah is an Arabic word that means peasant. Here, Wiley has transposed the female peasant depicted in Landelle's work with a young man. Though both subjects look out at the viewer, the figure from the original holds an urn as a signifier of her status, while the urn appears behind Wiley's subject. This transgendering of the subject is not in itself wholly unusual given deities of South Asian religions often are characterized as having more than one gender. Indeed, philosopher Rajesh Sampath suggests that the historic law passed by the Supreme Court in 2015 abolishing the binary gender system in India can be partly connected to the latter.[101] The court passed a law that created a protected third gender that covers transgender and intersex-identified subjects as well as *hijras*.[102] (Sampath notes there has been similar legislation in Nepal, Bangladesh and Pakistan.) At the same

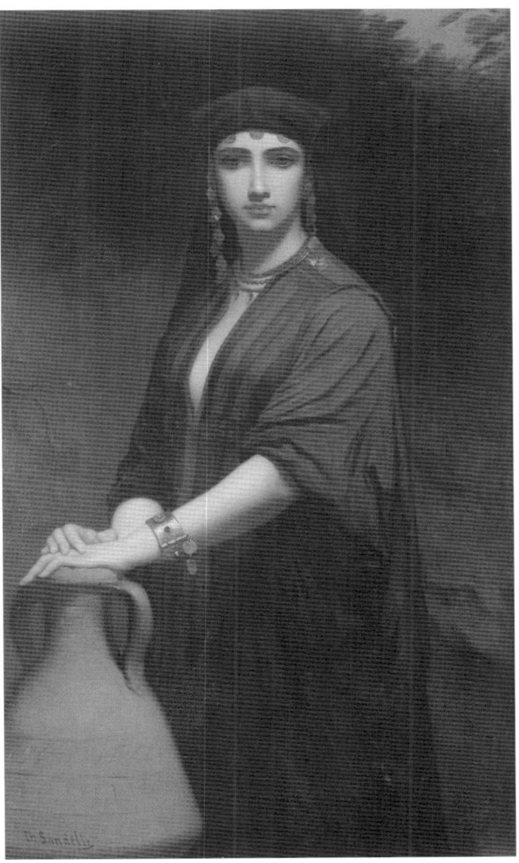

Charles Zacharie Landelle, *Femme Fellah*, 1866. Oil on canvas, 131 × 84 cm. 4.3

time, after a brief period during which sex acts between same-sex subjects was legal (2009–13), it has returned to being a crime in India, and it continues to be a crime in Sri Lanka.[103] Because Wiley's works were made in 2010, they would have had a different resonance due to the political realities at that time. Overall, significant discussion of homosexuality has largely been missing from most art historical writing and art criticism on Wiley's work. An exception is a chapter in Derek Conrad Murray's book *Queering Post-Black Art: Artists Transforming African-American Identity after Civil Rights* (2016).[104]

The *The World Stage: India, Sri Lanka* series is an anomaly in Wiley's oeuvre because he has forgone the bombast and flair of most of his work; the depicted subjects often are in yogic poses, those connected to deities or lithe young men. Though none of the men in the series are explicitly connected to hip hop, one impetus for Wiley for this series was a fascination for how people around the world – in his estimation – 'interact with American culture … through black American expression'.[105] He was particularly drawn to what he saw as the prevalence of 'black American hip hop culture' in southern India: 'to see it [black American hip hop culture] in sharp relief on these brown bodies in south Asia is something extraordinary'.[106] Though hip hop might not be signified in the *India, Sri Lanka* series it is difficult not to consider it when exploring these paintings, given its predominance in his other works. I would argue that the masculinity that is sometimes critiqued in his other work has a different resonance here – it bolsters the recovery of the South Asian male from the enduring and emasculating colonized gaze. Historian Mrinalini Sinha notes, for example, that British colonialists naturalized white supremacy in nineteenth-century Bengal through the production of 'manly' Englishmen in contrast to the 'unmanly' Bengali-educated men. Even a 'corrected' colonial era masculinity was still constructed as discrepant and certainly not virile.[107] Moreover, the construction of 'manly' Englishmen can be read as implicitly further shoring up their heterosexuality and deflecting the spectre of an effectively effeminized homosexuality onto the 'unmanly' Bengali-educated men. Postcolonial studies scholar Sara Suleri Goodyear provocatively notes that the colonial gaze was specifically directed at the 'sexual ambivalence of the effeminate male groom', rather than the 'inscrutability of an Eastern bride'.[108] Chapter 5 further explores artwork concerned with issues of sexuality as well as gender head-on. Also, whereas my use of queer theory has been largely theoretical up to this point, I now focus on queer bodies and subjectivities.

Notes

1 I could have used the word 'content' instead of 'subject matter' given they are often used interchangeably. (See, for instance, The Museum of Modern Art's website: s.v. 'subject matter' and 'content': 'Glossary of Art Terms', *Museum of Modern Art*, accessed 15 January 2016, www.moma.org/learn/moma_learning/glossary.) However, given the 'content', what is in the works, is not the same across the board, I have opted to use 'subject matter'.

2 Richard Dyer, *White: Essays on Race and Culture* (London; New York: Routledge, 1997), 4.

3 Ibid., 48.

4 The definition of the Greek word can be found here: Jacques Derrida, *Dissemination*, trans. Barbara Johnson (London: Continuum, 2004), xxiv. In his essay 'Plato's Pharmacy', Derrida discusses the slipperiness of the way in which translators have reckoned with the word *pharmakon* in Plato's *Phaedrus*, a Platonic dialogue between Phaedrus and Socrates. See ibid., 95–117, section titled 'The Pharmakon'. Originally published as Jacques Derrida, *La dissemination* (Paris: Éditions du Seuil, 1972). The word is used in a story

Socrates recounts concerning Thamus, the king of Gods, and the Egyptian god Theuth, the inventor of astronomy, geometry and calculation. Theuth says that he has a 'recipe for both memory and wisdom' that he believes Thamus should consider for all his subjects. Derrida, *Dissemination*, 75. Here, the *pharmakon* translated as 'recipe' is tantamount to 'writing'. To explain, Thamus, who cannot write and has no need for it in his vaulted position, argues that writing paradoxically will enable forgetfulness because it obviates the need for memory. In this way, Derrida points out, 'This *pharmakon*, this "medicine," this philter [or potion] … can be – alternately or simultaneously – beneficent or maleficent.' See ibid., 70.

5 Donald Preziosi, *Rethinking Art History: Meditations on a Coy Science* (New Haven, CT: Yale University Press, 1989), 23. In a footnote to this point, he further writes that 'Derrida's text is central to any serious consideration of the object of art history as a domain of disciplinary knowledge.' See ibid., 188 (note 8).

6 See Vida A. Robertson's doctoral dissertation in which she theorizes 'racial *pharmakon*' in the context of literature: Vida A. Robertson, 'The Racial Pharmakon: Investigating Albinism in African American Literature' (PhD dissertation, Miami University, 2006), https://etd.ohiolink.edu/ap/10?0::NO:10:P10_ACCESSION_NUM:miami1146224861#abstract-files.

7 Derrida, *Dissemination*, 129.

8 Ibid., 110. On the same page, he writes that the 'dangerous *supplément* that breaks into the thing that would have liked to do without it yet lets itself *at once* be breached, roughed up, fulfilled, and replaced, completed by the very trace through which the present increases itself in the act of disappearing'. Emphasis in original.

9 Ibid., xiii.

10 Emphasis in original. Ibid., 109.

11 Emphasis in original. Immanuel Kant, *The Critique of Judgement*, trans. James Creed Meredith (Oxford: Clarendon Press, 1911), 67–8.

12 David Batchelor, *Chromophobia* (London: Reaktion, 2000), 22–3. Batchelor refers to the West's denigration of colour exemplary of what he terms is tantamount to a fear of colour or 'chromophobia'. In his book *What Color Is the Sacred?*, anthropologist Michael Taussig conjectures that chromophobia stretches back as far as a millennium. See Michael T. Taussig, *What Color Is the Sacred?* (Chicago; London: University of Chicago Press, 2009), 12.

13 Johann Wolfgang von Goethe, *Theory of Colours*, trans. Charles Locke Eastlake (Cambridge, MA: MIT Press, 1970), 55. Originally published in German in 1810 as *Zur Farbenlehre*.

14 Jacques Derrida, *Of Grammatology* (Baltimore: Johns Hopkins University Press, 1976), 206. Derrida's deconstruction of Kantian aesthetics in his 1978 book *The Truth in Painting* illustrates that in aesthetics that which is inside the frame is always already a '*supplément*'. See Jacques Derrida, *The Truth in Painting* (Chicago: University of Chicago Press, 1987), see especially 'The Parergon', 37–82.

15 Dyer, *White*, 47.
16 Ibid.
17 That Dean's work functions as a *pharmakon* is embedded in the work's subject matter: the rainbow-like mounds of pigment used to celebrate contemporary *Holi*. Once created from ground flowers, they are now created from toxic chemicals that give the illusion of nature. See T. Velpandian et al., 'Ocular Hazards of the Colors Used during the Festival-of-Colors (Holi) in India – Malachite Green Toxicity', *Journal of Hazardous Materials* 139, no. 2 (10 January 2007): 204–8, doi:10.1016/j.jhazmat.2006.06.046; T. Dada, N. Sharma and A. Kumar 'Chemical Injury due to Colours Used at the Festival of Holi', *The National Medical Journal of India* 10, no. 5 (1996): 256. Indeed, the air was so thick with these chemical pigments when Dean's team filmed the festival that several of them, including his wife, suffered from mild lead poisoning (Stephen Dean, interview by Alpesh Kantilal Patel, March 2005). The deleterious pigments, meant to usher in spring and fresh beginnings, thus flit between symbolizing life and being literally poisonous.
18 Peter Plagens, 'This Man Will Decide What Art Is: But Will Anyone Else Agree? The Whitney Museum's Larry Rinder Is out to Break Down the Traditional Boundaries in His New Biennial Exhibition', *Newsweek*, 4 March 2002, www.highbeam.com/doc/1G1–83283918.html.
19 Bob Nickas et al., 'Mild About Larry: 2002 Whitney Biennial', *Artforum* 40, no. 9 (2002): 162.
20 Thomas McEvilley, William Rubin and Kirk Varnedoe, 'Doctor Lawyer Indian Chief: "'Primitivism' in 20th Century Art" at the Museum of Modern Art', *Artforum* 23 (1984): 59. See Chapter 2, note 10.
21 This could be read as an exoticization of the Other but again in my experience the abstraction of Dean's work prevents these identifications from being stable. Elisabeth Kley, 'Mystical Cosmetics: Oliver Herring, Stephen Dean, Berni Searle', *PAJ: A Journal of Performance and Art*, no. 72 (2002): 103.
22 Peter Schjeldahl, 'Do It Yourself: Biennial Follies at the Whitney', *The New Yorker*, 25 March 2002, www.newyorker.com/magazine/2002/03/25/do-it-yourself-2.
23 Ibid.
24 Dean's next installation, *Volta* (2002–3), continues his exploration of colour as a way in which to represent emotionally charged and colourful cultural phenomena. In *Volta* he captures the energy of the audiences of Brazilian soccer games by filming the colourful banners and handkerchiefs they are waving – eschewing any shots of the actual game. Again, masses of bodies become pure colour. Reviewers of *Volta* did not accuse Dean of appropriating Brazilians in the way some critics of *Pulse* accused the artist of appropriating South Asians.
25 See J. K. Puar and A. S. Rai, 'The Remaking of a Model Minority: Perverse Projectiles under the Specter of (Counter)Terrorism', *Social Text* 80 (2004): 75–104. Despite the heterogeneity of South Asian-American subjects, they were often positioned as 'the model minority' along with the much more

visible Chinese-, Japanese- and Korean-American communities. See Vijay Prashad, *The Karma of Brown Folk* (Minneapolis: University of Minnesota Press, 2000), 6–7. See also Tamar Lewin, 'Report Takes Aim at "Model Minority" Stereotype of Asian-American Students', *The New York Times*, 10 June 2008, sec. Education, www.nytimes.com/2008/06/10/education/10asians.html. Lewin's article summarizing the report, 'Facts, Not Fiction: Setting the Record Straight', authored by Robert T. Teranishi, New York University education professor, in collaboration with the College Board as well as Asian-American educators and community leaders, indicates that 'more Asian-Americans and Pacific Islanders were enrolled in community colleges than in either public or private four-year colleges. But the idea that Asian-American "model minority" students are edging out all others is so ubiquitous that quips like "UCLA really stands for United Caucasians Lost Among Asians" or "MIT means Made in Taiwan" have become common, the report said'. Prashad has also argued that South Asian-American subjects were constructed as a counterpoint to African-Americans. See also 'Success Story of One Minority Group in US', *U.S. News & World Report*, 26 December 1966. The article focuses on Chinese-Americans, though South Asians were quickly folded into the stereotype of the model minority; and argues that Chinese-Americans believed in the 'old idea that people should depend on their own efforts – not a welfare check' as a foil for the 'hundreds of billions of dollars be[ing] spent to uplift Negroes and other minorities'.

26 Susanne Gaensheimer and Bernd Reiss (eds), 'In Conversation: Susanne Gaensheimer and Mario Pfeifer', in *A Formal Film in Nine Episodes, Prologue and Epilogue: A Critical Reader* (Leipzig: Spector Books, 2013), 62.

27 For quotations, see Gaensheimer and Reiss, 'In Conversation: Susanne Gaensheimer and Mario Pfeifer', 62. The official name of the city is Mumbai, a variant of the guardian deity Mumbadevi. The city's former official title 'Bombay' came from a Portuguese term meaning 'good bay'. The inhabitants of the city and India use either of these names. See Suprio Bhattacharjee, 'Lost Landscapes: On Bombay's Urban Development', in *A Formal Film in Nine Episodes, Prologue and Epilogue: A Critical Reader*, ed. Susanne Gaensheimer and Bernd Reiss (Leipzig: Spector Books, 2013), 218.

28 Ibid., 78.

29 Ibid., 72.

30 More specifically, his locations included a barber shop, an eye clinic, an ice factory, Crawford market, Sanjay Gandhi National Park, an auto rickshaw, Vashi Bridge and various interior apartments.

31 Gaensheimer and Reiss, 'In Conversation: Susanne Gaensheimer and Mario Pfeifer', 76.

32 Ibid., 74. In addition to an assistant and a cameraman, Pfeifer had a film crew of roughly twenty-five individuals who had experience with documentary and feature films, as well as advertising. Prior to this, he had not collaborated with any more than a few individuals.

33 Ibid., and Shanay Jhaveri, '"Inside" and "Outside" a Frame of Historical and Cultural Referentiality?', in *A Formal Film in Nine Episodes, Prologue and Epilogue: A Critical Reader*, ed. Susanne Gaensheimer and Bernd Reiss (Leipzig: Spector Books, 2013), 44.
34 Ibid.
35 Susanne Gaensheimer and Bernd Reiss (eds), 'In Conversation: Shuddhabrata Sengupta and Nikolaus Hirsch with Mario Pfeifer [New York, September 30, 2012]', in *A Formal Film in Nine Episodes, Prologue and Epilogue: A Critical Reader*, ed. Susanne Gaensheimer and Bernd Reiss, 206.
36 The work was also presented as a linear film for film festivals at the Anthology Film Archives in New York City and the London International Documentary Film Festival. For these, Pfeifer had to choose a sequence for the episodes. See Gaensheimer and Reiss, 'In Conversation: Susanne Gaensheimer and Mario Pfeifer', 82.
37 Amira Gad, 'Blurring the Boundaries', in *A Formal Film in Nine Episodes, Prologue and Epilogue: A Critical Reader*, ed. Susanne Gaensheimer and Bernd Reiss, 140.
38 Ibid., 142.
39 Ibid., 144.
40 Ibid., 138. Gad makes brief mention of the repetition of certain colours across episodes but her essay is concerned primarily with physical space.
41 Gaensheimer and Reiss, 'In Conversation: Susanne Gaensheimer and Mario Pfeifer', 74.
42 Emphasis in original. Natasha Eaton, *Colour, Art and Empire: Visual Culture and the Nomadism of Representation* (London: I. B. Tauris, 2013), 3.
43 Leatrice Eiseman and Keith Recker, *PANTONE®: The 20th Century in Color* (San Francisco: Chronicle Books, 2011), 8.
44 Ibid.
45 Cinematographer Avijit Mukul Kishore shot these meticulously framed moving images.
46 Eaton, *Colour, Art and Empire*, 3.
47 Roc Morin, 'India's "Third Gender" Is Marginalized and Sanctified', *VICE*, 29 June 2015, www.vice.com/read/indias-third-gender-is-marginalized-and-sanctified-456.
48 Mario Pfeifer, *A Formal Film in Nine Episodes, Prologue and Epilogue: A Critical Reader*, ed. Susanne Gaensheimer and Bernd Reiss.
49 Shanay Jhaveri considers the artwork through the lens of the various European filmmakers who turned their cameras on to India since the early twentieth century. He also maps out Germany's long-standing fascination with India through a brief discussion of Fritz Lang's *Tiger of Eschnapur* and *The Indian Tomb* (both 1959) and Werner Herzog's *Jag Mandir* (1991). He discusses Roberto Rossellini's *India: Matri Bhumi* (1959) and Louis Malle's 378-minute film *Phantom India* (1969), which resulted in the BBC's Indian bureau being shut down, and the BBC being banned from filming in India for a short period, too. See Suzanne Franks, '"India's Daughter": The Latest

Episode in New Delhi's Fraught Relationship with the BBC', *International Policy Digest*, 6 March 2015, www.intpolicydigest.org/2015/03/06/india-s-daughter-the-latest-episode-in-new-delhi-fraught-relationship-with-the-bbc/. Summarizing, Jhaveri notes, 'What emerges … is a set of responses, which have consistently ranged, in equal measure, from the orientalist and camp to the documentarian and poetic assuming varying degrees of self-awareness.' Jhaveri, '"Inside" and "Outside" a Frame of Historical and Cultural Referentiality?', 38–59; quote on 44. Finally, Jhaveri notes two other contemporary art projects that use South Asia as subject matter: Doug Aitken's *Into the Sun* (1999) and *Kimsooja's Mumbai: A Laundry Field* (2008).

50 Joan Kee, 'The World in Plain View: Form in the Service of the Global', in *Contemporary Art: 1989 to the Present*, ed. Alexander Blair Dumbadze and Suzanne Perling Hudson (Chichester, West Sussex: Wiley-Blackwell, 2013), 101–2.

51 Amelia Jones, *Seeing Differently: A History and Theory of Identification and the Visual Arts* (London: Routledge, 2012), 11–12. Jones is carefully mapping the shift from binary identity politics to more dispersed theories of identification.

52 John P. Bowles, 'Forum: Blinded by the White: Art and History at the Limits of Whiteness', *Art Journal* 60, no. 4 (1 December 2001): 38–43; Adrian Margaret Smith Piper, 'Whiteless', *Art Journal* 60, no. 4 (1 December 2001): 62–5; Ellen Fernandez-Sacco, 'Check Your Baggage: Resisting Whiteness in Art History', *Art Journal* 60, no. 4 (1 December 2001): 58–61; Olu Oguibe, 'Whiteness and "The Canon"', *Art Journal* 60, no. 4 (1 December 2001): 44–7, doi:10.1080/00043249.2001.10792093; Maurice Berger, 'Picturing Whiteness: Nikki S. Lee's Yuppie Project', *Art Journal* 60, no. 4 (1 December 2001): 54–7; Martin A. Berger, *Sight Unseen Whiteness and American Visual Culture* (Berkeley: University of California Press, 2005).

53 Piper, 'Whiteless', 63.

54 Adrian Margaret Smith Piper, 'The Color Wheel Series', 2004, 2, www.adrianpiper.com/art/docs/2004TheColorWheelSeries.pdf.

55 Holland Cotter, 'ART IN REVIEW; Adrian Piper', *The New York Times*, 12 January 2001, sec. Arts, www.nytimes.com/2001/01/12/arts/art-in-review-adrian-piper.html.

56 Adrian Margaret Smith Piper, 'Removed and Reconstructed en.Wikipedia Biography', artist website, *Adrian Piper*, accessed 18 August 2015, www.adrianpiper.com/removed-and-reconstructed-en.wikipedia-biography.shtml.

57 Adrian Margaret Smith Piper, 'News', artist website, *Adrian Piper* (26 September 2012), www.adrianpiper.com/news_sep_2012.shtml.

58 Emiko Ohnuki-Tierney, *The Monkey as Mirror: Symbolic Transformations in Japanese History and Ritual* (Princeton, NJ: Princeton University Press, 1987), 69.

59 Herman Ooms, *Tokugawa Ideology: Early Constructs, 1570–1680* (Princeton, NJ: Princeton University Press, 1985), 407–8, as quoted in Ohnuki-Tierney,

The Monkey as Mirror, 69. Of course, the interpretation of the three-monkey theme among the non-elite/non-privileged in Japan was entirely different. Ohnuki-Tierney notes that for the latter it essentially meant that they should give up fighting the system and by the Early Modern period it became a recommended code of conduct. She further writes that this is more or less what the three monkeys signify in contemporary culture. Interestingly, Gandhi had been gifted a small wooden sculpture of the three monkeys by Chinese devotees. He was so enamoured of it that it famously became one of his few material possessions. Gandhi not surprisingly had a more pacifist spin on the three monkeys. He said, 'This guru [the monkeys] of mine always teaches me never to see evil in others. That is why it has its eyes closed. The other one has closed its ears because one should hear no evil of others. The third one has closed its mouth because one should neither speak evil of others nor utter a single word which might hurt anyone.' See Mahatma Gandhi, *The Collected Works of Mahatma Gandhi*, vol. 87 (New Delhi: Publications Division, Ministry of Information and Broadcasting, Government of India, 1983), 286. More recently, artist Subodh Gupta permanently installed in Katara (the cultural village of Doha, Qatar) three large monkey heads constructed of bronze, chrome and his signature materials, everyday utensils such as lunch boxes and cooking utensils used in India. One monkey wears a soldier's helmet, another a gas mask and a third a terrorist hood. Titled *Gandhi's Three Monkeys* (2007–8), the work is a trenchant critique of and wry commentary on what Gandhian pacifism has unintentionally wrought. See Subodh Gupta et al., *Subodh Gupta: Gandhi's Three Monkeys* (New York: Jack Shainman Gallery, 2008).

60 Emphasis in original. Henry Louis Gates, Jr, *The Signifying Monkey: A Theory of African-American Literary Criticism* (New York: Oxford University Press, 1988), 47.

61 Piper, 'The Color Wheel Series', 1.

62 Ibid., 2.

63 'Pantone Publishes 1998 Color Trends for Graphic and Web Design; *Pantone Celebrates 35 Years of the PANTONE MATCHING SYSTEM® with Authoritative ColorTrends Guide and Software*', press release, *PANTONE®* (1997), www.pantone.com/pages/pantone/pantone.aspx?pg=20127&ca=10. In the latter, the PANTONE MATCHING SYSTEM® is described as 'an international printing, publishing and packaging color language providing an accurate method for the selection, presentation, specification, communication, reproduction, matching and control of color'. For additional information on the PANTONE MATCHING SYSTEM®, see: 'The PANTONE MATCHING SYSTEM®: Always Show Your True Colors', *PANTONE®*, accessed 26 August 2015, www.pantone.com/the-pantone-matching-system. Finally, for a description of how the colours are numbered, see: 'Color Intelligence – PANTONE® Numbering Explained', *PANTONE®*, accessed 26 August 2015, www.pantone.com/pantone-numbering-explained.

64 'PANTONE® Formula Guide Color Palette History', *myPANTONE*™, 19 March 2013, http://pantone.custhelp.com/app/answers/detail/a_id/1327/~/pantone-formula-guide-color-palette-history. There are currently 1,755 PANTONE® colours: 'FORMULA GUIDE Solid Coated & Solid Uncoated', *PANTONE*®, accessed 26 August 2015, www.pantone.com/formula-guide?gclid=CjoKEQjw3auuBRDj1LnQyLjy-4sBEiQAKPU_vfWaDhsAKUj88oP3yKwbEdOF-CrHiBQOJ3rMukck9CIkaAogy8P8HAQ.
65 Piper, 'The Color Wheel Series', 2.
66 Emphasis in original; ibid., 1.
67 Ibid.
68 Ibid., 2.
69 Roberta Smith, 'Review: "Kehinde Wiley: A New Republic" at the Brooklyn Museum', *The New York Times*, 19 February 2015, www.nytimes.com/2015/02/20/arts/design/review-kehinde-wiley-a-new-republic-at-the-brooklyn-museum.html.
70 In addition to his paintings, his early mid-career retrospective at the Brooklyn Museum in 2015 presented bronze portrait busts, portraits in stained glass and portable altarpieces reminiscent of Northern Renaissance works. Along with experimentation in media beyond painting, he had begun to explore black female subjects in 2012 with his *Economy of Grace* exhibition at Sean Kelly Gallery in New York City.
71 Kehinde Wiley, 'Frequently Asked Questions', Artist website, *Kehinde Wiley*, accessed 11 June 2015, www.kehindewiley.com/faq.html.
72 Robert Hobbs, 'Kehinde Wiley's Conceptual Realism', in *Kehinde Wiley* (New York: Rizzoli, 2012), 61.
73 Wiley, 'Frequently Asked Questions'.
74 *Kehinde Wiley: The World Stage: China* (Sheboygan, WI: John Michael Kohler Arts Center, 2007); Krista A. Thompson, Thelma Golden and Robert Hobbs, *Kehinde Wiley: The World Stage: Africa, Lagos-Dakar* (New York: Studio Museum in Harlem, 2008); Brian Keith Jackson and Kimberly Cleveland, *Kehinde Wiley: The World Stage: Brazil = O Estágio Do Mundo* (Culver City, CA: Roberts & Tilton, 2009); Gayatri Sinha and Paul D. Miller, *Kehinde Wiley: The World Stage: India, Sri Lanka* (Chicago: Rhona Hoffman Gallery, 2011); Ruth Eglash, Claudia J. Nahson and Dr. Shalva Weil, *Kehinde Wiley: The World Stage: Israel = Bamat Ha-'olam: Yiśra'el* (Culver City, CA: Roberts & Tilton, 2012); *Kehinde Wiley: The World Stage: France 1880–1960 = La scène mondiale: La France 1880–1960* (Paris: Galerie Daniel Templon, 2015); Ekow Eshun, *Kehinde Wiley: The World Stage: Jamaica* (London: Stephen Friedman Gallery, 2013); M. Cynthia Oliver and Mike Rogge, *Kehinde Wiley: The World Stage: Haiti = Sèn mondyal la Ayiti* (Culver City, CA: Roberts & Tilton, 2015).
75 Molly Nesbit, 'Fourteen Years Ago at Yale', in *Kehinde Wiley: A New Republic*, ed. Eugenie Tsai (New York: Brooklyn Museum in association with Del-Monico Books & Prestel, 2015), 63. In addition to the Goldman Sachs report,

Nesbit notes that the catalyst for his series was the 1982 experimental film *Sans Soleil*, directed by Chris Marker, that explores time, memory and place.

76 Martin Heidegger, 'The Age of the World Picture', in *The Question Concerning Technology and Other Essays*, trans. William Lovitt (New York: Harper & Row, 1977), 115–54. The essay was originally delivered as a lecture on 9 June 1938, under the title 'The Establishing by Metaphysics of the Modern World Picture', as the last of a series that was arranged by the Society for Aesthetics, Natural Philosophy, and Medicine in Freiburg im Breisgau, Germany.

77 Ibid., 129.

78 Gayatri Chakravorty Spivak, 'Three Women's Texts and a Critique of Imperialism', *Critical Inquiry* 12, no. 1 (Autumn 1985): 243–61.

79 Martin Heidegger, 'The Origin of the Work of Art', in *Philosophies of Art and Beauty: Selected Readings in Aesthetics from Plato to Heidegger*, ed. Albert Hofstadter and Richard Kuhns, trans. Albert Hofstadter (Chicago: University of Chicago Press, 1964), 649–701.

80 Gayatri Chakravorty Spivak, 'Interview with Elizabeth Grosz: Criticism, Feminism, and the Institution', in *The Post-Colonial Critic: Interviews, Strategies, Dialogues*, ed. Sarah Harasym (New York: Routledge, 1990), 1.

81 Jean Sorabella, 'The Grand Tour', in *Heilbrunn Timeline of Art History* (New York: The Metropolitan Museum of Art, 2003), www.metmuseum.org/toah/hd/grtr/hd_grtr.htm.

82 See Alissa Guzman, 'Kehinde Wiley's "Politics of Perception"', *Hyperallergic*, 22 April 2015, http://hyperallergic.com/200742/kehinde-wileys-politics-of-perception/. For a particularly nuanced argument regarding some of the issues with Wiley's project *The World Stage* through the lens of his exhibition of works resulting from his trip to Israel, see: Jillian Steinhauser, 'Kehinde Wiley Paints Israelis in Color', *The Forward*, 14 March 2012, http://forward.com/culture/152951/kehinde-wiley-paints-israelis-in-color/.

83 Gayatri Sinha, 'Archaeology & Subversion: Kehinde Wiley in India', in *Kehinde Wiley: The World Stage: India, Sri Lanka* (Chicago: Rhona Hoffman Gallery, 2011), 10.

84 Derrida, *Dissemination*, 141.

85 Ibid., 129.

86 Roberta Smith, 'A Hot Conceptualist Finds the Secret of Skin', *The New York Times*, 4 September 2008, sec. Arts / Art & Design, www.nytimes.com/2008/09/05/arts/design/05stud.html.

87 See James Adams, 'Artist Kehinde Wiley and "the Call of the Avant-Garde"', *The Globe and Mail*, accessed 6 October 2015, www.theglobeandmail.com/arts/film/artist-kehinde-wiley-and-the-call-of-the-avant-garde/article17003136/.

88 He goes on to say, 'And so that was in a way part of my training. I see now how I critique and embrace the same traditions, like sibling histories. I like to think of history as a rhetorical device.' See Christine Y. Kim, 'Faux Real: Interview with Kehinde Wiley', *Issue Magazine*, December 2003, http://issuemagazine.com/kehinde-wiley-faux-real/#/. He does not specifically

name his teacher Joseph Gotto here but he does later in his interview with the Smithsonian. See Kehinde Wiley, Oral history interview with Kehinde Wiley, Archives of American Art, Smithsonian Institution, interview by Anne Louise Bayly Berman, recorded and transcribed, 29 September 2010, www.aaa.si.edu/collections/interviews/oral-history-interview-kehinde-wiley-15882.

89 Dyer, *White*, 82–144; Hobbs, 'Kehinde Wiley's Conceptual Realism', 33, 247 (note 64); Krista Thompson, 'The Sound of Light Reflections on Art History in the Visual Culture of Hip-Hop', *Art Bulletin* 91, no. 4 (December 2007), 490.

90 Dyer, *White*, 89.

91 Ibid.

92 Ibid.

93 Ibid., 14.

94 See Martha Schwendener, 'The Diaspora Is Remixed', *The New York Times*, 22 March 2012, www.nytimes.com/2012/03/23/arts/design/the-diaspora-is-remixed.html. Wiley has assistants who often complete the backgrounds; and it has been posited that this is why some of his works look bland. However, I would argue that these assistants work under the direction of Wiley and were asked to paint this way.

95 Sinha, 'Archaeology & Subversion: Kehinde Wiley in India', 15.

96 Murtaza Vali, 'The White Slave', in *Kehinde Wiley: A New Republic*, ed. Eugenie Tsai (New York: Brooklyn Museum in association with DelMonico Books & Prestel, 2015), 102.

97 Derek Conrad Murray, *Queering Post-Black Art: Artists Transforming African-American Identity after Civil Rights* (London: I.B. Taurus, 2016), 84.

98 Ibid.

99 Ibid.

100 Jamilah King, 'The Art of Masculinity', *Colorlines*, 24 February 2015, www.colorlines.com/articles/art-masculinity. Also, as Deborah Solomon writes incorporating Wiley's words: 'His paintings all begin with an exchange of glances between artist and subject. Mr. Wiley describes the process as "this serendipitous thing where I am in the streets running into people who resonate with me, whether for cultural or sexual reasons. My type is rooted in my own sexual desire."' See Deborah Solomon, 'Kehinde Wiley Puts a Classical Spin on His Contemporary Subjects', *The New York Times*, 28 January 2015, www.nytimes.com/2015/02/01/arts/design/kehinde-wiley-puts-a-classical-spin-on-his-contemporary-subjects.html.

101 Rajesh Sampath, 'India Has Outlawed Homosexuality. But It's Better to Be Transgender There than in the U.S.', *The Washington Post*, 29 January 2015, www.washingtonpost.com/posteverything/wp/2015/01/29/india-has-outlawed-homosexuality-but-its-better-to-be-transgender-there-than-in-the-u-s/.

102 Ibid.

103 Nilanjana Bhowmick, 'Homosexuality Is Criminal Again as India's Top Court Reinstates Ban', *Time*, accessed 1 February 2016, http://world.time.com/2013/

12/11/homosexuality-is-criminal-again-as-indias-top-court-reinstates-ban/; Jo Eckersley, 'Coming out Is Never Easy. But in Sri Lanka and Much of Surrounding South Asia It's Dangerous', *Gay Times*, 31 December 2015, www.gaytimes.co.uk/life/21742/coming-out-is-never-easy-but-in-sri-lanka-and-much-of-surrounding-south-asia-its-dangerous/. See also my discussion of homosexuality in my article on Raqib Shaw's artworks that was written during the short period the colonial-era 1860 law was abolished: Alpesh Kantilal Patel, 'Open Secrets in "Post-Identity" Era Art Criticism/History: Raqib Shaw's Queer Garden of Earthly Delights', *Darkmatter: In the Ruins of Imperial Culture* 9, no. 2 (29 November 2012), www.darkmatter101.org/site/2012/11/29/open-secrets-in-post-identity-era-art-criticism-history-raqib-shaws-queer-garden-of-earthly-delights.

104 Murray, *Queering Post-Black Art*, 74–110. See also: Brian Keith Jackson, 'Quiet as It's Kept', in *Kehinde Wiley* (New York: Rizzoli, 2012), 110–55.

105 Wiley, 'Frequently Asked Questions'.

106 Ibid.

107 See Mrinalini Sinha, *Colonial Masculinity: The 'Manly Englishman' and the 'Effeminate Bengali' in the Late Nineteenth Century* (Manchester: Manchester University Press, 1995).

108 Sara Suleri Goodyear, *The Rhetoric of English India* (Chicago: University of Chicago Press, 1992), 16.

5 Space/site: writing queer feminist transnational South Asian art histories

In 2003 the city of Manchester, England, was deemed the most 'bohemian' and 'creative' city according to the 'Boho (or Bohemian) Britain Index' of 40 UK cities.[1] The Boho Index uses three indices – ethnic diversity, proportion of gay residents and number of patent applications per head – as key indicators of the city's economic health, and Manchester unsurprisingly scores high in all these areas.[2] Indeed, its reputation once based on a thriving industrial centre, the city of Manchester has become just as well known for giving rise to punk and 'new wave' music in the 1980s and for being the post-millennial, commercial epicentre of gay life in the northwest of England. For instance, the city has many gay clubs, bars and restaurants, which make up the area known as the Gay Village, and became the first British city to host Europride in 2003. Manchester has a diverse ethnic population, too, evidenced most conspicuously in the commercialized spaces of Chinatown and Curry Mile, so named for its many South Asian restaurants and shops.

Urban geographer Steve Quilley notes that since at least the early 1990s, those involved in 'all aspects of urban regeneration' adhered to a 'Manchester script' that characterized the city as 'post-modern, post-industrial and cosmopolitan'.[3] In this chapter, of crucial importance is a consideration of the larger implications of this shift to marketing the city as 'cosmopolitan' for subjects traversing the Gay Village, in particular the lesbian, bisexual and trans*-identified women of South Asian descent of the collective Sphere around whose artwork *Sphere:dreamz* this chapter pivots. In other words, I am referring here not to cosmopolitanism as an intellectual attitude but rather the material determinants that produce and set limits to it.[4]

Organized under the creative direction of cofounder Jaheda Choudhury, multimedia artist Shanaz Gulzar and writer Maya Chowdhry, *Sphere:dreamz* was installed in spring 2006 near Canal Street, the epicentre of the Gay Village. At least partially, the work is a response to the space of the Gay Village that the women of the collective experienced as largely gay, white, middle class and male. Outside of my doctoral thesis and that of queer and gender studies scholar Elisavet Pakis, this project has received no academic attention.[5]

However, my interest is not just in a straightforward recording of my experience viewing the artwork for posterity. Instead, I present my own research into the material culture and histories of both the Gay Village and Curry Mile in Manchester, where I lived from 2005 to 2008, as entangled with my writing about *Sphere:dreamz.*

Before describing *Sphere:dreamz*, I explore theories of urban space and then the construction of the Gay Village as place, given it is where the collective decided to locate its work. At the end of the chapter, I explore the space of Curry Mile, which I argue is integral to further understanding the work, if only implicitly so. All the evidence was collected during the time I lived in Manchester and therefore refers only to the period up to May 2008.[6] Overall, my aim is to deepen, enrich and broaden the meaning of the work of Sphere as part of writing specifically *queer* and *feminist* transnational South Asian art histories. I embed the work simultaneously within the complex production of space in Manchester, by intertwining it with a broad range of theory, and by making visible my specific subjectivity as a queer transnational South Asian.

I am especially mindful that by incorporating autobiographical, anecdotal evidence, I run the danger of persuading my audience of a particular agenda, or worse, losing my academic objectivity. I therefore lay bare my own subjectivity without privileging it as somehow authentic. I toggle between academic prose and descriptions of personal experience in the same spirit as self-identified Chicana-lesbian feminist Gloria Anzaldúa in her book on diasporic identities, *Borderlands/La Frontera: The New Mestiza* (1999).[7] Art historian Russell Ferguson notes that through Anzaldúa's specific use of Spanish and English and prose and poetry she presents the 'expression of a deterritorialization which she feels physically, in her mouth, her tongue, her teeth'.[8] While Ferguson is referring to the particular variation in physical sensations associated with speaking different languages, I hope to encompass the sensations of the entire corporeal body. It is significant in this regard that French sociologist Henri Lefebvre chooses the body to elaborate upon his theory of space that it 'is at once conceived, perceived, and directly lived',[9] I explore this theory in the next section. He notes that 'social practice presupposes the use of the body', including the 'sensory organs'.[10] However, I am not concurring with his belief that bodily, lived experience is more authentic than visual representation. Art historian Amelia Jones notes that Lefebvre is operating 'on a belief system that is … based on an oppositional model of the "real" being opposed to (and superseding) representation'.[11] Imagistic representations – whether artworks like *Sphere:dreamz* or other types of representations – cannot be so easily extricated from bodily, lived experience, as they are both chiasmically intertwined.[12] Given this point, it seems difficult writing about *Sphere:dreamz* without also considering lived experience. The art history I write is necessarily syncretic and embodied.

Space as perceived, conceived and directly lived

Henri Lefebvre sketches out a compelling conceptual framework for collecting and examining data in relation to the production of urban space in his seminal book *The Production of Space* (1974). He notes that three types of 'practice' produce space – spatial practice, practices of representation of space and the everyday practices of appropriation of space or spaces of representations.[13] These in turn equate to the production of space as 'perceived', or the routine spatial behaviours that can be perceived in the physical transformations of space; of space as 'conceived', or those conceptions of space which order our knowledge of what is possible, such as maps and official hegemonic, or intellectual, narratives; and of space as 'directly lived'. Drawing on Lefebvre's conceptual model, I attempt to elucidate the relationships among the perceived, conceived and directly lived socio-spatial sub-spaces of the Gay Village through a range of evidentiary material, including the work of Sphere.

Lefebvre's characterization of the relationship among his various types of spatial production is ambiguous, though he does note that it is 'dialectical'.[14] As one potential application of Lefebvre's theory for urban analysis, architectural historian and Lefebvre scholar Łukasz Stanek suggests exploring how the products of one practice of production of space – in this case mass media representations – are used as tools for other practices of the production of space.[15] Drawing on Stanek's approach and expanding on it, I consider how the products of each type of spatial production reinforce, become the condition for, or serve as the tools to subvert the products of other types of spatial production. Rather than distilling the products of different types of space into specific cause-and-effect relationships, I focus on producing an *impressionist montage* of the Gay Village.

I specifically explore civic representations of the Gay Village as 'conceived' through various marketing materials, as well as the commercial production of space as 'conceived' through Canal Street gay and lesbian club websites and party flyers. To explore space as 'perceived', I describe the economic, political and social forces underpinning the historical physical transformation of the geographical areas now known as the Gay Village. Finally, I offer my own and others' explorations of space as 'directly lived' in dialogue with the aforementioned evidence to complete Lefebvre's model of the production of space.

Queer, women's studies and literature scholar Dianne Chisholm's exploration of a variety of literary queer (gay and lesbian) readings of city spaces in her compelling 2005 book, *Queer Constellations: Subcultural Space in the Wake of the City*, suggests further what my approach might afford. Though Chisholm does reference Lefebvre's scholarship, of most relevance here is her observation that the queer texts she explores approximate German philosopher Walter Benjamin's method of presenting various ephemera from the city in a 'dialectical image' – or in montage to unearth the contradictions within urban space – that closely approximates my overall presentation of evidence.[16] In particular, I am filtering Benjamin's concept of dialectical imaging or montage through Lefebvre's perceived, conceived and directly lived triad.

Chisholm offers American writer and literary critic Samuel L. Delaney's book *Times Square Red, Times Square Blue* (1999) as one of several examples to further illustrate her concepts. Delaney's book is a memoir of his coming out as a gay and black man in 1960s Times Square, as well as a Marxian critique of the civic 'renewal' of Times Square in the 1990s and the associated destruction of subcultural queer space.[17] Chisholm notes that by 'blast[ing] apart' dominant narratives of urban progress through both a queer and black subjectivity, Delaney 'reassembl[es] fragments of collective history into dialectical images' in a way that rejects the possibility of achieving an exhaustive, unified account of developing city space.[18] I hope my own writing will similarly destabilize the dominant civic and commercial production of the Gay Village. Moreover, Delaney's account of the gentrification of Times Square was written *before* the influx of gays in the post-2000 period in the area known as Hell's Kitchen, bordering Times Square, and the concomitant proliferation of glossy gay bars and restaurants in that area.[19] These bars and clubs are themselves part of the redevelopment that he would undoubtedly decry, and would have provided a different perspective from which to read the redevelopment of Times Square.[20] Following on this point, I explore the broader implications of Manchester's own consolidation of its Gay Village as an important ingredient in the city's official re-imagination.[21]

The Gay Village can be understood more in terms of what it *does* than what it *is* at any given time and place – what queer and performance studies scholar José Esteban Muñoz describes as '*racial performativity*'.[22] Muñoz describes the latter as generated by an 'affective particularity' that 'is supposed to be descriptive of the receptors we use to hear each other and the frequencies on which certain subalterns speak and are heard, or more importantly, *felt*'.[23] Moreover, he posits 'ethnicity as "a structure of feeling", as a way of being in the world, a path that does not conform to the conventions of a majoritarian public sphere' to theorize 'feeling brown' as a useful mode of understanding *latinidad*, which can be defined as characteristics that those of Latin American origin might share without reducing them to essentialized traits.[24] Muñoz is drawing here on the work of British cultural theorist Raymond Williams, who describes a 'structure of feeling' as connecting different groups – the Marxist Williams was referring to working-class groups – to social experiences that can be 'in process' and yet historically situated.[25] Therefore, though Muñoz theorizes 'brown' in 'feeling brown' through a viewpoint that is *latinidad* and not South Asian, he notes that 'feeling brown' is meant to 'surpas[s] … epistemological renderings of race'.[26]

My interpretation of my South Asian-ness is closely allied with Muñoz's 'feeling brown'. 'Feeling South Asian' would be simply that which might allow groups to unite across geographical/national, as well as racial, gendered, class, faith-based and sexual categories – among other affiliations that have yet to be named and are merely 'experienced' or 'felt' – against a 'majoritarian affect'. On Canal Street, the majoritarian affect I describe is gay, white, middle class and male.

(De)construction of the Gay Village

The idea for a distinct 'Gay Village' can be traced to the 1960s, though it was not until 1991 that *City Planning News* – a now defunct free newspaper delivered to all Manchester households – referred to the Village as an explicit planning entity.[27] Since then, the city of Manchester has invested large amounts of capital into the Gay Village as part of its long-term economic revitalization goals. In fact, the conspicuous success of the Gay Village has encouraged many other UK city councils, such as that of Birmingham, to outline similar civic revitalization plans connected to queer commercial areas.[28] By the mid- to late 1990s, the Gay Village – with its bars and clubs aplenty as well as restaurants – was well trafficked day and night. The darkened windows of many of the bars found in the area in the early 1990s, which presumably protected patrons' privacy, gave way to large, transparent windows that are often ajar during the day and early evening hours in the summer.

In the late 1990s, the city's veritable epicentre of gay life, Canal Street, became the subject matter of Channel 4's critically acclaimed miniseries *Queer as Folk* (Red Production Company, 1999), solidifying the already visible mainstreaming of Manchester's queer scene.[29] By 2006, students across the UK voted Manchester Metropolitan University the best place for gays to study, ahead of all London-based universities.[30] Moreover, in 2007 the Manchester City Council and the Greater Manchester Police (GMP) department ranked third and thirteenth, respectively, in a list of the top 100 gay employers in the UK compiled by the gay rights group Stonewall.[31] It is therefore no surprise that the city's gay scene figures prominently in the informational brochures produced by Marketing Manchester. Established in 1997, Marketing Manchester is the city's official tourist board for Greater Manchester and the agency charged with promoting the region on the national and international stage. As an example of the extent to which the organization actively markets the Village, a 40-page, full-colour, glossy informational brochure marketing the city in 2006 and 2007 to gay and lesbian visitors is widely disseminated in North America and Western Europe and has a production run of 10,000.[32] Moreover, in Marketing Manchester's 2006/7 brochure, *Manchester: Where to Stay 2006/07*, the annual Pride event is mentioned under the 'Events' section, and Canal Street is listed as one of the numerous places one should visit in the city in a '48 hour period'.[33] The brochure also indicates that the 'Gay Village boasts a range of stylish bars' and the 'mixed and friendly crowd makes a unique party atmosphere … it's the perfect place to dance the night away'.[34] The word 'stylish' and the phrase 'mixed and friendly crowd' are important in underscoring that the Gay Village is being marketed as hip, trendy and for gays *and* straights alike. The term 'mixed' might also refer to ethnic mix, while the use of the adjective 'friendly' defuses any sense of 'danger' that the Village might elicit for tourists.

The 'gentrification' of the Gay Village, signalled by these strategies of depicting the Village as a 'safe, usable other, but … still different' enough to be exciting, has met with some degree of backlash from the gay community.[35] In September 2006 the comedy club Jongleurs was closed down and converted into residential space. It was the third such proposal in as many months to convert an entertainment venue in the Gay Village into housing developments in the area. Nigel Martin-Smith, owner of the now defunct Gay Village nightclub Essential, describes this most recent proposal as a threat to the existence of the Village itself. Martin-Smith has said that '"we [presumably gays] will not allow anyone to destroy it [the Village]"'. Furthermore, Martin-Smith sets up a class divide between the gay Villagers and the '*posh* architects and *rich* property developers'. Interestingly, many of the potential 'middle-class' property owners for whom the houses are being built are themselves gay and might easily be neighbours with these very same property developers and architects.[36] Most of the patrons of the Gay Village are white, male and middle (to upper) class – the profile of the ideal tenant for these city centre spaces.

To counteract the gentrification, certain bars now make it clear on their websites that many of their nights are primarily for gays only. For instance, the name of the gay club Essential already foreshadows the essentialist door policy stated on the club's website, which reads: 'We have a strict policy of majority Gay and Lesbian customers. We do admit some straight people on the condition that they respect the safe gay space that is Essential.'[37] The language on the website of another venue in the Gay Village, Falcon Men's Bar, anticipates that the bar's 'gay and bisexual men only' policy might offend a public that is now used to wandering freely through most of the Gay Village:

> The Gay Village is now fully integrated – and rightly so – with gay men, lesbians and their gay-friendly straight friends all enjoying each other's company … [but] just as some women want to enjoy a space of their own in bars like 'vanilla' so some gay and bisexual men want to socialize in male only company.[38]

However, invoking women-only spaces in the Village to justify the bar's policies is not completely analogical. Many of the spaces in the Village are arguably de facto more or less gay, male spaces already. As the only venue that explicitly markets itself for lesbians in the Village, vanilla fulfils more of a need rather than claiming a right, which Falcon is doing.[39] Moreover, both Essential's and Falcon Bar's policies are incredibly essentializing. They do not account, for example, for a transgendered 'male' with an anatomically female body.

A side effect of the move towards recovering a more gay presence in response to the upturn in the economic growth and mainstreaming of the Gay Village has been the reification of 'gay' as white, middle class and mostly male, which has had a decided impact on the diversity of people circulating on and near Canal Street as well. In fact, the *Queer as Folk* series, which brought significant international attention to Canal Street, presents a gay Manchester in which all of the main characters are white. The minor character of colour, Lance, who is marrying the lesbian character Romy for UK citizenship, is constituted outside of the gay, white family, and ultimately turns out to be abusive. His questionable character is a red herring. As queer studies and literature scholar David Alderson explains, Lance 'cannot be assimilated' easily into a homosexual family because of his other differences – racial and national.[40] Alderson notes that the specifically queer variant of cosmopolitanism depicted in *Queer as Folk* demands conformity to a white, male and middle-class subjectivity that is recognizable '*despite* cultural differences'.[41]

Marketing Manchester: sites/sights of knowledge and the visual as performative

Urban geographer Dereka Rushbrook notes that queer spaces are constructed and marketed as 'ethnic' spaces – especially by what she calls 'secondary cities', like Manchester, or 'wannabe world cities'.[42] Indeed, London's overwhelming dominance in terms of funding, tourism and visibility has left other UK cities grappling for some kind of angle to distinguish themselves – for Manchester, the Gay Village has fulfilled that function.[43] Rushbrook observes, however, that when a queer space is marketed like a traditional ethnic space, the complexities of the 'differential mobilities of the bodies' that inhabit both spaces are effectively erased.[44]

In the context of the Gay Village, Manchester-based civic marketing ephemera exemplify Rushbrook's point by eliding subjects of colour as well as gender. The 'See what the *locals* think' section under the 'gay and lesbian' tab of Greater Manchester's official tourism website, *Visit Manchester*, includes head shots of three individuals canvassed for opinions – two male and one female, who are all apparently white.[45] Three other photos are at the bottom of the website – a medium close-up of two white women, a long shot of Canal

Street and a head shot of a black man. Only one woman appears on the main body of the web page, and no people of colour. When the smaller photos on the bottom of the web page are considered, the male–female ratio is split evenly, but the number of people of colour remains the same.[46] South Asians are apparently not represented at all, nor are any women of colour. The same goes for the brochure *Manchester: A Guide for LGBT Visitors 2006/07*, produced by Marketing Manchester.[47]

To explore further how the Gay Village is 'conceived' and is 'directly lived', I examine commercial queer bar and club websites and flyers, and draw on the experiences of subjects, which sometimes circulates as unverifiable fact, innuendo or gossip. Art historian Irit Rogoff specifically notes how gossip in visual studies can be productive as an object of analysis: 'In Foucauldian terms it [gossip] serves the purpose through negative differentiation, of constituting a category of respectable knowledge … In Derridean terms gossip allows for the constitution of the formal boundaries of the genre and its outlawed, excessive and uncontrollable narratives.' Rogoff compellingly argues that a consideration of gossip can be useful in reassessing the mechanisms that bound and define certain knowledge as 'true', such as who is and is not queer, as I explore in the next section.[48]

Many doormen of Canal Street bars and clubs vet patrons to ensure that only perceived gay and lesbian patrons are admitted. If, as British cultural studies scholar Stuart Hall argues, 'identification is in the end conditional, lodged in contingency', then this can often lead to misrecognition.[49] Indeed, Mancunian gays and lesbians of South Asian descent have shared their difficulties in getting past the door of various bars and clubs on Canal Street.[50] Their experiences suggest that when doormen encounter a queer subject of South Asian descent, their 'gaydar' – defined as 'the ability to recognize homosexuals through observation or intuition' – is temporarily obfuscated, giving them a moment of pause.[51] Embedded within the definition of 'gaydar' is the centrality of embodied vision to the process of visual recognition. Thus, the doormen of Canal Street respond to subjects through a particularly affectual, reflexive response – what Maurice Merleau-Ponty would describe as a 'corporal or postural schema', which can be 'habitual' – a default position the body assumes in various commonly experienced circumstances.[52] People of colour thus disrupt a postural schema that on Canal Street is characterized as habitually white, male and gay.[53] The brownness of a subject's skin could serve to effectively render invisible his or her queerness, if only temporarily.

Women of colour hold the most compromised position on Canal Street. The co-founder of the collective Sphere, Jaheda Choudhury, who identifies as a lesbian of South Asian descent, has said that she felt not only (hetero)sexualized, but also 'exoticised' by doormen so that her gender and ethnicity combined to make her an object of what could be described as a neo-colonial, sexist and misogynistic gaze.[54] Even when gender is explored on Canal Street in academic research, issues of race become subsumed.[55] In addition, flyers archived online for parties of the lesbian club vanilla – which describes itself as 'the lesbian mecca of the North' on its website – depict subjects who are all apparently white, as ironically signalled by the name of the bar itself.[56] This also applies to a poster advertising one of the rare joint parties co-hosted by vanilla and the gay club Essential, organized to destabilize the divide between 'gay' and 'lesbian' spaces.[57] Even the light flesh tones of the four computer-generated women who are part of the banner of vanilla's homepage appear to be white.[58]

I am mindful of the irony of my falling back on appearance to construct identifications – as with my descriptions of the photos in the city marketing materials – having just outlined the shortcomings of such visually constructed knowledge. However, I want to emphasize that all visual knowledge is always already partial – there is no stable, unchanging or 'correct' reading. In this case, I am placing my interpretation of the identification of subjects on websites in dialogue with the other products of practices of space as commercially constructed – such as flyers for Canal Street clubs.

Flyers advertising parties at the gay club Essential in March 2007 all have apparently white male subjects with one notable, and I argue problematic, exception, the 'Chav Bender' party flyer.[59] 'Chav' is a derogatory term used to describe white, lower-class, young British men (or 'chavettes' for women).[60] They model their behaviour on stereotypes associated with black gangsters and rappers and often wear caps, tracksuits, heavy jewellery and knock-off designer wear – most notoriously Burberry clothing.[61] The background of the poster advertising the queer Chav Bender party is a standard Burberry clothing design print overlaid with the image of a shirtless young man wearing a baseball cap on his head, heavy jewellery around his neck and pants that reveal his Calvin Klein underwear. The sepia tone wash, which matches one of the colours of the Burberry print, implicitly gives the male body on the poster a non-white, perhaps black ethnic, appearance. Given that the term 'chav' is normally reserved for low-class whites, the flyer implicitly classes the only apparently ethnic subject on Essential's flyers as 'low'. Moreover, the archetype for the pose – authoritative, aggressive, and yet meant to be provocatively titillating – is the early 1990s Calvin Klein commercial advertisement featuring Mark Wahlberg, then known as Marky Mark.[62] The tough guy pose of Wahlberg – who headlined the band Marky Mark and the Funky Bunch, one of the first white rap bands in the early 1990s to have mainstream appeal – draws on the stereotype of an urban, African-American male rapper. In this way, the source image, itself, for the Chav party poster is also problematic for its appropriation of the black body.

Persons who appear to be of colour are also sparse in the photos archived on websites of Canal Street clubs. Websites, including vanilla's, also make clear the relative lack of women of colour on Canal Street.[63] Canal Street clubs hire photographers to take photos of patrons attending their club nights and often post the photographs on their websites, leaving traces of the ephemeral parties and becoming part of the club's marketing. Performance and queer studies scholar José Esteban Muñoz articulates the virtues of 'ephemera as evidence' as a valid object of inquiry, especially in the absence of any more traditional evidentiary material.[64] Although the photos obviously do not stand in for the events themselves, they can serve as one of presumably many historical archives documenting the clubs and exposing how they want to promote themselves.

Each of the subjects in the photos has already been filtered up to four times – by patrons who self-select or exclude themselves, based on their interpretations of official or unofficial club door policies; by doormen who make decisions on which patrons to permit into the club; by the photographer; and by club owners who choose the photos to post on their websites. The photos selected for uploading reflect a careful process of editing that is hardly random. Of course I cannot know how the subjects in the photographs define themselves in terms of race, gender and sexuality – only their apparent identities, which have been constructed by the club through multiple gazes/edits.

The incessant posting of photos on Canal Street club websites, some of which upload daily, betrays an almost obsessive cataloguing/archiving that seems to reinforce and perpetuate an endless cycle of performance of homosexuality as materially gay, white, middle class and male, and therefore ultimately made visually apparent as such. The latter is reinforced by the flyers, as well. Ironically, this reiteration creates its own 'norm' within this supposedly radical, marginal 'queer' community. Judith Butler theorizes this repeated, compulsive citation of a norm in terms of performativity, which she describes 'not as the act by which a subject brings into being what she/he names, but, rather, as that reiterative power of discourse to produce the phenomena that it regulates and constrains.'[65] This helps explain how a club like vanilla, which has one of the more lax door policies on Canal Street, still has a dearth of people of colour represented on its website. The club self-regulates by producing a normative discourse of lesbianism as white and middle class on which it is ultimately based.

Judith Butler is concerned with the discursive production of bodies – which is not to say that there is no material body, but that it is not produced prior to or outside of discourse – and the dominant constructions of gender and sexuality, achieved through continual reiteration and performance of particular discourses. In this way, I am using Butler, perhaps perversely, to comment on normative homosexuality, rather than heterosexuality.[66]

Sphere:dreamz

Henri Lefebvre notes provocatively in *The Production of Space* that: 'To change life … we must first change space.'[67] I now explore the role that the public art project *Sphere:dreamz* plays to 'change space' and thereby 'change life' for the subjects who traverse those spaces. *Sphere:dreamz* – an outdoor installation which consisted of thirteen beds all placed in a circle – provided a foil, or counter narrative, to the gay, white and male narrative of Canal Street. In late 2005 Sphere put out a call for women of South Asian descent from the north-west of England who identify as lesbian, bisexual, transgender and queer to share their 'dreams' and 'hopes'.[68] Poetry written by Maya Chowdhry about the many responses received became the foundation of the installation, which was strategically situated in Sackville Park, next to the epicentre of the Gay Village, Canal Street. The installation was just up for a few hours as part of that year's queerupnorth – a Manchester-based annual international arts festival (now defunct) dedicated to promoting queer arts and culture in the northwest of England.[69]

The installation highlighted the limits of the commercial and civic production of Canal Street as a public spatial identification by surfacing issues of gender, faith and race as intersectional with sexuality (Plate 10 and Figure 5.1). The work foregrounded the lives of queer South Asian women. For example, the headboard of one of the beds in *Sphere:dreamz* had been replaced with a women's bathroom door from a queer bar or club, while the bedspread and pillow of another were composed of a patchwork of clothing items, such as jeans, a *choli* (the part of a sari worn on the upper body), or short-sleeve blouse, skirt and a golden-coloured *salwar kameez* (Figures 5.2–3 and Plate 11). The juxtaposition of the queer club/bar bathroom door and jeans with traditional South Asian clothes not only highlighted the invisibility of South Asian women in Canal Street bars and clubs, but also confused the presence of these subjects on Canal Street as non-normative.

The beds also functioned as sites of intimacy between the viewer and the artist. That is, each bed reflected its creator's particular concerns and interests, but was presented in such a way that the bodies of visitors became intertwined with the bed and therefore with the creator's decidedly queer, female and South Asian subjectivity as well. For instance, visitors were encouraged to sit or lie on the beds – many of which were not only infused with incense but also had recorded poetry piped up through their bases – ensuring that the bodily experience of 'viewing' the artwork elicited a multi-sensory engagement, directly incorporating every sense except taste.

In another example, a bed was covered with plush comforters and sheets that moulded to the contours of the subject who was enveloped within them, allowing each subject who lay on the bed to leave an imprint of her or his body and creating a complex, ever-shifting topography of embodied hills, valleys or clouds. The allusion to clouds was also signalled by the silver ink used to write words such as 'security', 'love', 'dream', 'safety' and 'peace' on the sheets in both English and Urdu (Figures 5.4–5). Light and airy, the bed

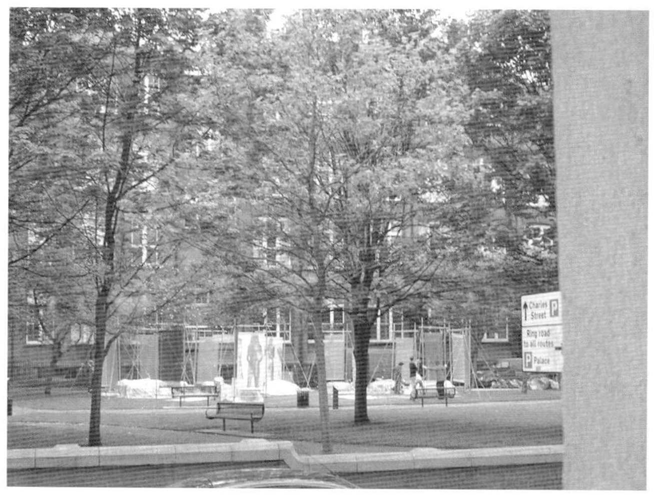

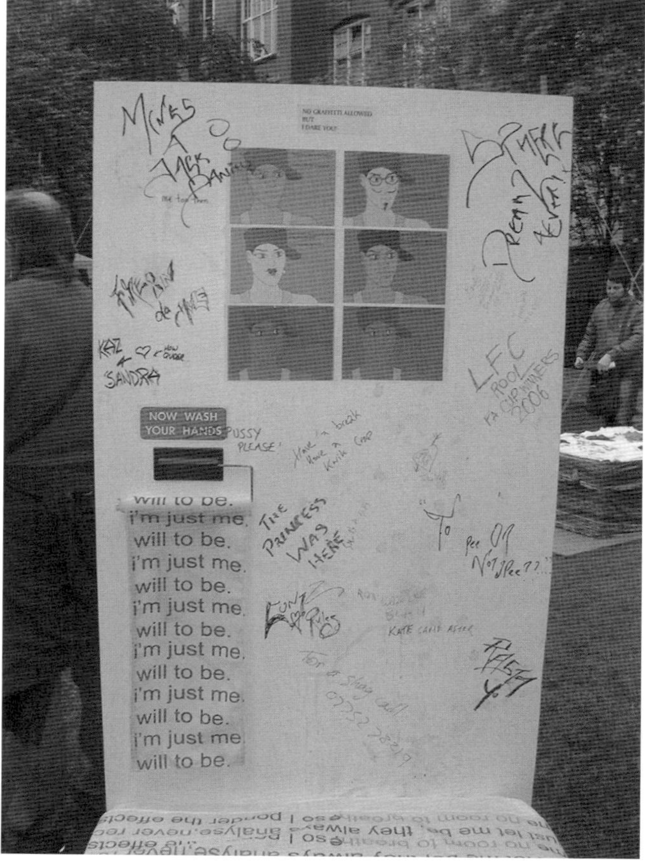

5.1–7 Sphere, *Sphere:dreamz*, Sackville Park, Manchester, England.

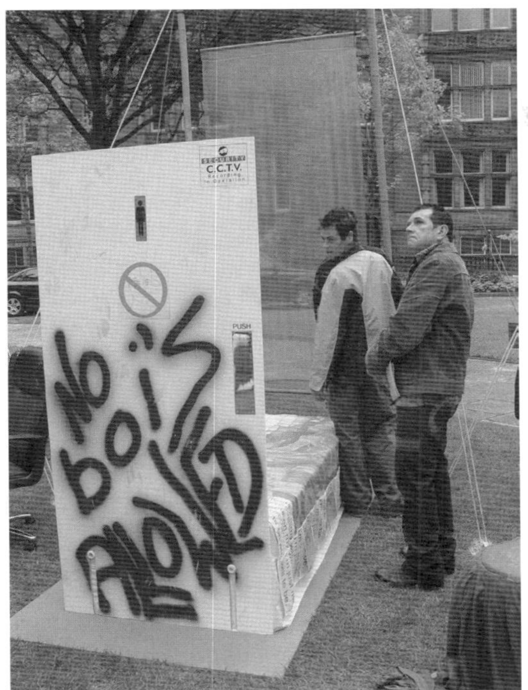

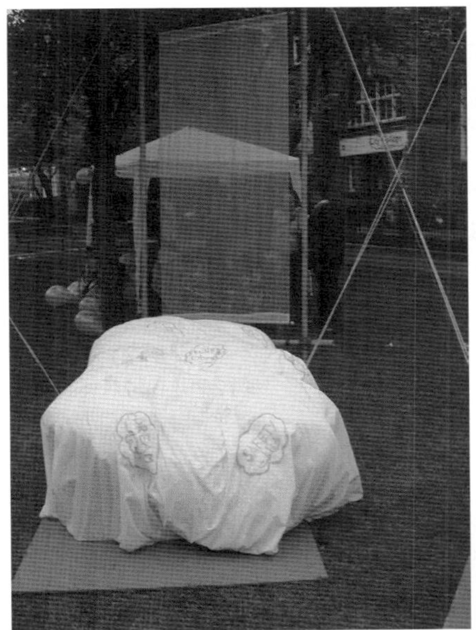

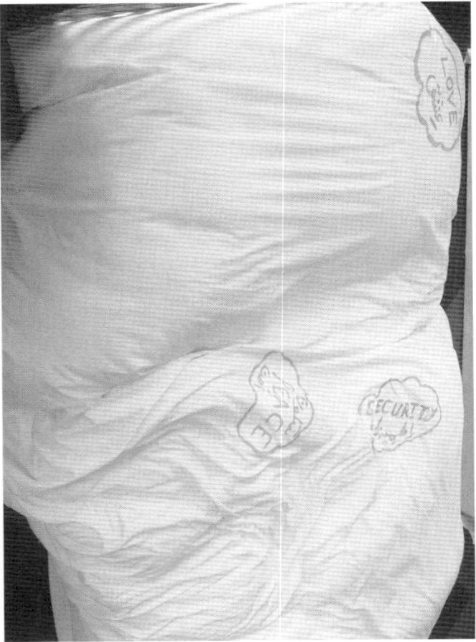

Continued

5.1–7

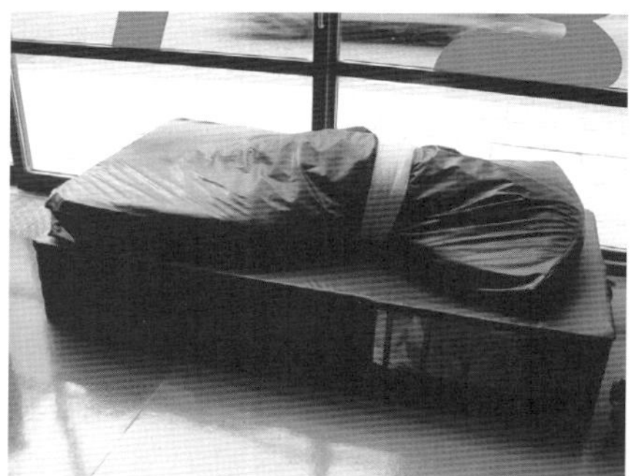

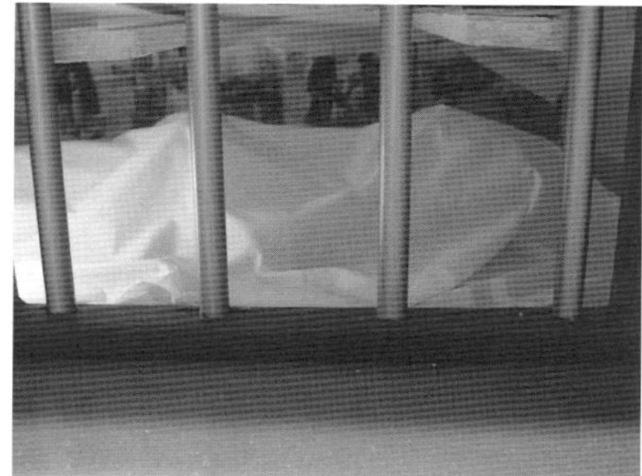

5.1–7 Continued

depicted the metaphoric and literal 'silver lining in every cloud', giving it a utopian quality, or an escapist feeling. Another bed in which a tree was planted and covered in a verdant fitted sheet was similarly life-affirming in its suggestion of the bed as a celebratory site of fertility (Plate 12).

Other beds were more confrontational, such as the stark, black vinyl-clad, minimalist mattress that warped into what appeared to be a body, the waist of which was forcibly formed by a surgical bandage wrapped around the centre of the beds. Through a grated opening on the side of the platform, another body covered by a shroud-like white sheet was visible (Figures 5.6–7). This bed implicitly highlighted the metaphoric difficulties and constraints of navigating Canal Street as a queer, female and transnational South Asian, or straddling normative gendered, queer and South Asian subjectivities, all of which place a collective queer, South Asian gendered subjectivity at the margins.

On yet another bed, bejewelled, flesh-like materials resembling footprints were interspersed with splashes of red paint to suggest the ritual of new Indian brides dipping the soles of their feet in red dye to literally mark their first entry into their new homes. In the context of the larger installation, this bed underscored the presumptive heteronormativity of the ritual, which excludes lesbian women from the home (Plate 13). The splotches of red paint could also be considered vaginal blood, hinting at the expectation that a Muslim woman must be a virgin when she marries and that her husband should break her hymen on their first night of marriage. Many British Muslim women have gone to great lengths to ensure the appearance of virginity through medical reconstruction of broken hymens. Furthermore, given that the breaking of the hymen is not always accompanied by blood even if the bride is a virgin, fake blood capsules are often inserted into the lining of the repaired hymen.[70]

All the beds were situated around a central *rangoli* floor design comprised of flowers, incense, rice and powdered chalk (Plate 14). The practice of rangoli-making can be traced back to the Indus Valley (c.3000 BC) and is typically executed by women in India as an offering to the Hindu goddess of rice and wealth, Lakshmi, to stave off poverty and protect the home.[71] However, the installation as a whole was not exclusively connected to Hinduism; another bed incorporated depictions of Christ on the cross alongside the 'om' symbol utilized in the Hindu, Jain and Buddhist faiths, thereby underscoring a few of the many faiths connected to a queer, transnational South Asian female subjectivity (Plate 15).

On the pillow and sheet of this bed depicting multiple religions, the following excerpt from the 'Bhagavad-Gita' (song of God) from the Sanskrit epic *Mahabharata* was written in both Sanskrit and English: 'For one who sees Me everywhere and sees everything in Me, I am never lost, nor is he ever lost to Me.'[72] Attributed to Lord Krishna, this statement in the context of Sphere's project was as an affront to the heterodoxy typically associated with Hindu faith, in particular, and the assumption that being queer is not compatible with religious doctrines, more generally. Furthermore, the flags of India, Australia and the United Kingdom on this particular bed sheet indicated the complex connections between the women of Sphere and these nations – whether by birth, residence or perhaps tourism. Indeed, the snorkelling gear on the bed could be another reference to Australia, known for its Great Barrier Reef.

(De)constructing Curry Mile

The *Sphere:dreamz* installation helped to underscore the profound possibilities of artworks to queer the manner in which urban subjects experience or feel public spaces – in this case the public spaces of Canal Street. I became interested in how this work might have functioned near Curry Mile, which is connected to the Gay Village by the same artery, Oxford Road. The two spaces are a half-hour walk from each other (Figure 5.8). In my conversation with Sphere collective co-founder Jaheda Choudhury – whom I had met several months earlier at a conference – she indicated that though none of the women of Sphere had experienced any overt homophobia in Curry Mile, they nonetheless *felt* out of place, and over time some of them had stopped going to the area altogether.

In December 2006, I approached Sphere to discuss the possibility of positioning several of the beds and associated ephemera from the original installation in various sites including Curry Mile.[73] Sphere was eager to support the overall concept of my exhibition idea, but Choudhury expressed reservations about involving Curry Mile. She was particularly concerned about the hate an overt queer presence in Curry Mile could potentially elicit from restaurant owners.[74] I argue that to fully understand why *Sphere:dreamz* was not sited in Curry Mile, it is important to understand how exclusion works using Lefebvre's model of understanding space, theory and my and others' experiences

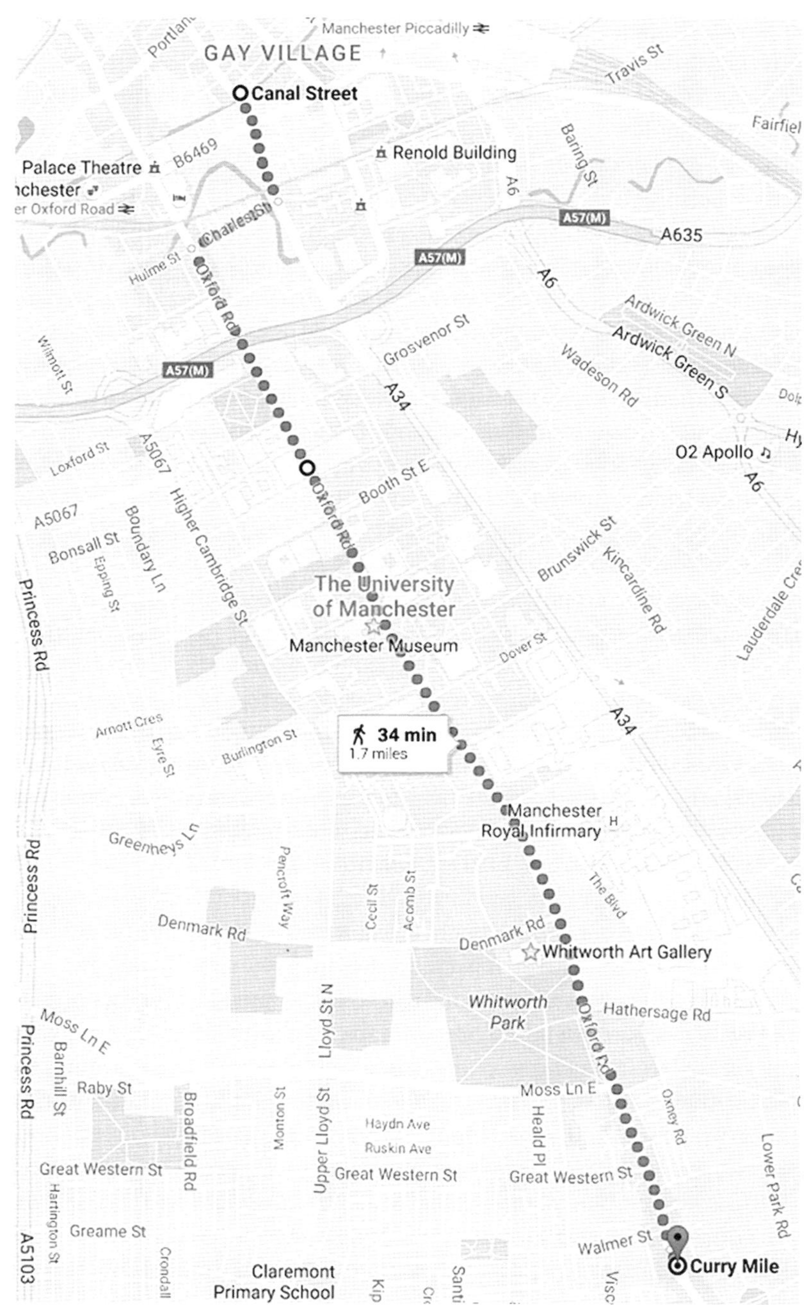

5.8 Map of distance between Curry Mile and Gay Village, Manchester, England.

in these spaces to create an impressionist montage of this commercialized space.

Since the early 1960s, thousands of immigrant families, mostly from Pakistan, have settled in and around Curry Mile. The restaurants that first sprang up during this period on Wilmslow Road initially catered to and were run by Pakistani immigrant men, and later their families, who wanted foods they could not otherwise find in Manchester.[75] From a handful of sweet-centres, cafes and kebab houses, the neighbourhood Rusholme exploded into a neon shrine to Britain's love of curry. More than 150 other types of businesses also operate along Wilmslow Road – Asian grocers, kebab houses, sari shops, eclectic Asian music, video and bookshops and jewellers selling golden goods. Moreover, the growth spurt in the 1980s and 1990s that gave rise to the contemporary Curry Mile was driven primarily by the growth in the university student population, who found the curry restaurants' affordable dining options in close proximity to student housing.[76] Indeed, the clientele of a contemporary Curry Mile restaurant is not largely South Asian, but white and middle class. More recently, refugee communities and social groups – Eastern European, Kurdish and Islamic – have settled on the side streets off the Wilmslow Road main corridor, making Curry Mile Manchester's most ethnically diverse neighbourhood.

The moniker 'Curry' Mile itself belies the topography of the strip, which includes a smorgasbord of diverse restaurants. Even *Visit Manchester*, the official tourism website for Greater Manchester, mentions Curry Mile under its 'international cuisine' section without any indication that the area offers more than the eponymous 'curry', which in the British context is a term that stands in for all South Asian food.[77] In addition to the more than fifty restaurants, takeaways and sweet houses that offer the varied delicacies of Bangladesh, Pakistan, India and Iran, the area also has a sizeable number of Middle Eastern, Greek, Chinese and Caribbean restaurants. Some restaurants serve food from more than one geographical region, such as Pink Garlic, which serves both Chinese and Indian dishes.[78] Also, the food served is often inflected by a diasporic sensibility, such as a hybrid of South Asian and Middle Eastern foods or British Asian food.

Chicken tikka masala, perhaps the epitome of a hybrid British Asian dish, was declared a 'true national dish' in 2001 by the UK's then Foreign Secretary Robin Cook.[79] According to an article in the *Guardian* in 2004, chicken tikka masala is 'served an estimated 23m times a year in Britain's 9,000 curry houses. Millions eat packaged equivalents from supermarkets – Sainsbury's alone sells 32,000 packs a week.'[80] The exact provenance of the popular dish remains nebulous, but it is generally thought that in response to customer requests a curry restaurant owner in the UK – some report Glasgow, others insist on a more English connection – added a sweet, tomato-based sauce to the chicken as a sort of 'gravy' to cut the spiciness of the dish.[81]

Despite the panoply of cuisine offered by curry restaurants, a large body of evidence – perhaps innuendo or gossip is the better descriptor – points to the perceived, homogenous experience of dining in any of Rusholme's curry restaurants.[82] For instance, a user posted the following on a discussion forum suggesting that the restaurants were actually part of a larger conglomerate: 'All of the curries I've been out for recently have been almost carbon copies of each other … It's as if there is only *one kitchen* shared between all the restaurants.'[83] Channel 4's 2000 documentary, which focused on Curry Mile as part of a larger investigation of Britain's curry houses in the northwest of England, also insinuated the latter.[84] Mukhtar Ahmed, Chairman of the Rusholme Business Association, notes that almost all Curry Mile restaurants are independently run.[85] Nonetheless, the circulation of 'knowledge' countering such facts is interesting because it reflects the perceived *sameness* of the dining experience at each curry restaurant in which differences are flattened out, rendering the restaurants indistinguishable.

Geraldine Bedell notes the striking homogeneity of curry restaurant menus across the UK in the *Guardian* newspaper. She writes that:

> The most extraordinary thing about the Balti Houses and Rajput Tandooris up and down the country is that each and every one of them has the same menu. You can find more or less identical lamb pasandas and chicken vindaloos in Bradford and Brick Lane, Alderley Edge and Virginia Water.[86]

Curry restaurateurs have themselves contributed to this apparent homogenization through the curious addition of food colouring to the sauces of chicken tikka masala dishes to give them a distinctive but standardized bright orange-red hue. A 2004 Trading Standards Office investigation in Surrey found 'illegal and dangerous' levels of food-colouring additives in 57 per cent of the restaurants surveyed in the area despite earlier 'educational campaigns' revealing the degree of almost obsessive-compulsive attention to colour.[87] The Surrey Council points out that 'part of the problem undoubtedly stems from a consumer preference for *strong colours*.'[88] Chad Rahman, UK's National Curry Chef of the Year in 2002 and 2003, also indicates that the strong desire to conform to a perceived visual standard was an aesthetic choice driven by a presumed consumer preference rather than related to the taste of the food:

> The reason why these restaurants do it is because the customer will say: 'This is not a chicken tikka masala, it's not *bright red*,' and the restaurants fear they will lose trade … a lot of people eat with their eyes.[89]

When Chef Rahman says above that 'a lot of people eat with their eyes', he is signalling the importance of embodied visuality to any dining experience.

Consumers of food at Curry Mile restaurants take on what Maurice Merleau-Ponty describes as a corporal or postural schema, which can be habitual – a default position the body assumes in various commonly experienced circumstances. In this case, the absence of a bright, colourful sauce would confuse the expected bodily sensation normally associated with eating chicken tikka masala. The disconnect between seeing and feeling is similar to the one described earlier on Canal Street, where people of colour (especially women of colour) disrupt a postural schema characterized as habitually white, male and gay. The fastidious attention to aesthetics of sauce colour therefore serves to prevent a similar sort of disruption.

I argue that curry restaurants have not only 'strategically essentialized' colour to authenticate chicken tikka masala as 'South Asian' – ironic given that the dish is the epitome of hybridity as noted earlier – but also the broader experience of dining in a curry restaurant. In this way, the sameness of curry restaurants in Rusholme can be linked to a commercial performance of South Asian-ness. I do not want to imply a simplistic cause and effect between consumer preference and the homogenization of the dining experience – indeed, the two have probably developed in a mutually reinforcing fashion. Moreover, when postcolonial scholar Gayatri Chakravorty Spivak argues for a 'strategic use of … essentialism', she specifically argues this should be done for 'a scrupulously visible political interest' rather than a commercial one.[90] As queer studies scholar Diana Fuss also notes, an assessment of not only the motivation of strategic deployments of essentialism is important, but also a consideration of their 'political and textual effects' – intended or not.[91] In this vein, I flesh out the commercial performance of the curry restaurants as 'South Asian' and consider this performance's broader political effects, especially for queer-identified subjects who traverse Curry Mile.

Judith Butler's reworking of Freud's use of 'melancholia' to theorize heterosexual, gendered subjects is fruitful in further theorizing the performance of Curry Mile as a space. Freud describes melancholia as that condition in which the ego refuses to acknowledge the loss of the object, ingests the object into itself and therefore comes to disparage itself. The lost object becomes incorporated into the psychic life as part of the ego, instead of being surrendered as in healthy 'mourning'.[92] Butler applies Freud's term discursively, characterizing heterosexual, gendered subjects as being formed through 'the psychic and performative practices by which heterosexualized genders form themselves through the renunciation of the *possibility* of homosexuality, a foreclosure that produces a field of heterosexual objects at the same time that it produces a domain of those whom it would be impossible *to love*'.[93] She also provocatively argues that the '"truest" lesbian melancholic' is the 'strictly straight woman' and the '"truest" gay male melancholic' is the 'strictly straight man'.[94] The former has not mourned the loss of the woman she has disavowed from loving and the latter has never mourned the loss of the man he has disavowed from loving. Both thereby preserve their melancholic object.

Butler says in an interview that diasporic subjects are characterized by a discursive, melancholic formation – in this case one that forecloses the possibility of returning 'home'.[95] She notes that 'to the extent that the history of "race" is linked to a history of diasporic displacement it seems to me that melancholia is there, that there is, as it were, inscribed in "race" a lost and ungrievable origin, one might say, an impossibility of return, but also an impossibility of an essence'.[96] Following Butler's argument, the 'truest' queer, transnational South Asian melancholic would be the strictly straight, 'South Asian' woman or man: a heterosexual subject who both refuses to acknowledge the loss of the same-sex subject he or she foreclosed from loving, and refuses to mourn the 'impossibility of a return' to a bounded homeland, or an 'impossibility of an essence'.[97] In the next few sections, I describe how the products of the commercialized space of Curry Mile perform a variant of what could be considered a commercial projection of the characteristics of the truest queer, transnational South Asian melancholic subject – in particular, a space that is performed as strictly 'South Asian' and heterosexualist.

Theorizing queer and transnational South Asian flânerie

One of the methods I use includes describing my own walk down Curry Mile. Dianne Chisholm argues that queer writers often employ flânerie, which 'plots the city-on-the-move in fleeting physiognomies of city spaces and types' and in the process makes visible contradictions in space. Drawing particularly on Walter Benjamin's flâneur, rather than 'the self-composed aloofness of Balzac's hero', Chisholm notes that the 'disjointed notes of flâneries' of Benjamin, like those of contemporary queer writers, 'crystallize the contradictions of the era'.[98] Chisholm also notes that Delaney 'returns, again and again, to *his* Times Square, countering devastation with a projection of urban possibility'.[99] By logging my own participant-based observations as a queer and transnational South Asian flâneur through the various public spaces of *my* Manchester, I hope to 'crystallize the contradictions' of Manchester's narrative of progress.

Walking through a public space as a form of 'social practice' would not only produce a montage of optical images, but also embodied images, or what I argue might be described more accurately as 'haptic' images. In his 1901 book *Late Roman Art Industry*, Viennese art historian Alois Riegl employs 'haptic' to describe Persian textiles (among other things), the sight of which elicits for him a tactile, bodily response as opposed to the strictly 'optical' character of Late Roman art. Riegl specifically borrows the term from physiology – in which *haptein* means to fasten – to avoid constructing the tactile and visual as oppositional, and to underscore that haptic is much more expansive than merely touch.[100] For instance, the *Oxford English Dictionary* (OED) notes that 'haptic' has been used to refer to 'kinaesthetic experiences', which is particularly significant given my focus on the movement of the body in urban space.[101]

Walter Benjamin invokes Riegl in his seminal essay 'The Work of Art in the Age of Mechanical Reproduction', and implies the connection between haptic and kinaesthesia when he notes that: 'Buildings are appropriated in a twofold manner: by use and by perception – or rather, by touch and sight.' Benjamin's observation that the often distracted manner in which subjects experience buildings is also paradoxically embodied – buildings 'are mastered gradually by habit'. The latter is his metaphor for how the distracted gaze elicited by the medium of modernist cinema – 'No sooner has his eye grasped a scene than it is already changed' – can also physically 'assail the spectator'. He even goes as far as to characterize cinema as primarily a 'tactile' medium.[102] Given that my own strategy of presenting an impressionistic montage of images closely approximates montage as a method of film editing, in the context of his writings on flânerie and city writing, Benjamin's metaphor suggests that the dialectical imaging through which he unpacks urban space can also be seen as having a haptic dimension. While Riegl primarily saw the form of the object as the catalyst for the embodied response, Benjamin suggests a much more expansive use of haptic as enfolding the maker and perceiver of the object, as film scholar Antonia Lant points out.[103]

Film and visual studies scholar Laura U. Marks's scholarship makes explicit the connection between Riegl's scholarship and cinema spectatorship as embodied. She theorizes 'haptic visuality' to refer to a specific mode of reception of cinematic images in which vision is located in the body. Marks argues that though a cinematic image might be classed as optical in terms of form, it can still be received in an embodied manner, for 'haptic images invite a multisensory, intimate and embodied perception, even when the perceptions to which they appeal are vision and hearing alone'.[104] Marks arrives at her theory of haptic visuality through a careful investigation of avant-garde film and video of artists based in the United States and Canada – artists she further describes as 'intercultural', or between two cultures.[105] She notes how these films challenge the often facile categorization of cultural anthropologists, who evacuate the sensuous potential of engaging with the most visual of objects in Western cultures and displace or ascribe 'the fullness of sensory experience only to "non-Western" cultures by invit[ing] an intimate, sensuous, and memory-based relationship'.[106] Marks specifically references anthropologist David Howes's comparison of two images – an Albrecht Dürer engraving of an artist looking through an Albertian perspectival grid in order to draw a woman, and an abstract-looking design used by shamans of the Shipibo-Conibo Indians of Eastern Peru. She notes that Howe translates the former into a purely visual experience, whereas the latter 'embodies many forms of sensory experience'.[107] Indeed, even Riegl's teleological organization of art renders the haptical character of textiles and Egyptian art as having necessarily to give way to the optical character of Western art. Marks states that 'Howes deplores the separation of the senses and overvalorization of the visual in Western societies in a way that is partly accurate and partly romantic.' To be fair, since Marks wrote her diatribe against Howes as part of her book *The Skin of the Film*, he has been part of an initiative that has complicated this binarism that evacuates the sensual potential of Western objects. Specifically, as part of this initiative/project, Howes explores the sensuous potentialities *within* Western urban space, which dovetails with my own interests.[108]

To further flesh out my use of haptic theory, I draw on the scholarship of French philosophers Gilles Deleuze and Félix Guattari, who apply Riegl's theories to space most directly. In particular, they suggest the intimate and embodied manner in which subjects can traverse space through their theorization of haptic, or 'smooth', space, which is moved through by constant reference to the immediate environment – such as walking through an expanse of sand or snow. In contrast, they note that 'striated space' relates to a 'more distant vision, and a more optical space'. Like Riegl, they are careful not to imply a facile dichotomy of the sense organs. Deleuze and Guattari argue not only 'that the eye itself can perform a nonoptical function', and thereby produce smooth or haptic space, but also that the 'eye in turn is not the only organ' to produce striated or optical space.[109] In addition, though many of the examples of smooth space they give are rural, they also note that '[e]ven the most striated city gives rise to smooth spaces'.[110] For instance, my descriptions of Curry Mile in the next section illustrates how multi-sensory experiences produce a striated space by preventing more intimate engagement with the surroundings. The latter is particularly important in better understanding the experience of the women of Sphere. Indeed, in terms of the latter, underlying Benjamin's observation that the reception of filmic images is embodied is an implicit warning of the invasive manner in which fascistic ideology can penetrate the viewing subject. Thus, haptic theory can be useful in further characterizing how the subject both evades *and* can become enfolded into ideology.

Curry Mile as striated space: performance of South Asian-ness

I tease out the characteristics of the commercial performance of South Asian-ness of Curry Mile by presenting my own walk down Wilmslow Road, as well as my dining experience at the restaurant Shahenshah. I follow this with a more critical analysis of the 'textual effects' of such a performance.[111] My walk is by no means illustrative of a cartographic map, but rather a series of 'pedestrian speech-acts'.[112] French philosopher Michel de Certeau notes in his book

The Practice of Everyday Life that just as the act of enunciation can alter the meaning of words in a language, a spatial act of enunciation can shift the meaning of walking in an urban system. He argues that the act of speaking is to language as the act of walking is to the city. De Certeau also articulates the spatial use of two linguistic terms that describe aspects of my walk – synecdoche and asyndeton. The former 'expands a spatial element in order to make it play the role of a "more" (a totality)' and the latter 'by elision, creates a "less", opens gaps in the spatial continuum'. While synecdoche amplifies and focuses on details, asyndeton cuts them out. Thus, I do not describe a graphic trail of my walk or an exhaustive description of every detail of my experience dining at the restaurant. Instead, I describe a series of non-linear moments, some of which are amplified more than others, that nonetheless provide a totalizing experiential image.[113]

My stroll down Wilmslow Road as a queer and transnational South Asian flâneur to the restaurant Shahenshah includes the following montage of felt experiences and sights: the bright neon flashing lights of the restaurants, the electric rush of passers-by that was both invigorating and claustrophobic, the confluence of Bollywood, sitar, British Asian, Caribbean and Arabic music – piping out of restaurants and music shops – and the smells of a variety of pungent curries and kebabs. The sights of South Asian confectionery, such as rainbow-coloured *burfi* and electric orange-coloured *jalebi* – stacked on cake trays in the storefront windows – evoke a rush of different bodily responses: the rich, doughy taste and crumbly but soft texture of the former and the syrupy sweet taste of the latter, which always leaves one's hands sticky. The sights of colourful saris and the plethora of glittering, gold jewellery displayed in street-front windows are equally dramatic – I can almost feel the silky thread of the saris and the slightly heavier weight, usually 18k or 22k, of the ceremonial gold jewellery (Plate 16).

I pass the restaurant King Cobra on my way to Shahenshah and notice two sculptures of elephants in the street-facing windows of another restaurant. The two men standing at the threshold of Shahenshah cajole me inside to dine with welcoming grins and gesticulating arms – a frequent scene at many Curry Mile restaurants that stands in stark contrast to the unwelcoming doormen found in the Gay Village. The waiters are dressed in 'traditional' kafni pyjamas. Once inside, I am seated at a table and immediately notice that the interior décor consists of a series of paintings hung on the wall. Three of the paintings are harvest scenes, and one depicts what appears to be a celebration of the Sikh Baisakhi harvest festival.[114] The other three are similarly pastoral – two depict scenes of cooking and farm animals, and another is a portrait of a rural Sikh family (Plate 17 and Figures 5.9–12).

The overall experience of my walk prior to entering the restaurant reflects an elision – consistent with de Certeau's characterization of asyndeton – of

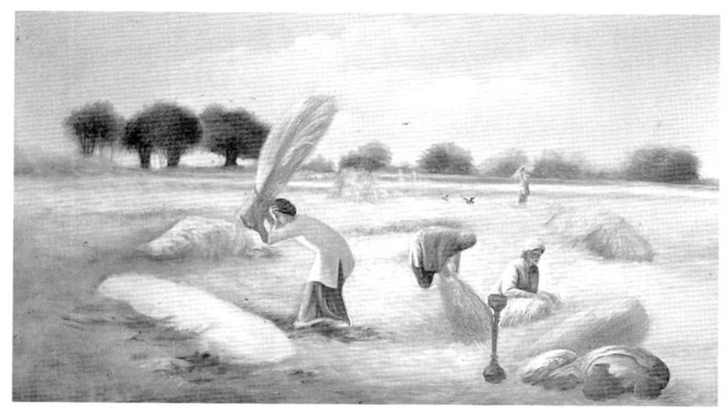

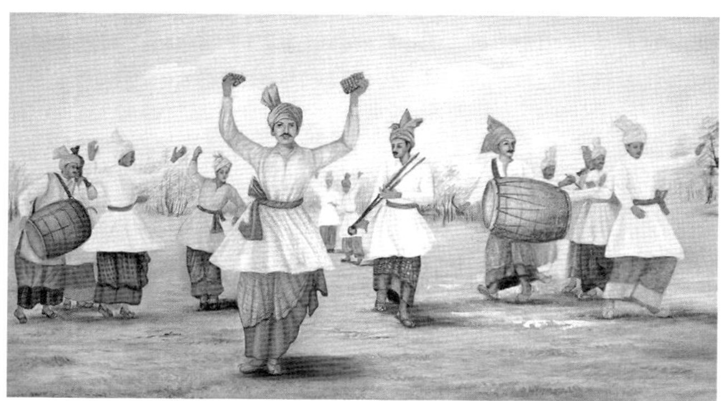

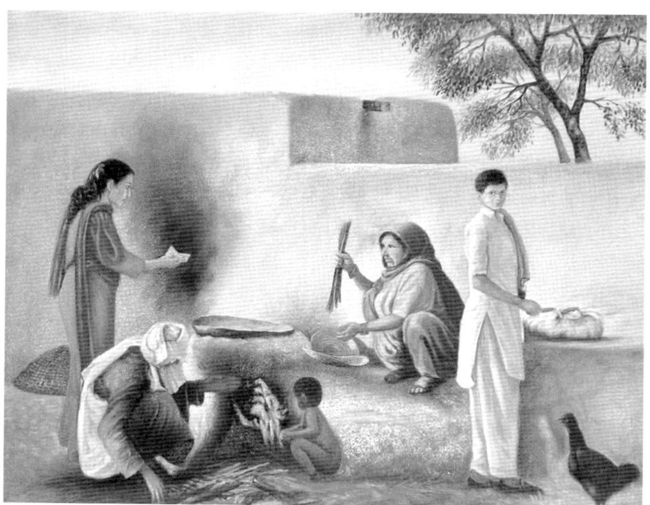

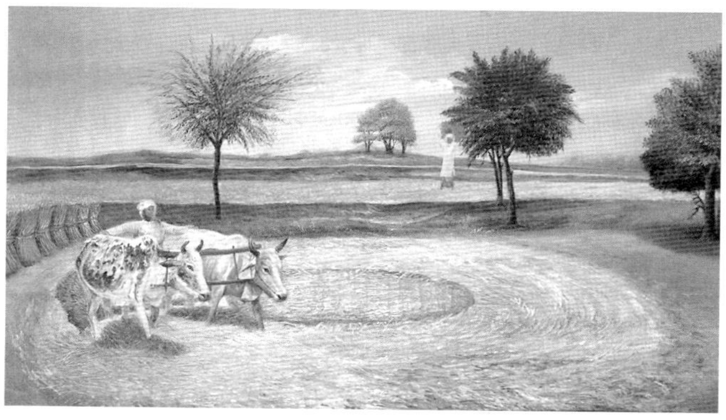

5.9–12 Paintings installed in Shahenshah restaurant. Manchester, England, 2008.

the sights of non-South Asian restaurants and shops and sounds of Caribbean, Arabic and even British Asian music; and an amplification – consistent with de Certeau's characterization of synecdoche – of the sounds of sitars and Bollywood music, smells of curries, and sights of jewellery, saris and confectionery. In particular, the latter sights – which evoked my personal memories of tasting, touching and consuming *burfi* and *jelabi* and handling jewellery and saris – function to subsume the sounds, sights and smells of non-South Asian music, restaurants and food, respectively.

The haptic 'South Asian' image generated by my walk has the potential to produce the type of space that Deleuze and Guattari describe as 'smooth', or potentially liberatory. Indeed, the sights of confectionery, in particular, evoke warm memories of my mother making a fresh batch of *burfi* every week. However, my experience of the performance of the restaurant prevents these memories from being anything more than ephemeral by bringing into being a more constrained, or what Deleuze and Guattari refer to as 'striated', space – one that, I argue, can be further characterized as exotic, primitive and patriarchal (heterosexualist and masculinist).

All the paintings in the restaurant appear to depict nondescript rural locations that are still readable as being located in South Asia, most likely Punjab, but not necessarily in a more specific place or time. Instead, South Asia is depicted as 'timeless'. The latter is perhaps underscored by the naked child, which seems to evoke the Orientalist stereotypes of the colonial subject as innocent and childlike.[115] Urban studies and globalization scholar Andreas Huyssen warns that 'when the imagined past is sucked into the timeless present of the all-pervasive virtual space of consumer culture' – such as that of Curry Mile – cultural '[m]emory as re-presentation, as making *present*, is always in danger of collapsing the constitutive tension between past and present', or in this case eliding the uglier aspects of British colonial subjugation of South Asia.[116] Moreover, as the raison d'être for Curry Mile continues to shift away from being a place operated by and for its first-generation South Asian immigrant population, nostalgic representations of 'South Asia' reconfigure the geographical space of Curry Mile into more of a 'commodity spectacle'.[117]

In so doing, Curry Mile restaurants careen towards performing a specifically *exotic* self. The omnipresence of enduring visual signifiers of the subcontinent contributes to a production of a particularly exotic commodity spectacle. For instance, the elephant is a popular signifier of the South Asian subcontinent that figures importantly in Buddhist and Hindu religions, and an elephant motif appears in many of the curry restaurants. The cobra, a signifier that evokes the Orientalist stereotype of snake charmers, is another motif found in curry restaurants, such as the restaurant King Cobra, whose signage is composed of images of three king cobras. Aural signifiers of the subcontinent, such as the sitar music which I heard playing on my way to and in the restaurant, also contribute to the exoticization of Curry Mile. Indeed, *New York Times* reporter Henry Shukman notes how 'whining sitars' have become almost 'inseparable from Indian food' for him – a fact reinforced by the sitar music that plays at the beginning and the end of the online slideshow accompanying his article on Indian restaurants in London. He also suggests that his reaction to sitar music is so habitual that even when he hears sitar music outside the context of a South Asian restaurant he begins to salivate: 'even today I only have to hear sitar music and it brings on a Pavlovian salivation, with olfactory hallucinations of cumin'.[118] His conditioned olfactory response to the aural stimulus of sitar music can be described as another kind of postural schema related to dining in a curry restaurant. As I noted earlier, though Deleuze and Guattari theorize striated space as 'optical', which implies a 'constitution of a central perspective', they also note that 'the eye … is not the only organ to have this capacity'.[119] The sounds of the sitar music work in tandem with the sights of representations of cobras and elephants to produce Curry Mile as striated space, or specifically as exotic in this case.

Moreover, the restaurant paintings depicting a space and time unspoiled by globalization, or even modernity, suggest that the restaurants perform not only an exotic commodity spectacle, but also a *primitive* one. Gender and colonial studies scholar Anne McClintock explains in her book *Imperial Leather: Race, Gender, and Sexuality in the Colonial Contest* that one of the paradoxes of the colonial enterprise is that the journey into 'new' lands was 'figured as proceeding *forward* in geographical space but *backward* in historical time'.[120] In this way, the paintings symbolically displace 'indigenous peoples' to 'anachronistic space', which is characterized as primitive. This colonial trope of primitivizing its subjects 'to what is figured as a prehistoric zone of racial and gender difference' is worth further exploring in the restaurant space in terms of gender and sexuality.

From the male waiters on the streets beckoning me to dine at their restaurant to the male waiting staff inside the restaurant space itself, the restaurant space of Shahenshah is male-dominated. This creates a privileging of a space/time that is not only primitive or ancient, but also patriarchal – that is, bound by presumed, traditional constructions of gender (male-dominated) and sexuality (heterosexualist). The restaurant space implicitly naturalizes the arbitrariness of masculine domination over women and of heterosexuality through an accumulation of subtle, performative visual acts. Moreover, the incessant iterative performance of South Asian-ness as exotic, primitive and patriarchal creates a 'norm' on which it (the norm) is based.

I do not want to imply that Curry Mile restaurants are sexist or homophobic in any simple way. Indeed, my first University of Manchester Lesbian, Gay, Bisexual and Transgendered (LGBT) Society meeting was held there. Instead,

I argue that Curry Mile as a patriarchal space is consolidated through what French sociologist Pierre Bourdieu has described as 'symbolic violence', or 'gentle violence, imperceptible and invisible … exerted for the most part through the purely symbolic channels of communication and cognition (more precisely, misrecognition), recognition, or even feeling'.[121] In this way, the 'symbolic violence' of the space of the curry restaurant as heterosexualist – which is otherwise typically 'undetectable', yet pervasive – became much more pronounced and felt at the LGBT meeting on Curry Mile.

Politics of performance of racial masculinity, Curry Mile

Perhaps the most illustrative example of the space of Curry Mile becoming a masculinist and heterosexualist space occurs every year during the well-attended religious Islamic Eid festivals.[122] The festivals regularly attract thousands of revellers – up to 10,000 in 2006, for instance. Late in the evenings, the festivals switch from more 'family-oriented' affairs – I return to this term shortly – to celebrations that have become notorious for 'groups of young men squaring up to each other' in a 'territorial' fashion.[123] The men speed up and down Wilmslow Road in high performance sports cars or stretch limousines, revving their engines, doing 'dangerous handbrake turns', ceremoniously waving Pakistani flags, playing loud music and cruising the streets.[124] Through these acts, cultural studies scholar Rajinder Dudrah suggests in his discussions of similar religious festivals in Birmingham, UK, that '[a] reclaiming of urban spaces occurs … and a performance of masculinities takes place which shout out against racist discourses of the inner city, including some of the derisory practices of police stop-and-search procedures and the popular perception of Asians as passive.'[125]

The performance of a specifically racialized, heterosexual masculinity during Eid has resulted in increased tensions between the young Muslim men and the Greater Manchester Police (GMP). Police made 30 arrests and citations in October 2006, and have made up to 70 at other festivals.[126] By December 2006, 360 police officers were stationed in and around Curry Mile with police helicopters and planes on call if needed to quell any rowdy crowds.[127] To help support a trouble-free Eid, the police enlisted pugilist Amir Khan, British 2004 Olympic silver medallist in boxing. Khan was thus made to serve as an example of the contained British-Muslim, male subject par excellence.[128]

In January 2007, the Rusholme Business Association (RBA) and the GMP formed a rare alliance to help curb the problems associated with Eid by closing down Curry Mile restaurants at 11 p.m. – an unusually early hour, as they usually remain open as late as 4.30 a.m., Thursdays to Saturdays. Indeed, both the GMP and RBA have decried the posturing of young Muslim males during Eid:

> However, this year, law abiding people have made it clear that they will not tolerate unacceptable behaviour and the celebrations are changing into a *family orientated event* that *everyone* can enjoy. (John Graves, Chief Inspector, Greater Manchester Police (GMP))

> My wife was ill last year and I wanted to get home. It took me two hours to get from Wilmslow Road to Chorlton … It's bad for *our community*. That's why we suggested we need to stop it somehow. (Mukhtar Ahmed, Chairman of the Rusholme Business Association (RBA))[129]

I argue that the excessive displays of homosocial masculinity during Eid position young Muslim males as the constitutive limit of the 'family' unit (assumed heterosexual) and the behaved British/Asian 'community'.[130] The containment of homosociality of Muslim males by both the GMP and the RBA is a contemporary variant of the colonialist discourses discussed in the context of Kehinde Wiley's artworks in Chapter 4 – particularly the construction of South Asian male subjects as effeminate or 'unmanly', which implicitly projects the fear of homosexuality of British colonials onto their subjects.[131] The GMP emasculates and thereby displaces fears of homophobia onto Muslim males through its vigilance; the RBA perversely co-opts the GMP's policies to contain the threat of homosexuality within the British Asian community.

Production of (ephemeral) queer, transnational South Asian space

In the shoring-up of boundaries in the restaurants as well as religious events such as Eid on Curry Mile and bars and clubs of the Gay Village, a queer, transnational South Asian presence slips through the cracks and is rendered invisible or particularly problematic. However, as Deleuze and Guattari note, '[t]he striated itself might disappear … opening the way for a new smooth space'.[132] I conclude this chapter on writing queer feminist transnational South Asian art histories by bringing attention to these smooth spaces. Club Zindagi (or 'life' in Hindi), for instance, opened in Manchester in early 2003 and is one of a number of gay and lesbian South Asian clubs that emerged in the 1990s and early 2000s in the UK as well as the United States.[133] Queer South Asian parties are located on Canal Street – however, unlike the static urban spaces that Henri Lefebvre discusses, these parties are often roaming and examples of spaces described as 'heterotopias' by Michel Foucault.[134] A heterotopia is a single place that juxtaposes several places that are in themselves incompatible. The floating nature of Club Zindagi is therefore a reflection of the incompatibility of queerness and South Asian-ness described in this chapter as existing together in a static place.

Club Zindagi has often promoted events with the 'HomieSexual'[135] parties, described as 'a weekly urban music night for GLBTs' by the group's website, and created a fusion party known as 'Ghetto Superstars'.[136] The latter party queers the homophobia and misogyny of most urban (and to a lesser degree bhangra) music, while it simultaneously 'butches up' feminized South Asian male identities and makes less threatening urban, black male ones.[137] At a Ghetto Superstar party during Manchester Pride in 2006, one room played R&B, hip-hop, ragga funk, and dancehall, while another played bhangra, giddha (the female counterpart to bhangra) and Bollywood.[138] The organization of these parties across ethnic or racial groups brings together not only British South Asians, black Britons and other ethnic groups, for instance, but also with the inclusion and queering of giddha they end up crossing gender lines much more successfully than the bifurcated gay and lesbian community of Canal Street.

In sharp contrast to the photos posted on Canal Street websites, the photos on HomieSexual's website indicate a broad range of not only male and female ethnic minorities, but also white subjects.[139] I also present two flyers from Manchester's HomieSexual parties as a foil for the aforementioned Essential Canal Street club flyers. One flyer, entitled 'The Lord of the Bling: The Return of the Mack', reworks the title of British rapper Mark Morrison's hit 1996 single *Return of the Mack* via the 2003 film *The Lord of the Rings: The Return of the King*.[140] The poster is a biting commentary on the racism of the latter epic series, as well as a nod to the literal return of Morrison with his first new album since his 1996 debut. Another flyer, entitled 'Chitti Chitti Bling Bling', references the lyrics of the 1995 live freestyle collaboration between artists Scoob Lo, Notorious B.I.G., 2Pac, and Big Daddy Kane entitled 'Chitty Chitty Bang Bang'.[141] The flyer reworks the poster of the film *Chitty Chitty Bang Bang* (1968) by replacing the all-white cast of the original poster in the flying car with the rotund B.I.G., and replacing 'GEN 11' on the license plate with 'Pac 2'.[142] The flyers not only recover the ethnic in queer that was absent in the Essential club flyers, but also attend to the homophobia (less so misogyny) typically ascribed to urban music.

The *Sphere:dreamz* project I am writing into a provisional queer feminist transnational South Asian art history must also be seen as part of a larger network of events in the city like the ones above that are feminist, anti-racist and queer. At the same time, it is important to note that like *Sphere:dreamz* these parties and events take place on Canal Street – not on Curry Mile. This point becomes the impetus for the next chapter.

Notes

1 London and Leicester tied for second: see Helen Carter, 'Gritty City Wins the Boho Crown', *Guardian*, 26 May 2003, www.theguardian.com/uk/2003/may/26/communities.arts.

2 'Manchester Is Favourite with "New Bohemians"', press release, *DEMOS (London-Based Cross-Party Think Tank)* (26 May 2003), www.demos.co.uk/media/pressreleases/bohobritain. The high number of patents is most likely a direct result of the fact that the city is home to a number of higher education institutions, including Manchester Metropolitan University (MMU) and the University of Manchester – the largest university in the UK.
3 Steve Quilley, 'Entrepreneurial Turns: Municipal Socialism and After', in *City of Revolution Restructuring Manchester*, ed. Jamie Peck and Kevin Ward (Manchester; New York: Manchester University Press, 2002), 91.
4 See, for instance, Pheng Cheah and Bruce Robbins (eds), *Cosmopolitics: Thinking and Feeling beyond the Nation*, Cultural Politics 14 (Minneapolis: University of Minnesota Press, 1998); Timothy Brennan, *At Home in the World: Cosmopolitanism Now*, Convergences (Cambridge, MA: Harvard University Press, 1997); John Tomlinson, *Globalization and Culture* (Oxford: Polity, 1999).
5 Elisavet Pakis, 'Playing in the Dark: Performing (Im)possible Lesbian Subjects' (PhD dissertation, Lancaster University, 2010), http://ethos.bl.uk/OrderDetails.do?uin=uk.bl.ethos.547939. See chapter 5. She does a wonderful analysis of the recorded poetry being piped up through the various beds.
6 This is before 'austerity measures' took hold in England in 2010. For discussion of them in 2015 see Amelia Gentleman, 'Austerity Cuts Will Bite Even Harder in 2015 – Another £12bn Will Go', *Guardian*, 1 January 2015, sec. Society, www.theguardian.com/society/2015/jan/01/austerity-cuts-2015–12-billion-britain-protest.
7 Gloria Anzaldúa, *Borderlands/La Frontera* (San Francisco: Aunt Lute Books, 1999).
8 Russell Ferguson, 'Introduction: Invisible Center', in *Out There: Marginalization and Contemporary Cultures*, ed. Russell Ferguson et al. (New York and Cambridge, MA: New Museum of Contemporary Art; MIT Press, 1990), 13.
9 Henri Lefebvre, *The Production of Space*, trans. Donald Nicholson-Smith (Oxford; Cambridge, MA: Blackwell, 1991), 356. Originally published in 1974.
10 Ibid., 40.
11 Amelia Jones, *Self/Image: Technology, Representation, and the Contemporary Subject* (London and New York: Routledge, 2006), 84–5.
12 French philosopher Maurice Merleau-Ponty notes that seeing involves both the viewing and the viewed subjects, who are importantly both the seen and the seer. He refers to the site of reciprocal interpenetration between and within embodied subjects as the 'chiasmus'. Maurice Merleau-Ponty, *The Visible and the Invisible; Followed by Working Notes*, ed. Claude Lefort, trans. Alphonso Lingis, Northwestern University Studies in Phenomenology & Existential Philosophy (Evanston, IL: Northwestern University Press, 1968), 138, 140–1.
13 Ibid., 38–40.
14 Ibid., 38.

15 Łukasz Stanek, 'The Production of Urban Space by Mass Media Storytelling Practices: Nowa Huta as a Case Study' (fourth media in transition conference, Boston, MA: Massachusetts Institute of Technology, 2005), 2, http://web.mit.edu/comm-forum/mit4/papers/stanek.pdf.

16 Dianne Chisholm, *Queer Constellations: Subcultural Space in the Wake of the City* (Minneapolis: University of Minnesota Press, 2005), 26–9, 68 (for discussion of Lefebvre); ix, 10–11 (for discussion of Benjamin's dialectical image).

17 See the following on gentrification of Times Square: Neil Smith, 'Giuliani Time: The Revanchist 1990s', *Social Text* 57, vol. 16, no. 4 (Winter 1998): 1–20.

18 Chisholm, *Queer Constellations*, 30.

19 Gay.com, 'New York City: Introduction', accessed 31 May 2008, www.gay.com/travel/premium/?coll=adult_articles&sernum=173&page=2.

20 In the penultimate chapter of her book, *Queer Constellations*, Chisholm offers another example of a writer who through her writings destabilizes dominant modes of urban progress, in this case the commercialization of the bohemia of NYC's East Village in the 1980s. In particular, Chisholm describes how Sarah Schulman's novels destabilize the latter through her specifically queer and gendered perspective. See Chisholm, *Queer Constellations*, 195–244. Also see Benjamin's 'The Bohème' which Chisholm draws upon: Walter Benjamin, '"The Bohème," the first part of his essay, "The Paris of the Second Empire in Baudelaire" (1938; translation, 1969)', in *Walter Benjamin: Selected Writings: Volume 4, 1938–1940*, ed. Howard Eiland and Michael W. Jennings, trans. Edmund Jephcott and others (Cambridge, MA; London: Belknap Press of Harvard University Press, 2006), 3–18.

21 Quilley notes that the Gay Village has figured prominently in Manchester's post-industrial cosmopolitanism, especially the '"village in the city" ethos which now dominates urban residential developments in the city'. See Steve Quilley, 'Constructing Manchester's "New Urban Village": Gay Space in the Entrepreneurial City', in *Queers in Space: Communities, Public Places, Sites of Resistance*, ed. Gordon Brent Ingram, Anne-Marie Bouthillette and Yolanda Retter (Seattle: Bay Press, 1997), 285.

22 Emphasis in original. José Esteban Muñoz, 'Feeling Brown, Feeling Down: Latina Affect, the Performativity of Race, and the Depressive Position', *Signs*, 31, no. 3 (Spring 2006): 678.

23 Emphasis mine. Ibid., 677.

24 José Esteban Muñoz, 'Feeling Brown: Ethnicity and Affect in Ricardo Bracho's *The Sweetest Hangover (and Other STDs)*', *Theatre Journal* 52, no. 1 (2000): 67–8, 79.

25 See Raymond Williams, *Marxism and Literature*, Marxist Introductions (Oxford: Oxford University Press, 1977), 133. For a study that probes structures of feeling in working-class Manchester and Sheffield, see Ian R. Taylor, Karen Evans and Penny Fraser, *A Tale of Two Cities: Global Change, Local Feeling and Everyday Life in the North of England: A Study in Manchester and Sheffield* (International Library of Sociology. London; New York: Routledge, 1994). An entire chapter is devoted to exploring the structure of feeling of the

Gay Village: ibid., 180–97. However, Curry Mile and Rusholme do not figure prominently in their scholarly investigation. Manchester has been a locus of study of the working class since the 1800s when Friedrich Engels used his experiences living in Manchester as the basis for his *The Condition of the Working-Class in England in 1844*, trans. Florence Kelley Wischnewtzky (London: S. Sonnenschein & Co., 1892). Engels frequently collaborated with Karl Marx, as well.

26 Muñoz, 'Feeling Brown, Feeling Down: Latina Affect, the Performativity of Race, and the Depressive Position', 687.

27 *City Planning News* 2:4 (Summer 1991): 1, as quoted in Quilley, 'Constructing Manchester's "New Urban Village": Gay Space in the Entrepreneurial City', 284; Marketing Manchester, *Manchester: A Guide for LGBT Visitors, 2006/07*, brochure (40 pp.), 6.

28 'Corporate Strategy for Lesbian, Gay, Bisexual and Trans People Equality, 2003–2006', *Birmingham City Council*, accessed 23 October 2008, www.birmingham.gov.uk/ELibrary?E_LIBRARY_ID=174.

29 Russell T. Davies's miniseries spawned an American equivalent, which has added to the original series's international notoriety.

30 Gary Ryan, 'City Which Spawned Queer as Folk and Canal Street Wins Ultimate Gay Student Accolade', *Guardian*, 10 August 2005, sec. UK news, www.theguardian.com/uk/2005/aug/11/gayrights.highereducation.

31 See John Scheerhout, 'Force Wins Praise from Gay Group', *Manchester Evening News*, 18 March 2007, www.manchestereveningnews.co.uk/news/greater-manchester-news/force-wins-praise-from-gay-group-985583; 'Manchester Wins Double Accolade as UK's Top Gay-Friendly Local Authority', press release, *Manchester City Council* (9 January 2007), www.manchester.gov.uk.

32 Marketing Manchester, *Manchester: A Guide for LGBT Visitors, 2006/07*. The specific locations in which the brochure is distributed are: New York, Chicago, Los Angeles, San Francisco, Scandinavia, Germany, Italy and the UK. See Marketing Manchester, *Leisure Tourism*, accessed 22 August 2008, www.marketingmanchester.com; Marketing Manchester, *Greater Manchester Destination Management Plan: The Visitor Economy Action Plan, 2008–2011*, 2008, 24, www.marketingmanchester.com.

33 Marketing Manchester, *Manchester: Where to Stay 2006/07*, brochure (40 pp.), 6.

34 Ibid., 4.

35 Jon Binnie and Beverley Skeggs, 'Cosmopolitan Knowledge and the Production and Consumption of Sexualized Space: Manchester's Gay Village', *Sociological Review* 52, no. 1 (February 2004): 50.

36 Emphasis mine. Dianne Bourne, 'Village Boss Hits out at Jongleurs Closure', *Manchester Evening News*, 15 February 2007, www.manchestereveningnews.co.uk/whats-on/comedy-gigs/village-boss-hits-out-at-jongleurs-1041188.

37 'Frequently Asked Questions', *Essential*, accessed 11 March 2007, www.essentialmanchester.com/faqs.php.

38 *Falcon Men's Bar*, accessed 20 February 2005, www.falconmensbar.com.
39 Coyotes Bar is the other well-known lesbian bar in the Village. It does not market itself, however, like vanilla as 'lesbian'. The pictures of clientele at nights at Coyotes Bar on its website indicate a much more apparently diverse crowd (men, women and people of colour) than pictures of clientele at nights on vanilla's website. *Coyotes Bar*, accessed 31 May 2008, www.coyotesbar.co.uk.
40 David Alderson, 'Queer Cosmopolitanism: Place, Politics, Citizenship and *Queer as Folk*', *New Formations* 55 (2005): 84.
41 Emphasis in original. Ibid., 76.
42 See Dereka Rushbrook, 'Cities, Queer Space, and the Cosmopolitan Tourist', *GLQ: A Journal of Lesbian and Gay Studies* 8, no. 1 (2002): 188. Rushbrook skilfully illustrates how racial and sexual diversity are posited as mutually exclusive within the wording of a description of a nightclub in Berlin in an international travel book. She notes that, 'queers of color are erased from the discourses of cosmopolitanism and globalization, as consumers and commodities.' See ibid., 184.
43 I return to this point in the context of culture in the next chapter.
44 Rushbrook, 'Cities, Queer Space, and the Cosmopolitan Tourist', 188.
45 Emphasis mine. *Visit Manchester*, accessed 17 March 2007, www.visitmanchester.com.
46 I realize my visual identifications are facile (I do not know how these subjects identify themselves), but as I hope to underscore throughout this chapter visual identification is always already partial. Here, I offer this evidence in the context of a larger body of evidence, which I present as connected to the marketing of the Village.
47 Marketing Manchester, *Manchester: A Guide for LGBT Visitors, 2006/07*.
48 Rogoff, 'Gossip as Testimony: A Postmodern Signature', 272. Gavin Butt, drawing on Rogoff, also uses gossip to reconsider art world practices, especially in relation to homosexuality: Butt, *Between You and Me: Queer Disclosures in the New York Art World, 1948–1963* (Durham, NC: Duke University Press, 2005).
49 Stuart Hall, 'Introduction: Who Needs "Identity?"', in *Questions of Cultural Identity*, ed. Stuart Hall and Paul du Gay (London and Thousand Oaks, CA: Sage, 1996), 3.
50 Various personal conversations, 2005–8. Queers of colour, along with others who feel marginalized on Canal Street, have even created an organization, Kaffequeeria, which hosts support groups and holds an alternative Pride event. See 'An Alternative to Pride', *Manchester Evening News*, 23 August 2005, www.manchestereveningnews.co.uk/whats-on/going-out/music/an-alternative-to-pride-1081267.
51 *Merriam-Webster Dictionary*, s.v. 'Gaydar', accessed 15 February 2007, www.merriam-webster.com/dictionary/gaydar.
52 Maurice Merleau-Ponty, *Phenomenology of Perception*, trans. Colin Smith, International Library of Philosophy and Scientific Method (New York:

Humanities Press, 1962), 5, 152 (for the 'habitual' reference). Cultural anthropology scholar Kira Kosnick's ethnographic research of queer clubs in Germany evinces how bouncers often rely on an implicit gaydar, which not surprisingly results in misrecognition. See Kira Kosnick, 'Selecta at the Door', digital commons, *openDemocracy* (29 November 2004), www.opendemocracy.net/arts-multiculturalism/article_2248.jsp.

53 Frantz Fanon takes Merleau-Ponty's notion of a habitual, postural body and applies it specifically to race: the 'Negro, because of his body, impedes the closing of the postural schema for the white man'. See Frantz Fanon, *Black Skin, White Masks*, trans. by Charles Lam Markmann. Evergreen Black Cat Book. (New York: Grove Press, 1968), 160.

54 Personal communication with Jaheda Choudhury, March 2006 and March 2007.

55 For instance, in a 2000 article on lesbian space in Manchester's Gay Village, the authors provocatively indicate in the introduction that 'human status characteristics such as class, race and ethnicity, sexuality, and disability *combine* to create points of empowerment or oppression in women's leisure worlds', but then they proceed to exclude completely any other factor than gender in their analysis (page 106). Emphasis mine. See Annette Pritchard, Nigel Morgan and Diane Sedgley. 'In Search of Lesbian Space? The Experience of Manchester's Gay Village'. *Leisure Studies* 21, no. 2 (2002): 105–23.

56 *vanilla*, accessed 7 March 2007, www.vanillagirls.co.uk/html/gossip.php. As in the gay club websites I discuss later in this section, there is a curious lack of (apparent) subjects of colour in the photos the club has posted online for various events, as well. However, unlike most gay bars, entry is not nearly as regimented so the group is largely self-selected. Alpesh Kantilal Patel, 'Queer Desi Visual Culture Across the "Brown Atlantic"' (PhD dissertation, Manchester University, 2009), 218.

57 Ibid., 219.

58 Ibid.

59 Ibid., 220–1.

60 Chav is sometimes described as an acronym for 'Council Housed and Violent'. See Anoop Nayak and Steve Drayton, 'Charvers Webchat', Q and A with public, *BBC Inside Out* (21 February 2005), www.bbc.co.uk/insideout/northeast/series7/webchat_charvers.shtml.

61 *Urban Dictionary*, s.v. 'Chav', accessed 1 January 2016, www.urbandictionary.com/define.php?term=chav. See also 'Chavscum: A User's Guide to Britain's ASBO Generation', *Chavscum*, accessed 12 June 2007, www.chavscum.co.uk/index.php. It refers to chavs as 'Britain's peasant underclass'. ASBO is the acronym for the Anti-Social Behavioural Ordinance on the basis of which British police can regulate a wide range of citizens' behaviours, up to and including restrictions on movement within certain areas, for instance. For more information, see Research, Development and Statistics Directorate, 'Defining and Measuring Anti-Social Behaviour', Development and Practice

Report (London: Home Office, 2004), www.gov.uk/government/uploads/system/uploads/attachment_data/file/116655/dpr26.pdf

62 Patel, 'Queer Desi Visual Culture Across the "Brown Atlantic"', 221.

63 See photos archived on the following websites of Canal Street gay clubs: *Essential*, 13 January 2007, accessed 7 March 2007, www.essentialmanchester.com/show_gallery.php?id=250; *Cruz 101*, Easter 2006, accessed 7 March 2007, www.cruz101.com/gallerythumbs.aspx?id=54; *Queer*, accessed 7 March 2007, www.queer-manchester.com/gallery/Default.asp?offset=36; and *vanilla*, accessed 7 March 2007, www.vanillagirls.co.uk/gallery/index.php.

64 José Esteban Muñoz, 'Ephemera as Evidence: Introductory Notes to Queer Acts', *Women & Performance: A Journal of Feminist Theory* 8, no. 2 (1996): 5–16.

65 Judith Butler, *Bodies That Matter: On the Discursive Limits of 'Sex'* (New York: Routledge, 1993), 2.

66 I discuss at length how the visual might be performative in my doctoral dissertation. See Patel, 'Queer Desi Visual Culture Across the "Brown Atlantic"'. Chapter 5, section titled 'Theorizing queer desi visuality as performative'.

67 Lefebvre, *The Production of Space*, 190, 419.

68 This information was culled from the leaflet available on the day of the installation.

69 The archive of queerupnorth (1992–2006), Manchester's international festival of lesbian, gay and queer arts, is housed at Manchester Archives and Local Studies, accessed 16 January, 2016, http://discovery.nationalarchives.gov.uk/details/rd/b4aaf4cf-e3a2–4f4e-bd3b-8e8e22abe3f6.

70 James Chapman, 'Women Get "Virginity Fix" NHS Operations in Muslim-Driven Trend | Daily Mail Online', *Daily Mail*, 15 November 2007, www.dailymail.co.uk/news/article-494118/Women-virginity-fix-NHS-operations-Muslim-driven-trend.html.

71 Sita Anantha Raman, *Women in India: A Social and Cultural History*, vol. 1 (ABC-CLIO, 2009), 104–5.

72 His Divine Grace A. C. Bhaktivedanta Swami Prabhupada, *Bhagavad-Gita As It Is* (The Bhaktivedanta Book Trust, 1989), 300.

73 Part of the original Sackville Park installation was installed in Manchester Museum, Contact Theatre and the greenroom. However, the points I wished to draw out regarding the effect of geography and type of space remained implicit.

74 Personal conversation with members of Sphere, December 2006.

75 Nida Kirmani, 'Rusholme', in *A Postcolonial People: South Asians in Britain*, ed. Nasreen Ali, Virinder S. Kalra and S. Sayyid (New York: Columbia University Press, 2008), 327–8.

76 Ibid.

77 *Visit Manchester*, accessed 8 March 2007, http://visitmanchester.com/.

78 *Pink Garlic*, accessed 22 May 2007, www.pinkgarlic.com/3.html.

79 Sophie Ahmed, 'Chicken Tikka Masala', in *A Postcolonial People: South Asians in Britain*, ed. Nasreen Ali, Virinder S. Kalra and S. Sayyid (New York: Columbia University Press, 2008), 62–3.
80 James Meikle, 'The Colour of a Curry May Make It Look Better – but Is It Good for You?', *Guardian*, 24 March 2004, sec. UK news, www.theguardian.com/uk/2004/mar/24/foodanddrink.
81 Geraldine Bedell, 'It's Curry, but Not as We Know It', *Guardian*, accessed 3 November 2005, www.theguardian.com/lifeandstyle/2002/may/12/foodanddrink.shopping2.
82 Rogoff, 'Gossip as Testimony: A Postmodern Signature', 272.
83 Emphasis in original. *YakYak* (discussion forum), accessed 24 April 2007, http://66.102.9.104/search?q=cache:AZHoLod8x8MJ:www.yakyak.org/viewtopic.php%3Ft%3D17600%26highlight%3D%26sid%3D4bf0b599ca740f13afe6e4fe28a629d1+%22curry+mile%22+%22one+kitchen%22&hl=en&ct=clnk&cd=1.
84 Iain B. MacDonald, 'Argi Bhaji', episode, *Cutting Edge* (UK: Channel 4, 1999).
85 Personal interview, Mukhtar Ahmed, Sangam Restaurant, Rusholme, 24 May 2007.
86 Bedell, 'It's Curry, but Not as We Know It'.
87 Press Association, '"Dangerous Dye Levels" Found in Tikka', *Guardian*, 23 March 2004, www.theguardian.com/uk/2004/mar/23/foodanddrink.
88 Emphasis mine. Meikle, 'The Colour of a Curry May Make It Look Better – but Is It Good for You?'
89 Emphasis mine. Press Association, '"Dangerous Dye Levels" Found in Tikka'.
90 Gayatri Chakravorty Spivak, *In Other Worlds: Essays in Cultural Politics* (New York: Routledge, 1988), 281. She makes this point in her discussion of reading the work of Subaltern Studies against the grain. In an interview in 1993, Spivak said that 'strategic essentialism' was one of her most widely used, yet, most misunderstood terms. She also said that she had given up on 'strategic essentialism' as a term, but not as a project. She found herself 'much more interested in seeing the differences among these so-called essences in various cultural inscriptions.' See Gayatri Chakravorty Spivak, Sara Danius and Stefan Jonsson, 'An Interview with Gayatri Chakravorty Spivak', *boundary 2* 20, no. 2 (1993): 24–50.
91 Diana Fuss, *Essentially Speaking: Feminism, Nature & Difference* (New York: Routledge, 1989), xi.
92 Sigmund Freud, 'Mourning and Melancholia (1917)', in *The Standard Edition of the Complete Psychological Works of Sigmund Freud*, trans. James Strachey, Vol. XIV, 1914–1916 (London: Hogarth Press/Institute of Psycho-Analysis, 1957).
93 Emphasis in the original. Butler, *Bodies That Matter*, 235. Moreover, Julia Kristeva notes that each heterosexual subject is formed through a domain of exclusion or abjection. Kristeva writes: 'I expel *myself*, I spit *myself* out, I abject *myself* within the same motion through which "I" claim to establish *myself* … it is that *they* see that "I" am in the process of becoming an other

at the expense of my own death.' Emphasis in original. Julia Kristeva, *Powers of Horror: An Essay on Abjection*, trans. Leon S. Roudiez (New York: Columbia University Press, 1982), 3.

94 Butler, *Bodies That Matter*, 235.

95 Vicki Bell, 'On Speech, Race and Melancholia: An Interview with Judith Butler', *Theory, Culture & Society* 16, no. 2 (1999): 170.

96 Ibid., 169–70.

97 Ibid. Butler notes that heterosexual melancholy is 'less *the refusal* to grieve (a formulation that accents the choice involved) than a preemption of grief performed by the absence of cultural conventions for avowing the loss of homosexual loss'. Emphasis in original. Butler, *Bodies That Matter*, 236. My choice of the word 'refusal', then, in my description of a queer, transnational South Asian melancholic subject produced by Curry Mile is purposeful. I argue that Curry Mile performs itself in a particularly strategic manner, and therefore presupposes a certain degree of agency, if only commercially driven. At the same time, I do not want to imply that the strategic performance of Curry Mile is not conditioned by certain cultural norms and power structures (residues of colonialist stereotypes, for instance, which continue to stubbornly and powerfully circulate in the West).

98 Chisholm, *Queer Constellations*, 46–7; Walter Benjamin, '"The Flâneur," the first part of his essay, "The Paris of the Second Empire in Baudelaire" (1938; translation, 1969)', in *Walter Benjamin: Selected Writings: Vol. 4, 1938–1940*, ed. Howard Eiland and Michael Jennings, trans. Edmund Jephcott and others, vol. 4 (Cambridge, MA; London: Belknap Press of Harvard University Press, 2006), 18–39.

99 Chisholm, *Queer Constellations*, 7.

100 Alois Riegl, 'Late Roman or Oriental? (1902)', in *German Essays on Art History: Winckelmann, Burckhardt, Panofsky, and Others*, ed. Gert Schiff, trans. Peter Wortsman (New York: Continuum, 1988), 190.

101 *Oxford English Dictionary*, s.v. 'Haptic', accessed 1 December 2016, http://dictionary.oed.com/.

102 Walter Benjamin, 'The Work of Art in the Age of Mechanical Reproduction (1936)', in *Illuminations*, trans. Harry Zohn (New York: Schocken Books, 1986), 231, 233.

103 Antonia Lant, 'Haptical Cinema', *October* 74 (1995): 69.

104 Laura U. Marks, *Touch Sensuous Theory and Multisensory Media* (Minneapolis: University of Minnesota Press, 2002), 133.

105 Laura U. Marks, *The Skin of the Film: Intercultural Cinema, Embodiment, and the Senses* (Durham, NC: Duke University Press, 2000), 1. How these artists describe and identify themselves is less clear.

106 Laura U. Marks, 'Haptic Visuality: Touching with the Eyes', *Framework: The Finnish Art Review* 2 (November 2004), www.framework.fi/2_2004/visitor/artikkelit/marks.html (no longer available). Second quote in sentence and all other quotes in this paragraph from Marks, *The Skin of the Film: Intercultural Cinema, Embodiment, and the Senses*, 208.

107 Marks, *The Skin of the Film: Intercultural Cinema, Embodiment, and the Senses*, 185.
108 See Concordia Sensoria Research Team (CONSERT), Concordia University, Canada. Sensing the City: Sensuous Explorations of the Urban Landscape, accessed 11 January 2008, http://alcor.concordia.ca/~senses/sensing-the-city-index.htm.
109 Gilles Deleuze and Félix Guattari, *A Thousand Plateaus: Capitalism and Schizophrenia* (Minneapolis: University of Minnesota Press, 1987), 492–4; quote 493.
110 Ibid., 500.
111 Michel de Certeau, *The Practice of Everyday Life*, trans. Steven Rendall (Berkeley: University of California Press, 1984).
112 Ibid., 119.
113 Ibid., 101.
114 *All About Sikhs*, 'The Sikh Festivals: Baisakhi', accessed 8 August 2008, www.allaboutsikhs.com/index.php?option=com_content&task=view&id=1155.
115 This construction is perhaps best embodied in early to mid-twentieth century Hollywood and British cinema actor Sabu, originally from Mysore, India, whose penultimate role at the age of 38 was, tellingly, as a native 'boy' sidekick opposite Robert Mitchum in the 1963 jungle adventure film *Rampage*. See Gayatri Gopinath's brilliant discussion of Iain Rashid's film *Surviving Sabu* in her *Impossible Desires: Queer Diasporas and South Asian Public Cultures* (Durham, NC: Duke University Press, 2005), 65–77.
116 Emphasis mine. Andreas Huyssen, *Present Pasts: Urban Palimpsests and the Politics of Memory* (Stanford, CA: Stanford University Press, 2003), 10.
117 Anne McClintock, *Imperial Leather: Race, Gender, and Sexuality in the Colonial Contest* (New York: Routledge, 1995), 33.
118 Henry Shukman, 'CHOICE TABLES | LONDON; Where Indian Cuisine Reaches for the Stars', *The New York Times*, 4 March 2007, www.nytimes.com/2007/03/04/travel/04Choice.html?_r=0. The Russian Nobel Prize winner Ivan Pavlov, whom Shukman invokes, is known for having articulated that reflex responses, like salivation, can occur conditionally on specific previous experiences. See Nobelstiftelsen, *Physiology or Medicine, 1901–1921* (Amsterdam; London; New York: Elsevier Publishing Company, 1967), www.nobelprize.org/nobel_prizes/medicine/laureates/1904/pavlov-bio.html. His conditioned olfactory response to the aural stimulus of sitar music can be described as another example of a postural schema related to dining in a curry restaurant.
119 Deleuze and Guattari, *A Thousand Plateaus*, 493–4.
120 Emphasis mine. McClintock, *Imperial Leather*, 30. All quotations in the remainder of this paragraph are from the same page.
121 Bourdieu, *Masculine Domination*, 1–2. Originally published as Pierre Bourdieu, *La domination masculine* (Paris: Éditions du Seuil, 1998).
122 There are two Eid festivals in a year. One is called 'Eid-ul-Fitr' and the other, which comes about 10 weeks later, is called 'Eid-ul-Adha'. I am referring to

the former, celebrated at the end of the month of fasting. Eid-ul-Adha is celebrated on the 10th of the month of Thul-Haj to commemorate the obedience of Hadhrat Ibrahim and his son Hadhrat Ishmael. See 'Eid-Ul-Fitr and Eid-Ul-Adha Festivals', *Ahmadiyya Muslim Community*, accessed 2 January 2016, www.alislam.org/books/salat/11.html.

123 Riazat Butt, 'Manchester Police Prepare for Double Celebration', *Guardian*, 29 December 2006, sec. UK news, www.theguardian.com/uk/2006/dec/29/religion.world.

124 'Eid Show-Offs Will Lose Cars', *Manchester Evening News*, 14 August 2007, www.manchestereveningnews.co.uk/news/local-news/eid-show-offs-will-lose-cars-1155851; 'Eid Mubarak!', *BBC News*, 11 December 2004, www.bbc.co.uk/manchester/content/articles/2004/11/11/eid_2004_comments_feature.shtml. Although the word 'cruising' has several connotations, here it refers to the act of walking or driving in specific pursuit of a partner, in this case for women.

125 Rajinder Kumar Dudrah, 'Birmingham (UK): Constructing City Spaces through Black Popular Cultures and the Black Public Sphere', *City: Analysis of Urban Trends, Culture, Theory, Policy, Action* 6, no. 3 (2002): 343.

126 Butt, 'Manchester Police Prepare for Double Celebration'.

127 Ibid.

128 'Khan Appeals for Trouble-Free Eid', *BBC*, 2 November 2005, sec. Manchester, http://news.bbc.co.uk/2/hi/uk_news/england/manchester/4401138.stm. This is somewhat ironic given Khan was charged with speeding at almost twice the legal limit and for not producing a licence or insurance documents on New Year's Eve of 2006. See 'Top Boxer's Speed Charge', *Manchester Evening News*, 13 August 2007, www.manchestereveningnews.co.uk/news/local-news/top-boxers-speed-charge-990680.

129 Emphasis mine. 'Early Closing Brought Eid Peace', *Manchester Evening News*, 14 August 2007, www.manchestereveningnews.co.uk/news/local-news/early-closing-brought-eid-peace-1018892.

130 Moreover, both the racialized performance of masculinity and the language used by the GMP and RBA above render women invisible, or as linchpins of heteronormative families at best. This is particularly ironic given one of the more successful business owners on Curry Mile is a woman, Nighat Awan, chief executive and co-owner of the Shere Khan Group, which owns Indian restaurants throughout the UK. Awan was also awarded an OBE by the Queen for her business achievements and philanthropy. See *Women Speakers*, accessed 20 August 2007, www.womenspeakers.co.uk/speakerdetail2.asp?speakerid=19. See also 'Nighat Awan Wins "Outstanding Contribution" Award', *Redhotcurry*, 12 October 2004, http://redhotcurry.com/food_and_drink/other/nighat_awan_award.htm.

131 See Chapter 4, p. 98 and Mrinalini Sinha, *Colonial Masculinity: The 'Manly Englishman' and the 'Effeminate Bengali' in the Late Nineteenth Century* (Manchester: Manchester University Press, 1995).

132 Deleuze and Guattari, *A Thousand Plateaus*, 493.

133 *Club Zindagi, Manchester* (started in 2003), accessed 27 March 2007, www.clubzindagi.com/.

134 Michel Foucault, 'Text/Context: Of Other Spaces', in *Grasping the World: The Idea of the Museum*, ed. Donald Preziosi and Claire J Farago, trans. Jay Miskowiec (Aldershot: Ashgate, 2003), 371–9. Originally published in English as 'Of Other Spaces', *Diacritics* 16, no. 1 (Spring 1986): 22–7, doi:10.2307/464648. First published in French two years earlier: Michel Foucault, 'Des Espaces Autres (Basis of Lecture given in 1967)', *Architecture, Mouvement, Continuité*, no. 5 (October 1984): 46–9.

135 *HomieSexual*, accessed 9 March 2007, www.shlomp.com/homiesexual/home/folder/1/About_HomieSexual.html. 'Homie' is urban slang for close friend. Combined with 'homosexual', 'HomieSexual' refers to an urban queer who is black or another person of colour. See the plethora of meanings on *Urban Dictionary*, s.v. 'Homie', accessed 9 March 2007, www.urbandictionary.com/define.php?term=homie.

136 *Ghetto Superstars,* accessed 12 August 2007, www.ghetto-superstars.co.uk/. London's equivalent of this party is called 'Spice', a union of London-based parties, Club Desi and Club Urban. At Spice, Club Urban plays R&B, reggaeton, hip-hop and soul in one room, and Club Desi plays Bollywood, bhangra and Arabic music in another. The inclusion of Arab music as part of the music mix broadens the appeal of these partygoers potentially even further than their Manchester counterpart. See *Urban Desi*, accessed 27 March 2007, www.urban-desi.co.uk. Furthermore, in 2005 the 'Bolly Lolly' queer party in London evinces, again, how an alliance of homosexual politics enables the breaking down of borders, in this case violently formed national ones, such as India (as referenced through *Bolly*wood) and Pakistan (as referenced through *Lolly*wood, the term for Pakistan's equivalent of Bollywood based in the capital city of Lahore).

137 Malkani articulates a new breed of British Asian masculinity re-claimed through urban music: see Gautam Malkani, *Londonstani* (New York: Penguin Press, 2006). In London, for instance, the club party, Bombay Bronx, is quite popular and is the heterosexual version of the Ghetto Superstar party in Manchester or London's Spice party. (These parties are not as radical about gender and sexuality, though, as their queer equivalent.)

138 Email to CZcrew (Club Zindagi Crew) distribution list, 5 August 2006.

139 See archive of club photos on *HomieSexual*, accessed 9 March 2007, www.shlomp.com/homiesexual/home/album/20/HomieSexual_Flyers-photos.html.

140 Patel, 'Queer Desi Visual Culture Across the "Brown Atlantic"', 228.

141 Ibid. For the 'Chitty Chitty Bang Bang' freestyle lyrics, see '2Pac – Chitty Chitty Bang Bang Freestyle Lyrics', *Metro Lyrics*, accessed 2 January 2016, www.metrolyrics.com/chitty-chitty-bang-bang-freestyle-lyrics-2pac.html.

142 The poster is also no doubt a tongue in cheek reference to the fact that both 2Pac and Notorious B.I.G. were killed in drive-by shootings in 1996 and 1997,

respectively. See Randall Sullivan, 'The Unsolved Mystery of the Notorious B.I.G.', *Rolling Stone*, 15 December 2005, www.rollingstone.com/music/news/the-unsolved-mystery-of-the-notorious-b-i-g-20110107; 'Tupac Shakur Biography', *Rolling Stone*, accessed 3 January 2016, www.rollingstone.com/music/artists/tupac-shakur/biography. Portions of this biography appeared in *The Rolling Stone Encyclopedia of Rock & Roll* (New York: Simon & Schuster, 2001).

'Practice-led': producing art, producing art history

6

In this chapter, I explore the range of public artistic events comprising the project *Mixing It Up: Queering Curry Mile and Currying Canal Street* that I organized in autumn 2007.[1] Created by Manchester-based art and music collectives on the basis of my conception of using culture to subvert, confuse, or 'mix up' the production of a rationalized Manchester – and thereby (I hoped) potentially shift expectations about the people generally found in Curry Mile and the Gay Village – the public art projects I commissioned for *Mixing It Up* took place in these two areas of the city. Art historian Gavin Butt's observation of the importance of a critic's 'engagement with – and response to – the contingencies encountered whilst undertaking the act of criticism itself' in the introduction to his anthology exploring new models of art criticism describes how experiencing *Sphere:dreamz* and my concomitant investigation of the material production of the city of Manchester led to *Mixing It Up*.[2] In fact, given much of the evidence collecting for the previous chapter overlapped with the production and execution of the projects discussed here, the chapters mutually informed each other.

Chapter 5 pivoted around *Sphere:dreamz* and my material investigation of the Gay Village and Curry Mile as bounded spaces in my exploration of how to write queer feminist transnational art histories. This chapter explores *Mixing It Up*, the general and cultural marketing of the Gay Village *relative* to Curry Mile and the notion of 'practice-led' research and how it relates to writing transnational South Asian art histories – not just feminist ones although many of the works do deal with queer feminism in this chapter.

Criticality, the curatorial, and practice-led research

In many ways this chapter is a seamless extension of the previous one, especially the shift from negative critique to actively producing the transnational South Asian art histories I want to see written. However, the fact that I brought into being the very material I want to historicize requires further reflection. That is, I am even more entangled here than in the previous chapter with the subject matter about which I hope to write. Visual culture scholar Irit Rogoff's conceptualization of 'criticality' as distinct from criticism is useful in further thinking through my entanglement. She writes that:

> … criticality, is a state of duality in which one is at one and the same time, both empowered and disempowered, knowing and unknowing … So it would seem that criticality is in itself a mode of embodiment, a state from which one cannot exit or gain a critical distance but which rather marries our knowledge and our experience in ways that are not complimentary.[3]

Crucial here is that a lack of critical distance does not mean that critical reflection is thrown to the wayside but that it takes a more protean form. Critical reflection is able to adapt and reshape itself when necessary rather than forcefully adapting, reshaping or acting on evidence (seen as being distinct from the theorist rather than imbricated with him or her). Indeed, Rogoff further writes that '"criticality" … brings together that being studied and those doing the studying, in an indelible unity'.[4] I am embracing a state of both 'knowing and unknowing' and thereby being both 'empowered and disempowered'.

In this chapter, I move even closer to criticality than in Chapter 5 because I am producing the art projects that I historicize. To clarify, the writing in this chapter is not merely documentary. It also includes an analysis of the reception of the projects. In this way, the exhibition should not be seen as a temporally fixed event and this notion is something with which I believe art history as a discipline is in a position to contend and process. For instance, as art historian Carrie Lambert-Beatty writes: 'Art history is characterized by delay, decontextualization, and mediation: seeming weaknesses that we might instead celebrate as correctives to a condition of art [in my case the exhibition] as event.'[5] She also makes a fascinating parallel between 'the critique of presence' in performance studies that brought to the fore the complex relationship between a performance and its document and the importance of reassessing 'the role of contemporary art history in relation to art's production and dissemination'.[6] By doing so, contemporary art history is performative and this is made more explicit through a practice that toggles between production and theorization of 'art' – the line between the two is not clear in the first place as Lambert-Beatty implies – as I do in this chapter. As Lambert-Beatty half-jokingly writes, 'Academia isn't contemporary art's funeral parlor. It is its current address.'[7]

Producing art projects could be described as 'practice-led' research.[8] Of course, my descriptions of walks in the city in Chapter 5 and my affective engagement with visual culture in Chapter 7 also constitute such research. However, in this chapter my jumping-off point as a frame of reference is practice-led. There is often a sharp line drawn between practice and research or practice and theory.[9] Curating is seen as a practice but theory and the writing of art history are not. At the same time, curating is not seen as research or theory in the way writing might. In this chapter, I move away from these binaries. The writing of art history is a practice or a way of working ideas out in the same way as the manipulation of space by curators. While there are differences between practice and theory or practice and research, at their best they share a curiosity and interest in questions, answers which are shaped through the practice of doing – whether through writing or curating.

Rogoff's delineation between 'curating' and the 'curatorial' is instructive in further characterizing practice-led research. She describes curating as 'the practice of putting on exhibitions and the various professional expertises it involves' and the curatorial as follows:

> In the realm of 'the curatorial' we see various principles that might not be associated with displaying works of art; principles of the production of knowledge, of activism, of cultural circulations and translations that begin to shape and determine other forms by which arts can engage. In a sense 'the curatorial' is thought and critical thought at that, that does not rush to embody itself, does not rush to concretise itself.[10]

The 'curatorial' dovetails with my approach to curating that does not begin and end with the event itself. Her note that the curatorial is 'critical thought' but that it 'does not rush to embody itself' is particularly evocative. I would also note that writing and theorizing can enable critical thought in the context of the curatorial by slowing down the process of meaning-making.

Rogoff articulates that specificity of place (a kind of boundedness) and embodiment need not to be abstracted. She notes how exhibitions she has seen such as *Vilnius[Lithuania]/New York* or *Tokyo/Paris*, are driven by a desire to inhabit worlds 'they admire or to which they aspire', preventing them from being banal or disembodied'.[11] These exhibitions are driven by a 'desire' in inhabiting worlds 'they admire or to which they aspire', preventing them from being banal or disembodied.[12] We could easily replace the cities Rogoff brings up with sites such as Curry Mile and the Gay Village, which are worlds that the women of Sphere would like 'to inhabit' or should be able to inhabit.

Marketing Manchester

While Curry Mile and the Gay Village are located in close proximity within the urban fabric of Manchester, they are not only geographically distinct from each other, but also discursively defined as separate by the city's marketing and – as described in the last chapter – internalized by urban subjects as felt separation. It is also worth noting that while scholars have explored the Gay Village in the context of Manchester's post-industrial cosmopolitanism, the absence of a discussion of Curry Mile from academic discussions is itself indicative of the cleaving of the space from the Gay Village.[13]

In comparison to Curry Mile, Manchester marketing brochures give the Gay Village a metonymically privileged position. Other ethnic spaces, such as Chinatown, also fare much better than Curry Mile. For instance, the 2006/7 brochure, *Manchester: Where to Stay 2006/07*, produced by Marketing Manchester, mentions both the Gay Village and Chinatown in the 'What to Do in 48 Hours in Manchester' section.[14] Curry Mile is curiously missing from the list, even though it is as dynamic as the Village, and much larger and arguably more vibrant than Chinatown – many restaurants are open until about 4.30 a.m. on Curry Mile, whereas Chinatown is shut down normally by midnight. Furthermore, the Manchester Visitor Information Centre's *Manchester: Guided Walks & Tours 2007* brochure lists an 'Out in the Past Trail', which explores over 200 years of gay and lesbian history in Manchester, under its 'Regular Walks and Tours' section, as well as two separate walks in Chinatown under its 'Cultural Manchester' section, but no walks have been constructed around Curry Mile.[15]

On the website *Visit Manchester*, the official tourism website for Greater Manchester, the 'Cityscapes' tab mentions 'the colourful Gay Village' and Chinatown, 'one of the city centre's most distinctive areas', but again excludes Curry Mile.[16] Moreover, 'Gay and Lesbian'-related material fills an entire tab of the site in addition to being highlighted in the 'Nightlife' section, while Curry Mile is referenced in only one sentence in the 'International Cuisine' sub-section of the 'Food and Drink' tab.[17] In addition, Rusholme, the area in which Curry Mile is situated, and Chinatown are given equal nods in the following description:

> You can eat your way around the world in Manchester, sampling everything from Armenian to Australian to African. There are the sights and smells of Chinatown and Rusholme's Curry Mile, upmarket and traditional takes on Italian, Spanish and French, and a host of international restaurants offering gourmet global fare.[18]

The 88-page full-colour glossy guide *Manchester – The Destination* omits Curry Mile completely. The 'Places to Eat' section begins with a description of the diversity of restaurants available in the city including 'Italian, Greek, Mexican, Armenian, Cantonese, Thai and Japanese', but does not mention Indian, Pakistani or Middle Eastern cuisines, which make up many of the restaurants on Curry Mile.[19]

In the 'Culture' section, 'Manchester Pride', 'Manchester Irish Festival 2007' and 'Chinese New Year' are included, but not Manchester's Eid festivities.[20] A full-page colour photo of the Chinese New Year is also included in both the guide and the glossy pocketbook-size pamphlet 'Manchester: Short Breaks'.[21] Given that only three sides of the latter were available for non-advertising material, this inclusion is as significant as the exclusion (once again) of images of Curry Mile.[22] Curry Mile is given a textual mention, but as an equivalent of Chinatown.[23]

The fact that Chinatown is in the city centre and Curry Mile is not can explain part of the invisibility of Curry Mile in the output of Marketing Manchester. For instance, photos of the Gay Village and Chinatown are included in the section 'Manchester – the neighbourhood' in *Manchester – The Destination*, but the latter is limited to city centre neighbourhoods, explaining the elision of Curry Mile in this instance.[24] Nonetheless, the brochure includes other spaces and venues that are at least as far away from the city centre as Curry Mile, making the latter's invisibility not completely attributable to its location outside of the city centre. For instance, in *Manchester: Where to Stay 2006/07*, The Lowry and the Daniel Libeskind-designed Imperial War Museum North – both significantly further away from the city centre than Curry Mile – are included in the 'What to Do in 48 Hours in Manchester' section, but not Curry Mile. The document also includes a photo of the museum and Chinatown.[25]

The lack of textual and visual reference to Curry Mile in the marketing output of the city suggests important class distinctions. For instance, despite Curry Mile's relative proximity to the city centre, the sale prices of homes over the 2004–6 period in the M1 postal code (City Centre/Gay Village) range from roughly £130,000 to £470,000 – twice that of homes in the M13 postal code (Rusholme), which range from £83,000 to £205,000.[26] At the same time, the low property values in Rusholme compared to the city centre undoubtedly contributed to the emergence of Curry Mile in that location. However, the history of Rusholme – which was incorporated into the city in 1885 – does not indicate that the area was always such an economically underprivileged area. City historian Ed Glinert described Rusholme as being 'a once quiet middle-class suburb' in reference to the newly monied families that settled in the area and the contiguous Victoria Park in the mid-nineteenth century.[27] By the beginning of the twentieth century, though, families began to move to other more fashionable areas in town, such as Didsbury, and property values began to drop as some homes were converted into apartments and others fell into disrepair.

The contemporary ideological and literal exclusion of Curry Mile from the civic marketing of the city, therefore, cannot be seen as a seamless legacy of the historical class structure of the area. Instead, it seems clear that the low property values in Rusholme and the invisibility of Curry Mile in the city's marketing material can be linked to the construction of Curry Mile as 'ethnic' – and darker-skinned subjects become synonymous with a lower class. Even within South Asian communities, those with darker skin are often discriminated against and are considered of a lower class.[28]

The asymmetry in marketing coverage between Curry Mile and the Gay Village has been particularly exacerbated by the move away from municipal socialism – or 'people-based' and 'bottom up' governmental and economic policies – that Manchester has undergone since the late 1980s, which has resulted in a more entrepreneurial mandate with a focus on 'place-marketing' and 'property-led regeneration'.[29] This shift favours the Gay Village, the economic success of which has given rise to the frequent use of the term 'the pink pound' in reference to the area's economic significance to the city.[30] Indeed, members of Marketing Manchester's staff were featured speakers at the 2006 'The Pink Pound Conference', a forum devoted to exploring the 'Latest marketing insight into a UK consumer market worth £70 billion'.[31] According to the conference programme, Marketing Manchester's talk was meant to take '[a] look at how Manchester successfully regenerated and transformed their leisure business to create a vibrant, inclusive offering and highly profitable means of regenerating a city'.[32] Marketing Manchester is also one of the principle backers of Manchester's Pride parade, held in and around the Gay Village. To further underscore the potential for the blurring of queer political organizing and the marketing of the city, Andrew Stokes, the Chief Executive of Marketing Manchester from 2003 to 2015 and a long-time board member of Manchester Pride Ltd, was appointed the latter's chairman in 2003 (a post he held until 2009).[33]

Marxist urban geographer David Harvey notes that public–private partnerships – such as Marketing Manchester, a private company, which frequently collaborates with civic bodies, in particular the city council – inscribe within their logic unequal distribution of urban development. They are more concerned with construction of place (the image of a specific place) and the enhancement of property values rather than the amelioration of conditions (housing, health, poverty, etc.) of the city where the place is located.[34] Urban geography scholars Craig Young, Martina Diep and Stephanie Drabble, for instance, note that property developers' and estate agents' brochures for the city centre construct 'a geography of difference in which definitions of the "cosmopolitan city value or pathologise and *spatialise* certain forms of difference'.[35] The low property values in Rusholme can be seen, at least partially, as a by-product of the municipal entrepreneurialism associated with the city's post-industrial cosmopolitanism. In other words, the boosterism of other parts of the city has kept property values low.[36]

Ironically, the move away from municipal socialism that places some focus on the most vulnerable members of a community has also meant that support has been siphoned away from *non*-commercial gay and lesbian support centres – the few places that those who are probably less likely to frequent the commercialized Gay Village might go to.[37] As recently as 2007, the Manchester City Council sent a notice to the city's Sidney Street LGBT centre – which serves as a meeting place for a variety of different groups marginalized within the larger queer community, such as ethnic minorities, the disabled, the elderly and women – to vacate the city-owned building in which it has been located since 1988.[38]

Cultural marketing, Canal Street and Curry Mile

Another point of departure for the genesis of *Mixing It Up* was my research into the role of culture, and public art more specifically, in the marketing and re-branding of Manchester as a cosmopolitan city in the post-1990s period. As in Chapter 5, I discuss evidence collected up to 2008, shortly after all the various projects of *Mixing It Up* had taken place; and when I moved back to the United States. During the 1990s and early 2000s, a confluence of factors spurred the city of Manchester to embark on a massive project of civic regeneration tied to various cultural projects. These factors included embracing entrepreneurship over municipal socialism that gave rise to the Gay Village as an economic centre, the 1996 IRA bombing of the city centre that jump-started its rebuilding, and civic interest in hosting the Olympics and the Commonwealth Games. By the time the 2002 Commonwealth Games were held in Manchester, a slew of new iconic buildings – including The Lowry, Daniel Libeskind's Imperial War Museum North, and Urbis: Museum of the City – had led to what *The New York Times* referred to as the 'architectural rebirth' of Manchester.[39]

By 2002, the development agency 'Manchester: Knowledge Capital' (M:KC), comprised of a mixture of health, public, private and academic constituencies, had also been formed to promote both economic and cultural growth in the Greater Manchester region.[40] Given its concentration of higher education and cultural institutions, Oxford Road became a focal point for the agency's larger activities to promote Manchester as a knowledge capital. For instance, the Royal Northern School of Music, the University of Manchester and Manchester Metropolitan University (MMU) can all be found on Oxford Road, as well as a number of cultural institutions – the University of Manchester's Whitworth Art Gallery, Manchester Museum, Contact Theatre, MMU's Holden Art Gallery and Cornerhouse, a contemporary art space and film venue.[41]

The sheer density of cultural institutions along Oxford Road resulted in the branding of the area stretching from town hall just north of Oxford Road to the Whitworth Art Gallery, the southern terminus of Oxford Road, as the Oxford Road Cultural Corridor (ORC). In 2003, a public art policy report prepared by John Hyatt, chair of the public art sub-committee of the ORC Executive Group, noted that public art could be instrumental in consolidating the ORC as a knowledge and cultural centre.[42] Based on Hyatt's report, the

Manchester City South Partnership, a public–private partnership which aimed to deliver part of the vision plan outlined by Manchester: Knowledge Capital, unveiled details for a public art project, the 'Avenue of Giants', in March 2008.[43]

The 'Avenue of Giants' was envisioned as 'a linear open air art gallery themed to honour the intellectual giants who have lived, worked or studied in the [Oxford Road] area',[44] such as the Victorian novelist Elizabeth Gaskell and social historian Friedrich Engels, both of whom lived off Oxford Road in the mid-nineteenth century; Karl Marx, with whom Engels would frequently collaborate and who is cited as having developed part of his communist theory in Manchester; and a number of important scientists, such as Nobel Prize winners Lord Ernest Rutherford (Chemistry, 1908) and German physicist Niels Bohr (Physics, 1922) and Hans Geiger, whose name is immortalized in the Geiger counter radiation detector he devised.[45] The fact that all of these figures are white and, with the exception of Gaskell, male is not surprising given the socio-historical context.

What bears further reflection, however, is the fact that both Oxford Street, which leads to town hall and the city centre, and Wilmslow Road, on which Curry Mile is located, bookend and are seamless with Oxford Road, yet only Oxford Street is part of the explicit, official parameters of the ORC and the aforementioned public art proposal. Though Oxford Street is north of Oxford Road and therefore closer to the city centre than Wilmslow Road, which is south of Oxford Road, the inclusion of the former and exclusion of the latter cannot be completely ascribed to their relative distance from the city centre. For instance, the city centre map on the official Manchester City Council website lists the Gallery of Costume, which is located even further south than Curry Mile on Wilmslow Road, among the 'cultural destinations' south of the city centre.[46] The exclusion of Wilmslow Road from the ORC could also be considered somewhat tautological, given that the word 'Oxford' appears in the ORC title. Yet even the Manchester City South Partnership, which has slightly less restrictive parameters than the ORC and emphasizes areas 'south' of the city centre, shares the same southern terminus as the ORC and therefore stops short of including Wilmslow Road.

It is also worth noting that though a desert-like, concrete expanse separated Wilmslow and Oxford roads as recently as the late 1980s, the division has since become softened and much more seamless with the construction in the post-2000 period of both university dormitories and a variety of commercial shops.[47] By 2007, the exteriors of several Rusholme restaurants and shops echoed the sleek, minimalistic décor of high-end, city centre eateries, thereby further blurring the distinctions between Curry Mile and the city centre. In the context of the latter, the exclusion of Rusholme – the larger area in which Curry Mile and Wilmslow Road are situated – from the cultural marketing and public art strategies of the city is particularly peculiar.

The ideological and literal separation of Rusholme from civic culture can be linked to the contemporary class construction of the area as 'low', as argued earlier. The history of Rusholme, however, indicates that the area was not always so divorced from culture. By 1947, Rusholme had arguably become Manchester's most culturally avant-garde area, when John E. Blakeley opened a film studio just off Dickenson Street at the southern point of contemporary Curry Mile.[48] Popularly known as 'Jollywood' for the number of commercially successful comedies the studio produced, it served as a focal point for the city's creative community. The studio was ultimately sold to the BBC in 1953 when Blakeley retired.[49] Its sale signalled a shift to a more popular cultural focus, with the inaugural episode of the popular *Top of the Pops* series broadcast from the Rusholme studio in 1964. However, the studio was deemed too small, and the series was absorbed into the main BBC studio in London in 1967.[50] A number of cinema houses, including the Trocadero and Capital Cinema (both now defunct), also cropped up in Rusholme during the 1960s. Significantly, the cinema houses began to cater to the increasing number of Asian immigrants entering Manchester during this period by screening Bollywood films at weekends. British sociologist Nida Kirmani has identified this trend as an important factor in the eventual construction of curry restaurants in Rusholme, as Asian immigrant families would see movies and then share a meal out.[51]

Rather than being characterized as a site of cultural experimentation as in the heyday of Jollywood, or a site of pop culture as it was at the height of the BBC's takeover of the latter studio and the rise of the local cinema houses, Rusholme is now known for its less prestigious *multi*culturalism, as indicated by the language of Hyatt's 2003 report on public art. The report explains that '*Manchester Oxford Road* has the potential, because of its rich cultural mix of "art" venues, the super campus [a reference to the many universities] and the multi-cultural dimension of Rusholme to become a cultural destination of choice.'[52] Rusholme is important to the construction of Oxford Road's Cultural Corridor as a knowledge/culture centre, but only in so far as it fills a pared-down role of contributing ethnic diversity *tout court* that, to complete the perverse logic, constructs the ORC, composed of the 'super campus' and 'art venues', as otherwise white.[53] In this context, the exclusion of Curry Mile detaches Curry Mile and Rusholme from the city's larger post-1990s cultural renaissance and serves, if only implicitly, to naturalize the whiteness of the 'Avenue of Giants'.

The Gay Village is also not part of the ORC, and Canal Street is not even physically a continuation of Oxford Road like Curry Mile. Nevertheless, the Gay Village and the people expected to be traversing it are not as detached from 'culture' in the script of the city marketing materials as Curry Mile.[54] For example, a section of the full-colour, glossy 40-page brochure on queer

Manchester produced by Marketing Manchester, entitled *A Touch of Culture*, includes a range of different cultural destinations of putative interest to queers, such as the Opera House, the Urbis, then an exhibition centre focusing on city life, and the Cornerhouse contemporary art space and film venue.[55] Also, the 'Gay & Lesbian' tab of the official tourism website for Greater Manchester, *Visit Manchester*, lists a number of cultural venues located all over the city centre.[56] Moreover, parts of the Gay Village and Chinatown fall within the official parameters of the Manchester City South Partnership, too.[57]

Art historian Miwon Kwon's scholarship on public art as tied to civic identities is instructive in further considering the spatial parameters and civic use of public artworks to manufacture a spatial identity for Oxford Road as a cultural corridor. She has noted that 'the appropriation of site-specific public art for the valorization of urban identities' has come with a larger shift in the manner in which urban cities create singular identities. Instead of architecture and urban planning, she notes that 'other media more intimate to marketing and advertising' have become dominant and are linked to the commissioning of public art. Kwon further argues that public art supplies 'distinction of place', 'locational identity', and: 'Under the pretext of their articulation or resuscitation, site-specific public art can be mobilized to expedite the erasure of differences via the commodification and serialization of places.' In this way, the 'Avenue of Giants' and the Oxford Road Cultural Corridor ultimately expedite what Kwon terms 'the erasure of difference' in its omission of Curry Mile, while celebrating the difference of queer in its embrace of the Gay Village.[58]

The extensive promotion of Manchester's 'locational identity' and 'distinction of place' through public art strategies and print publications is not surprising in the context of the overwhelming dominance of London, which has left other UK cities endlessly grappling for some kind of national, international and cultural visibility, as well as funding. For instance, a 'Core Cities Group' was formed in the mid-1990s as a strategic economic and cultural alliance among a number of UK cities, including Manchester, which work together to promote each other.[59] By 2007, a *BBC News* poll indicated that Manchester was unofficially regarded as England's 'second city' behind London and ahead of Birmingham, its long-time erstwhile and sometimes contemporary rival, and in this way has at least fared better than other UK cities more recently.[60]

In the next few sections, I describe in more detail the performances and installations, as well as an educational project, connected to *Mixing It Up* that aimed to reveal the queer in Curry Mile and the transnational South Asian in Canal Street, thereby confusing the implicit assumptions on which the city's post-millennial cultural renaissance is ultimately based.[61] My specific role as the creator of *Mixing It Up* included writing grant proposals, securing in-kind support from each of the five major venues, and generally nurturing the individual projects, although the artists retained ultimate creative control over their individual art installations and performances.

Individual projects, which took place from September to December 2007, were designed to be self-contained but were also linked to each other. To underscore the connections among the different projects, full-colour, glossy postcards listing all the projects were made available at each event, at every venue that hosted a project and at various establishments in both Curry Mile and the Gay Village, as well as at other locations throughout the city (Figures 6.1–2). Explanatory placards and wall labels were also produced to draw in as broad an audience as possible and to make explicit the connections I was hoping to make.

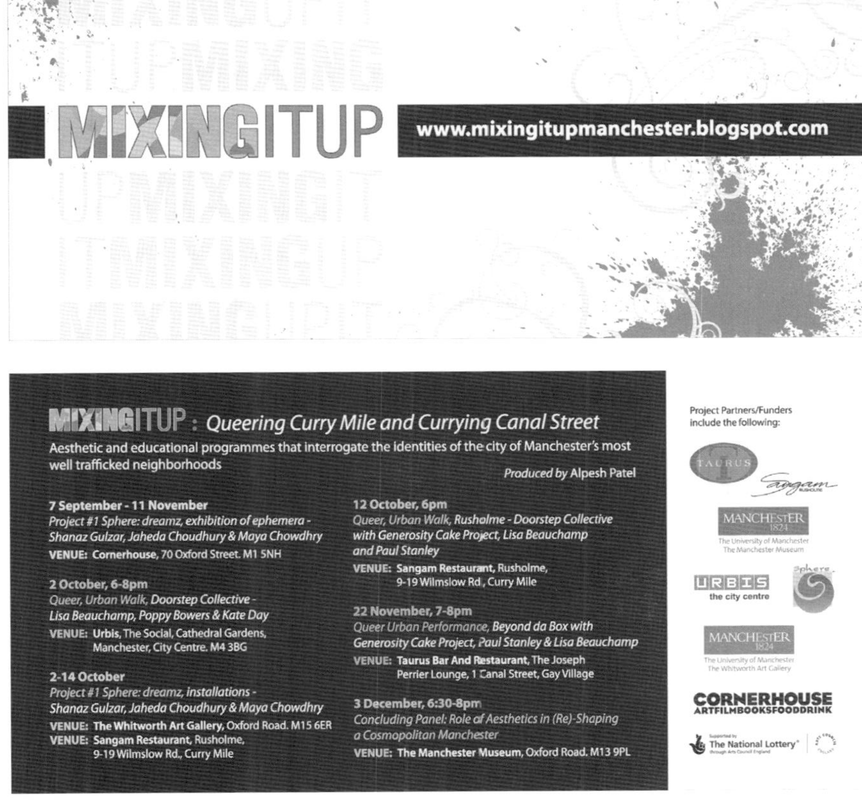

Mixing It Up postcard (front and back). **6.1–2**

Sphere:dreamz re-sited: queering Curry Mile and the Oxford Road cultural corridor

Whereas the cultural industries of Manchester, more generally, have a strong connection to the commercial businesses of Canal Street, as noted by Sam McCormick, former Cultural Regeneration Officer of the Manchester City Council, the former do not yet have strong ties to the commercial restaurants of Curry Mile.[62] Indeed, the placement of Sphere's original project near the Gay Village does not entirely reflect Sphere's apprehension regarding Curry Mile. On the contrary, its placement can be attributed to the fact that Queer Up North, the organization that partially produced *Sphere:dreamz*, has a considerable network of contacts in the Gay Village, and therefore was able to secure Sackville Park as a location for the installation.[63]

Fortunately, finding support from Curry Mile restaurateurs for *Mixing It Up* and a suitable location for the placement of one of Sphere's beds in a restaurant on Curry Mile was relatively uncomplicated. Mukhtar Ahmed, chairman of the Rusholme Business Association, with whom I first met to discuss the overall concept of *Mixing It Up*, welcomed Sphere's project and even offered to host a bed in his own restaurant, Sangam, which appropriately means 'meeting place' in Hindi.[64] Sangam's involvement in *Mixing It Up* marked the first queer art project in Curry Mile, according to McCormick.[65] Ahmed also contributed the following unsolicited statement for a press release regarding the bed in Curry Mile prepared by the University of Manchester's Press Office on behalf of *Mixing It Up*:

> We're over the moon to be involved in … [the] project and think it will be a brilliant experience for our customers … This project will help to widen people's perceptions of the people of Rusholme … This is a powerful way to show how open minded and tolerant we are as a community.[66]

Ahmed's support underscored the facileness of the tendency to interpret the restaurant owners and workers of Curry Mile as masculinist and heterosexist in their approach to potential clients. Furthermore, his indication that the 'project will help to widen people's perceptions of the people of Rusholme … [and] to show how open minded and tolerant we are as a community' reveals a keen understanding, on his part, that the identification of Curry Mile often becomes conflated with that of Rusholme, the wider geographical area in which Curry Mile is situated, and those that live within it, as well as the South Asian community, more generally. Undoubtedly, Ahmed's wish to be involved with the project was perhaps also commercially motivated. Whether this was true (or even partially true), however, does not diminish or somehow vitiate his support for *Mixing It Up*, which he was willing to put in print.

Originally, the beds were going to be placed in multiple restaurant spaces, however, given that a year and a half had passed since the original installation, many of the beds required significant conservation for which funds were not available. Furthermore, the desire to place the artwork in a restaurant had to be balanced with the potential for damage to the artwork. Therefore, in the end only one bed was displayed in Curry Mile and only for one week to minimize wear and tear (Plate 18).

Sangam Restaurant was an especially advantageous site to install one of Sphere's beds given that it sits on the edge of Curry Mile and the Oxford Road Cultural Corridor. The placement of the artwork de facto troubled the arbitrary construction of the former and latter as mutually exclusive. Sphere's bed was placed near the entrance of the restaurant so that customers could sit on it while waiting for tables, for instance. The material use of the bed, itself, with its connotations of intimacy and safety contrasted with the otherwise public, commercial space of the Curry Mile restaurant, which is frequented by large numbers of students. The bodies of visitors who sat on the bed became intertwined metaphorically with the creator's decidedly queer, female and transnational South Asian subjectivity, and in the process highlighted the potential shared identifications of, rather than differences among, the various visitors and the woman who created the bed.

The Urdu poem written on the bed by one of the women associated with Sphere and the placards contextualizing the project made explicit and visible a representation of female, transnational South Asian queerness where it might not be otherwise expected. The bed not only threw into relief the notion that South Asian cultures and queerness were irreconcilable, but also that queerness was largely male and culturally 'white'. In addition, many of the restaurant's waiters helped to point out the bed to customers, and often enthusiastically described its queer content.[67] The experience of seeing the waiters in a Curry Mile restaurant enjoy such work and hearing them advertising an art project concerned with queer, transnational South Asian women's issues further challenged the dominant construction of Curry Mile restaurants as implicitly masculinist and heterosexualist.

Another of *Sphere:dreamz*'s beds was installed in the Whitworth Art Gallery, part of the University of Manchester, a short walk north of Sangam Restaurant and closer to the city centre and Canal Street. The Whitworth Art Gallery sits on the edge of the Oxford Road Cultural Corridor and Curry Mile. The *Sphere:dreamz* bed was incorporated into an exhibition broadly exploring 'the body' (Plate 19). With the exception of Sphere's bed, all the artworks in the exhibition were drawings and paintings – primarily portraits and some self-portraits – from the gallery's permanent collection. A sample of the artworks included: Pablo Picasso's *Femme Vue du Dos* (*Woman Seen from Behind*), 1922, Edgar Degas's *Study of Four Dancers*, c.1895–1900, Lucian Freud's *Man's*

Head (Self Portrait I), 1963, and Camille Pissaro's *La Petite Bonne* (*The Young Maid*), 1896.[68]

The bed in the exhibition was also a self-portrait, although an abstract one. Col Bashir, one of the few individuals of Sphere who attached her name to the bed she made, made palpable the difficulty of being self-identified as queer, South Asian, and a woman within the corporate world by depicting a ghostly body pushing out from under the sheets of the bed. The bed also doubled as a boardroom table on which folders were placed. Visitors could sit on the bed, or in the swivel chair positioned next to it, and listen to recorded poetry being piped in from the bottom of the chair. The crisp, white sheets served to heighten the sterility or implied homogeneity (white, male and heterosexual) of the corporate boardroom.

Part of the rationale of placing the bed within the museum context was to situate the artwork among broader issues in the history of Western art. For instance, the bed served as a corrective to the archetypal artist's model used by many of the other artists in the exhibition. The depicted body in Sphere's artwork was androgynous and not sexualized, as opposed to the white, female nude depicted by many of the other artists in the exhibition. Sphere's artwork was also the sole artwork by an artist of South Asian descent in the exhibition. The description of the artwork above and the otherwise implicit connections I am outlining were detailed in a pithy manner on a didactic wall label.[69]

Finally, ephemera related to *Sphere:dreamz* were also installed in the public space of Cornerhouse as part of 'Cornerhouse projects', a series of exhibitions in and around the first-floor café and ground-floor bar areas featuring new work by emerging artists based in the Northwest. Cornerhouse was located roughly where Oxford Road becomes Oxford Street and sits at the opposite end of the ORC from the Whitworth Art Gallery.[70] Gauze-like organza screens, which originally stood in 8-ft tall bamboo frames besides the corresponding creator's bed of *Sphere:dreamz*, were strategically placed in the floor to ceiling windows of the first floor (Plate 20). A central screen featuring an abstracted image of one of the queer, South Asian women of Sphere was flanked by two coloured screens (magenta and yellow). The windows of the eastern façade in which the screens were installed faced out towards Canal Street, which is a short walk from Cornerhouse. The screens served to metaphorically unveil the artifice of the construct of the commercial and civic performance of the Gay Village as largely gay, white, male and middle class, as well as to protect (or veil) the identity of the queer, South Asian woman depicted. An extended wall label highlighted the geographical location of Cornerhouse in relation to Canal Street and noted that the abstracted image was of a queer, South Asian woman.

Many of the women associated with Sphere are not public about their sexuality, and therefore silhouettes, profiles and abstracted forms, such as in those on the organza screens, became leitmotifs for the other two newly created artworks installed in Cornerhouse – a short video entitled *A Wakening* and an untitled mural. Visitors were able to identify the bodies as queer only via wall labels.[71] Both the video and the mural were installed in the busy ground-floor space of the gallery. The video included a silhouette of one of the queer South Asian women associated with Sphere putting on and taking off a variety of different clothes and accessories, from baseball caps to underwear to dresses. The silhouette was represented as a figure floating within various scenes, ranging from the domestic to nightlife on Canal Street, and shifting in bright colours from green to blue to orange; at other times, these scenes were played within the outline of a silhouette (Figure 6.3). The digitally produced mural was constructed through serial repetition of anonymous profiles of queer, South Asian women from the video and was installed on the ground floor on the wall facing the well-trafficked Oxford Road (Plate 21). The bright, neon colours of the mural (highly visible from across the street) and

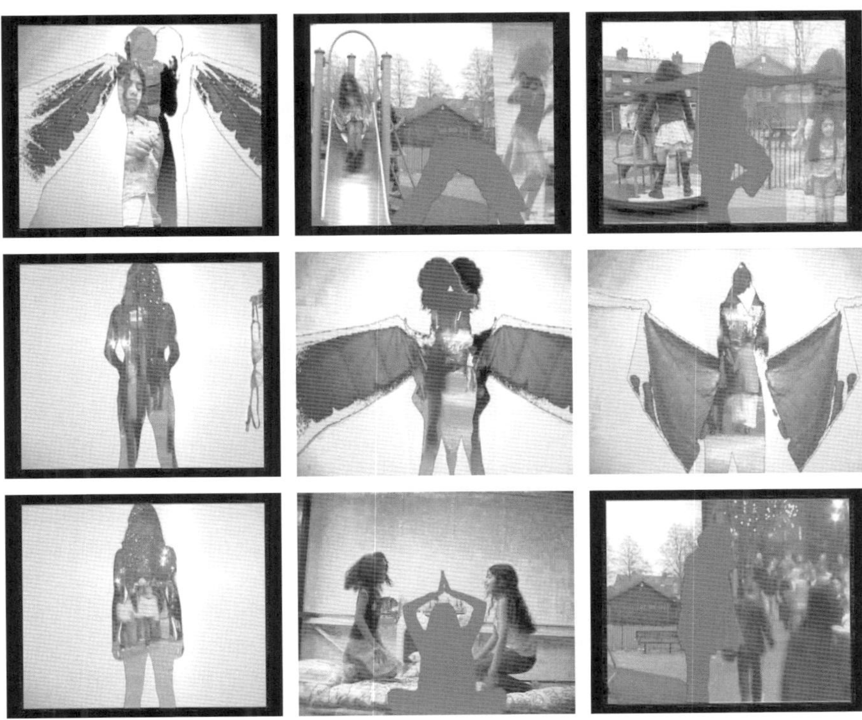

Sphere, Stills from *A Wakening*, single-channel video, Cornerhouse, Manchester, England, September–November 2007. 6.3

video acted as a foil for the profiles of the former and the use of silhouettes in the latter and the organza screens.

The women purposefully brought attention to their queer bodies in the well-trafficked ground and first floors of Cornerhouse, but the use of silhouettes and abstraction also allowed them to maintain control of their own representations. All the installations in Cornerhouse were on display from 7 September to 11 November 2007. The long run of the installation for these artworks in a space that is heavily trafficked served to maximize the presence, however abstracted, of a queer, gendered and South Asian subjectivity.

Queer Urban Walk, *Dérives* and psychogeographies

A series of *Mixing It Up* projects were also scheduled to coincide with the end of the Muslim religious observance of Ramadan, including Sphere's project in Sangam Restaurant and the Whitworth Art Gallery, as well as Paul Stanley's *Generosity Cake Project* and the Doorstep Collective's *Queer Urban Walk*. The last day of Ramadan, 12 October 2007, was strategically chosen as the day and time for an event exploring intersecting issues of faith in relation to both queer and transnational South Asian as identifications. Also the art projects aimed to challenge the omission of the Eid al-Fitr festivities in any of the city's marketing materials, which reinforces a narrow definition of subjects of Muslim faith as disconnected from civic cosmopolitanism.[72]

The first portion of the evening included a *Queer Urban Walk* in and around the space of Curry Mile that was organized by the Manchester-based Doorstep Collective, comprised of Lisa Beauchamp, Poppy Bowers and Kate Day (Figure 6.4). The genesis of this project was an academic talk I had given at Urbis, then an exhibition centre focusing on city life in Manchester, on my own performative walk down Curry Mile that one of the members of the collective, Beauchamp, had attended. Doorstep, founded in 2006, was an ideal *Mixing It Up* partner given that it had been formed to interrogate the ways that urban citizens navigate and produce individualized mappings of space.

As part of the preparation for the walk, Doorstep asked subjects in Curry Mile and Canal Street to share their best and worst memories in connection with the space over a period of several weeks. The walk began at Sangam Restaurant an hour before sundown on the day on which Muslims break their fast to celebrate the end of Ramadan. The Collective gave out envelopes to the fifteen to twenty participants who came on the walk, eighteen of which contained the culled responses and three of which were labelled 'navigator'. None of the responses were altered in any way in terms of length or content. Each of the individuals with a 'navigator' envelope was given an opportunity to lead the larger group along any route he or she wished within a prescribed stretch of geographical space around Curry Mile and its surroundings to an arbitrary

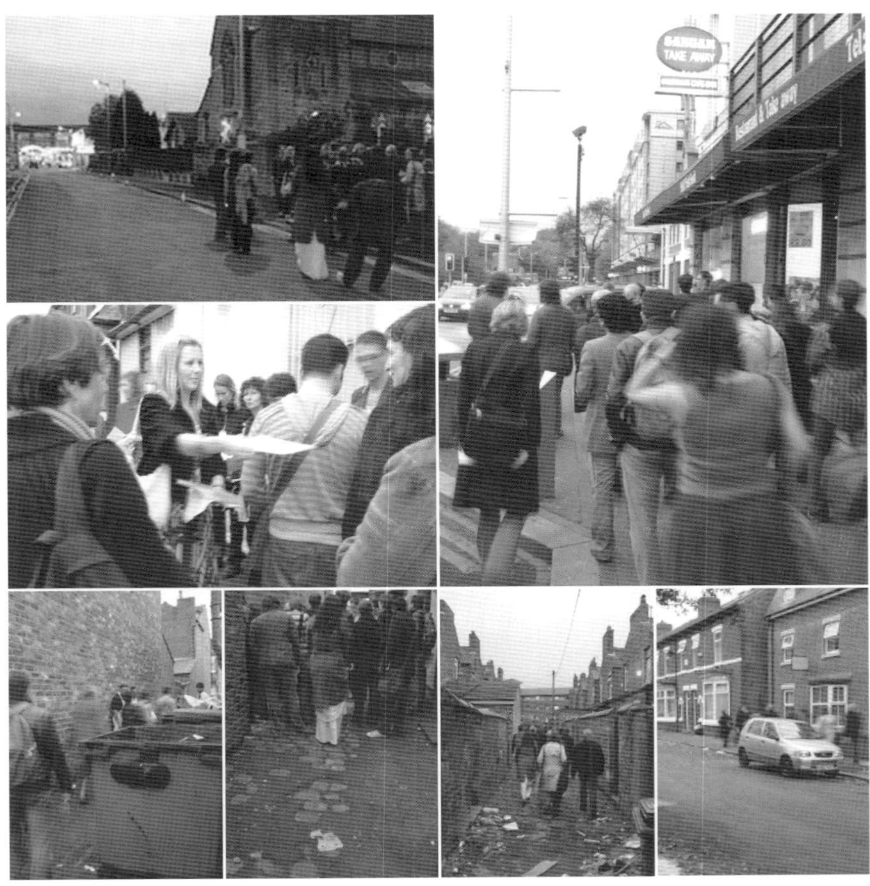

Doorstep Collective, *Queer Urban Walk, Curry Mile*, Manchester, England, 2007 (end of Ramadan). 6.4

fixed destination. When the navigator reached the latter, the second navigator would take over and so on.

Each navigator was asked to stop randomly three times during their journey; at each stop, two individuals who had envelopes containing the anonymous written memories were asked to read these memories out to the larger group. The slips of paper in the envelopes indicated whether each memory was a best or worst moment and the particular space (Gay Village or Curry Mile) to which it pertained. The comments that were read aloud were alternatively silly and poignant, trivial and reflective. Some specifically referred to issues of sexuality and the site of Curry Mile or the Gay Village; others were much more abstract in relation to either identity or space. The pastiche of collected memories and stories projected out into the space in and around

Curry Mile served to collapse the conceptual and geographical divide between the space and Canal Street.

The *Queer Urban Walk* in Curry Mile not only lay bare and queered dominant assumptions built into the space, specifically regarding issues of sexuality and race, but also provided enough spontaneity in the walk itself to prevent it from becoming prescriptive. As the Collective notes on its website, the use of navigators, in particular, allowed the walk to become 'directly responsive to the surrounding urban environment in a way that would only happen at that time, on that day'.[73] The loose structure of the walk engendered a sensibility of ambling, rather than purposeful, directed walking. In particular, the readings that punctuated the walk focused the group's attention from time to time, whereas the temporal and spatial gaps between readings encouraged conversation among participants or more personalized mappings of space.

The walk helped some participants recall personal memories connected to the space. As British urban studies scholar Steve Pile notes, the network of streets of urban cities 'both produce and contain memories … in a flash, the past, the present and the future are combined and recombined'.[74] One individual was reminded of her experiences as a student living in Rusholme in the 1980s, and was struck by how much the topography of the area now known as Curry Mile had shifted since that time. For instance, she vividly remembered the sight and smell of the butchers' shops that are no longer there.[75]

In his book *The Body and the City: Psychoanalysis, Space and Subjectivity* Pile provides an inroad into more rigorously theorizing the relationship between psychic processes and space, or psycho-spatiality. He rereads Lefebvre's *Production of Space* through a psychoanalytic lens and expands considerably on Freud's suggestion in his *Civilization and Its Discontents* (1930) that the traces of the past embedded in the architecture of urban spaces are similar to the ways in which our minds preserve traces of the past alongside new memories.[76] Pile argues cogently that 'if mental processes are analogous to the city, then its location … needs to be foregrounded'.[77]

The walk was implicitly organized in the spirit of the French Situationists International (SI), successor to the Letterist International, which was founded in 1957 by activists, artists and writers committed not only to exploring urbanism and socio-spatial relations, but also to changing them.[78] In particular, the Letterist International coined the term 'psychogeographies' to describe the exploration of the cities on foot through '*dérives*', or wanderings, by members of the organization. Although Doorstep's walk did not result in literal 'maps', it did attempt to reveal and question the politics of the spatial identification of Curry Mile in terms of race and sexuality. In this way, Doorstep's walk underscored the 'rights to the city',[79] which Situationist associate Henri Lefebvre argued, related to the right to dwell in and inhabit the city. For instance, some of the members of Sphere *felt* their right to inhabit Curry Mile was compromised.

In connection with the walk, I also organized an educational workshop, 'Mapping Art', for a group of local Year 12 students at Cornerhouse.[80] The students, who were around 17 years old, put together psychogeographies relating to their tour of the Cornerhouse exhibitions, including the Sphere bed that was installed in Cornerhouse at that time. In the morning, I led an hour-long session regarding the complex manner in which art conveys meaning, including discussing form, socio-historical context, synaesthesia, intersectional identifications (of the viewing and implied/explicit authorial subjects) and psycho-spatiality through many of the artworks I have discussed in this book, as well as those of *Mixing It Up*. In addition, we discussed psychogeographies through a series done by contemporary artists related to Manhattan.

In the afternoon, a staff member gave the students a tour of the exhibition *Outside the Box*, which was on display at Cornerhouse, while I gave a tour of Sphere's artworks. More importantly, students created psychogeographical maps of the exhibitions using magazines, newspapers, glue sticks, scissors and coloured markers. Their representations of their *dérives* were a mixture of the literal maps of the paths they took through the exhibitions and mental maps of particular places, time periods or abstract thoughts invoked by the tour. The diversity of the visual maps highlighted the ability of urban subjects to re-map space – in this case an art space – and even tours, no matter how scripted.

Some of the maps were also multi-sensorial and explicitly participatory. One student incorporated his iPod into his map, directing the viewer to listen to particular songs at several points. Another student sprayed perfume on her map. Indeed, the students' maps were much more multi-sensorial than those produced by the pioneers of the Situationist movement in the 1960s in Paris, which tended to be organized by what they saw or a disembodied sight.[81]

Currying Canal Street

After the *Queer Urban Walk* concluded, participants were invited to visit the exhibition in which Sphere's bed was placed at the Whitworth Art Gallery, about a 15-minute walk from the endpoint of the walk. The final project in the series of events held on Ramadan took place at Sangam Restaurant. As a reflection of the generosity central to Eid al-Fitr and the breaking of the fast at the end of Ramadan, each of the participants was given an assortment of appetizers and a chance to continue discussions related to the project. At least one of the participants also broke his fast with us.[82]

At the end of the meal, artist Paul Stanley, whose artworks I encountered through my association with the Doorstep Collective, gave out slices of cake/

artwork as part of a series of performances exploring the connection between visual and embodied knowledge. Stanley appropriated an image of a chicken tikka kebab for the surface of his cake (Plate 22). The bodily sensation typically evoked by the image confounded the sugary sweetness expected of the confectionery on which it was found. Stanley did not choose the image specifically for *Mixing It Up*; he had been using it in his larger series for some time. This is not surprising given that food in general, and Asian food in particular, is approached visually as well as through taste and smell.[83]

Responses to the cake illustrated the power of the visual to affect taste and smell. For instance, many participants were somewhat disgusted by the idea of consuming a cake they initially assumed would taste like chicken tikka. Even after some participants learned that the cake was not chicken tikka flavoured, they noted that the embodied response to the sight of the chicken tikka overpowered any of their rational faculties; they still tasted chicken tikka. Moreover, the artwork drew attention to the connection between visual and socially constructed knowledge embedded in the body by subverting how subjects habitually responded to visual stimuli – for instance perceived 'South Asian' or 'gay' subjects in the city.

The final two projects associated with *Mixing It Up* were situated in and around the spaces of Canal Street – another performative walk organized by the Doorstep Collective and a performance by Ajha, a Manchester-based musical collective that included Sphere member Jaheda Choudhury, Samira Arhin-Acquaah (aka Lucid) and Jaydev Mistry. Doorstep Collective's *Queer Urban Walk* was similar to the Curry Mile walk, but covered Canal Street instead. The walk took place on 2 October 2007, two weeks before the walk on Curry Mile, and the 'navigator' had not yet been incorporated into the project. Instead, the Collective steered the group to arbitrary locations around Canal Street. Participants' readings of the best and worst memories culled from subjects from both Curry Mile and Canal Street served to punctuate the overall walk, much like the walk situated around Curry Mile, with breaks to focus everyone's attention from time to time.

The Ajha collective performed an hour of songs I commissioned on 22 November 2007 at the Joseph Perrier Lounge of Taurus Bar and Restaurant on Canal Street.[84] The songs incorporated multilingual lyrics (English, Bengali and Hindi) and incorporated a range of styles, such as spoken word, hip-hop, rock, funk, bangla folk and Bollywood. The pastiche of various musical styles destabilized any of them as distinct, and also reworked dominant associations of misogyny and homophobia connected to hip-hop, in particular. More importantly, the music served as a counterpoint to the homogenous, English-language club and pop music drifting out of most Canal Street venues, and underscored the importance of the aural in the construction of urban spatial identification. Indeed, like the student's psychogeographical map utilizing an

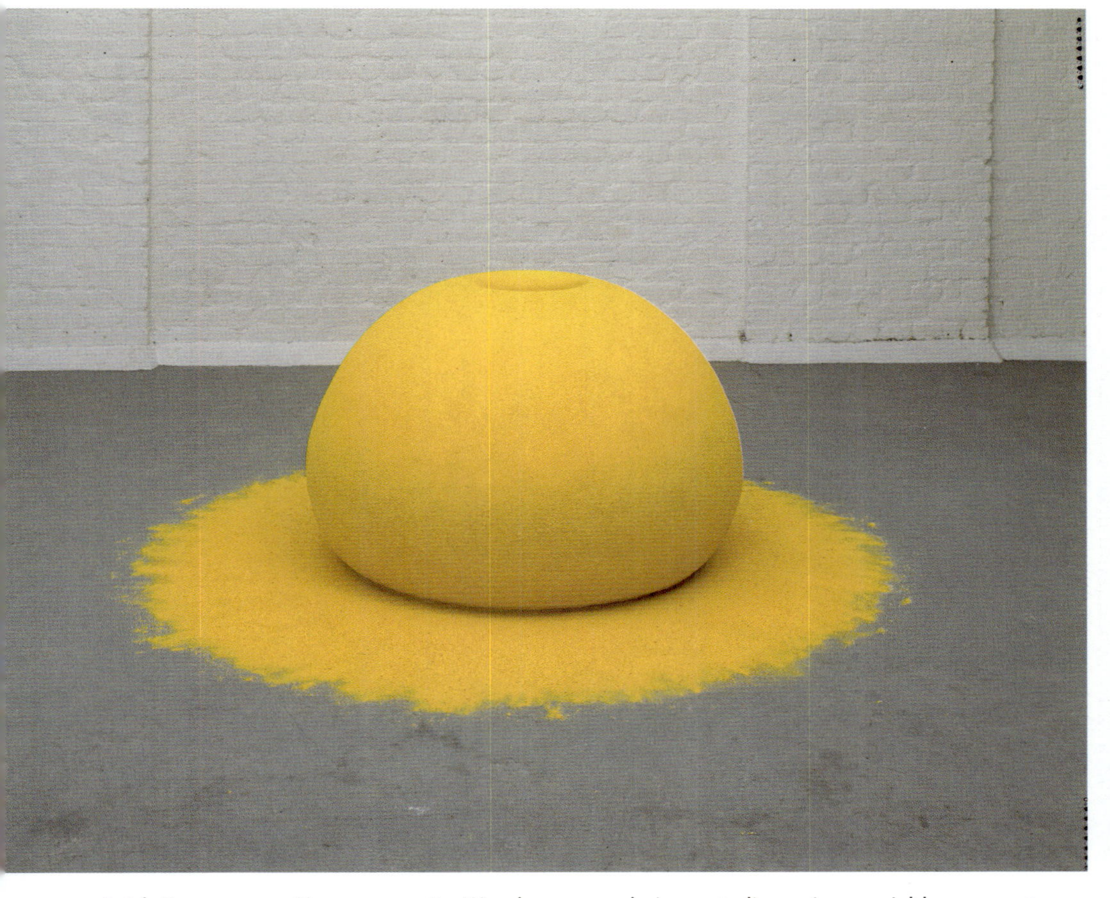

Anish Kapoor, *1000 Names*, 1979–80. Wood, gesso and pigment, dimensions variable. 1

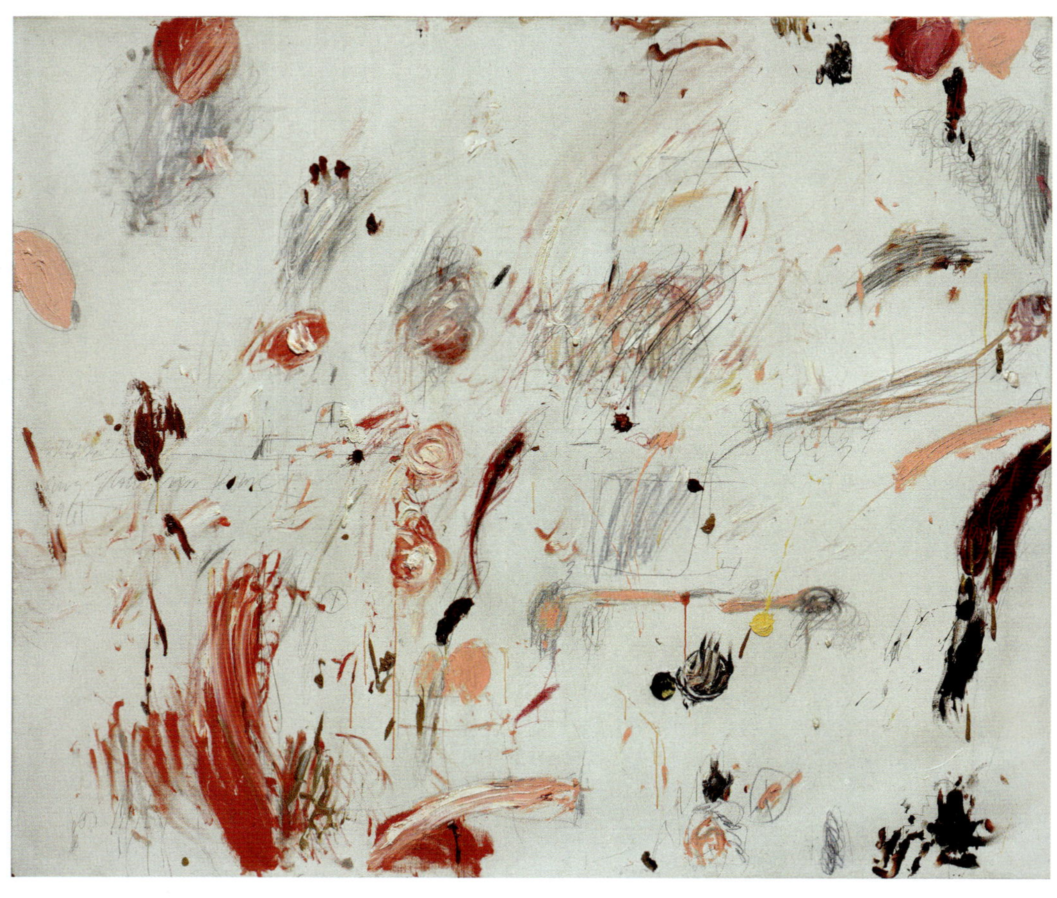

2 Cy Twombly, *Ferragosto II*, 1961. Oil, oil crayon and pencil on canvas, 64¾ × 78⅞ in. (164.5 × 200.3 cm).

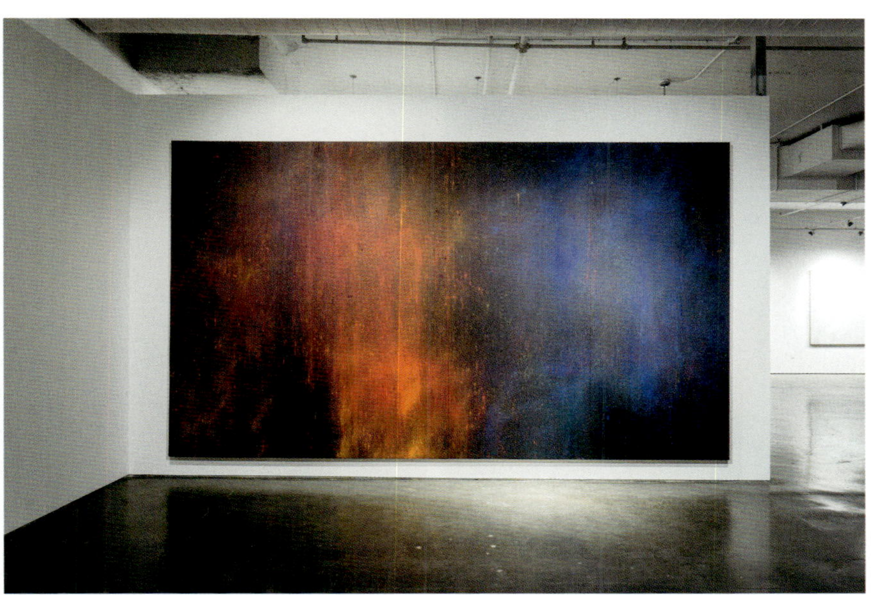

Natvar Bhavsar, *VAATRI*, 1969. Pigment, oil and acrylic on canvas, 108 × 192 in. 3

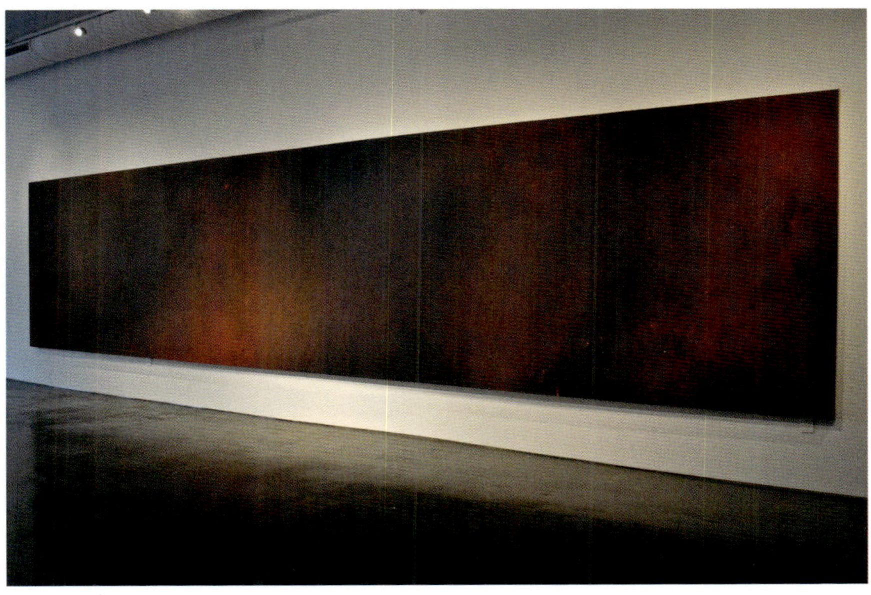

Natvar Bhavsar, *THEER-A-THEER-A*, 1969. Pure pigment, oil and acrylic on canvas, 81.5 × 360 in. 4

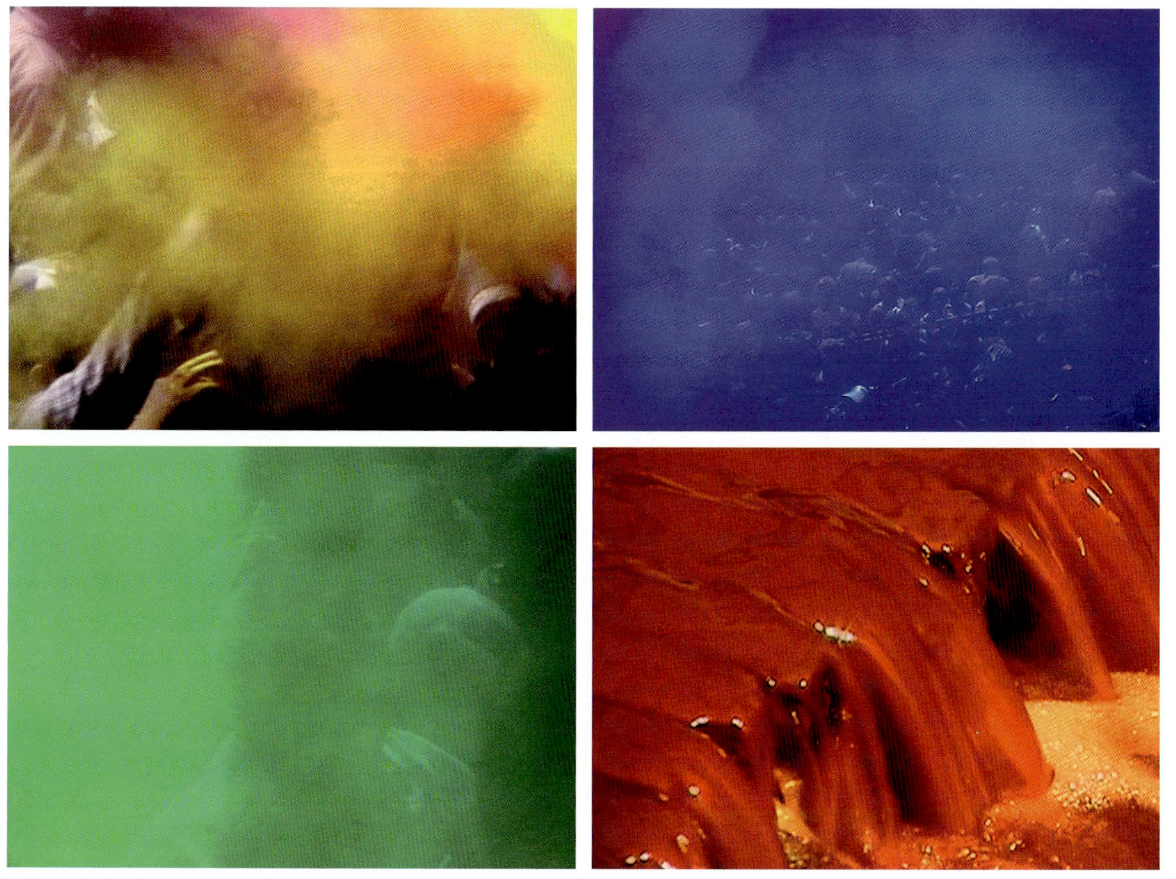

Stephen Dean, Stills from *Pulse*, 2001. Video installation, sound, 7:20 min.

5

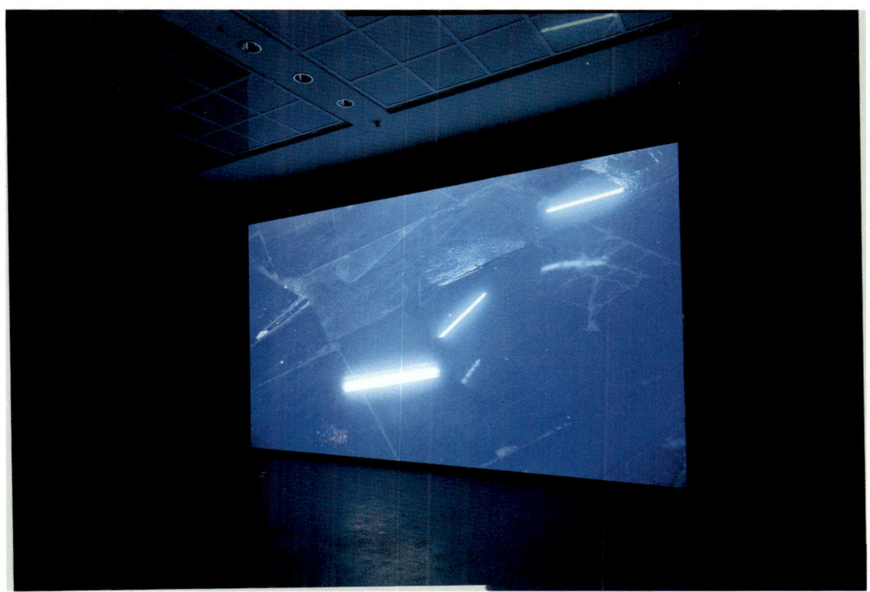

Mario Pfeifer, *A Formal Film in Nine Episodes, Prologue & Epilogue*, 2010. 35 mm film transferred to HD video; stereo, 52 min; multiple projections for exhibition space (variable). Hindi, Tamil with English subtitles. Installation view: MMK Museum für Moderne Kunst, Frankfurt am Main, 2012–13. **6**

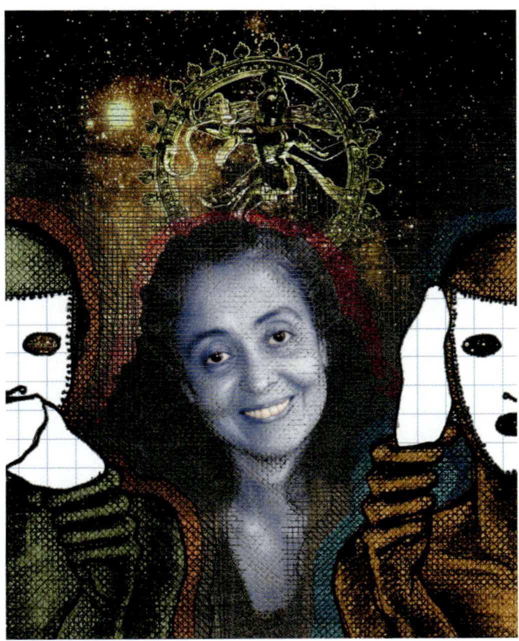

Adrian Piper, *The Color Wheel Series, Second Adhyasa: Pranamayakosha II. 102 (Adrian Piper)* (7/31/01). 8.25 × 10 in. 600 dpi. Pantone #5767 CVC, 287 CVC, 1385 CVC. **7**

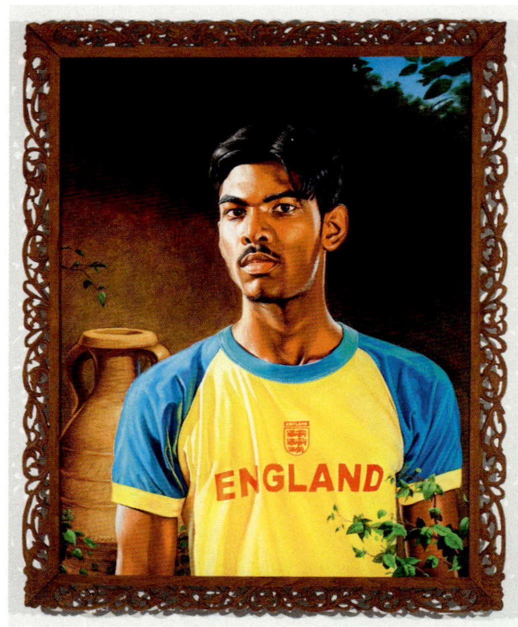

8 Kehinde Wiley, *Femme Fellah*, 2010. Oil on canvas, 45 × 36 in.

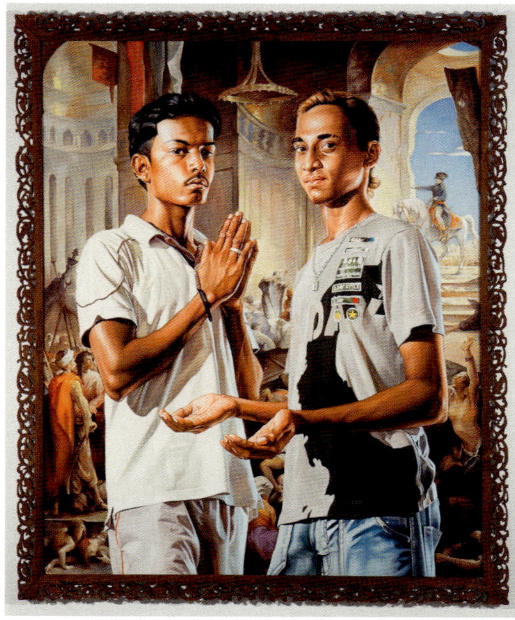

9 Kehinde Wiley, *Bonaparte in the Great Mosque of Cairo*, 2010. Oil on canvas, 60 × 72 in.

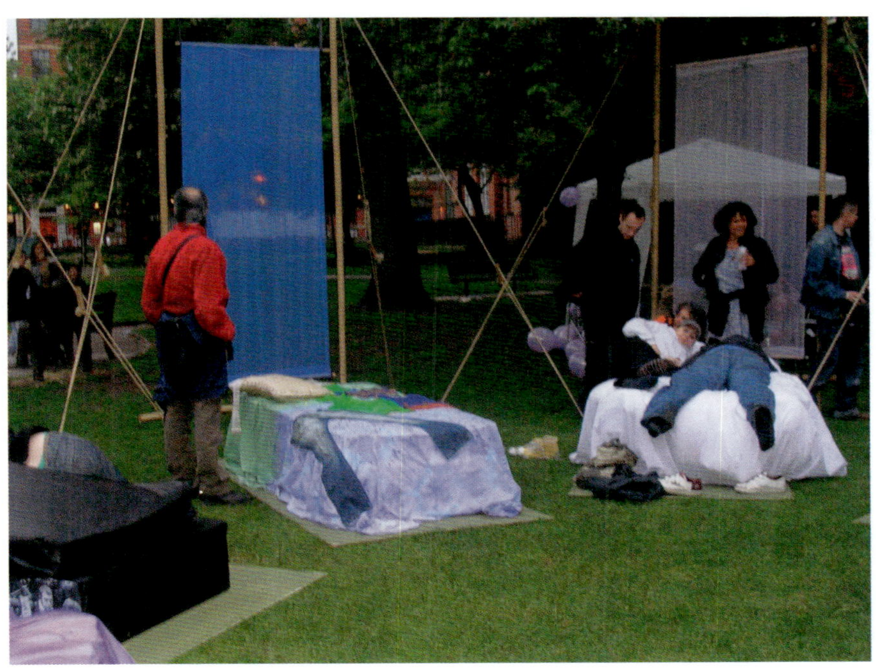

Sphere *Sphere:dreamz*, Sackville Park, Manchester, England, Spring 2006.  10

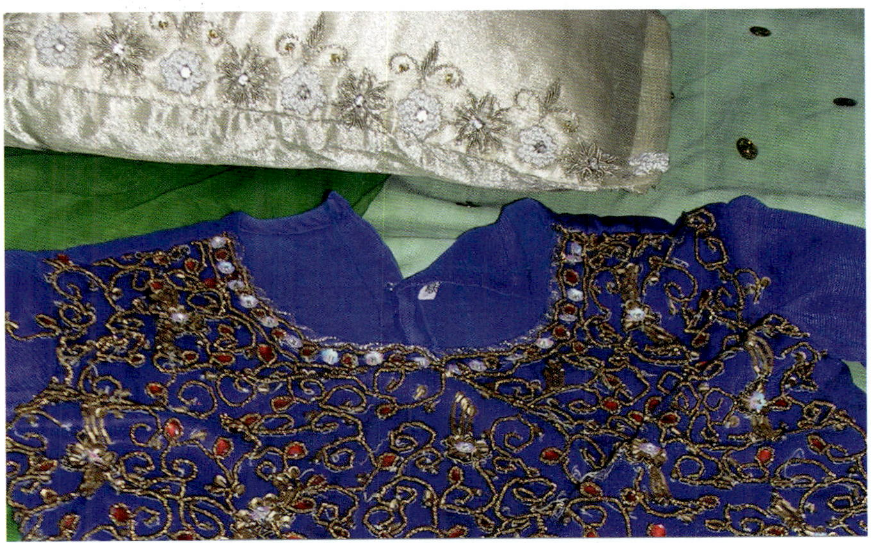

Sphere, *Sphere:dreamz*, Sackville Park, Manchester, England, Spring 2006. 11

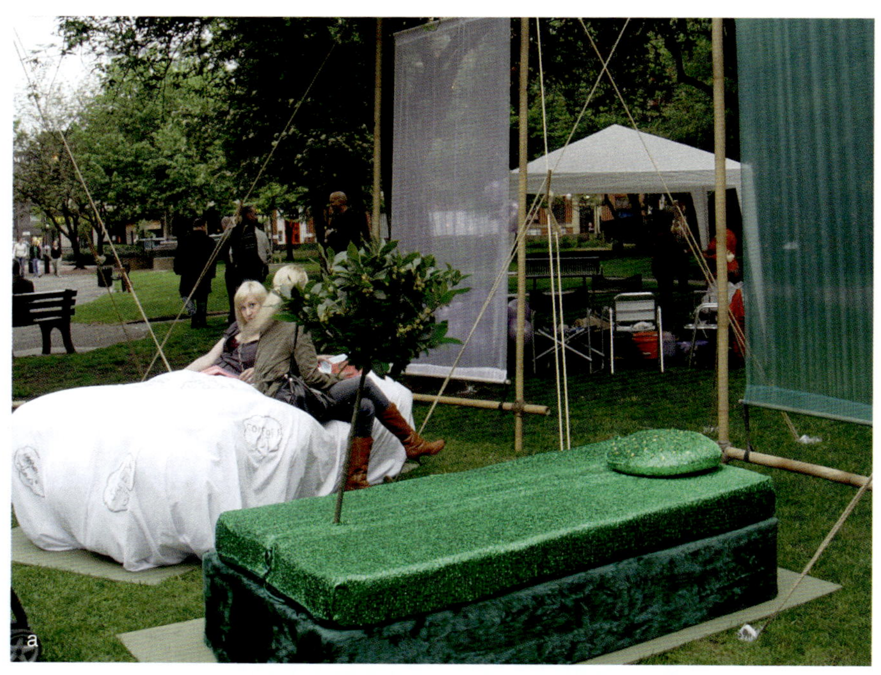

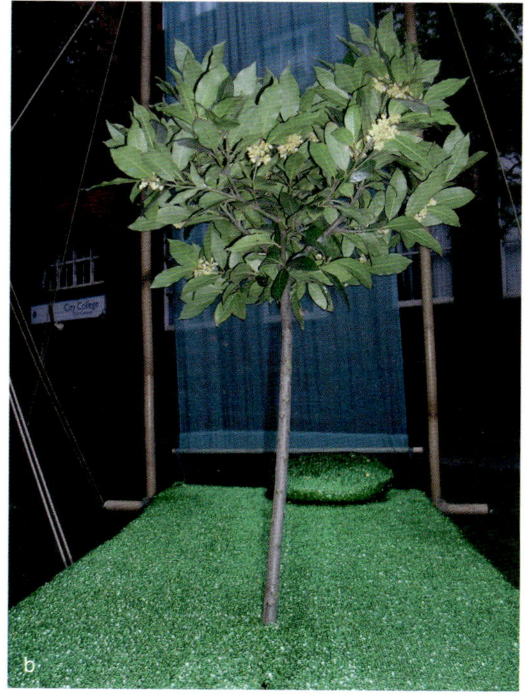

12 Sphere, *Sphere:dreamz*, Sackville Park, Manchester, England, Spring 2006.

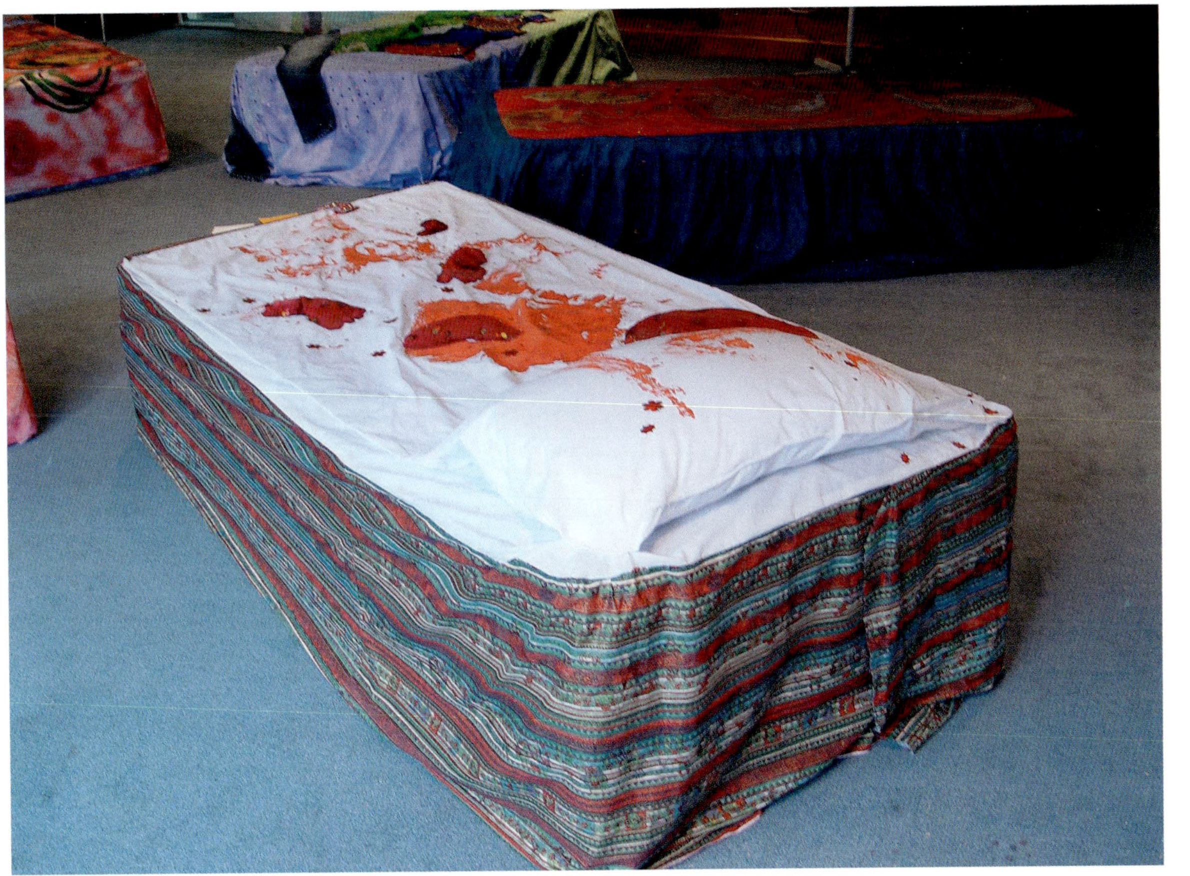

Sphere, *Sphere:dreamz*, Sackville Park, Manchester, England, Spring 2006.

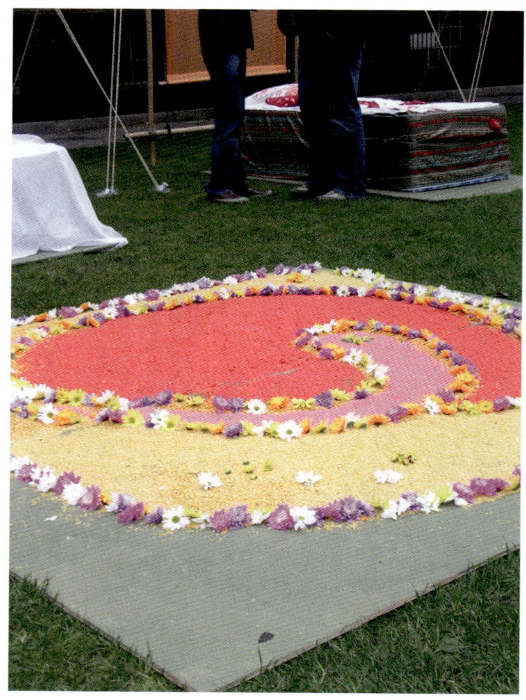

14 Sphere, *Sphere:dreamz*, Sackville Park, Manchester, England, Spring 2006.

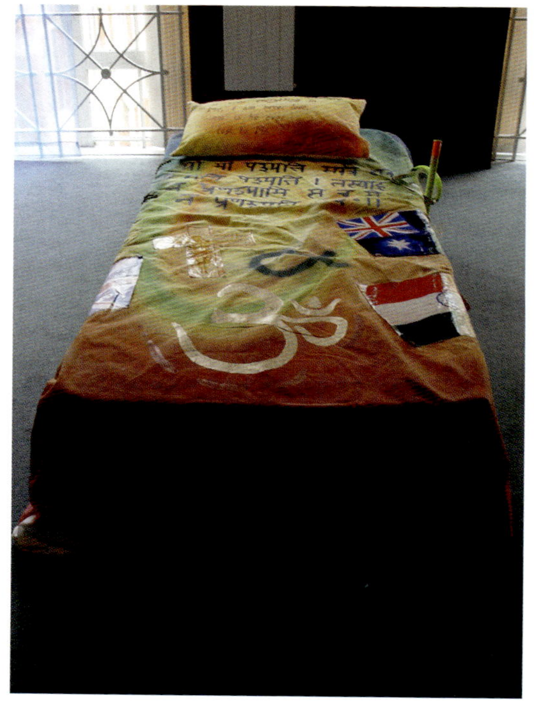

15 Sphere, *Sphere:dreamz*, Sackville Park, Manchester, England, Spring 2006.

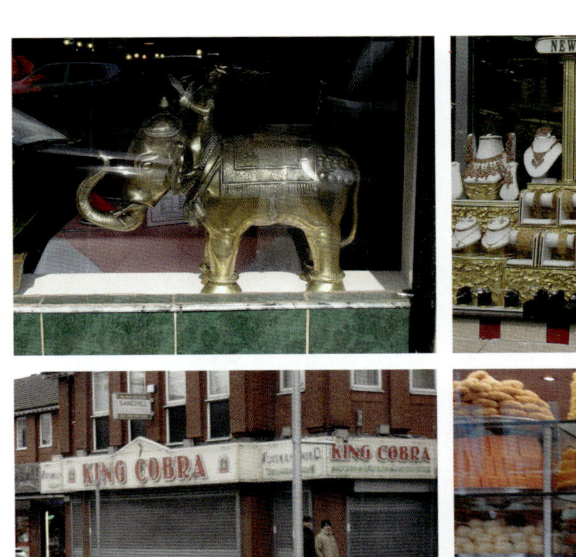

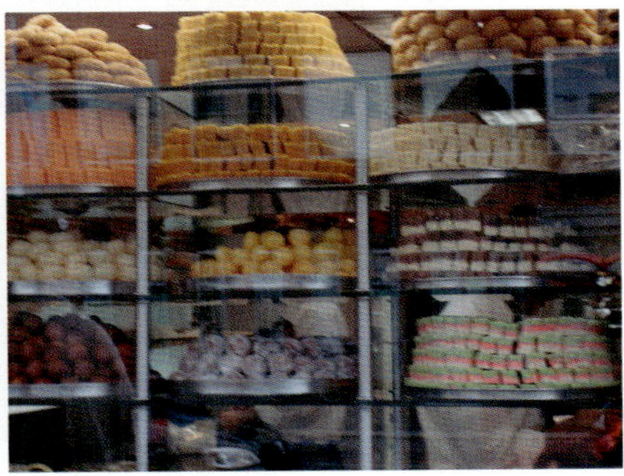

Photos of walk down Curry Mile, Manchester, England, 2007. **16**

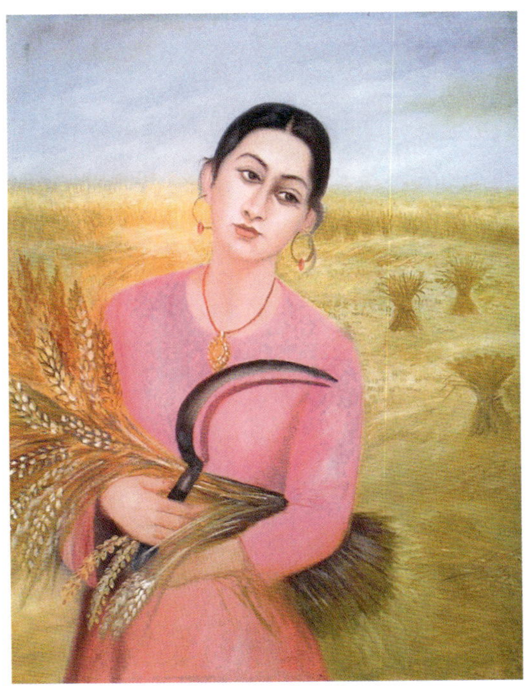

Painting installed in Shahenshah restaurant. Manchester, England, 2008. **17**

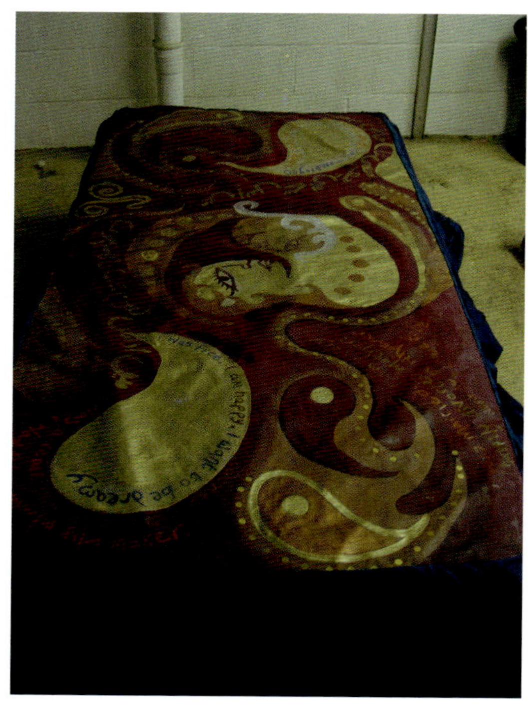

18 Sphere, Bed placed in Sangam Restaurant, Manchester, England, October 2007.

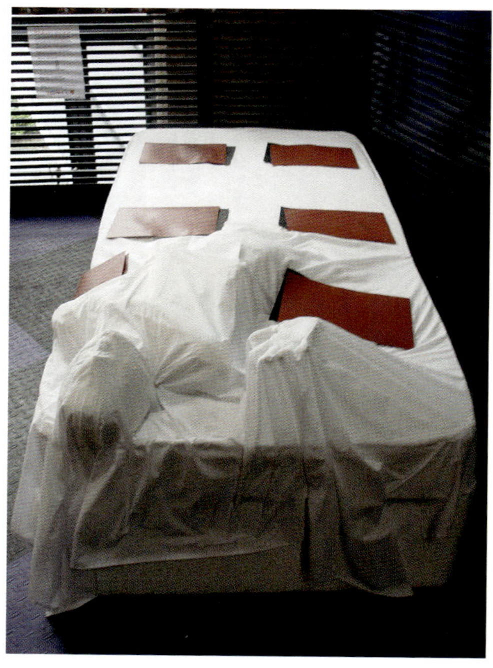

19 Sphere, Detail of *Sphere:dreamz* installation, Whitworth Art Gallery, The University of Manchester, Manchester, England, October 2007.

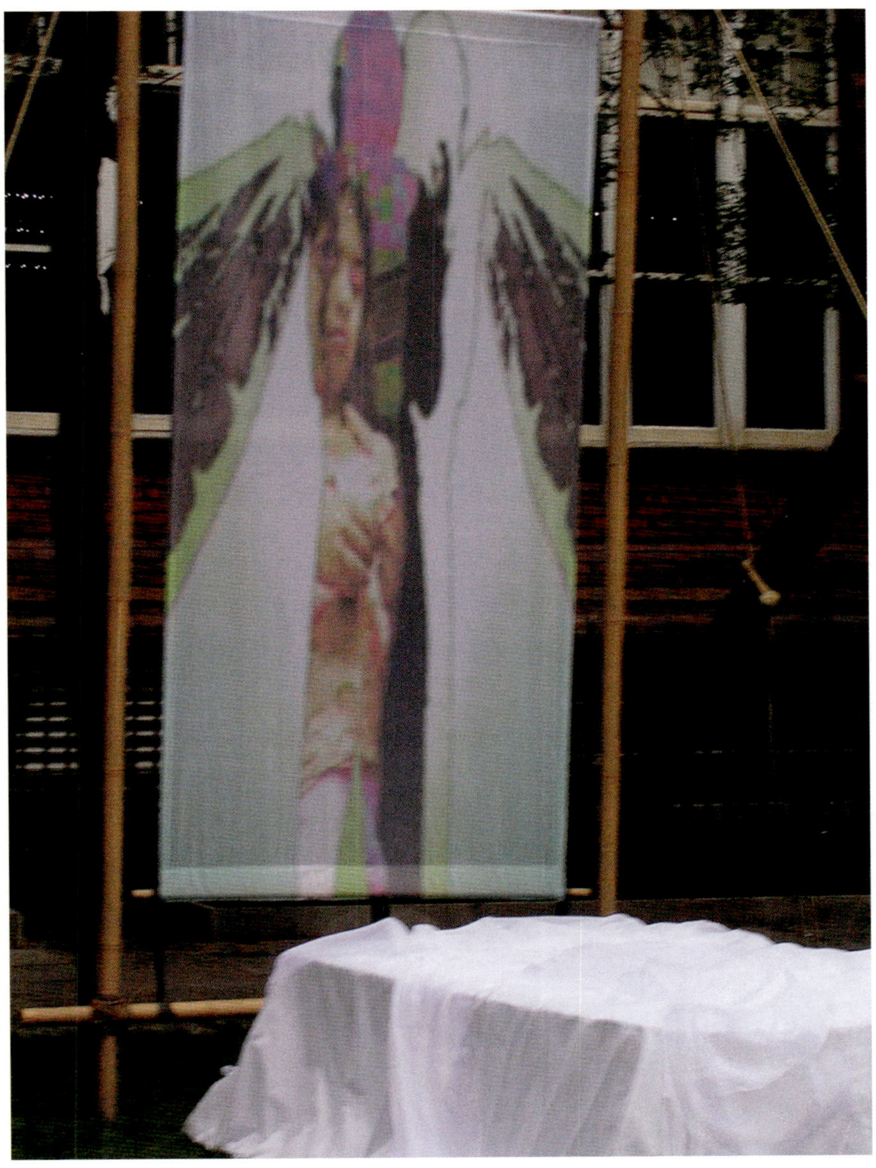

Sphere, Organza screens from bed frames of *Sphere:dreamz* re-sited to Cornerhouse, Manchester, England, September–November 2007. **20**

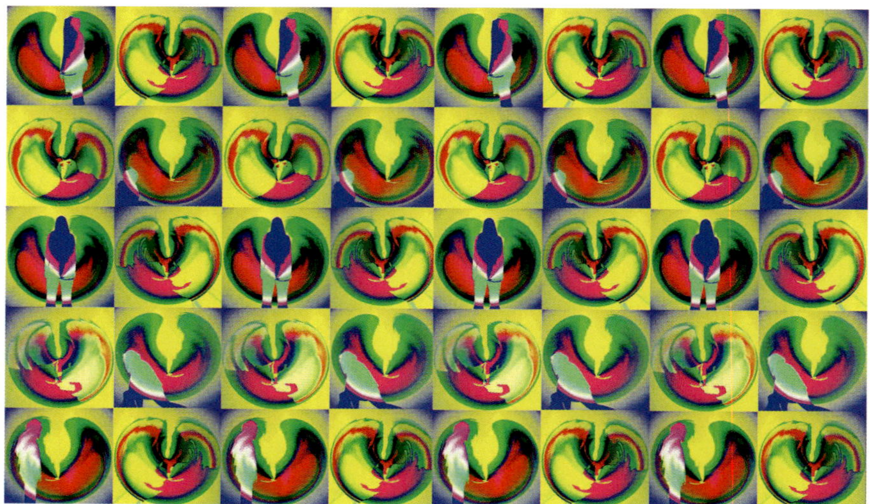

21 Sphere, *Untitled* (wall mural), Cornerhouse, Manchester, England, September–November 2007.

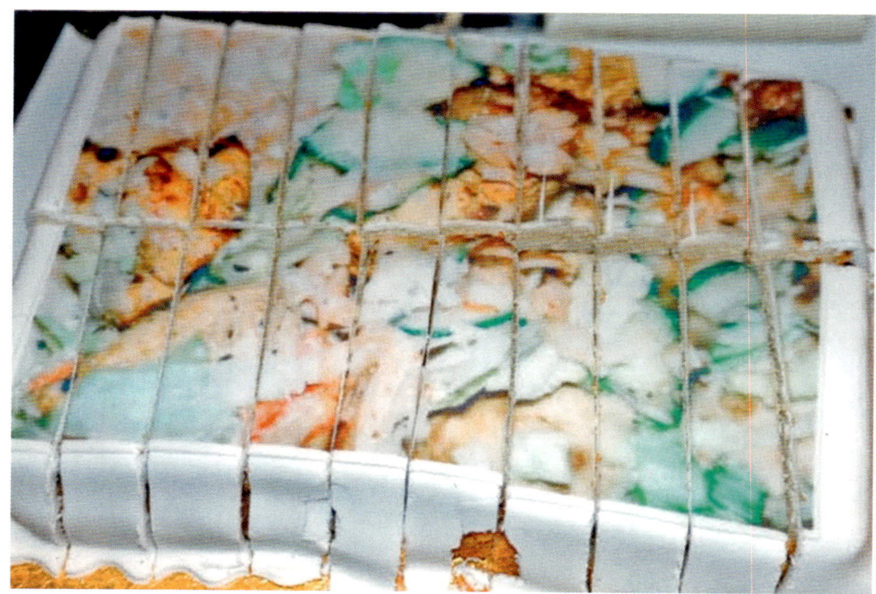

22 Paul Stanley, *Generosity Cake Project*, Sangam Restaurant, Manchester, England, 2007 (end of Ramadan).

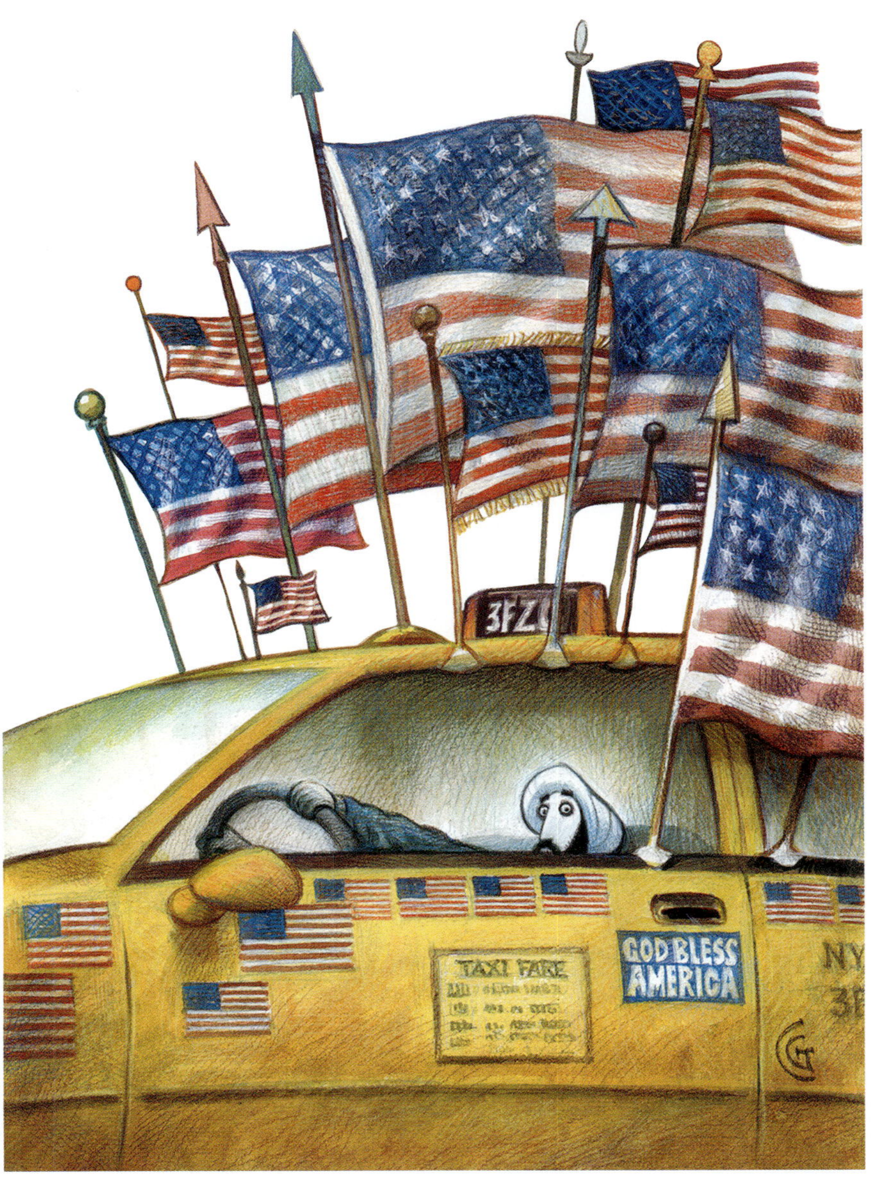

Carter Goodrich, *Untitled*, 2001. Watercolour and coloured pencil. Cartoon used for cover of 5 November 2001 issue of *The New Yorker*.

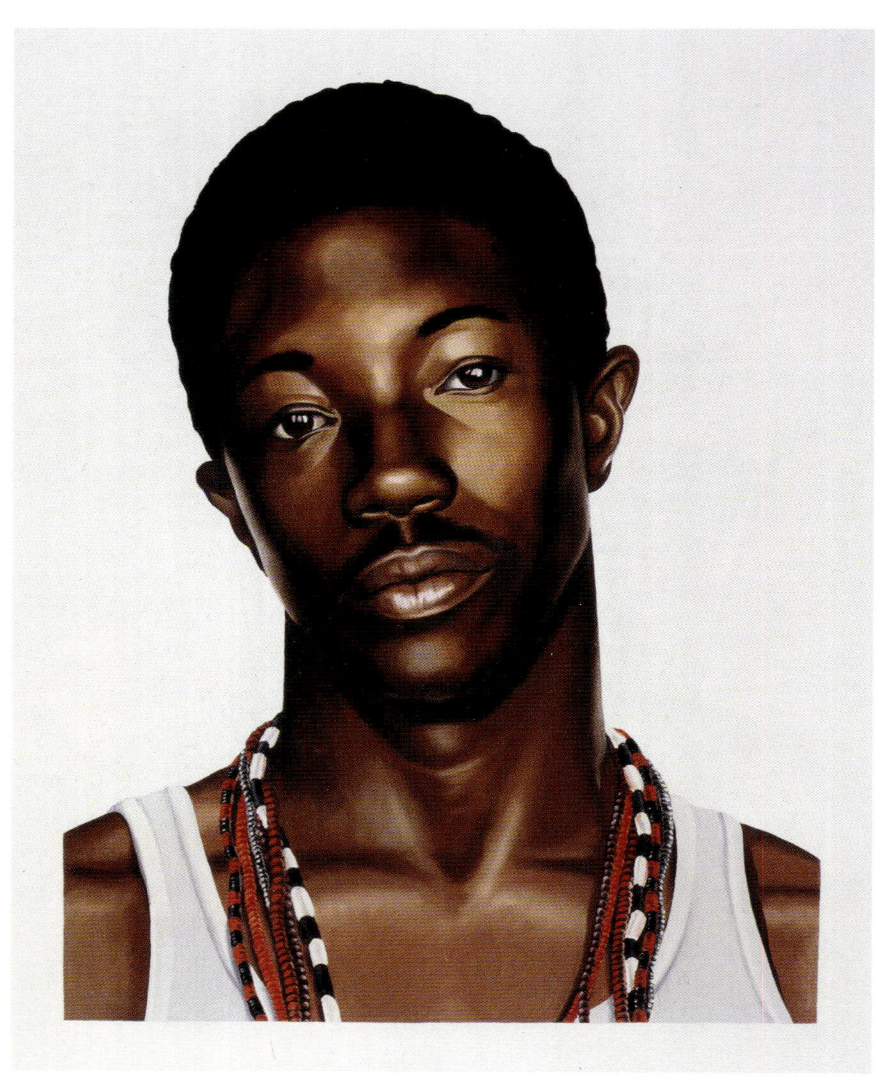

24 Kehinde Wiley, *Mugshot Study*, 2006. Oil on canvas, 36 × 24 in. The Sender Collection, New York.

iPod, Ajha's project was particularly useful in highlighting the manner in which sound, and song in particular, plays in the formation of subjects in urban space.

Towards a theorization of an ethical and embodied public sphere

German philosopher Jürgen Habermas's theory of the 'public sphere' and the copious critiques it has generated are instructive in unpacking how the various projects *Mixing It Up* might have reshaped the dominant spatial identifications of the Gay Village. Habermas theorized the public sphere as a socio-historical specific democratic space that emerged in the wake of, or in contestation of, absolutist monarchism in seventeenth- and eighteenth-century Europe.[85] Within this public sphere – which included coffeehouses, newspapers and museums, for instance – the rising bourgeois middle class debated matters of 'public' interest and acted as a watchdog to oversee the government.

Habermas's theory, based on a specific moment in European history, has been difficult to transplant into a contemporary context for a number of reasons, such as its presumptive disembodied, but still normatively white, heterosexual male subject, and its idealist notions of equal access to the public sphere – all of which have been highlighted by a plethora of scholars whose work has influenced my own theorization of an embodied public sphere. For instance, German sociologist Oskar Negt and filmmaker Alexander Kluge have described the public sphere as a site of competing public spheres, or 'counterpublics', and feminist literature scholar Nancy Fraser has articulated a more specific variant of the latter, 'subaltern counterpublics', to describe the manner in which marginalized groups contest or compete with the dominant public sphere.[86] Fraser conjoins Negt and Kluge's counterpublic with Gayatri Chakravorty Spivak's 'subaltern', a discursive category to describe a broad range of subjects who are constructed as having no agency.[87]

Habermas himself has noted that his conception of the public sphere would have been different had he considered 'the dynamics of those processes of communication … excluded from the dominant public sphere'.[88] Both Fraser's and Negt and Kluge's models supplant Habermas's utopic mono-public sphere with a persuasive but perhaps equally undesirable scenario of incessantly multiplying public spheres that do not overlap. As queer and literary theorist Michael Warner has astutely noted, 'there are contradictions and perversities inherent in the organization of *all* publics, tensions that are not captured by critiques of the dominant public's exclusions or ideological limitations. Counterpublics are publics, too.'[89]

Perhaps more useful than the counterpublic model noted above is Carol Breckenridge and Arjun Appadurai's theorization of a 'public culture' in the context of India as a '*zone* of cultural debate' in which the tensions and contradictions between various cultural processes play out.[90] Also compelling is Belgian political theorist Chantal Mouffe's theorization of an agonistic public sphere. An 'agon' is an ancient Greek word that refers to a contest or struggle, the end result of which is not as important as the process itself.[91] Mouffe's agonistic public sphere highlights *conflictual* consensus in the spirit of agon. She further notes that, 'While there is no underlying principle of unity' in her public sphere, she is also not advocating 'the kind of dispersion envisaged by some postmodernist thinkers.'[92] Both Breckenridge and Appadurai's 'public culture' and Mouffe's 'agonistic public sphere' envisage fragmentation of a mono-public culture/sphere into smaller *counter* public cultures/spheres, as well as potential connections among these smaller counter public cultures/spheres.

The reworking of Habermas's public sphere can also be linked to a much larger debate that has positioned his theorization in opposition to the post-structuralist theories of both Jacques Derrida and Michel Foucault. Given my reliance on deconstruction and notions of discourse early in the book, it is worth considering this debate further. Whereas Habermas's public sphere theory stems from his strong belief that the project of modernity and enlightenment is not complete and that further work on rational critique remains to be done, Foucauldian discourse theory and Derridean deconstruction are based on an inherent pessimism toward such totalistic and rational positions.[93] In this way, my exploration of reworking the dominant public sphere is somewhat at odds with my invocation of Habermas's public sphere.

Despite this apparent contradiction, Foucault has downplayed the philosophical differences between himself and Habermas in at least one interview by noting that 'one must not be for nonconsensuality, but one must be against consensuality'.[94] Although Foucault's statement is admittedly abstruse, it suggests that the non-consensuality of theories of discourse and deconstruction and the consensuality of Habermas's public sphere cannot be simplified to a facile Manichean opposition. For instance, Habermas's later theorization of a public sphere based on 'communicative actions' – or actions oriented to understanding, as opposed to 'instrumental actions', or actions oriented towards success – rather than a public sphere based on consensuality, indicates that the public sphere is formed through difference and is always in flux.[95]

Art historian Frazer Ward sums up nicely why Habermas's public sphere cannot be completely jettisoned. He explains that 'given on the one hand the contemporary dominance of mass media, and on the other, the balkanization of identity politics and its tendency to degenerate into a field of clashing particularized claims … a necessarily modified Habermasian scheme demands attention'.[96] Therefore, I straddle the admittedly fine line between consensuality and non-consensuality towards my theorization of a visible and embodied, queer and transnational South Asian public sphere.

Drawing on the scholarship of Negt and Kluge in 1972 in which they emphasized modes of communication ('publicity') over the resulting site of communication ('public sphere'), Ward has encouraged a shift in thinking about the function of artwork as a form of publicity.[97] Ward defines publicity in the context of art as 'all those practices of intervention in economies of cultural production and reception that go to realize conceptions of the public sphere'.[98] As forms of publicity, *Sphere:dreamz* aimed to give 'rise to debates and opinions' that could contribute to altering the public sphere. Thus, the work allowed 'both conceptions of the public sphere and of collective identifications within and across categories of social difference [to] coalesce'.[99]

In fact, all of the projects of *Mixing it Up* functioned in a similar way.[100] The projects also aimed to yoke together the civic and commercial rational construction of the Gay Village and Curry Mile with their supposedly irrational other – the transnational South Asian in the former and the queer in the latter. In so doing, the projects attempted to uncover the irrationality, itself, of the supposedly normative constructions of both spaces.

Art historian Miwon Kwon refers to Fraser's work in noting that 'an effort to imagine a democratic public sphere anew is necessarily an exercise in abstraction, the (art) work to be done seems to be located in the space of coming together of this different sort of intimacy and publicity'.[101] Warner also underscores the need to flesh out a public sphere (whether agonistic or counter) 'in which embodied sociability, affect, and play have a more defining role than they do in the opinion-transposing frame of rational-critical dialogue'.[102] British sociologist Nick Crossley theorizes an embodied public sphere. Crossley combines Habermasian public sphere theory and Maurice Merleau-Ponty's phenomenology in order to construct a model of a more embodied public sphere, as well as a more ethical phenomenology.[103] Crossley's scholarship helps to bridge the various theories of the public sphere I have recounted, if only implicitly. His public sphere is not only an affective and embodied one (per Warner and Kwon), but also one in which artwork as publicity (per Negt and Kluge and Ward) can be envisioned as making felt – if only transient – connections among different, perhaps conflicting, counterpublics or subjects within a public culture (per Mouffe and Breckenridge and Appadurai); such a public sphere is both ethical and embodied, but ultimately also processual.

To add traction to my descriptions and interpretations of the various projects presented, I conclude with a section presenting evidence on *Mixing It Up*'s impact – such as responses culled from those who experienced the art projects, as well as radio and print press – even if this paradoxically requires me to admit that my hopes and 'intentions' were not always realized. The latter both reveals and attempts to minimize potential conflict between my roles as producer and evaluator of *Mixing It Up*.

By presenting responses to *Mixing It Up* in tandem with my own descriptions and interpretations of the various projects, I am indeed attempting to straddle the fine line I noted earlier between the consensuality of Habermas's public sphere model, a variant of which I theorized, and the non-consensuality of deconstruction and discourse. The former is politically important in elucidating how a queer and transnational South Asian subjectivity can become more visible and felt in both Curry Mile and the Gay Village, whereas the latter ensures that the visibility of queer transnational South Asian identifications as sometimes achieved by the *Mixing It Up* projects does not become normalized or imply a facile stability.

Notes on reception of *Mixing It Up*

Ajha's music and Stanley's *Generosity Cake Project* were especially useful in providing insight into theorizing subject formation in urban space as multisensorial. Doorstep Collective's walks, as well as the psychogeographies produced by the students who were part of the 'Mapping Art' workshop, highlighted the effect of site/place on subject formation and the ways in which subjects queer urban spaces everyday in perhaps small ways. Meanwhile, Sphere's projects helped to consider the very different effects *types* of space, institutional or commercial, can have on artistic meaning, as well as the tensions inherent among queer, transnational South Asian and gender identifications, which underscored the importance of an intersectional approach.

Responses to the various art projects that indicated that the aims of the projects were not quite achieved were similarly useful in informing the critical writing of this book. For example, a participant in a feedback session about the walk on Canal Street assumed most of the stories being read were authored by gay men. However, none of the stories belied their creator's identification. Her assumption seemed to confirm the dominant construction of Canal Street as gay, and thereby reinforced the importance of site or place to visual identification, albeit unwittingly. In another example, a member of the audience at Ajha's performance on Canal Street misidentified one of the members of the collective, Lucid, as a man, and therefore misinterpreted a romantic duet between Lucid and Choudhury, two queer-identified women, as one between a heterosexual couple.[104] Her misidentification indicated the supplementarity, or slippage, of queer, transnational South Asian as an identification and that visual identification is always negotiated between and within viewing and viewed subjects.

Feedback about the trio of art events on Ramadan also revealed an issue that remained largely implicit in all the *Mixing It Up* projects: the tacit manner in which the politics of whiteness functions in art projects concerning race.[105] For instance, one participant noted the following in reference to the *Queer Urban Walk* and the dinner:

> A friend and I discussed the unsettling appearance of a group of (mostly) white, or at least arty-type people taking up the back streets of Rusholme and even our 'private' party upstairs at Sangam.[106]

Though an official survey of how participants identified themselves in terms of class, race, sexuality or gender was not conducted, the comment above is fairly accurate in terms of my own memory of the apparent class and ethnic appearance of the participants. Furthermore, whereas Sphere's installations generally involved the intimate participation of one person with a bed – this was more the case with the bed in the Whitworth Art Gallery than in Sangam Restaurant – the *Generosity Cake Project* and the *Queer Urban Walk* were group participatory events in which the apparent class status and whiteness of the participants inevitably became much more pronounced.

Another participant that evening noted the relative vocal, visual and felt absence of the queer South Asian women connected with Sphere, which perhaps further highlighted the apparent non-presence of ethnic subjects. The latter is partly an unfortunate result of the fact that, unlike Sphere's artworks, the *Generosity Cake Project* and the *Queer Urban Walk* involved the artists, who happened to be white, in a more literally visible manner in the execution of the projects.[107] Sphere's artworks, which were installations, required visitor participation, but not necessarily direct artist involvement. The issue of whiteness triggered by some of the projects informed my theorization of the intertwining of the viewing subject, artwork and implied authorial subject in the production of artistic meaning and, in particular, helped me to flesh out my discussion of whiteness in Chapter 4.

In terms of press, Sphere's bed in Curry Mile, in particular, received a significant amount of attention from Asian newspapers, lesbian and queer-focused websites and publications, and queer and South Asian-focused radio programmes.[108] On the other hand, *Mixing It Up* projects connected to Canal Street and the ORC did not receive much attention at all. The projects on Canal Street and the ORC were implicitly folded into the progressive but facile view of the Gay Village and cultural institutions as open to difference, and therefore perhaps less newsworthy. Furthermore, during my interviews with both Manchester-based BBC radio news programmes, *LGBT Citizen Manchester* and *Indus* (focused on Asian issues), the interviewers steered the discussion to homophobia within the dominant construction of the British South

Asian community, as opposed to issues of racism in Canal Street or sexism in either Canal Street or Curry Mile.[109]

The notes above I offer to prevent my descriptions and interpretations of the artworks as creator of the projects from becoming implicitly totalizing, or, perhaps even worse, from flattening out the complex identity politics underpinning the project. British sociologist Virinder Kalra has provocatively suggested that the *Mixing It Up* projects, specifically Sphere's project in Curry Mile, might become easily enfolded into the 'normative account of the sheen and shine of multicultural Asian Britain'. He writes that:

> South Manchester is produced through a dominant narrative of vibrancy, in the economic and cultural sphere, with Rusholme and the Curry Mile an iconic space in which the City Council can celebrate multiculturalism … In the Northwest, cultural policy in this area has written extensively about Asian exclusion from the arts. Yet Wilmslow Road is also the site where a visual arts project … [of] a South Asian lesbian and gay group (Sphere) can 'mix-it-up'. Indeed, it is the ways in which academic, policy and cultural texts entwine to create a normative account of the sheen and shine of multicultural Asian Britain that creates a blurring, at the level of production as well as creation, of the various genres of writing about Asian Manchester.[110]

Indeed, 'at the level of production as well as creation' it is worth noting that the institutional and governmental funders (University of Manchester, Manchester City Council and Arts Council England) of *Mixing It Up* produce the rhetoric of cosmopolitanism I am critiquing. My hope is that my writings on *Mixing It Up* would work against becoming part of the 'academic, policy and cultural texts [that] entwine to create a normative account of the sheen and shine of multicultural Asian Britain'.

Nonetheless, at the risk of putting a final, polished 'sheen and shine' on the projects of *Mixing It Up* I share the following compelling and optimistic anecdote from the women of Sphere about the installation of the bed in Curry Mile.[111] At the conclusion of the *Mixing It Up* project, when it emerged that some of the waiters of Sangam Restaurant needed beds on which to sleep, the artists donated all eleven beds used in their art project to them. Passing something as intimate as a bed between two camps that had not previously 'mixed' openly, though a simple gesture, indicated the transformative role artworks can play in creating a more intimate and ethical public sphere.

Notes

1 My many thanks to Amelia Jones for her many thoughtful suggestions (including 'Mixing It Up' as a title for the project) and careful reads of multiple drafts of grant proposals, the success of which ultimately made the project possible. Thanks also to Dr Piotr Bienkowski, former Deputy

Director, Manchester Museum, and Professor of Archaeology and Museology, University of Manchester, for his early support and encouragement, as well. In particular, *Mixing It Up* projects were funded by an Arts Council England grant; a Neighbourhood Renewal Funding Culture grant from the Manchester City Council; and a grant from the University of Manchester's Migration, Diaspora and Cultural Studies Network. Major in-kind support was received from the Manchester Museum and the Whitworth Art Gallery, both part of the University of Manchester; Cornerhouse; Sangam Restaurant, Curry Mile; Taurus Bar and Restaurant, Canal Street; and the art collectives Sphere and Doorstep Collective.

2 Gavin Butt (ed.), *After Criticism: New Responses to Art and Performance* (Malden, MA: Blackwell, 2005), 17.

3 Irit Rogoff, '"Smuggling" – An Embodied Criticality', European Institute for Progressive Cultural Policies, *Transversal* (August 2006), 2, http://eipcp.net/transversal/0806/rogoff1/en.

4 Ibid.

5 Carrie Lambert-Beatty, 'The Academic Condition of Contemporary Art', in *Contemporary Art: 1989 to the Present*, ed. Alexander Blair Dumbadze and Suzanne Perling Hudson (Chichester, West Sussex: Wiley-Blackwell, 2013), 463. Though not explicitly cited, I presume Lambert-Beatty is referring to scholarship such as: Amelia Jones, '"Presence" in Absentia: Experiencing Performance as Documentation', *Art Journal* 56, no 4 (Winter 1997): 11–18.

6 Lambert-Beatty, 'The Academic Condition of Contemporary Art', 462.

7 Ibid., 465.

8 'Practice-led research' doctoral programmes emerged in the 1990s for the most part in the UK, mainland Europe and Australia although they developed in different ways in each of these regions. It has a slippery meaning across these geographies as well as disciplinary formations. Though there has been plenty of discussion concerning the legitimacy of doctorates in the visual arts in the United States, they have not flourished there. See, for instance, James Elkins, *Artists with PhDs: On the New Doctoral Degree in Studio Art* (Washington, DC: New Academia Publishing, 2009). For more sources regarding practice-led research in the UK educational system, see the bibliography of the following 2007 report on practice-led research for the Arts & Humanities Research Council (AHRC) – the major governing body for academic research in the arts and humanities in the UK: Chris Rust, Judith Mottram and Jeremy Till, 'AHRC Review of Practice-Led Research in Art, Design & Architecture', Review (Arts & Humanities Research Council, 2 November 2007), http://arts.brighton.ac.uk/__data/assets/pdf_file/0018/43065/Practice-Led_Review_Nov07.pdf.

Discussions about practice-led research are usually focused on studio art practices rather than curating. In my own research developing a curatorial practice programme as part of an existing Master in Fine Arts of Visual Arts degree at Florida International University (FIU), most curatorial programs are closer to art history in character.

9 The mutual exclusivity of 'research' and 'practice' is interrogated in the following: Hazel Smith and R. T. Dean (eds), *Practice-Led Research, Research-Led Practice in the Creative Arts* (Edinburgh: Edinburgh University Press, 2009). See also Michael Ann Holly and Marquard Smith (eds), *What Is Research in the Visual Arts?: Obsession, Archive, Encounter* (New Haven, CT: Yale University Press, 2008). Based on the proceedings of the Clark Conference 'What is research in the visual arts?: obsession, archive, encounter' held on 27 and 28 April 2007 at the Sterling and Francine Clark Institute, Williamstown, Massachusetts.

10 Rogoff, '"Smuggling" – An Embodied Criticality', 3 [in full]. She writes further on the same page: 'Moving to "the curatorial" then, is an opportunity to "unbound" the work from all of those categories and practices that limit its ability to explore that which we do not yet know or that which is not yet a subject in the world.'

11 Ibid.

12 Ibid.

13 See David Alderson, 'Queer Cosmopolitanism: Place, Politics, Citizenship and *Queer as Folk*', *New Formations* 55 (2005): 73–88; Jon Binnie and Beverley Skeggs, 'Cosmopolitan Knowledge and the Production and Consumption of Sexualized Space: Manchester's Gay Village', *Sociological Review* 52, no. 1 (February 2004): 39–61; Annette Pritchard, Nigel Morgan and Diane Sedgley, 'In Search of Lesbian Space? The Experience of Manchester's Gay Village', *Leisure Studies* 21, no. 2 (2002): 105–23; Quilley, 'Entrepreneurial Turns: Municipal Socialism and After', in *City of Revolution: Restructuring Manchester*, ed. Jamie Peck and Kevin Ward (Manchester: Manchester University Press, 2002), 91; Steve Quilley, 'Constructing Manchester's "New Urban Village": Gay Space in the Entrepreneurial City', in *Queers in Space: Communities, Public Places, Sites of Resistance*, ed. Gordon Brent Ingram, Anne-Marie Bouthillette and Yolanda Retter (Seattle: Bay Press, 1997), 275–92; Dereka Rushbrook, 'Cities, Queer Space, and the Cosmopolitan Tourist', *GLQ: A Journal of Lesbian and Gay Studies* 8, no. 1 (2002): 183–206; Ian R. Taylor, Karen Evans and Penny Fraser, *A Tale of Two Cities: Global Change, Local Feeling and Everyday Life in the North of England: A Study in Manchester and Sheffield*, International Library of Sociology (London and New York: Routledge, 1996); Craig Young, Martina Diep and Stephanie Drabble, 'Living with Difference? The "Cosmopolitan City" and Urban Reimaging in Manchester, UK', *Urban Studies* 43, no. 10 (1 September 2006): 1687–1714.

14 Marketing Manchester, *Manchester: Where to Stay 2006/07*, brochure (40 pp.).

15 Marketing Manchester, *Manchester: Guided Walks & Tours 2007*, pamphlet (7 pp.).

16 *Visit Manchester*, accessed 7 March 2007, www.visitmanchester.com.

17 Ibid.

18 Emphasis mine. Ibid.

19 Marking Manchester, *Manchester – The Destination*, October 2007, see pp. 54–5 (Culture section) and 26–7 (Places to Eat section).
20 I return to the role of culture in Manchester's civic marketing later in this chapter.
21 Marketing Manchester, *Manchester: Short Breaks*, 2007, fold-out pamphlet.
22 Ibid.
23 This disparity is present in non-Manchester City generated materials, as well. For instance, see Simon Jenkins, 'British Politics Can't Survive If It Treats Provincial Cities as Overseas Colonies', *Guardian*, 5 October 2006, sec. Opinion, www.theguardian.com/commentisfree/2006/oct/06/comment.labourconference. Jenkins praises the cultural diversity of Manchester (including mention of Chinatown and the Gay Village, what he refers to as the 'gay quarter'), but completely forgets to mention Curry Mile. Thanks to Amelia Jones for pointing this article out to me.
24 Marking Manchester, *Manchester – The Destination*, 10–12.
25 Marketing Manchester, *Manchester: Where to Stay 2006/07*, 2–5.
26 *Our Property*, accessed 4 January 2007, www.ourproperty.co.uk.
27 Ed Glinert, *The Manchester Compendium: A Street-by-Street History of England's Greatest Industrial City* (London: Penguin, 2009), 170.
28 The following contains summaries of academic research on issues of skin colour in specific relation to class and subjects of the South Asian diaspora: Francis C. Assisi, 'Color Complex In The South Asian Diaspora', *INDOlink: The Best of Both Worlds*, no date, www.indolink.com/displayArticleS.php?id=062204065913.
29 Quilley, 'Constructing Manchester's "New Urban Village": Gay Space in the Entrepreneurial City', 287. See also his article 'Entrepreneurial Turns: Municipal Socialism and After', 76–94. In the latter, he indicates that the break from municipal socialism to entrepreneurialism can be dated at least partially to Margaret Thatcher's third victory in the general election in June 1987. The latter signalled the defeat of the Labour Party, but also its municipal socialist experiments. See ibid., 87.
30 Gwyndaf Williams, *The Enterprising City Centre : Manchester's Development Challenge* (London and New York: Spon Press, 2003), 249.
31 'The Pink Pound: The Definitive Marketeers Guide to Understanding and Attracting the Gay Consumer', social marketing company, programme for conference held on 22 June 2006 in Westminster, London, *Ingenious Group*, 1, accessed 1 January 2016, http://ingenious-group.com/IGpageimages/pinkpound/Pink_pound_conference.pdf.
32 Ibid., 3.
33 See Andrew Stokes, 'Andrew Stokes', professional networking website, *LinkedIn*, accessed 1 January 2016, https://uk.linkedin.com/in/andrew-stokes-016bb04; 'Andrew Stokes and Steven Small to Leave Marketing Manchester', press release, *Marketing Manchester* (2015), www.marketingmanchester.com/what-we-do/members/andrew-stokes-and-steven-small-to-leave-marketing-manchester.aspx.

34 David Harvey, *The Condition of Postmodernity: An Enquiry into the Origins of Cultural Change* (Oxford; Cambridge, MA: Blackwell, 1989); 'What Are Public Private Partnerships?', *BBC*, 12 February 2003, sec. UK, http://news.bbc.co.uk/2/hi/uk_news/1518523.stm.

35 Emphasis mine. Young, Diep and Drabble, 'Living with Difference? The "Cosmopolitan City" and Urban Reimaging in Manchester, UK', 1688.

36 Rosemary Mellor has argued that the 'hypocritical plan' (Friedrich Engels's phrase) of Manchester during its industrial era can also be evinced in contemporary Manchester's leisure-led re-generation. See Rosemary Mellor, 'Hypocritical City: Cycles of Urban Exclusion', in *City of Revolution Restructuring Manchester*, ed. Jamie Peck and Kevin Ward (Manchester and New York: Manchester University Press, 2002), 214–35.

37 Quilley, 'Entrepreneurial Turns: Municipal Socialism and After'.

38 See 'Save the Gay Centre Manchester Collective', accessed 15 April 2008, http://profile.myspace.com/index.cfm?fuseaction=user.viewprofile&friendid=237110768. Also see 'Save The Gay Centre Manchester Campaign Collective 2007', *YouTube*, accessed 1 January 2016, www.youtube.com/user/savethegaycentremcr.

39 Alan Riding, 'An Industrial City's Architectural Rebirth; New Museums Brighten Manchester', *The New York Times*, 18 July 2002, sec. Arts, www.nytimes.com/2002/07/18/arts/an-industrial-city-s-architectural-rebirth-new-museums-brighten-manchester.html. The Lowry was even cited as 'The British Building of the Year' in 2000 by The Royal Fine Art Commission Trust, ahead of London's Tate Modern, also completed that year.

40 Head of economic and urban policy, 'Manchester: Knowledge Capital, Innovation Nation' (Manchester: Manchester City Council, 10 December 2008), www.manchester.gov.uk/egov_downloads/6_%28MKC%29.pdf.

41 Cornerhouse in 2012 merged with the Library Theatre Company to become 'HOME'. See: http://homemcr.org/about/.

42 John Hyatt, 'Avenue of the Giants: A Public Art Strategy for Manchester Oxford Road', November 2003, www.miriad.mmu.ac.uk/innovation/oxfordroad/ The%20Avenue%20of%20the%20Giants%20text.pdf.

43 Manchester City South Partnership., 'Strategic Development Framework', March 2008, 7, 52, www.corridormanchester.com/_filestore/corridormanchester/city-south-framework-pdf/original/city_south_framework.pdf. The partnership includes Manchester City Council, University of Manchester, Manchester Metropolitan University, North West Regional Development Agency, NHS Trust and Central Manchester and Manchester Children's University Hospitals. The spatial parameters of the Manchester City South Partnership are slightly different from those of the Oxford Road Cultural Corridor Group. The former extends north a little further than the latter to St Peter's Square. However, the southern end of the prescribed area for the Partnership remains identical to that of the Cultural Corridor Group: Whitworth Park. Manchester City South Partnership, 'New Agency Established to Unlock Manchester's Economic Potential – MIDAS', press release (archived), *Invest*

in Manchester (5 March 2008), www.investinmanchester.com/news/archive/new-agency-established-to-unlock-manchesters-economic-potential/.

44 Manchester City South Partnership, 'Strategic Development Framework', 52.

45 Yakub Qureshi, 'Oxford Road to Become an Avenue of Giants', *Manchester Evening News*, 15 February 2007, www.manchestereveningnews.co.uk/news/greater-manchester-news/oxford-road-to-become-an-avenue-of-giants-982151.

46 Manchester City Council, City Centre Map, accessed 4 January 2007, www.manchester.gov.uk/visitorcentre/images/maps/CityCentreMap.pdf.

47 These commercial shops include: Tesco Express and Lidl, both grocery stores; Blockbuster video rental shop; Subway; Café Nero; and Wetherspoons and Varsity, both bars/eateries, for instance.

48 Jeffrey Richards, *Films and British National Identity: From Dickens to Dad's Army* (Manchester: Manchester University Press, 1997), 267. See also Philip Martin Williams and David L. Williams, *Hooray for Jollywood: The Life of John E. Blakeley and the Mancunian Film Corporation* (Ashton-under-Lyne: History on Your Doorstep, 2001).

49 Richards, *Films and British National Identity*, 267.

50 John Mundy, *Popular Music On Screen: From Hollywood Musical to Music Video* (Manchester: Manchester University Press, 1999), 205.

51 Nida Kirmani, 'Rusholme', in *A Postcolonial People: South Asians in Britain*, ed. Nasreen Ali, Virinder S. Kalra and S. Sayyid (New York: Columbia University Press, 2008), 327.

52 Emphasis in original. John Hyatt, 'Manchester's Mile: Where Culture, Ideas, Creativity and Learning Meet' (The Manchester Oxford Road Cultural Corridor Group, September 2003), 3, http://smartermanchester.org/resources/.

53 Ibid. See also Misela Kunda (photographer) and Tim Birch, 'The F-Word', *All Saints, No Sinners: The Culture and Sub-Culture of Manchester's Oxford Road*, Spring/Summer 2006. The variety of foods available on Curry Mile is used as a metaphor to illustrate the number of 'hyphenated identities' that Manchester boasts, but these never go beyond ethnicity or nationality (British Chinese/Muslim/Indian). Nonetheless, it is encouraging that Rusholme is explicitly written into the map of the Corridor appearing on the last page of the magazine – this is the only map I have seen so far that does so. For more information on the quarterly magazine see the interview of its founder here: Richard Turner and Susie Stubbs, 'All Saints, No Sinners', *BBC Manchester*, 13 January 2006, www.bbc.co.uk/manchester/content/articles/2006/01/13/130106_saints_sinners_interview_feature.shtml.

54 See Chapter 5, p. 109, regarding the 'Manchester script'. In the early 1990s, the Manchester City Council commissioned a study to assess the city's cultural economy and the manner in which culture could be utilized to raise the city's profile on a national and international stage, as well as improve access of the city's inhabitants to culture. See Gwyndaf Williams, *The Enterprising City Centre: Manchester's Development Challenge* (London; New York: Spon Press, 2003) chapter 9 titled 'Urban Consumption and Cultural Vitality'.

55 Marketing Manchester, *Manchester: A Guide for LGBT Visitors, 2006/07*, brochure, 10. As noted in Chapter 5, the length and production qualities of the brochure are a startling testament to the importance of the difference of queer to the city of Manchester's cosmopolitanism.

56 Specifically, the following are listed under the 'Culture' section: The Palace Theatre, Royal Exchange Theatre, Opera House, Contact Theatre, the Library Theatre, the greenroom, The Lowry and The Bridgewater Hall.

57 See Chapter 5, pp. 154–5, for a deeper discussion regarding the relative inclusion of Chinatown in the marketing materials of the city in comparison to Curry Mile.

58 Miwon Kwon, 'Public Art and Urban Identities', special issue: pre_public, European Institute for Progressive Cultural Policies, *Transversal* (January 2002), http://eipcp.net/transversal/0102/kwon/en. Originally published as 'For Hamburg: Public Art and Urban Identities' in the exhibition catalogue *Public Art is Everywhere* (Hamburg, Germany: Kunstverein Hamburg and Kulturbehörde Hamburg, 1997), 95–109; Kwon also cites cultural critic Sharon Zukin, who has noted, 'it seemed to be official policy [by the 1990s] that making a place for art in the city went along with establishing a marketable identity for the city as a whole.' Sharon Zukin, *The Cultures of Cities* (Cambridge, MA: Blackwell, 1995), 23.

59 The cities that are part of the alliance include Birmingham, Bristol, Leeds, Liverpool, Manchester, Newcastle, Nottingham and Sheffield. See 'Core Cities', accessed 4 October 2008, www.corecities.com/dev07/Introduction/about.html.

60 'Manchester "England's Second City"', *BBC*, 12 September 2002, sec. England, http://news.bbc.co.uk/2/hi/uk_news/england/2253035.stm.; 'Manchester Tops Second City Poll', *BBC*, 10 February 2007, sec. England, http://news.bbc.co.uk/2/hi/uk_news/england/6349501.stm.

61 I do not discuss the academic panel 'Role of aesthetics in (re-)shaping a cosmopolitan Manchester', though the conversations certainly inform much of my writing on Manchester. It took place at Manchester Museum, part of the University of Manchester, on 3 December 2007 as part of *Mixing It Up*. The panel provided a public format to discuss tensions inherent in marketing the city as 'cosmopolitan' and the marketing of culture. I am especially indebted to the panellists for sharing their insights on the latter, including Dr Piotr Bienkowski, former Deputy Director, Manchester Museum and Professor of Archaeology and Museology, University of Manchester; Jaheda Choudhury, artist, musician and educator; and Andrew Stokes, former Chief Executive, Marketing Manchester, Chairman, Manchester Pride Ltd and Chair, Queer Up North. Thanks also to Anna Bunney, Engagement Manager (and former Curator of Public Programmes), Manchester Museum, for coordinating and marketing the panel.

62 Personal conversation with Sam McCormick, April 2007.

63 Personal conversation with Jaheda Choudhury, February 2007.

64 I 'cold-called' the restaurant and after several months had a meeting with Ahmed. I was certainly a little jittery the day of the meeting about

approaching a curry restaurant regarding a queer project. However, Ahmed allayed any concerns I might have had with this courteousness. He sent me home with a complimentary meal, as well.

65 Personal conversation with Sam McCormick, December 2007.

66 'Move Over Tracy Emin, Queer Bed Comes to Curry Capital' (University of Manchester Press Office, 2 October 2007), www.manchester.ac.uk/discover/news/article/?id=3153. Thanks to Michael Addleman, Media Relations Officer for the University of Manchester's Faculty of Humanities, for drafting this press release and for helping to publicize the overall project.

67 Exhibition wall text can be found here: Alpesh Kantilal Patel, 'Queer Desi Visual Culture Across the "Brown Atlantic"' (PhD dissertation, Manchester University, 2009), 255–6.

68 This exhibition was curated by Mary Griffiths, Curator, Modern Art, Whitworth Art Gallery. My thanks to her, as well as to Maria Balshaw, former Director, Whitworth Art Gallery.

69 Exhibition wall text can be found here: Patel, 'Queer Desi Visual Culture Across the "Brown Atlantic"', 256–7.

70 Thanks to Kathy Rae Huffman, former Curator, Cornerhouse, who commissioned the project; Tereza Kotyk, former Exhibitions Officer, Cornerhouse; and David Moutrey, former Director, Cornerhouse.

71 Exhibition wall text can be found here: Patel, 'Queer Desi Visual Culture Across the "Brown Atlantic"', 257–8.

72 See Chapter 5, p. 154.

73 Kate Day, Poppy Bowers and Lisa Beauchamp, 'Doorstep Collective: Curry Mile Walk', *Doorstep Collective*, November 2007, http://doorstepcollective.blogspot.com/2007/11/curry-mile-walk.html; Kate Day, Poppy Bowers, and Lisa Beauchamp, 'Doorstep Collective: Curry Mile Walk (Photos)', *Doorstep Collective*, November 2007, http://doorstepcollective.blogspot.com/2007/11/blog-post.html.

74 Steve Pile, 'Memory and the City', in *Temporalities, Autobiography and Everyday Life*, ed. Jan Campbell and Janet Harbord (Manchester and New York: Manchester University Press, 2002), 115.

75 Personal conversation with anonymous participant, November 2007.

76 Sigmund Freud, *Civilization and Its Discontents*, trans. James Strachey, Standard edn (New York: W. W. Norton, 1961), 17–19.

77 Steve Pile, *The Body and the City: Psychoanalysis, Space and Subjectivity* (London; New York: Routledge, 1996), 250.

78 For links between Situationists and contemporary art practices, see the following: David Pinder, 'Arts of Urban Exploration', *Cultural Geographies* 12 (2005): 383–411; David Pinder, 'Ghostly Footsteps: Voices, Memories and Walks in the City', *Ecumene* 8, no. 1 (2001): 1–19; Amelia Jones, *Self/Image: Technology, Representation and the Contemporary Subject* (London; New York: Routledge, 2006), 87–127.

79 Henri Lefebvre, 'Right to the City', in *Writings on Cities*, trans. Eleonore Kofman and Elizabeth Lebas, English translation (Oxford; Cambridge, MA: Blackwell, 1996 [1968]).

80 Thanks to Chris Clarke, former Engagement Manager, Cornerhouse, for his assistance in organizing this educational programme.
81 Caroline A. Jones, 'The Mediated Sensorium', in *Sensorium: Embodied Experience, Technology, and Contemporary Art*, ed. Caroline A. Jones (Cambridge, MA: MIT Press; MIT List Visual Arts Center, 2006), 18. She also notes that Guy Debord addressed what he saw – the society of the spectacle.
82 Personal conversation with anonymous participant, November 2007.
83 As described in the previous chapter, when UK National Curry Chef of the Year for 2002 and 2003 Chad Rahman indicated in the context of discussing the colour of chicken tikka masala that 'a lot of people eat with their eyes', he was signalling the importance of embodied visuality to any dining experience, with specific reference to South Asian food. See Chapter 5, pp. 126–7.
84 Thanks to Iain Scott, owner of Taurus Bar and Restaurant for donating his space.
85 Jürgen Habermas, *The Structural Transformation of the Public Sphere: An Inquiry into a Category of Bourgeois Society*, trans. Thomas Burger with the assistance of Frederick Lawrence (Cambridge, MA: MIT Press, 1989).
86 'Counterpublic' first appeared in 1972 as *Gegenöffentlichkeit* in the German-language work of Oskar Negt and Alexander Kluge, *Public Sphere and Experience: Toward an Analysis of the Bourgeois and Proletarian Public Sphere*, trans. Peter Labanyi, Assenka Oksiloff and Jamie Owen Daniel (Minneapolis: University of Minnesota Press, 1993) [German original 1972]; Nancy Fraser, *Rethinking the Public Sphere: A Contribution to the Critique of Actually Existing Democracy* (Milwaukee: University of Wisconsin-Milwaukee, Center for Twentieth Century Studies, 1990), 123.
87 Gayatri Chakravorty Spivak, 'Can the Subaltern Speak?', in *Marxism and the Interpretation of Culture*, ed. Cary Nelson and Lawrence Grossberg (Basingstoke: Macmillan, 1988), 271–313.
88 Habermas, *The Structural Transformation of the Public Sphere*, 425.
89 Michael Warner, 'Publics and Counterpublics', *Public Culture* 14, no. 1 (2002): 81.
90 Emphasis in original. Carol A. Breckenridge, 'Public Modernity in India', in *Consuming Modernity Public Culture in a South Asian World* (Minneapolis: University of Minnesota Press, 1995), 5, http://site.ebrary.com/id/10159480.
91 Chantal Mouffe, 'For an Agonistic Public Sphere', in *Democracy Unrealized: Documenta 11_Platform1*, ed. Mark Nash et al. (Ostfildern-Ruit, Germany: Hatje Cantz Publishers, 2002), 87–97. For a more elaborate theoretical account of the notion of 'agonism', see Chantal Mouffe, *The Democratic Paradox* (London; New York: Verso, 2000). See chapter 4.
92 Chantal Mouffe, 'Artistic Activism and Agonistic Spaces', *Art & Research: A Journal of Ideas, Contexts and Methods* 1, no. 2 (Summer 2007).
93 Hal Foster and Jürgen Habermas (eds), 'Modernity-An Incomplete Project', in *The Anti-Aesthetic: Essays on Postmodern Culture* (Port Townsend, WA:

Bay Press, 1983), 3–15. This essay was originally presented as a speech on Habermas's reception of the Adorno Prize, given by the city of Frankfurt. A translation of this essay later appeared in *New German Critique* 22 (Winter 1981) under the title, 'Modernity Versus Postmodernity'.

94 Michel Foucault et al., 'Politics and Ethics: An Interview', in *The Foucault Reader*, ed. Paul Rabinow, trans. Catherine Porter (New York: Random House, 1984), 379.

95 Jürgen Habermas, *The Theory of Communicative Action. Vol. 1* (London: Heinemann, 1984); Jürgen Habermas, *The Theory of Communicative Action. Vol. 2* (Cambridge: Polity, 1987).

96 Frazer Ward, 'Haunted Museum: Institutional Critique and Publicity', *October* 73 (Summer 1995): 75 (note 9).

97 Negt and Kluge, *Public Sphere and Experience*. See especially 'The Public Sphere as the Organization of Collective Experience', 1–53.

98 Ward, 'Haunted Museum: Institutional Critique and Publicity', 72.

99 Ibid.

100 Ibid.

101 Miwon Kwon, 'Public Art as Publicity', in *In the Place of the Public Sphere? On the Establishment of Publics and Counter-Publics*, ed. Simon Sheikh (Berlin: b_books, 2005), http://republicart.net/disc/publicum/kwon01_en.htm.

102 Warner, 'Publics and Counterpublics', 88.

103 Nick Crossley, 'Corporeality and Communicative Action: Embodying the Renewal of Critical Theory', *Body and Society* 3, no. 1 (1997): 17–46. Crossley combines Merleau-Ponty's theorizations of the body-subject and intercorporeity (discussed in Chapter 7) with Habermas's critical theory.

104 Personal conversation with anonymous audience member, December 2007.

105 For a more detailed discussion of the notion of 'community' in artistic practices, see Miwon Kwon, *One Place After Another: Site Specific Art and Locational Identity* (Cambridge, MA: The MIT Press, 2002), chapter 5, 'The (Un) sitings of Community;' and Grant H. Kester, *Conversation Pieces: Community and Communication in Modern Art* (Berkeley and London: University of California Press, 2004), chapter 5, 'Community and Communicability.'

106 Anonymous response #3.

107 In fact, when the Doorstep Collective was invited to give a lecture by an outside organization, the audience members interrogated the Collective's whiteness in the context of the *Queer Urban Walk* in Curry Mile; once members of the Collective explained that I had specifically commissioned them to do the artwork, there was no longer an issue.

108 Publication/radio programme organized by dominant target audiences or interests: LESBIAN/WOMEN'S INTEREST (2): *Diva Magazine* (October 2007); 'Curry in Bed, How Queer?', women's lifestyle blog, *Dolly Mix* (October 2007), www.dollymix.tv/2007/10/curry_in_bed_how_queer.html.GAY/QUEER (3): Alpesh Kantilal Patel, LGBT Citizen Manchester, interview by Ashley Byrne, BBC Radio Manchester, 20 November 2007; 'Queer

Bed Comes To Curry Capital', *Rainbow Network*, 2 October 2007, link no longer available; 'Move over Tracy Emin: Queer Bed Comes to Curry Capital', *Hero*, 2 October 2007, link no longer available. ASIAN (2): 'Asian Gay Community Speaks out', *Manchester Evening News*, 31 August 2007, www.manchestereveningnews.co.uk/whats-on/going-out/asian-gay-community-speaks-out-1220265; Alpesh Kantilal Patel and Jaheda Choudhury, *Indus* (Asian Radio News Magazine), interview by Talat Awan, BBC Radio Manchester, 7 October 2007. ART (1): Caroline Lewis, 'Manchester Curry House Hosts Queer Bed and Chicken Tikka Cake', a Brighton-based, non-profit, digital cultural publishing organization, *Culture24* (6 October 2007), www.culture24.org.uk/art/art51159. OTHER: 'Move Over Tracy Emin, Queer Bed Comes to Curry Capital'; Caroline Lewis, 'Manchester Art Scene Mixes It Up', commissioned by Culture Online, part of the Department for Culture, Media and Sport from 2002–7, *Icons: A Portrait of England* (October 2007), www.icons.org.uk/news/icons-in-the-news/manchester-art-scene-mixes-it-up.

109 Patel, *LGBT Citizen Manchester*; Patel and Choudhury, *Indus* (Asian Radio News Magazine).

110 Virinder S. Kalra, 'Writing British-Asian (Greater) Manchester' (From diaspora to multi-locality: writing British-Asian cities Symposium, University of Leeds, England, 2008), 4, www.leeds.ac.uk/brasian/assets/Symp_Abs.doc.

111 Personal conversation with members of Sphere, December 2007.

Affect: belonging 7

Drawing on everything from artworks and a cartoon to police documents and a personal anecdote, I consider three temporally discontinuous events in the past to engender an ethical future across racial, ethnic and national lines. At stake in this chapter is the question of how certain subjects are considered as 'belonging' and others as not; and the role of art and writing in the reconstitution of notions of 'home' (not to mention art histories). I examine the fatal misrecognition of South Asians as 'terrorists' shortly after 9/11 in the United States; of Jean Charles de Menezes, an electrician originally from Brazil living in London, as a 'terrorist' after 7 July 2005 or '7/7' in the UK; and of teenager Trayvon Martin as a 'criminal' in Sanford, Florida, on 6 February 2012 in the United States.[1] I hone in on 'affect' to examine the complex manner in which visual identification – or misidentification in these cases – takes place and thereby connects these disparate events. 'Affect', roughly, refers to feeling before cognition.[2] To define it more specifically I draw on several theoretical models that mobilize the concept in relation to artistic practice and critical writing, in particular art historians Jill Bennett's conceptualization of 'practical aesthetics', Amelia Jones's theory of 'queer feminist durationality' and Marsha Meskimmon's 'affective criticality', respectively.[3]

To begin with, Bennett writes that practical aesthetics is 'defined by an orientation to real-world experience' and provides 'a means of inhabiting and moving through events'.[4] Given my focus on real-word experience, this is a particularly appropriate model to begin my discussion. As she also notes, practical aesthetics 'examines aesthetics of connection that posit links between events'.[5] By 'aesthetics' Bennett is specifically invoking the more recent use of the term as a 'general theory of sensori-emotional experience' which brings together art, psychology and the social rather than being concerned with judgement and highly fraught notions of beauty and taste.[6]

Bennett notes that since its origin, aesthetics has always promoted the idea of perception via senses, or *aisthesis*.[7] Affect, as the core feature of *aisthesis*, is the medium of practical aesthetics.[8] She further notes that affect is a defining feature of social, cultural and political relations; however, 'unlike meaning, iconography or a formal quality, affect is not easily anchored in an image.'[9] It is mobile, and in this way aesthetics is not 'a means of categorising and defining art'.[10] Rather, aesthetics traces 'the affective relations that animate art and real events'.[11] While affect is something activated in the social, it is ultimately experienced by the individual. 'Practical aesthetics', then, allows for a 'study of (art as a) means of apprehending the world via sense-based and affective processes – processes that touch bodies intimately and directly but that also underpin the emotions, sentiments and passions of public life'.[12]

The 'practical' in 'practical aesthetics' does not signify an interest in interrogating 'the philosophical ground of aesthetics or its historical determinations' but that which acknowledges 'an aesthetics informed by and derived from the practical, real-world encounters, an aesthetics that is in turn capable of being used or put into effect in a real situation'.[13] In this chapter, I weave together evidence that 'offers more than a record, a flashback or reconstruction; it generates a means of inhabiting and simultaneously reconfiguring the historical event as a radically different experience. Such an enquiry carries with it the possibility of reorienting the study of the *traumatic* event (that is, the shattering experience of a real event) away from the historiographical endeavour.'[14]

Bennett mobilizes the term 'contemporaneity' to further clarify that the 'event' is not temporally bound but 'a principle of connection to an unspecified present, to whatever might happen next'.[15] To explain this point, she writes that 9/11 cannot be reduced to a singular catastrophe. That is, 9/11 did not begin on that day and its effects continue to be felt in the present *and* the foreseeable future. In this way, practical aesthetics does not delineate a historical event but rather focuses on an extension of it – backwards and forwards in time. Her example is not incidental in that she argues that practical aesthetics itself emerges from 9/11, which demanded a crucial shift in the way in which the field of visual arts (broadly construed) operates.[16] Indeed, Bennett goes into great detail about how practical aesthetics cannot be explored in mainstream art history and visual cultural studies because of the constraining disciplinary foci of both.[17] In short, both are too rigid to tackle 9/11's endlessly mobile affective fallout. Instead she calls for a transdisciplinary aesthetics – or an investigation of aesthetics that crosses the disciplinary confines of visual culture and art history.[18]

As already noted, but worth underscoring again, Bennett argues 'an aesthetic reconfiguration of experience – to which affective connection is material – does not simply restore subjective experience to history but generates new ways of being in the event. It thereby holds out the possibility of reshaping the outcomes of a given event.'[19] However, she cautions that practical aesthetics should not be conflated with activism. Rather, 'Art becomes practical rather than abstract to the extent that it maintains a tension between aisthesis and signification.'[20] She writes that, 'It is this capacity to dwell in the interval and to untangle some of its complex operations (the links – and blockages or 'hesitations' – between apprehension and action, between feeling and believing, appearing, saying and doing) that makes a creative aesthetics so valuable to the study of social life.'[21] Drawing on literary theorist and poetry scholar Isobel Armstrong's scholarship, which draws parallels among theories of affect in discourses of phenomenology, psychoanalysis and other fields, Bennett also argues that, 'Art, like affect itself, inhabits an in-between space and is an agent of change.'[22] By exploring artwork and visual culture as nimbly occupying the 'in-between space', I aim to link 9/11, 7/7 and the death of Trayvon Martin by specifically bringing to the fore the manner in which visual identification takes place, a process that has been ill-explored in the context of any of these events. In so doing, I also suggest how artworks can be an 'agent of change'.

Art historian Amelia Jones in her book *Seeing Differently: A History and Theory of Identification and the Visual Arts* (2012) extensively explores visual identification in relation to artistic meaning. Of particular interest is Jones's theory of queer feminist durationality, which 'acknowledges the way in which identification still shadows and indeed deeply informs how we interpret, make meaning, and attribute value.'[23] Rather than suggesting an interest in time-based media, by 'durationality' Jones is referring to our embodied encounters with art objects, 'which opens into connections that are born of affect as tapped into, solicited, shaped, encouraged by the prick of memory and desire that constitutes the most powerful experiences we have in engaging with the things around us.'[24] Importantly, Jones insists on the identificatory aspects of affect in theorizing the encounter with an artwork that she notes both art historians Simon O'Sullivan and Jan Verwoert abstract.[25] She powerfully argues that:

> What is missing … is a sense of the alignment between the development of the possibility of *thinking* the rhizome … and what I am arguing to be among the crucial pressures that assisted in … the shattering of the … conventional perspectival system and the model of the subject it subtended and proposed: the decolonization of the so-called third world and the rise of identity politics in the post-Second World War period. Without recognizing this pressure, and the role in the shifts in informing postsructuralist theories of meaning, we are left with only an abstract (if elegant) description of a shift in ways of making and interpreting art.[26]

The 'rhizome' invoked here is that theorized by philosopher Gilles Deleuze and psychoanalyst Félix Guattari. The rhizome as conceptualized by them is a system without a centre and within which nodal points can connect but in a non-hierarchical manner.[27] Jones writes that the rhizome is precisely about the '*dispersals* of old binary systems' but without the emphasis on identity politics that arguably instantiated it.[28] In this way, my discussion of affect will be tied to thinking about identification.

Jones writes that 'the *queer feminist* aspect of durationality is as important as the performative, rhizomatic, or temporal angle'.[29] Jones's invocation of 'feminism' and 'queer' is specific but not essentialist, and it is useful to further articulate how identification is always already wrapped up with affect. For instance, she acknowledges how feminism has '*slowed down* the quick super-glue certainties of art criticism and its related discourse' and how '*queer is that which indicates the impossibility of a subject or a meaning staying still*'.[30] A queer feminist durational approach to practical aesthetics demands attention to visual identification as always already raced, sexed, classed and gendered as it emerges or erupts within the complex nexus of the 'performative, rhizomatic, or temporal' relationship of the viewer (in this case me) with the artwork. Indeed, invoking one's relationship to the artwork has been a feature of this entire book.

Drawing on historian Carolyn Dinshaw's and philosopher Henri Bergson's scholarship, Jones argues that temporality or durationality is powerful because it opens the present to the past and to the future.[31] Jones writes that, 'This is where ethics lie, of course, nudging us to attend to past histories in order to avoid future exploitation, pain and iniquity.'[32] Jones cites my research relating to 9/11 and 7/7 in her book.[33] I re-present my research in this chapter through her theory of queer feminist durationality, in particular by exploring my personal connection to these events (especially 9/11) with an eye towards a more ethical future.

Marsha Meskimmon's theory of 'affirmative criticality' in her important book *Contemporary Art and the Cosmopolitan Imagination* – the importance of which I explored in the preface – is crucial in further exploring ethics and its relation to aesthetics. Meskimmon draws on philosopher Jürgen Habermas's theory of the 'public sphere' and Deleuze's scholarship on ethics and aesthetics, but, like Jones, does not sacrifice discussions of identity/identification.[34] While Bennett's 'practical aesthetics' considers how artworks can re-shape real-world 'events' and Jones's 'queer feminist durationality' articulates a new of way of seeing – both of which allow glimpses of a more ethical future – Meskimmon's 'affirmative criticality' explores the possibilities of 'the potential of critical thinking to engender and affirm a hopeful, indeed better and more humane, future'.[35] This is particularly important in examining how an ethics can be produced through the writing of art histories, the core interest of this book.

Drawing on the scholarship of Rosalyn Diprose, Meskimmon invokes the Greek origins of the word ethics – *ethos* (or character and dwelling or habitat) – to suggest fascinating connections between home and home-making or place and place-making.[36] Meskimmon writes that ethics forges a link between the 'material constraints of our position in the world and our agency in making, maintaining and changing them'.[37] She further writes: 'The subject formed at the interstices of this critical modulation is an embodied, embedded and responsible subject – the subject who can inhabit a plurilocal, cosmopolitan home.'[38] Meskimmon argues that contemporary art has the potential to produce such an 'embedded and responsible subject' and the 'potential to make the world, not merely represent it'.[39]

In addition, she writes that affirmative criticality as 'a method of intellectual analysis and engagement' suggests that 'ethics and aesthetics have significant areas of intersection and, more strongly, mutual constitution' for the art historian, too: 'Where the response-ability of the subject meets a subject's responsibility with/in the world, aesthetics and ethics play in harmony.'[40] My hope is that readers' engagement with my text engenders his or her response-ability as co-extensive with his or her responsibility with/in the world. Of course, I have no delusions regarding the limits of my academic writing, which has a fairly circumscribed audience. However, I would argue that the instantiation of what might be described as 'micro-ethics' – ethics at the level of a subject – and its potential affective accretion over time can be powerful in its own regard.

The aim in this chapter is to *re*-present these horrific events – rather than representing them (not only impossible but also ethically dubious) – so as to engender the possibility of inhabiting them differently. In so doing, I draw resonances among them and suggest that these misidentifications are not a 'Brazilian', 'Sikh' or 'black' issue – although it must be noted that the latter two populations have been disproportionately targeted, though not in equivalent ways – but that they affect *all* of us who are interested in living in an ethical and just world.

Event #1: 9/11: towards multiple futures

I begin by considering a cartoon by Carter Goodrich that appeared on the cover of *The New Yorker* (Plate 23). Published roughly two months after 9/11 it explores the plight of taxi drivers after the attacks. The cartoon depicts a turbaned cab driver cowering in the seat of his yellow cab. A canopy of various sizes of American flags is mounted on the rooftop, and the cab is also covered with American flag stickers and a 'God Bless America' sticker. The hyperbolic use of the American flag in the cartoon underscores the equally excessive and overwhelming identification of turban-wearing Muslim and Sikh cab drivers as terrorists in a post-9/11 New York. Turbans not only became visual signifiers of terrorism, but also carried implicit presumptions of a lack of American citizenship. For instance, Frank S. Roque, who killed Balbir Singh Sodhi, an Indian Sikh from Arizona, on 15 September 2001 was heard saying that he would ‘kill the rag heads responsible for September 11’, prior to his assaults, and when handcuffed, he said, ‘I stand for America all the way! I’m an American. Go ahead. Arrest me and let those terrorists run wild!’[41]

Given that the terrorist attacks of 9/11 were ascribed to Middle Eastern and Islamic, or Muslim, radicals, American legal scholar Leti Volpp surmises that those who appear ‘Middle Eastern, or Muslim-looking’ – she mentions Latinos and African-Americans, for instance – practically became a new identity category in terms of United States citizenship.[42] Although the American flag became increasingly visible as a marker of patriotism after 9/11, the cartoon indicates that for some subjects, displaying the flag became a necessity to prevent any potential misidentification as not only a terrorist, but as ‘not’ American.[43] Indeed, this is at least part of the reason my own parents put various American flags – that are still up – in their dry cleaning business, especially after receiving at least one threatening phone call that I know of to ‘go back home’ after 9/11.

The visual conflation of turbans with terrorism also extends to issues of faith.[44] For instance, Sikh men do not cut their hair, including facial hair, and are required to wear turbans as an expression of their religion – ‘a Badge of [visual] Identity’, according to the website *SikhNet*.[45] Volpp further notes that the long beards and turbans of Sikh men were often ‘conflated with Osama bin Laden’, whose image with a beard and Afghani-style turban was heavily circulated online, on television screens and in print after the US terror attacks.[46] As a result, Sikhs were the most vulnerable to being visually misidentified as connected to the 9/11 attacks, despite the fact that Sikhs and Muslims have separate doctrinal views, different geographic homelands, different native languages and distinct turban styles, as noted by civil rights scholars Neha Singh Gohil and Dawinder S. Sidhu.[47] Indeed, Balbir Singh Sodhi was Sikh. The cab driver on *The New Yorker* cover is most likely Sikh rather than Muslim – as signalled by his turban, his dress and what appears to be a beard – yet he is clearly anticipating being visually misidentified as a Muslim.[48]

Interestingly, the US Department of Justice attempted to prevent the misidentification of Sikhs as Muslims by disseminating an educational poster among airport security staff in 2004 to educate them about Sikh head coverings.[49] Yet the poster obscured the larger problem of misrecognition of a much broader group of ‘Middle Eastern or Muslim looking men’ as terrorists signalled by Volpp above, and implicitly created a more appropriate object of post-9/11 animus. As American human rights and international law scholar Karen Engle notes, ‘Whether through government investigations and raids or “private” vigilance, the brunt of the internal war has fallen on Muslims, particularly those of Arab descent (now that Americans seem to have learned the difference between Sikhs and Muslims).’[50] In the same way, the fact that many Sikhs began to cut their hair and forgo wearing turbans altogether, though understandable, only seemed to reinforce the notion that turban-wearers more closely approximate 'the look' of a terrorist.[51]

This cartoon invariably takes me back to my own experience living in New York City during the terrorist attacks of 9/11. At the time, there had been reports of violence against South Asians who apparently looked like terrorists. In particular, there were three South Asians who were visually perceived to be Arab and killed in the United States within days of 9/11: a Pakistani from near Dallas, Texas, and an Indian Sikh from Mesa, Arizona, both on 15 September 2001; and a Gujarati Hindu from Mesquite, Texas, on 4 October 2001. Balbir Singh Sodhi, the Indian Sikh from Arizona, was landscaping the front of the gas station he owned when Roque fatally shot him in the back three times. Within a 30-minute period after shooting Singh, Roque also fired at Lebanese-American clerks at another gas station and into the home that he previously owned, which was then occupied by an Afghani couple.[52] Not surprisingly, for several weeks after 9/11 I really did not feel safe leaving my apartment alone. I started waking up a little earlier so I could head into Manhattan from Brooklyn with my roommate. I felt safe not only being with a good friend, but also one who was *not* brown. To explain, my skin colour was highly charged – capable of producing a strong affective reaction of repulsion, fear, or contempt on sight in a viewing subject. White skin, on the other hand, would produce no affect at all. By merely being proximal to someone with 'white' skin, I was hoping it would vitiate the affectivity of my brownness.

Approximately three weeks after 9/11, I finally did emerge alone to go meet friends of mine. It was a victory for me to be able to go out as I had always done before 9/11. At the time, I worked in a film company and I would often go to the theatre alone to watch movies. In New York City going solo to a movie theatre is not a big deal. That evening after having dinner with friends, I decided to go to a theatre near Broadway and 14th Street, a well-trafficked intersection near Union Square, which is a major hub for different subway lines and at the time a site of makeshift memorials for 9/11 victims.

Shortly before entering the theatre, I was hit with eggs which were thrown at me from a moving car. It was not really a violent attack in the sense that I was not physically harmed. Also, at first I was not even sure that any of the eggs had hit me. I did not see anything on my jacket – or perhaps more accurately I did not *want* to see anything because that would have it made it more real. I was hoping to escape the entire situation by going into a dark theatre. I first went to the automatic ticket machines but they were out of order so I had to get in line to get a ticket. While waiting, I decided to take off my jacket, the back of which of course was covered in egg yolk. I could no longer pretend nothing had happened, especially since at this point those behind me in line were staring at me. Incredibly embarrassed, I left the theatre and decided to take a taxi home. I did not want to spend money on a cab but I certainly did not want to take a 45-minute subway ride in public either. I had a feeling there was probably egg in my hair, too. Fortunately, it was not difficult to find a cab that night. I cannot remember if I sought out a driver who I thought was of South Asian descent but I did end up getting one who was. The irony is not lost on me that I typically would bristle when getting into a cab with a driver whom I thought was of South Asian descent. Often I would be asked by the drivers where I am from at which point I would indicate my family is from Gujarat but that I grew up in the United States. The conversation would usually end there – perhaps the drivers could feel my lack of interest in having a conversation or maybe they were looking to connect with someone who was from the same part of South Asia from which they came. In any case, I knew my annoyance was largely connected to the fact that I never felt I could approximate what being South Asian might generally signify – heterosexual.

That night, of course, all of the above was moot. There was no one else I would have wanted to be with than a South Asian taxi driver who I believed could sympathize with my situation. I did end up sharing what had just happened to me with the driver; I might have even initiated the conversation. When I got back to my apartment I threw my jacket away – it was an old Gap jacket. Really, though, I just did not want it around as a reminder of what had happened. I did not share my experience with anyone again for years.

The New Yorker cartoon invariably takes me back to my experience but it also allows me to inhabit the event through a very different lens – one that to a certain degree gives me back a measure of agency. Drawing on the scholarship of Jasbir K. Puar, the cartoon underscores that, 'Identity is one effect of affect, a capture that proposes what one is by masking its retrospective ordering and thus its ontogenetic dimension – what one was – through the guise of an illusory futurity: what one is and will continue to be.'[53] To explain, the cartoon effectively instantiates an affect of fear and paranoia in the viewing subject that we imagine drivers must have felt after 9/11. The cab driver is clearly anticipating that this affect could lead to his misidentification as a terrorist, and even to death. Through the hypervisual display of flags, he hopes he potentially avoids this future. Indeed, the visual identification of the driver as a 'terrorist' is intersectional with *other* visual presumptions of race, faith and citizenship as previously discussed. African-American feminist legal scholar Kimberlé Crenshaw in her important theory of intersectionality points to the importance of considering multiple categories of identity as constitutive of each other.[54] The cab driver hopes to redirect the dominant effect (being identified as a terrorist) of the affect of fear by redirecting one vector which is entangled with it: presumption of lack of citizenship. By doing so, he potentially breaks what Puar describes as the 'illusory futurity' that what one 'will continue to be', is the same not only as 'what one is' but also 'what one was'. Put another way, Puar's conceptualization of Crenshaw's theory as the 'becoming of intersectionality' is instructive.[55] Puar notes that Crenshaw's cogent description of cars meeting at an intersection is suggestive of intersectionality being an 'event'.[56] Puar writes that 'In this "becoming of intersectionality," there is emphasis on motion rather than gridlock; on how the halting of motion produces the demand to locate.'[57] The cartoon effectively focuses on the motion before multiple vectors – or cars per Crenshaw's analogy – come together to locate or identify the driver as a terrorist.

Event #2: 7/7: the right to opacity

On the morning of 7 July 2005, an atmosphere of fear and panic supplanted the celebratory mood in the city of London, which had been chosen as the site of the 2012 Olympics just 24 hours before, as a series of bombs exploded within the Greater London transport network during peak commuting hours. Police soon established that four suicide bombers were responsible for the tragedy – all of whom died in the blasts, along with 52 other innocent people.[58]

The city of London has survived numerous attacks over the decades, including most prominently the Nazi bombing campaign known as the Blitz from 1940 to 1941 and Irish Republican Army (IRA) bombing campaigns from the 1970s to the mid-1990s.[59] In April 1999 a lone perpetrator named David Copeland devised homemade nail bombs and deployed them in the Brixton and Brick Lane areas of London – targeting their black and South Asian communities, respectively – as well as in a gay pub in the Soho area of the city.[60] However, suicide bombings were relatively new to both the city of London and the entire UK. The media dubbed the coordinated terrorist attacks of 7 July 2005 '7/7', indelibly linking them in character to the terrorist attacks of 11 September 2001.

Just two weeks later on 21 July, terrorists targeted the London transport system again – this time unsuccessfully.[61] In one of the rucksacks containing an explosive, the police found a gym membership card with a photograph they judged to be 'a good likeness to' an image of one of the suspects, Hussain Osman, captured on closed-circuit television tapes at one of the sites where the bombs were recovered.[62] Based largely on this *visual* knowledge, the Metropolitan Police Service (MPS) decided to conduct surveillance on the apartment building where Osman was suspected to have resided.[63]

At 9.33 a.m. on the day after the failed attacks, an officer stationed in an observation van saw an individual leave the building. The officer checked the photographs of the suspects with which he had been provided. Police believed Osman to be Somali at the time, though it was later learned that he was in fact of Ethiopian descent.[64] The officer described the subject leaving the building as 'IC1' or 'Identity Code White'. However, he was unsure of his initial assessment and transmitted a message to his colleagues over the radio indicating 'that "it would be worth somebody else having a look"'.[65] Over the next three hours, undercover police officers followed the suspect onto a bus and into a tube station where he was fatally shot in the head twice, having been *visually* identified as the terrorist Osman by police.[66]

The person police spotted coming out of the apartment building would later be identified as Jean Charles de Menezes, a Brazilian man. The extensive 168-page report by the Independent Police Complaints Commission (IPCC) concerning the tragic events leading to de Menezes's death indicates that his misidentification as a terrorist was the last in a chain of misidentifications. During the time de Menezes was under surveillance, police had perceived him to be 'white', 'North African', 'Asian', 'Asian looking' and 'Asian/Pakistani'.[67] Many of the witnesses in the tube described de Menezes as 'Asian' and, in a case of double misidentification, frequently confused an undercover police officer, listed under the pseudonym 'Ivor' in the IPCC report, as the suspect.[68] In fact, police officers pinned Ivor to the ground and pointed a gun to his head before he was able to properly identify himself.[69] Thus, as the tragic events of 22 July unfolded in the immediate aftermath of two major acts of terrorism – one carried out and one thwarted – police officers and bystanders alike identified Osman, de Menezes and Ivor as Asian. According to the IPCC report, however, none of them are of Asian descent. This misidentification of all three men reveals an implicit visual conflation of Asian-ness with terrorism.[70]

The report provides important clues regarding how these identifications are made. For instance, one of the officers, identified as 'Harry' in the report, indicated that de Menezes was 'looking over his shoulder and acting in a wary manner. He appeared nervous'.[71] Officer Harry read de Menezes through what French philosopher Maurice Merleau-Ponty refers to as a 'corporeal or postural schema'[72] – a default position the body assumes in various commonly experienced circumstances that can be 'habitual'.[73] De Menezes's postural schema could be described as habitually associated with 'suspicious behaviour' in accordance with the officer's observation that de Menezes was 'acting in a wary manner' and 'appeared nervous'. This effectively rendered invisible de Menezes's identity as a Brazilian.[74]

Merleau-Ponty has theorized the inseparability of the body, the world and the mind. He writes that:

> Insofar as, when I reflect on the essence of subjectivity, I find it bound up with that of the body and that of the world, this is because my existence as subjectivity [= consciousness (translator's notes)] is merely one with my existence as a body and with the existence of the world, and because the subject that I am, when taken concretely, is inseparable from this body and this world.[75]

His indication of 'my existence as subjectivity' as 'bound up with that of the body and that of the world' is in direct opposition to the philosophical separation of the mind and body advocated most prominently by René Descartes, who wrote that 'the mind by which I am what I am, is wholly distinct from the body, and is even more easily known than the latter, and is such, that although the latter were not, it would still continue to be all that it is'.[76]

Merleau-Ponty further notes that seeing involves both the viewing and the viewed subjects, who are importantly both the seen and the seer. He describes 'this coiling over of the visible upon the visible' as 'intercorporeity', rendering oppositional terms such as 'subject' and 'object' as meaningless, as they are actually yoked together. Moreover, he writes that there is 'reciprocal insertion and intertwining of one [seeing body] and the other [seen or visible body]'.[77] The various identifications ascribed to de Menezes, as well as that of the terrorist suspect Hussain Osman, can be described as a chiasmic intertwining of de Menezes with each police officer's own psychic desires, fantasies and projections. Consequently, each officer's 'gut' or affective identification reflects a complex intermeshing of synaesthetic, or multisensory, visuality with psychic process. In another example, many attacks on turban-wearing citizens following 9/11 involved a bizarre intimacy, with turbans unceremoniously removed and hair often pulled at.[78] As the deaths of the Sikh Sodhi after 9/11 in the United States and the Brazilian de Menezes after 7/7 in the UK illustrate, 'subjects' (turban-wearing or not) are never fully able to visually embody an appropriate patriotism, citizenship or any other identification.[79]

While Goodrich's cartoon brought to the fore the becoming of intersectionality as crucial to understanding the mechanism of visual identification, the IPCC report illustrates in sobering detail how central location or site – it was de Menezes's emergence from the building in which the suspect was thought to have resided that set off a chain of reactions that lead to his death – as well as the affective readings of bodies are to this process. The permanent public memorial for de Menezes at Stockwell underground station in south London, where he was killed, provides another important way of reconsidering his tragic event (Figure 7.1). Created by artist Mary Edwards in 2010, the colourful mosaic includes an image of de Menezes surrounded by representations of flowers which replace the actual ones that overflowed from the site following his death.[80] His photographic image is composed of large and square tiles of the same size. British geographer Karen Wells has written that she is sceptical that the memorial can function beyond its 'recognition of a family's tragedy'.[81] That is, she writes: 'Despite the continuing ethical demand [from viewing subjects] of the image of the face [of de Menezes], what is demanded is now muted and slippery.'[82] At the same time, Wells writes that for all its 'foreclosure of political claims, [the memorial] may still be taken as simply a statement of presence, a refusal of erasure'.[83] Wells's reading of the memorial is compelling, but I question whether the work should be seen only through the lens of instrumentality – the demand for justice – and presence/visibility.

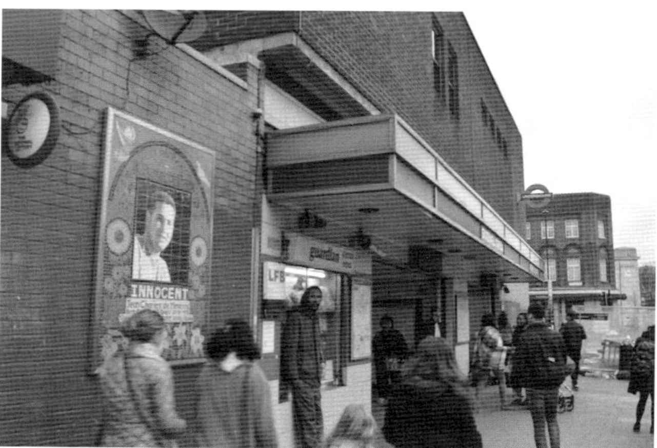

7.1 Mary Edwards, Jean Charles de Menezes memorial, Stockwell Tube Station, London, England. Unveiled on 7 January 2010.

To explain, when my colleague and friend took pictures of the memorial for this book he was having trouble getting a clear photograph of de Menezes's face. He first thought this was due to the lighting – it was a cloudy day when he decided to take the photographs – or that perhaps the angle of his shot needed to be adjusted. Eventually, he realized that the image itself is not entirely distinct. I was unable to find out if the artist or even the family had intended for the image's slight cloudiness. Whether intentional or not, I find this fascinating for two reasons. At first glance the square tiles of which his photograph is composed seem to 'locate' him on a grid, not to mention fragment him. However, the blurriness (even though slight) of the photograph allows him to transcend the locationary power of the grid and underscores that he was denied what Martinican philosopher Édouard Glissant would characterize as his right to 'opacity'.[84] Glissant's opacity is a concept he deploys to defend the right of the postcolonial subject not to be appropriated by discourses of power that originate elsewhere. He writes that opacity is 'the most perennial guarantee of participation and confluence'.[85] Glissant further notes that opacity is not the opaque or the obscure, 'though it is possible for it to be so and be accepted as such'.[86] Instead, he provocatively writes, 'The right to opacity … would be the real foundation of … freedoms.'[87] Here, he is referring to a non-hierarchical society in which equality is connected to respect of the 'other' as different. While the memorial is clearly labelled as being that of de Menezes, the opacity of the photograph places the viewer in the interval just before signification or identification takes place. This is the in-between space where the world, the body and mind that Merleau-Ponty so eloquently writes about are interconnected, and that Glissant further suggests includes a subject's right to opacity.

I briefly return to the work of Sphere in Chapter 6 in which opacity was at the core of the wallpaper, video, beds and screen, that incorporated silhouettes of the queer women of the collective. That is, I would extend Glissant's notion of opacity to issues of gender and sexuality, especially in this particular case. Through Glissant's lens, it can be argued that the dominant West's conflation of visibility and 'coming out' with freedom is reductive, even if well-meaning. Indeed, Sphere's work brings to the fore the notion that visibility is more than opticality.

Event #3: Trayvon Martin: fade to white

In early 2012 I learned that a 17-year-old African American male, by the name of Trayvon Martin, had been fatally shot in the chest as he had been walking home in Sanford, a city in Florida, located about an hour from where I grew up. Martin actually lived in south Florida with his mother – where I moved in late 2011 – but had been in Sanford visiting his father. Eventually it became clear that an overzealous community watch guard, George Zimmerman, followed Martin against police orders and murdered him for looking like a criminal.[88]

The scholarship of Jill Bennett, Amelia Jones and Marsha Meskimmon in different ways argue that artworks and critical writing can in fact be more than a mute mirror on the world. They may not achieve the goals of traditional activism but they can initiate micro-activism – not the grand-sweeping change on a macro level but at the level of the subject. However, when I heard about Trayvon Martin and decided to also include him in my thinking I could not help being a little disappointed at the apparent limits of academic writing. While I would neither claim that the validity of art historical writing lay in its instrumentality in the 'real world' nor that I had the power to prevent the death of Martin, I had at this point as part of my dissertation written about and linked together the deaths of Sodhi and de Menezes as visual misidentifications (though I did not explore affect). My aim was simply to underscore the stakes involved in the larger project in which I explored queer South Asian visual culture.

To explore this notion of micro-activism and to expand on my discussion of opacity, I consider Adrian Margaret Smith Piper's *Imagine [Trayvon Martin]* (2013) (Figure 7.2). Piper moved to Berlin in 2008 when she discovered her name on a US 'suspicious travelers' list.[89] She constructed this work after the acquittal of George Zimmerman – whom she describes as a 'Euroethnic

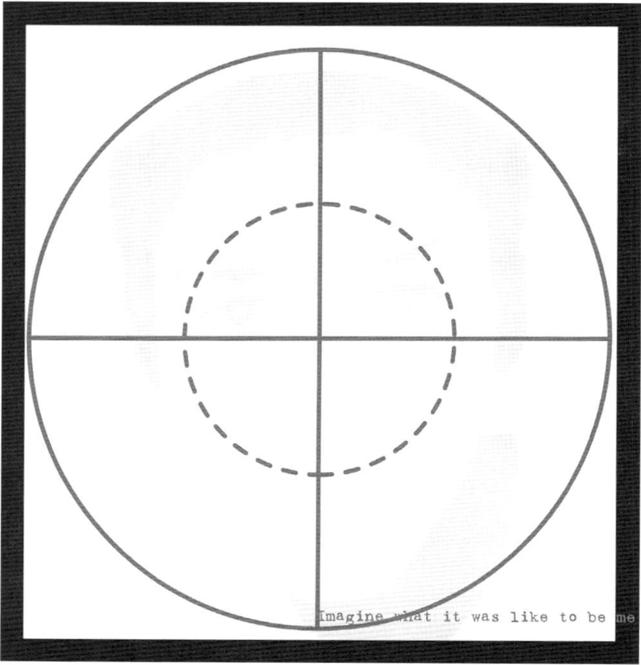

7.2 Adrian Piper, *Imagine [Trayvon Martin]*, 2013. Digital image for free download and printing from http://adrianpiper.com/art/index.shtml, 10.43 × 10.76 in., 300 dpi.

vigilante neighbour'.[90] She connects Martin's death to a number of deaths of unarmed African American males as follows:

> Trayvon Martin was not the first or only victim of police state-sponsored violence against unarmed African Americans. Several more recent cases have received the attention of the international press. Others, both before and since, have gone unnoticed or have been forgotten. But Trayvon Martin's shooting death was the wake-up call for many of those Euroethnic Americans for whom Barack Obama's presidency was supposedly conclusive proof that American racism was a thing of the past.[91]

Piper's work is constructed in a similar fashion to her work *The Color Wheel Series* (2000–4) discussed in Chapter 4 in that there is a target wheel in red, but gone are the acting heads and any other hues. The image is washed in white, though Piper does not consider this a colour.[92] Therefore, just as in the earlier work, there is an absence of colour as hue and as flesh. Moreover, the now well-known image of Martin in a hoodie is only faintly visible.[93] This suggests both how figures like Martin can become faint memories for the public *and* how they stubbornly refuse to disappear. More strikingly, the work seems to turn the portrait (if you will) on to the viewer. That is, by seeing almost nothing, the viewer becomes acutely aware of himself or herself looking. Once this happens, the possibility of the viewer to 'imagine what it was like to be me [Martin]', as Piper writes on the bottom of the target in blue text, becomes more likely. Martin becomes a subject rather than an object. Images of Martin in a hoodie circulated through the internet, print journalism and television with a speed that drains Martin's agency as a subject; Piper's work returns his right, but to opacity. Given that Martin is barely visible, Piper's work has even stronger connections to Glissant's concept of opacity than de Menezes's memorial.

Piper's Martin work is free and available to all to download from her website. As she writes:

> As an antidote to further memory loss, I have been distributing this work free of charge and as widely as possible. It is available for free download as a high-resolution PNG file at adrianpiper.com/art/index.shtml, and can be printed out in a variety of sizes and formats. Please take one, or many, and pass it on.[94]

More so than democratizing as an act – which it arguably is – Piper participates in the same circuits through which Martin's image has been circulated. By doing so, though, she counteracts the effect of the hyper-circulation. Rather than render the image affectless, the work accrues affective power through its circulation – it is a power consolidated through the instantiation of an embodied connection between the viewer and the work and what it does (or does not) represent. This connection is the one before the viewer signifies Martin; it again is that in-between in which meaning is held. Speed is often conflated with circulation; here we are slowed down.

Kehinde Wiley, another artist whose work I explored in Chapter 4, has explored the predicament of the black male in the United States. As critic Deborah Solomon writes, 'Wiley began thinking about the stereotypes that shadow black men long before events in Ferguson, Mo.'[95] Solomon is referring to the death of 18-year-old African American Michael Brown, Jr, after an encounter with police officer Darren Wilson on 19 August 2014 in Ferguson, part of the Greater St Louis area of the state of Missouri in the United States.[96] Brown's death happened a little over a year after Martin's. Wiley told Solomon in an interview: 'I know how young black men are seen … They're boys, scared little boys oftentimes. I was one of them. I was completely afraid of the Los Angeles Police Department.'[97]

While he was an artist-in-residence at the Studio Museum in Harlem, New York City, in 2001–2, Wiley came across a crumpled piece of paper on a street near the museum that turned out to be a New York Police Department (NYPD) mugshot of a young 'black' male.[98] The mugshot did not become source material for his work, though, until several years after his residency ended when he began thinking of it in the context of Western portraiture, posing and power as he explains in an interview with Roy Hurst for National Public Radio:

> I began thinking about this mug shot itself as portraiture in a very perverse sense, a type of marking, a recording of one's place in the world in time. And I began to start thinking about a lot of the portraiture that I had enjoyed from the eighteenth century and noticed the difference between the two: how one is positioned in a way that is totally outside their control, shutdown and relegated to those in power, whereas those in the other were positioning themselves in states of stately grace and self-possession.[99]

In 2006 he would finally do a portrait of the young man in the mugshot. Wiley's depiction of his subject's skin colour in *Mugshot Study* is lush and varied in tone (Plate 24). His subject is almost beatific. Directly under his portrait he faintly painted the sequence of numbers and letters that made up his New York State ID (NYSID) Number.[100] The digits are largely washed out and thereby become untethered signifiers. At the same time, Wiley's title for the work, *Mugshot Study*, subtly betrays the numbers' genealogy and specificity.

In this way, in Wiley's work the black male subject is both positioned in 'states of stately grace and self-possession' (subject) and depicted as a criminal (object).[101] This tension keeps his depicted subject between or trans (across) identifications instead of polarized as only productive reimaginations. Not surprisingly, Wiley refers to these works as 'anti-portrait paintings'.[102] In her thorough review of the criticism of Wiley's work, curator Connie Choi makes the astute point that his anti-portrait paintings are an 'ironic cultural criticism by the artist when thought of in relation to the historical depiction of African American bodies and its reduction of them to stereotypes'.[103] I would extend her argument to write that Wiley's work, by functioning between signs rather than at either pole, is about the past, present and future.

Wiley's works, much like that of Piper's digital work, Goodrich's cartoon and Martin's memorial, function at the in-between of significations. In so doing they hold out for more ethical futures – without insisting they will in fact happen – as much as they refuse to deny the politics and tragedy of real-world events. Empowering viewers to embrace this affective position is in fact more powerful than delivering either sharp criticism or blithely offering potentially false promises of the future.

Notes

1 National Commission on Terrorist Attacks Upon the United States, 'Executive Summary of "9/11 Commission Report: Final Report of the National

Commission on Terrorist Attacks Upon the United States"', accessed 22 July 2004, www.9–11commission.gov/report/911Report_Exec.pdf; 'Stockwell One: Investigation into the Shooting of Jean Charles de Menezes at Stockwell Underground Station on 22 July 2005' (London: Independent Police Complaints Commission (IPCC), 8 November 2007); CNN Library, 'Trayvon Martin Shooting Fast Facts', *CNN*, accessed 19 February 2016, www.cnn.com/2013/06/05/us/trayvon-martin-shooting-fast-facts/index.html.

2 Bennett summarizes several prevailing definitions of affect and what links them together as follows: 'Whether we think of affect in the term proposed by the American twentieth century psychologist Silvan Tompkins, as a subjectively originating energy that attaches itself to objects; or in the trans-subject terms of [French philosopher Gilles] Deleuze-inspired media studies, as a force within media itself; or, indeed, in [French psychoanalyst André] Green's … terms that cast affect as an aspect of the drives with a propensity to hook onto things real and imagined – we can concur that sometimes images and objects are simply in the path of an oncoming affect. Affect "enlivens" objects and experiences because it invests them with joy, sadness, wonder, rage.' See Jill Bennett, *Practical Aesthetics: Events, Affects and Art after 9/11* (London; New York: I. B. Tauris, 2012), 21–2.

3 Ibid.; Amelia Jones, *Seeing Differently: A History and Theory of Identification and the Visual Arts* (London: Routledge, 2012); Marsha Meskimmon, *Contemporary Art and the Cosmopolitan Imagination* (London and New York: Routledge, 2011).

4 Bennett, *Practical Aesthetics*, 36.

5 Ibid.

6 Ibid., 2. She further summarizes briefly other major scholars and how they have approached 'aesthetics'. She writes that philosopher 'Jacques Rancière reconfigures the aesthetic as the site for the systematic ordering of sense experience … which in turn establishes the political function of the aesthetic'; and that many media theorists (drawing on thinkers such as Deleuze and Guattari) have 'shifted the terms of aesthetic analysis to focus on media dynamics, affect and perception'.

7 Ibid., 1. See Alexander Gottlieb Baumgarten, *Aesthetica* (Hildesheim, Germany: G. Olms, 1961).

8 Bennett, *Practical Aesthetics*, 13.

9 Ibid., 21.

10 Ibid., 13.

11 Ibid.

12 Ibid., 3.

13 Ibid., 2.

14 Emphasis in original. Ibid., 40.

15 Ibid., 29. See also Terry Smith, Okwui Enwezor and Nancy Condee, *Antinomies of Art and Culture: Modernity, Postmodernity, Contemporaneity* (Durham, NC: Duke University Press, 2008).

16 Bennett, *Practical Aesthetics*, 18.
17 See ibid., 10–12. She writes that affect as a concept is problematic for visual culture in its disciplinary configuration. Visual culture is either still interested in exploring objects or has a fairly disembodied notion of the 'visual'. Bennett cites art historian James Elkins's writing several times regarding his wariness of visual culture as a field to explore 9/11 in particular. See ibid., 15–20 and James Elkins, *Visual Studies: A Skeptical Introduction* (New York: Routledge, 2003). Moreover despite the revival of interest in aesthetics in art history, the latter's separation of the former from postmodernism and postcolonialism has returned aesthetics to narrow formalist concerns.
18 Bennett, *Practical Aesthetics*, 28–9.
19 Ibid., 43.
20 Ibid., 46.
21 Ibid., 4.
22 Ibid., 26.
23 Jones, *Seeing Differently*, 236.
24 Ibid., 199.
25 Cf. Simon O'Sullivan, *Art Encounters: Deleuze and Guattari: Thought Beyond Representation* (Basingstoke: Palgrave Macmillan, 2006); Jan Verwoert, lecture at McGill University, 2011 as referenced in Jones, *Seeing Differently*, 214 (note 42).
26 Emphasis in original. See Jones, *Seeing Differently*, 188–9.
27 For a fuller discussion of the rhizome, see the introductory chapter appropriately titled 'Introduction: Rhizome' of Gilles Deleuze and Félix Guattari, *A Thousand Plateaus: Capitalism and Schizophrenia* (Minneapolis: University of Minnesota Press, 1987), 3–25.
28 Emphasis in original. Jones, *Seeing Differently*, 184. See also the final section titled 'Identification, and why we need queer feminist durational thinking' of the last chapter of Jones's book in which she elaborates on both the importance of the theory of the rhizome and how it falls short of anchoring its arguments in time and space; ibid., 233–9.
29 Emphasis in original. Jones, *Seeing Differently*, 232.
30 Emphasis in original. Ibid., 170–1.
31 Cf. Carolyn Dinshaw et al., 'Theorizing Queer Temporalities: A Roundtable Discussion', *GLQ: A Journal of Lesbian and Gay Studies* 13, nos 2–3 (2007): 177–95; Henri Bergson, *Matter and Memory*, trans. Nancy Margaret Paul and W. Scott Palmer (New York: Zone Books, 1988). Originally published as *Matière et mémoire: Essai sur la relation du corps à l'esprit* by Alcan in 1896 and again in 1908.
32 Jones, *Seeing Differently*, 171.
33 Ibid., xx.
34 Meskimmon, *Contemporary Art and the Cosmopolitan Imagination*, 90–3.
35 Ibid., 91.
36 Ibid., 19.
37 Ibid.

38 Ibid.
39 Ibid., 9.
40 Ibid., 91.
41 Human Rights Watch interview with Sergeant Mike Goulet of the Mesa, Arizona police department, 6 August 2002, as cited here: 'UNITED STATES: "WE ARE NOT THE ENEMY": Hate Crimes Against Arabs, Muslims, and Those Perceived to Be Arab or Muslim after September 11', *Human Rights Watch* 14, no. 6 (G) (November 2002): 18 (note 89).
42 L. Volpp, 'The Citizen and the Terrorist', *UCLA Law Review* 49 (2002): 1575. She notes, 'Persons of many different races and religions have been attacked as presumably appearing "Middle Eastern, Arab, or Muslim". South Asians, in particular, along with Arabs and persons of Middle Eastern descent, have been subject to attack, although Latinos and African Americans have also been so identified' (1599 (note 2)). See also Inderpal Grewal, *Transnational America: Feminisms, Diasporas, Neoliberalisms* (Durham, NC: Duke University Press, 2005). See chapter 5, 'Transnational America: Race and Gender After 9/11'.
43 Vijay Prashad, 'Shrouded by Flags', *Vietnam Veterans Against the War Anti-Imperialist*, 19 September 2001, http://vvawai.org/archive/afghan/shrouded-by-flags.html.
44 This section on faith and visual identification is inspired by the conference 'Faith & Identity in Contemporary Visual Culture', organized by Amelia Jones and coordinated in collaboration with Shisha, a Manchester-based agency for contemporary South Asian crafts and visual arts, among others. The conference was held on 10–11 November 2006 at the University of Manchester.
45 'Why Do Sikhs Wear Turbans?', *SikhNet*, accessed 30 January 2016, http://fateh.sikhnet.com/s/WhyTurbans.
46 Volpp, 'The Citizen and the Terrorist', 1590. See also Tamar Lewin and Gustav Niebuhr, 'A NATION CHALLENGED: VIOLENCE; Attacks and Harassment Continue on Middle Eastern People and Mosques', *The New York Times*, 18 September 2001, www.nytimes.com/2001/09/18/us/nation-challenged-violence-attacks-harassment-continue-middle-eastern-people.html. In addition, Mark Stromer notes that 'Since the terrorist attacks of September 11, 2001, videos and images of Osama bin Laden have created an air of hostility towards Sikhs, with an uninformed American public equating the appearance of Sikh men with bin Laden's beard and Afghani-style turban.' Mark Stromer, 'Combating Hate Crimes Against Sikhs: A Multi-Tentacled Approach', *The Journal of Gender, Race & Justice* 9, no. 3 (2006): 740.
47 Neha Singh Gohil and Dawinder S. Sidhu, 'The Sikh Turban, Post-911 Challenges to this Article of Faith', *Rutgers Journal of Law and Religion* 9:2 (Spring 2008): 19. Rajwant Singh, chief of the Sikh Council on Religion and Education (SCORE), a Washington DC-based Sikh advocacy group, noted that in a survey conducted by his organization in 2006, 'nine out of 10 educated Americans identified Sikhs with Muslims' See *The Financial Express*, 'Osama

becomes a Pain for American Sikhs', 10 July 2006, www.financialexpress.com/old/latest_full_story.php?content_id=133438.

48 The beard is occluded from full view given that he is cowering in fear.

49 'Common Sikh American Head Coverings', *US Department of Justice*, 2004, www.justice.gov/sites/default/files/crt/legacy/2008/10/21/sikh_poster.pdf. (accessed 28 May 2008).

50 Karen Engle, 'Constructing Good Aliens and Good Citizens: Legitimizing the War on Terror(ism)', *University of Colorado Law Review* 75, no. 1 (Winter 2004): 98.

51 Jeremy Page, 'Sikhs Head for the Barber and Turn Their Backs on Tradition', *The Times*, 24 November 2006, www.thetimes.co.uk/tto/news/world/asia/article2610612.ece.

52 'Frank S. Roque', *Arizona Republic*, 22 June 2004, http://archive.azcentral.com/specials/special32/articles/08030622roque-ON.html.

53 Jasbir K. Puar, *Terrorist Assemblages: Homonationalism in Queer Times* (Durham, NC: Duke University Press, 2007), 215.

54 Kimberlé Crenshaw, 'Mapping the Margins: Intersectionality, Identity Politics, and Violence Against Women of Color', in *The Public Nature of Private Violence: The Discovery of Domestic Abuse*, ed. Martha Albertson Fineman and Roxanne Mykitiuk (New York: Routledge, 1994), 94. Important scholarly forerunners to my own use of an intersectional framework in visual analysis include the collection of edited essays in *How Do I Look? Queer Film and Video* (1991); and the special journal issue of *Signs* (2006), which focused on intersectionality, feminism and visual culture. See Jennifer Doyle and Amelia Jones (eds), *Signs: Journal of Women in Culture and Society* 31:3 (Spring 2006). Special issue, 'New Feminist Theories of Visual Culture' and Bad Object Choices (organization), *How Do I Look? Queer Film and Video* (Seattle: Bay Press, 1991).

55 Jasbir K. Puar, '"I Would Rather Be a Cyborg than a Goddess": Intersectionality, Assemblage, and Affective Politics', European Institute for Progressive Cultural Policies, *Transversal* (2011), http://eipcp.net/transversal/0811/puar/en.

56 Ibid.

57 Ibid.

58 'Stockwell One: Investigation into the Shooting of Jean Charles de Menezes at Stockwell Underground Station on 22 July 2005'.

59 'Remembering the Blitz', *Museum of London*, accessed 30 January 2016, http://archive.museumoflondon.org.uk/archive/exhibits/blitz/index.html; Donald MacLeod, 'London: Past Terror Attacks', *Guardian*, 7 July 2005, sec. UK news, www.theguardian.com/uk/2005/jul/07/terrorism.july73.

60 Nick Hopkins, 'Bomber Gets Six Life Terms', *Guardian*, 30 June 2000, sec. UK news, www.theguardian.com/uk/2000/jul/01/uksecurity.nickhopkins.

61 'Stockwell One: Investigation into the Shooting of Jean Charles de Menezes at Stockwell Underground Station on 22 July 2005', 18.

62 Ibid., 20.

63 Ibid.
64 'Profile: Hussain Osman', *BBC News*, 9 July 2007, http://news.bbc.co.uk/2/hi/uk_news/6634923.stm.
65 The officer had been urinating in a plastic container in the van at the time, so he was unable to make a positive identification of any kind. See 'Stockwell One: Investigation into the Shooting of Jean Charles de Menezes at Stockwell Underground Station on 22 July 2005', 55.
66 Ibid., 81.
67 Ibid., 55, 64, 76.
68 Ibid., 66, 68, 69.
69 Ibid., 65.
70 This is not to imply, of course, that the conflation of terrorism with Arab-ness is any less problematic. See Human Rights Watch's 'UNITED STATES: "WE ARE NOT THE ENEMY": Hate Crimes Against Arabs, Muslims, and Those Perceived to Be Arab or Muslim after September 11'; Muneer Ahmad, 'Homeland Insecurities: Racial Violence the Day after September 11', *Social Text* 20, no. 3 (2002): 101–15.
71 'Stockwell One: Investigation into the Shooting of Jean Charles de Menezes at Stockwell Underground Station on 22 July 2005', 55–6.
72 'We grasp external space through our bodily situation. A "corporeal or postural schema" gives us at every moment a global, practical and implicit notion of the relation between our body and things.' See Maurice Merleau-Ponty, *Phenomenology of Perception*, trans. Colin Smith, International Library of Philosophy and Scientific Method (New York: Humanities Press, 1962), 5.
73 As Merleau-Ponty indicates, 'habit does not *consist* in interpreting the pressures of the stick on the hand as indications of certain positions of the stick, and these as signs of an external object, since it *relieves us of the necessity* of doing so.' Emphasis in original. Ibid., 152.
74 Whether or not de Menezes self-identified as Brazilian is unclear.
75 Merleau-Ponty, *Phenomenology of Perception*, 408.
76 René Descartes, *Discourse on Method: And, The Meditations*, trans. John Veitch (Amherst: Prometheus Books, 1989), 31. See also Antonio R. Damasio, *Descartes' Error: Emotion, Reason, and the Human Brain* (New York: G.P. Putnam, 1994). Damasio illustrates the central role of the body in cognition and emotion in both bodily and intellectual processes.
77 Maurice Merleau-Ponty, *The Visible and the Invisible; Followed by Working Notes*, ed. Claude Lefort, trans. Alphonso Lingis, Northwestern University Studies in Phenomenology & Existential Philosophy (Evanston, IL: Northwestern University Press, 1968), 130, 138, 140–1.
78 Nicole Bode, 'Teen Gets No Jail for Anti-Sikh Hate Crime', *NY Daily News*, 5 June 2008, www.nydailynews.com/new-york/queens/teen-no-jail-anti-sikh-hate-crime-article-1.292742. Women wearing the hijab were also affected, as noted in 'UNITED STATES: "WE ARE NOT THE ENEMY": Hate Crimes Against Arabs, Muslims, and Those Perceived to Be Arab or Muslim after September 11', 21.

79 To extend this argument, de Menezes's legality in the UK was still unclear days after his death, fuelled primarily by a statement from the Home Office that indicated that the stamp in his passport allowing him indefinite stay 'was not one that was in use by the Immigration and Nationality Directorate on the date given'. See Jenny Booth, 'Shot Brazilian Had Phoney Visa, Says Home Office (UK)', *The Times*, 28 July 2005, www.freerepublic.com/focus/news/1452554/posts. It was not until November 2007 when the IPCC's report into the death of de Menezes was published that his legal status was definitively confirmed: 'Evidence emerged during the course of the criminal trial into the Health and Safety charge that Mr de Menezes was lawfully in the country on 22 July 2005.' See 'Stockwell One: Investigation into the Shooting of Jean Charles de Menezes at Stockwell Underground Station on 22 July 2005', 21 (note 4). The information, however, was buried in a footnote.

80 Haroon Siddique, 'Jean Charles de Menezes Memorial Unveiled at Stockwell Station', *Guardian*, 7 January 2010, sec. UK news, www.theguardian.com/uk/2010/jan/07/jean-charles-de-menezes-memorial.

81 Karen Wells, 'Melancholic Memorialisation: The Ethical Demands of Grievable Lives', in *Visuality/Materiality: Images, Objects and Practices*, ed. Divya P. Tolia-Kelly and Gillian Rose (Farnham and Burlington: Ashgate, 2012), 165. Wells is drawing on poststructuralist scholars' (she cites Judith Butler and Paul Gilroy among others: see ibid., 162) readings of Sigmund Freud's essay 'Mourning and Melancholia'. See Sigmund Freud, 'Mourning and Melancholia (1917)', in *The Standard Edition of the Complete Psychological Works of Sigmund Freud*, trans. James Strachey, Vol. XIV, 1914–1916 (London: Hogarth Press / Institute of Psycho-Analysis, 1957). Wells argues that the 'moment between the burial and the erection of some permanent marker on the burial site' is one of melancholia 'when the meaning of a tragedy is located on the border between "private grief and public justice"'. Wells, 'Melancholic Memorialisation: The Ethical Demands of Grievable Lives', 160. Wells further explains that the transition from melancholia to mourning becomes the moment of 'recognition of the failure to make somebody take responsibility for his death'. Ibid., 161. This transition materializes at the moment of the erection of de Menezes's memorial. Wells does end her essay, though, with a more hopeful note. She writes that the 'analysis of memorials can … restore them to melancholia so that they may continue to provoke us to ask political questions about the unequal distribution of violence, risk and (in) security in the contemporary city'. Ibid., 166.

82 Wells, 'Melancholic Memorialisation: The Ethical Demands of Grievable Lives', 165.

83 Ibid., 166.

84 See the chapter titled 'For Opacity', in Édouard Glissant, *Poetics of Relation*, trans. Betsy Wing (Ann Arbor: University of Michigan Press, 1997), 189–94. Originally published in French by Gallimard in 1990.

85 Ibid., 191.

86 Ibid.
87 Ibid., 190.
88 CNN Library, 'Trayvon Martin Shooting Fast Facts'.
89 'Adrian Piper, Imagine [Trayvon Martin], 2013', 6 August 2013, http://creativetimereports.tumblr.com/post/57533582798/adrian-piper-imagine-trayvon-martin-2013.
90 Adrian Piper, 'Imagine What It Was Like To Be Me', *Creative Time Reports*, accessed 5 August 2015, http://creativetime.org/reports/2013/08/05/trayvon-martin-imagine-by-adrian-piper/.
91 Adrian Margaret Smith Piper, 'APRA Foundation Berlin: Adrian Piper's "Imagine [Trayvon Martin]" (2013) FREE', announcement archive, E-Artnow.org (30 January 2015), www.e-artnow.org/announcement-archive/archive/2015/1/article/ACTION/10789/.
92 Adrian Margaret Smith Piper, 'The Color Wheel Series', 2004, 2, www.adrianpiper.com/art/docs/2004TheColorWheelSeries.pdf.
93 Martin was wearing a grey hoodie the night he died and it has become an important signifier for his death, sometimes in problematic ways. For instance, Fox News correspondent Geraldo Rivera said: 'I am urging the parents of black and Latino youngsters, particularly, to not let their young children go out wearing hoodies. I think the hoodie is as much responsible for Trayvon Martin's death as George Zimmerman was.' While he is correct that the hoodie probably did have something to do with Martin's death what he unfortunately reinscribes with such a statement is that the victim is to blame or that by simply removing one's hoodie one is out of danger. See Erik Wemple, 'Geraldo's Hoodie Comments: Definitely Not a Hoax', *The Washington Post*, 23 March 2012, www.washingtonpost.com/blogs/erik-wemple/post/geraldos-hoodie-comments-definitely-not-a-hoax/2012/03/23/gIQAPmVGWS_blog.html?tid=a_inl. Perhaps more problematic, are the statements by Rivera's colleague Bill O'Reilly. He said that had Martin only been wearing a suit instead of looking like a 'gangsta' he would not have been killed. He also makes the provocative point that race had nothing to do with Martin's death. Both the latter points are incredibly reductive (not too mention racist) and do not take into consideration the complex manner in which visual identification works. See Eric Wemple, 'Fox News's Bill O'Reilly Blames Trayvon Martin's Death on Hoodie', newspaper, *The Washington Post* (16 September 2003), www.washingtonpost.com/blogs/erik-wemple/wp/2013/09/16/fox-newss-bill-oreilly-blames-trayvon-martins-death-on-hoodie/. In any case, the hoodie has become an important signifier for the death of Martin. At one point there was even speculation that the Smithsonian Museum was thinking of acquiring Martin's hoodie for its collection. See Jerriann Sullivan, 'Smithsonian Has "No Plans" to Display Trayvon Martin Hoodie', *Tribunedigital-Orlandosentinel*, 2 August 2013, http://articles.orlandosentinel.com/2013-08-02/news/os-trayvon-martin-hoodie-museum-20130802_1_trayvon-martin-francis-oliver-george-zimmerman. See also Emanuella Grinberg, 'Hoodie's Evolution from Fashion Mainstay to

Symbol of Injustice', *CNN*, 27 March 2012, www.cnn.com/2012/03/27/living/history-hoodie-trayvon-martin/index.html.

94 Piper, 'APRA Foundation Berlin: Adrian Piper's "Imagine [Trayvon Martin]" (2013) FREE'.

95 Deborah Solomon, 'Kehinde Wiley Puts a Classical Spin on His Contemporary Subjects', *The New York Times*, 28 January 2015, www.nytimes.com/2015/02/01/arts/design/kehinde-wiley-puts-a-classical-spin-on-his-contemporary-subjects.html.

96 See 'Timeline: Michael Brown Shooting in Ferguson, Mo.', *USA TODAY*, accessed 4 March 2016, www.usatoday.com/story/news/nation/2014/08/14/michael-brown-ferguson-missouri-timeline/14051827/.

97 Solomon, 'Kehinde Wiley Puts a Classical Spin on His Contemporary Subjects'.

98 Eugenie Tsai, 'Introduction', in *Kehinde Wiley: A New Republic*, ed. Eugenie Tsai (New York: Brooklyn Museum in association with DelMonico Books & Prestel, 2015), 12.

99 Kehinde Wiley, Interview with Roy Hurst, National Public Radio, 1 June 2005, as quoted in Robert Hobbs, 'Kehinde Wiley's Conceptual Realism', in *Kehinde Wiley* (New York: Rizzoli, 2012), 18.

100 A NYSID Number is 'a unique identifier assigned to an individual by the New York State Division of Criminal Justice Services (DCJS).' See: 'NYSID NUMBER – Data Element – NY DCJS', *NYS Division of Criminal Justice Services*, accessed 22 August 2015, www.criminaljustice.ny.gov/dict/dataelement295.htm.

101 Even at the level of reception, Wiley notes in an interview with curator Christine Y. Kim that he does not feel that he has to choose between a 'black-people-in-the-street audience' and 'a high-art audience'. Obviously, Wiley said this more to make a polemical point than to insinuate that the former could not be the latter. Put another way, he wants to engage the frequent museum visitor as much as someone who may have less knowledge of the history of art. See Christine Y. Kim, 'Faux Real: Interview with Kehinde Wiley', *Issue Magazine*, December 2003, http://issuemagazine.com/kehinde-wiley-faux-real/#/. This interview was published in its full version in Thelma Golden, *Black Romantic: The Figurative Impulse in African-American Art* (New York: Studio Museum in Harlem, 2002).

102 As quoted in Sarah Elizabeth Lewis, 'De(i)fying the Masters', *Art in America*, April 2005, 122.

103 Connie H. Choi, 'Kehinde Wiley: The Artist and Interpretation', in *Kehinde Wiley: A New Republic*, ed. Eugenie Tsai (New York: Brooklyn Museum in association with DelMonico Books & Prestel, 2015), 20–36.

Afterword

At the core of my approach to the writing of transnational South Asian art histories in this volume is a constant reassessment of belongingness. I argue that when belonging is kept open and porous, art histories (more broadly) can be dynamic and ever changing. The need or longing to belong is powerful but to what one belongs is best thought of as 'multiple and One' per Édouard Glissant.[1] In this way, the supplementarity of a transnational South Asian art history need not be one that is interminable. Rather, it can be recast as a constant mode of achieving South Asian-ness over and over again, each time in a different configuration. In this regard, I return to the concept of creolization as a process that results in incessant entanglement and constant renewal. Each point of renewal is not a moment of hybridization but rather of *indigenization* that cannot be traced back to discrete components. Indeed, sociologist Mimi Sheller points out that the word creole carries within it connotations of an 'achieved indigeneity'. She writes, 'Creolization (becoming Creole) can therefore be understood as a process of achieving an indigenous status of belonging to a locale through the migration and recombination of diverse elements that have been loosed from previous attachments and have reattached themselves to a new place of belonging.'[2] Though Sheller is not referring to writing art histories, I would argue that the chapters of this book are materializations of different kinds of belonging or iterations of what might be an achieved transnational South Asian indigeneity and art history.

At the same time, I want to tread lightly here. Many populations consider themselves as indigenous to certain lands and continue to work earnestly to be recognized as such by governments. My approach to indigeneity is certainly not meant to abstract the subjectivities of these individuals (or at worst be used as a tool to proclaim that we are post-indigineous!). In other words, there is an ethics that must go along with my theorization. In terms of the remit of this book, my use of indigeneity can marginalize histories of art that deal exclusively with works by artists of South Asian descent. That is, such histories could be implicitly cast as being too invested in a 'singular' root; and thereby diminishing the significance and value of such endeavours. This is certainly not my aim here, either: to do so would constitute a failure that is neither productive nor queer. Indeed, while Glissant challenges the notion of a totalitarian root, he does not give up on rootedness – just one borne through chaotic relations (broadly construed).

Expanding on Sheller's point, art historian Marsha Meskimmon describes how an artwork might engender an achieved indigeneity as the 'very possibility of a cosmopolitan imagination'.[3] Her link of the concept of cosmopolitanism 'to the concept of home and belonging … and to ethics' is particularly appropriate given my discussion above concerning the need for an ethics when writing transnational South Asian art histories as achieved indigeneity.[4] Meskimmon powerfully argues that the engagement of the viewer with an artwork can produce knowledge and even instantiate an ethics of being *a part* of the world rather than *apart* from it. Moreover, she explains, 'Achieved indigeneity understands the [viewing] subject who advances, moves on, never ceases to develop … Indeed I would argue more strongly that the longing for belonging is ambitious, productive and, importantly, political in its ramifications.'[5]

It is important to foreground that this notion of indigeneity is indebted not only to postcolonial but also queer and feminist theories. Indeed, Meskimmon's writing is informed by feminist philosophy on embodied subjectivity, situated knowledge, aesthetics and ethics. I am thinking here also of Amelia Jones's writings on the importance of feminist and queer theories to the genesis of conceptualizations of affect that I discuss in Chapter 7. In a similar way, I want to avoid this idea of achieved indigeneity from becoming too removed from lived experience, especially in relation to gender and sexuality, both of which have been central concerns of this book. In fact, cultural theorist E. K. Tan has suggested how creolization can be a useful concept through which to theorize transnational queer subjects.[6]

My production of transnational South Asian art histories has been equally informed by writing *with* rather than about artworks. This is most evident in my production of work for my project *Mixing It Up* but it is just as true with my engagement with extant work. This is a shift from only considering an artwork as something to be 'read' to something that co-produces thought and knowledge with the engagement of the art historian. As art historian Jill Bennett perspicaciously points out: 'We have rarely asked what it might mean to derive theory *from* the visual.'[7] Meskimmon has written that such an approach effectively shifts our understanding of theory from something disembodied and conceptual to one that is 'itself part of a critical exchange, responsive to material and able to be revised'.[8] In this way, she argues this critical exchange effectively 'corporealizes theory'.[9] Such a theory 'acknowledges the significance of thinking-in-making and encourages the emergence of a dynamic, process-based criticism between texts and images – as well as between subjects and objects'.[10]

Perhaps it is best to write that this book is about writing transnational South Asian histories not of and about artworks but with and through them. To be clear, I do not mean to instrumentalize artworks as inert objects from which theory can be extracted; this is just as problematic as the artwork that is put forth as an illustration of a theory. Rather, artworks slow down the historian to articulate the much more complex in-between of meaning and more specifically – in the context of this book – of transnational South Asian art histories.

Finally, I acknowledge there is potential for a kind of exhaustion in the unending nature of realizing art histories – even as achieved indigeneity. Stamina in the face of such unending multiplicity is vital. In feminist postcolonial literature scholar Gayatri Chakravorty Spivak's attempt to rethink the discipline of comparative literature, she mobilizes creolization theory and writes, 'Creolity assumes imperfection, even as it assures the survival of a rough future.'[11] If there is exhaustion, it is a queer one that neither ignores fatigue is a real condition nor considers fatigue as non-productive.[12] Endurance, strength and tenacity are key in navigating a 'rough future' of creolizing transnational South Asian art histories.

Notes

1 Édouard Glissant, *La cohée du Lamentin* (Paris: Gallimard, 2005), 15, as quoted in Jane Hiddleston, *Understanding Postcolonialism* (London; New York: Routledge, 2014), 146. First published in 2009.
2 Mimi Sheller, *Consuming the Caribbean: From Arawaks to Zombies* (London and New York: Routledge, 2003), 182, as cited in Marsha Meskimmon, *Contemporary Art and the Cosmopolitan Imagination* (London and New York: Routledge, 2011), 79, 100 (note 10).
3 Meskimmon, *Contemporary Art and the Cosmopolitan Imagination*, 79.
4 Ibid., 6–7. Meskimmon's more recent writing on artworks that through their agency of world-making bring into being 'precarious ecologies of cosmopolitanism' is also appealing. She writes, 'While the precarious does signal fragility, ephemerality, uncertainty and risk, its etymology further connects it with prayer or entreaty. That which is precarious is dependent upon the will or favour of another.' Marsha Meskimmon, 'The Precarious Ecologies of Cosmopolitanism', *Open Arts Journal* 1 (2013): 21, doi:10.5456/issn.5050-3679/2013s03mm.
5 Meskimmon, *Contemporary Art and the Cosmopolitan Imagination*, 79.
6 E. K. Tan, 'A Queer Journey Home in "Solos": Rethinking Kinship in Sinophone Singapore', in *Queer Sinophone Cultures*, ed. Howard Chiang and Ari Larissa Heinrich (New York: Routledge, 2013), 140–3.

7 Emphasis in original. Jill Bennett, *Empathic Vision: Affect, Trauma, and Contemporary Art* (Stanford, CA: Stanford University Press, 2005), 150.

8 Marsha Meskimmon, 'Corporeal Theory with/in Practice: Christine Borland's Winter Garden', *Art History* 26, no. 3 (1 June 2003): 451.

9 Ibid.

10 Ibid.

11 Gayatri Chakravorty Spivak, 'World Systems and the Creole, Rethought', in *Creolizing Europe: Legacies and Transformations*, ed. Encarnación Gutiérrez Rodríguez and Shirley Anne Tate (Liverpool: Liverpool University Press, 2015), 28. This is a revised version of chapter 21 of her book, *An Aesthetic Education in the Era of Globalization* (Cambridge, MA: Harvard University Press, 2012).

12 My writing here on queer exhaustion is indebted to performance artist Xandra Ibarra with whom I have had many conversations; and to artist and scholar Tina T. Takemoto, who co-chaired a panel with me on this topic at the 2016 annual conference of the College Art Association (CAA). The panel was sponsored by CAA's Queer Caucus for Art. Panellists included Nao Bustamante, Robert Summers and Tameka Norris. There is more to be written about 'queer exhaustion' but I leave that for another project.

Bibliography

'2Pac – Chitty Chitty Bang Bang Freestyle Lyrics'. *Metro Lyrics*. Accessed 2 January 2016. www.metrolyrics.com/chitty-chitty-bang-bang-freestyle-lyrics-2pac.html.

'A Grand Exhibition of U.S. Painting Comes to India'. *Statesman*, 26 March 1967.

Adams, James. 'Artist Kehinde Wiley and "the Call of the Avant-Garde"'. *The Globe and Mail*. Accessed 6 October 2015. www.theglobeandmail.com/arts/film/artist-kehinde-wiley-and-the-call-of-the-avant-garde/article17003136/.

Ahmad, Muneer. 'Homeland Insecurities: Racial Violence the Day after September 11'. *Social Text* 20, no. 3 (2002): 101–15.

Ahmed, Sophie. 'Chicken Tikka Masala'. In *A Postcolonial People: South Asians in Britain*, ed. Nasreen Ali, Virinder S. Kalra and S. Sayyid, 62–3. New York: Columbia University Press, 2008.

Alderson, David. 'Queer Cosmopolitanism: Place, Politics, Citizenship and *Queer as Folk*'. *New Formations* 55 (2005): 73–88.

Althusser, Louis. 'Ideology and Ideological State Apparatuses'. In *Lenin and Philosophy, and Other Essays*, translated by Ben Brewster, 127–86. New York: Monthly Review Press, 1972.

'An Alternative to Pride'. *Manchester Evening News*, 23 August 2005. www.manchestereveningnews.co.uk/whats-on/going-out/music/an-alternative-to-pride-1081267.

Andreae, Christopher. 'Beautiful Painting and Sculpture at the Jewish Museum'. *Christian Science Monitor*, 20 April 1970.

'Anish Kapoor, Interviewed by Shekhar Gupta'. *Walk the Talk*, 3 December 2010. www.ndtv.com/video/player/walk-the-talk/walk-the-talk-with-anish-kapoor/175606.

'Anish Kapoor: Delhi Mumbai'. Press release. British Council Visual Arts, 2010. http://visualarts.britishcouncil.org/exhibitions/exhibition/anish-kapoor-delhi-mumbai-2010.

'Anish Kapoor's Biography'. *Gladstone Gallery*. Accessed 2 January 2016. www.gladstonegallery.com/artist/anish-kapoor/biography.

Anzaldúa, Gloria. *Borderlands/La Frontera*. San Francisco: Aunt Lute Books, 1999.

'Asian American Art: A History, 1850–1970'. *Stanford University Press*. Accessed 8 May 2015. www.sup.org/books/title/?id=9403.

Association, Press. '"Dangerous Dye Levels" Found in Tikka'. *Guardian*, 23 March 2004. www.theguardian.com/uk/2004/mar/23/foodanddrink.

Austin, J. L. (John Langshaw). *How to Do Things with Words*. 2nd edn. The William James Lectures 1955. Cambridge, MA: Harvard University Press, 1975.

Barthes, Roland. 'Cy Twombly: Works on Paper'. In *The Responsibility of Forms: Critical Essays on Music, Art, and Representation*, translated by Richard Howard, 157–76. New York: Hill & Wang, 1985.

———. '"L'Express" Talks with Roland Barthes'. In *The Grain of the Voice: Interviews 1962–1980*, translated by Linda Coverdale, 88–108. New York: Hill & Wang, 1985.

———. 'Non Multa Sed Multum'. In *Cy Twombly: Fifty Years of Works on Paper*, translated by Henry Martin, 23–40. Munich: Schirmer/Mosel, 2004.

———. 'Preface to Renauld Camus's *Tricks*'. In *The Rustle of Language*, translated by Richard Howard, 291–5. Berkeley: University of California Press, 1989.

———. *Roland Barthes par Roland Barthes*. Paris: Seuil, 1975.

———. *Roland Barthes by Roland Barthes*. Translated by Richard Howard. New York: Hill & Wang, 1977.

Batchelor, David. *Chromophobia*. London: Reaktion, 2000.

Baumgarten, Alexander Gottlieb. *Aesthetica*. Hildesheim, Germany: G. Olms, 1961.

Bedell, Geraldine. 'It's Curry, but Not as We Know It'. *Guardian*. Accessed 3 November 2005. www.theguardian.com/lifeandstyle/2002/may/12/foodanddrink.shopping2.

Bell, Vikki. 'On Speech, Race and Melancholia: An Interview with Judith Butler'. *Theory, Culture & Society* 16, no. 2 (1999): 163–74.

Belting, Hans, Andrea Buddensieg and Emanoel Araújo, eds. *The Global Art World: Audiences, Markets, and Museums*. Ostfildern, Germany: Hatje Cantz, 2009.

Belting, Hans, Andrea Buddensieg and Peter Weibel, eds. *The Global Contemporary and the Rise of New Art Worlds*. Karlsruhe, Germany: ZKM/Center for Art and Media; Cambridge, MA; London: MIT Press, 2013.

Benjamin, Walter. '"The Bohème," the first part of his essay, "The Paris of the Second Empire in Baudelaire" (1938; translation, 1969)'. In *Walter Benjamin: Selected Writings: Volume 4, 1938–1940*, ed. Howard Eiland and Michael W. Jennings, translated by Edmund Jephcott and others, 3–18. Cambridge, MA; London: Belknap Press of Harvard University Press, 2006.

———. '"The Flâneur," the first part of his essay, "The Paris of the Second Empire in Baudelaire" (1938; translation, 1969)'. In *Walter Benjamin: Selected Writings: Volume 4, 1938–1940*, ed. Howard Eiland and Michael W. Jennings, translated by Edmund Jephcott and others, 18–39. Cambridge, MA; London: Belknap Press of Harvard University Press, 2006.

———. 'The Work of Art in the Age of Mechanical Reproduction (1936)'. In *Illuminations*, translated by Harry Zohn, 211–44. New York: Schocken Books, 1986.

Bennett, Jill. *Empathic Vision: Affect, Trauma, and Contemporary Art*. Stanford, CA.: Stanford University Press, 2005.

———. *Practical Aesthetics: Events, Affects and Art after 9/11*. London; New York: I. B. Tauris, 2012.

Berger, Martin A. *Sight Unseen Whiteness and American Visual Culture*. Berkeley: University of California Press, 2005.

Berger, Maurice. 'Picturing Whiteness: Nikki S. Lee's Yuppie Project'. *Art Journal* 60, no. 4 (1 December 2001): 54–7.

Bergson, Henri. *Matter and Memory*. Translated by Nancy Margaret Paul and W. Scott Palmer. New York: Zone Books, 1988.

Bernabé, Jean, Patrick Chamoiseau and Raphaël Confiant. 'In Praise of Creoleness'. Edited and translated by Mohamed B. Taleb Khyar. *Callaloo* 13, no. 4 (1990): 886–909. doi:10.2307/2931390.

Bhabha, Homi. 'Hybridité, identité et culture contemporaine'. In *Magiciens de la terre*, ed. Jean Hubert Martin and Homi Bhabha, 24–7. Paris: Editions du Centre Pompidou, 1989.

Bhattacharjee, Suprio. 'Lost Landscapes: On Bombay's Urban Development'. In *A Formal Film in Nine Episodes, Prologue and Epilogue: A Critical Reader*, ed. Susanne Gaensheimer and Bernd Reiss, 218–39. Leipzig: Spector Books, 2013.

Bhavsar, Natvar. 'Interview with Abeed Hossain. "The Metaphysics of Expression: A Conversation with Natvar Bhavsar"'. *South Asia Journal*, no. 4 (21 March 2012). http://southasiajournal.net/the-metaphysics-of-expression-a-conversation-with-natvar-bhavsar/.

———. Interview by Alpesh Kantilal Patel and Santhi Kavuri-Bauer, 17 July 2012.

———. Interview by Alpesh Kantilal Patel, 6 August 2015.

Bhowmick, Nilanjana. 'Homosexuality Is Criminal Again as India's Top Court Reinstates Ban'. *Time*. Accessed 1 February 2016. http://world.time.com/2013/12/11/homosexuality-is-criminal-again-as-indias-top-court-reinstates-ban/.

Binnie, Jon, and Beverley Skeggs. 'Cosmopolitan Knowledge and the Production and Consumption of Sexualized Space: Manchester's Gay Village'. *Sociological Review* 52, no. 1 (February 2004): 39–61.

Bird, Jon. 'Indeterminacy and (Dis)order in the Work of Cy Twombly'. *Oxford Art Journal* 30, no. 3 (1 October 2007): 484–504. doi:10.1093/oxartj/kcm024.

Booth, Jenny. 'Shot Brazilian Had Phoney Visa, Says Home Office (UK)'. *The Times*, 28 July 2005. www.freerepublic.com/focus/news/1452554/posts.

Bourdieu, Pierre. *La domination masculine*. Paris: Éditions du Seuil, 1998.

———. *Masculine Domination*. Translated by Richard Nice. Stanford, CA: Stanford University Press, 2001.

Bourne, Dianne. 'Village Boss Hits out at Jongleurs Closure'. *Manchester Evening News*, 15 February 2007. www.manchestereveningnews.co.uk/whats-on/comedy-gigs/village-boss-hits-out-at-jongleurs-1041188.

Bowles, John P. 'Forum: Blinded by the White: Art and History at the Limits of Whiteness'. *Art Journal* 60, no. 4 (1 December 2001): 38–43.

Breckenridge, Carol A. 'Public Modernity in India'. In *Consuming Modernity Public Culture in a South Asian World*, 1–20. Minneapolis: University of Minnesota Press, 1995. http://site.ebrary.com/id/10159480.

Brennan, Timothy. *At Home in the World: Cosmopolitanism Now*. Convergences. Cambridge, MA: Harvard University Press, 1997.

Browne, Kath, Sally R. Munt, and Andrew K.T. Yip. *Queer Spiritual Spaces: Sexuality and Sacred Places*. Farnham and Burlington, VT: Ashgate, 2010. http://public.eblib.com/choice/publicfullrecord.aspx?p=513923.

Butler, Judith. *Bodies That Matter: On the Discursive Limits of 'Sex'*. New York: Routledge, 1993.

———. 'Critically Queer'. *GLQ: A Journal of Lesbian and Gay Studies* 1, no. 1 (1 November 1993): 17–32. doi:10.1215/10642684-1-1-17.

Butt, Gavin. *Between You and Me: Queer Disclosures in the New York Art World, 1948–1963*. Durham, NC: Duke University Press, 2005.

———, ed. *After Criticism: New Responses to Art and Performance*. Malden, MA: Blackwell, 2005.

———. 'Introduction: The Paradoxes of Criticism'. In *After Criticism: New Responses to Art and Performance*, ed. Gavin Butt, 1–19. Malden, MA: Blackwell, 2005.

Butt, Riazat. 'Manchester Police Prepare for Double Celebration'. *Guardian*, 29 December 2006, sec. UK news. www.theguardian.com/uk/2006/dec/29/religion.world.

Carter, Helen. 'Gritty City Wins the Boho Crown'. *Guardian*, 26 May 2003. www.theguardian.com/uk/2003/may/26/communities.arts.

Casid, Jill H., and Aruna D'Souza, eds. *Art History in the Wake of the Global Turn*. Clark Studies in the Visual Arts. Williamstown, MA: Sterling and Francine Clark Art Institute, 2014.

Cassina, Irene, Marco Cassina and Akaash Mehta, eds. *Natvar Bhavsar: Five Decades*. New York: Cara Gallery, 2015.

Certeau, Michel de. *The Practice of Everyday Life*. Translated by Steven Rendall. Berkeley: University of California Press, 1984.

Chancé, Dominique. 'Creolization: Definition and Critique'. In *The Creolization of Theory*, ed. Françoise Lionnet and Shu-mei Shih, translated by Julin Everett, 262–8. Durham, NC: Duke University Press, 2011.

Chang, Gordon H., Mark Dean Johnson, Paul J. Karlstrom and Sharon Spain, eds. *Asian American Art: A History, 1850–1970*. Stanford, CA: Stanford University Press, 2008.

Chapman, James. 'Women Get "Virginity Fix" NHS Operations in Muslim-Driven Trend | Daily Mail Online'. *Daily Mail*, 15 November 2007. www.dailymail.co.uk/news/article-494118/Women-virginity-fix-NHS-operations-Muslim-driven-trend.html.

'Chavscum: A User's Guide to Britain's ASBO Generation'. *Chavscum*. Accessed 12 June 2007. www.chavscum.co.uk/index.php.

Cheah, Pheng, and Bruce Robbins, eds. *Cosmopolitics: Thinking and Feeling beyond the Nation*. Cultural Politics 14. Minneapolis: University of Minnesota Press, 1998.

Chisholm, Dianne. *Queer Constellations: Subcultural Space in the Wake of the City*. Minneapolis: University of Minnesota Press, 2005.

Choi, Connie H. 'Kehinde Wiley: The Artist and Interpretation'. In *Kehinde Wiley: A New Republic*, ed. Eugenie Tsai, 20–36. New York: Brooklyn Museum, in association with DelMonico Books & Prestel, 2015.

Chrisman, Laura. 'Re-Thinking Black Atlanticism'. *The Black Scholar* 30, nos 3/4 (Fall 2000): 12–18.

Chuh, Kandice. *Imagine Otherwise: On Asian Americanist Critique*. Durham, NC: Duke University Press, 2003.

Citron, Beth. 'Modernist Art from India'. Rubin Museum of Art, New York, 2012. Exhibition brochure.

'Color Intelligence – PANTONE® Numbering Explained'. *PANTONE®*. Accessed 26 August 2015. www.pantone.com/pantone-numbering-explained.

Connell, Kieran, and Matthew Hilton. 'The Working Practices of Birmingham's Centre for Contemporary Cultural Studies'. *Social History* 40, no. 3 (3 July 2015): 287–311. doi:10.1080/03071022.2015.1043191.

'Corporate Strategy for Lesbian, Gay, Bisexual and Trans People Equality, 2003–2006'. *Birmingham City Council*. Accessed 23 October 2008. www.birmingham.gov.uk/ELibrary?E_LIBRARY_ID=174.

Cotter, Holland. 'ART IN REVIEW; Adrian Piper'. *The New York Times*, 12 January 2001, sec. Arts. www.nytimes.com/2001/01/12/arts/art-in-review-adrian-piper.html.

———. 'V. S. Gaitonde Retrospective at the Guggenheim'. *The New York Times*, 1 January 2015. www.nytimes.com/2015/01/02/arts/design/v-s-gaitonde-retrospective-at-the-guggenheim.html.

Coyotes Bar. Accessed 31 May 2008. www.coyotesbar.co.uk/.

Crenshaw, Kimberlé. 'Mapping the Margins: Intersectionality, Identity Politics, and Violence Against Women of Color'. In *The Public Nature of Private Violence: The Discovery of Domestic Abuse*, ed. Martha Albertson Fineman and Roxanne Mykitiuk, 93–118. New York: Routledge, 1994.

Crossley, Nick. 'Corporeality and Communicative Action: Embodying the Renewal of Critical Theory'. *Body and Society* 3, no. 1 (1997): 17–46.

Cvetkovich, Ann. 'Queer Art of the Counterarchive'. In *Cruising the Archive: Queer Art and Culture in Los Angeles, 1945–1980*, ed. Sarah Kessler and Mia Locks, 32–5. Los Angeles: ONE National Gay & Lesbian Archives, 2011.

Dada, T., N. Sharma and A. Kumar. 'Chemical Injury due to Colours Used at the Festival of Holi'. *The National Medical Journal of India* 10, no. 5 (1996): 256.

Daigle, Claire. 'Biography'. *Cy Twombly*. Accessed 7 May 2015. www.cytwombly.info.

———. 'Cy Twombly: Lingering at the Threshold Between Word and Image'. *TATE ETC* 13 (2008): 62–9. www.tate.org.uk/context-comment/articles/lingering-threshold-between-word-and-image.

———. 'Reading Barthes/Writing Twombly'. PhD dissertation, City University of New York, 2004.

Damasio, Antonio R. *Descartes' Error: Emotion, Reason, and the Human Brain*. New York: G.P. Putnam, 1994.

Davé, Shilpa, Pawan Dhingra, Sunaina Maira, Partha Mazumdar, Lavina Dhingra Shankar, Jaideep Singh and Rajini Srikanth. 'De-Privileging Positions: Indian Americans, South Asian Americans, and the Politics of Asian American Studies'. *Journal of Asian American Studies* 3, no. 1 (2000): 67–100.

Dean, Stephen. Interview by Alpesh Kantilal Patel, March 2005.

Deleuze, Gilles, and Félix Guattari. *A Thousand Plateaus: Capitalism and Schizophrenia*. Minneapolis: University of Minnesota Press, 1987.

Derrida, Jacques. *Dissemination*. Translated by Barbara Johnson. London: Continuum, 2004.

———. *Of Grammatology*. Baltimore: Johns Hopkins University Press, 1976.

———. *Speech and Phenomena: And Other Essays on Husserl's Theory of Signs*. Translated by David B. Allison. Evanston, IL: Northwestern University Press, 1973.

———. *The Truth in Painting*. Chicago: University of Chicago Press, 1987.

Desai, Jigna. 'Homo on the Range: Mobile and Global Sexualities'. *Social Text* 20, no. 4 (2002): 65–89.

Devere Brody, Jennifer. 'Shading Meaning'. In *Performing the Body/Performing the Text*, ed. Amelia Jones and Andrew Stephenson, 89–106. London; New York: Routledge, 1999.

Dinshaw, Carolyn, Lee Edelman, Roderick A. Ferguson and Carla Freccero. 'Theorizing Queer Temporalities: A Roundtable Discussion.' *GLQ: A Journal of Lesbian and Gay Studies* 13, nos. 2–3 (2007): 177–95.

Doyle, Jennifer, and David Getsy. 'Queer Formalisms: Jennifer Doyle and David Getsy in Conversation'. *The Art Journal* 72 (2013): 58–71.

D'Souza, Aruna. 'Introduction'. In *Art History in the Wake of the Global Turn*, ed. Jill H. Casid and Aruna D'Souza, vii–xxiii. Clark Studies in the Visual Arts. Williamstown, MA: Sterling and Francine Clark Art Institute, 2014.

Dudrah, Rajinder Kumar. 'Birmingham (UK): Constructing City Spaces through Black Popular Cultures and the Black Public Sphere'. *City: Analysis of Urban Trends, Culture, Theory, Policy, Action* 6, no. 3 (2002): 335–50.

Dyer, Richard. *White: Essays on Race and Culture*. London and New York: Routledge, 1997.

Dyer, Sonya. 'Boxed in: How Cultural Diversity Policies Constrict Black Artists'. Manifesto Club Artistic Autonomy Hub, May 2007. www.manifestoclub.com/files/BOXEDIN.pdf.

'Early Closing Brought Eid Peace'. *Manchester Evening News*, 14 August 2007. www.manchestereveningnews.co.uk/news/local-news/early-closing-brought-eid-peace-1018892.

Eaton, Natasha. *Colour, Art and Empire: Visual Culture and the Nomadism of Representation*. London: I. B. Tauris, 2013.

Eckersley, Jo. 'Coming out Is Never Easy. But in Sri Lanka and Much of Surrounding South Asia It's Dangerous'. *Gay Times*, 31 December 2015. www.gaytimes.co.uk/life/21742/coming-out-is-never-easy-but-in-sri-lanka-and-much-of-surrounding-south-asia-its-dangerous/.

Edwards, Brent Hayes. 'The Uses of Diaspora'. *Social Text* 19, no. 1 66 (20 March 2001): 45–73. doi:10.1215/01642472–19–1_66–45.

Eglash, Ruth, Claudia J. Nahson and Dr. Shalva Weil. *Kehinde Wiley: The World Stage: Israel = Bamat Ha-'olam: Yiśra'el*. Culver City, CA: Roberts & Tilton, 2012.

'Eid Mubarak!' *BBC News*, 11 December 2004. www.bbc.co.uk/manchester/content/articles/2004/11/11/eid_2004_comments_feature.shtml.

'Eid Show-Offs Will Lose Cars'. *Manchester Evening News*, 14 August 2007. www.manchestereveningnews.co.uk/news/local-news/eid-show-offs-will-lose-cars-1155851.

'Eid-Ul-Fitr and Eid-Ul-Adha Festivals'. *Ahmadiyya Muslim Community*. Accessed 2 January 2016. www.alislam.org/books/salat/11.html.

Eiseman, Leatrice, and Keith Recker. *PANTONE®: The 20th Century in Color*. San Francisco: Chronicle Books, 2011.

Elkins, James. *Artists with PhDs: On the New Doctoral Degree in Studio Art*. Washington, DC: New Academia Publishing, 2009.

———. *Visual Studies: A Skeptical Introduction*. New York: Routledge, 2003.

———, ed. *Is Art History Global?* Art Seminar 3. New York; London: Routledge, 2007.

Elkins, James, and Michael Newman, eds. *The State of Art Criticism*. New York: Routledge, 2007.

Elkins, James, Zhivka Valiavicharska and Alice Kim, eds. *Art and Globalization*. The Stone Art Theory Institutes, v. 1. University Park, PA: Pennsylvania State University Press, 2010.

Elliott, John. 'Anish Kapoor on Show in India – a Permanent Public Sculpture Is Planned'. Blog. *Riding the Elephant*, 29 November 2010. https://ridingtheelephant.wordpress.com/2010/11/29/anish-kapoor-on-show-in-india-%e2%80%93-a-permanent-public-sculpture-is-planned/.

Engels, Friedrich. *The Condition of the Working-Class in England in 1844*. Translated by Florence Kelley Wischnewtzky. London: S. Sonnenschein & Co., 1892.

Engle, Karen. 'Constructing Good Aliens and Good Citizens: Legitimizing the War on Terror(ism)'. *University of Colorado Law Review* 75, no. 1 (Winter 2004).

Enwezor, Okwui, Carlos Basualdo, Ute Meta Bauer, Susanne Ghez, Sarat Maharaj, Mark Nash and Octavio Zaya, eds. *Créolité and Creolization: Documenta11_Platform3*. Ostfildern-Ruit, Germany: Hatje Cantz, 2003.

———. 'Introduction'. In *Créolité and Creolization: Documenta11_Platform3*, 13–16. Ostfildern-Ruit, Germany: Hatje Cantz, 2003.

Eshun, Ekow. *Kehinde Wiley: The World Stage: Jamaica*. London: Stephen Friedman Gallery, 2013.

Falcon Men's Bar. Accessed 20 February 2005. www.falconmensbar.com.

Fanon, Frantz. *Black Skin, White Masks*. Translated by Charles Lam Markmann. Evergreen Black Cat Book. New York: Grove Press, 1968.

———. *The Wretched of the Earth*. Translated by Constance Farrington. New York: Grove Press, 1965.

Ferguson, Russell. 'Introduction: Invisible Center'. In *Out There: Marginalization and Contemporary Cultures*, ed. Russell Ferguson, Cornel West, Martha Gever and Trinh T. Minh-Ha, 9–14. New York; Cambridge, MA: New Museum of Contemporary Art; MIT Press, 1990.

Fernandez-Sacco, Ellen. 'Check Your Baggage: Resisting Whiteness in Art History'. *Art Journal* 60, no. 4 (1 December 2001): 58–61.

Fernie, Eric. 'The History of Art and Archaeology in England Now'. In *The Art Historian: National Traditions and Institutional Practices*, ed. Michael F. Zimmermann, 160–6. Williamstown, MA: Sterling and Francine Clark Art Institute, 2003.

Fisher, Jean. 'Dialogues'. In *Shades of Black: Assembling Black Arts in 1980s Britain*, ed. David A. Bailey, Ian Baucom and Sonia Boyce, 167–96. Durham, NC: Duke University Press in association with the Institute of International Visual Arts and the African and Asian Visual Artists' Archive, London, 2005.

'FORMULA GUIDE Solid Coated & Solid Uncoated'. *PANTONE®*. Accessed 26 August 2015. www.pantone.com/formula-guide?gclid=CjoKEQjw3auuBRDj1LnQyLjy-4sBEiQAKPU_vfWaDhsAKUj88oP3yKwbEdOFCrHiBQOJ3rMukck9CIkaAo-gy8P8HAQ.

Foucault, Michel. *The Archaeology of Knowledge and the Discourse on Language*. Translated by A. M. Sheridan Smith. New York: Pantheon Books, 1972.

———. 'Des Espaces Autres (Basis of Lecture given in 1967)'. *Architecture, Mouvement, Continuité*, no. 5 (October 1984): 46–9.

———. 'Text/Context: Of Other Spaces'. In *Grasping the World: The Idea of the Museum*, ed. Donald Preziosi and Claire J Farago, translated by Jay Miskowiec, 371–9. Aldershot: Ashgate, 2003.

———. 'What Is an Author?' In *Language, Counter-Memory, Practice: Selected Essays and Interviews*, ed. Donald F. Bouchard, translated by Donald F. Bouchard and Sherry Simon, 113–38. Ithaca, NY: Cornell University Press, 1977.

Foucault, Michel, and Jay Miskowiec. 'Of Other Spaces'. *Diacritics* 16, no. 1 (Spring 1986): 22–7. doi:10.2307/464648.

Foucault, Michel, Paul Rabinow, Charles Taylor, Martin Jay, Leo Lowenthal and Richard Rorty. 'Politics and Ethics: An Interview'. In *The Foucault Reader*, ed. Paul Rabinow, translated by Catherine Porter, 373–80. New York: Random House, 1984.

Franks, Suzanne. ' "India's Daughter": The Latest Episode in New Delhi's Fraught Relationship with the BBC'. *International Policy Digest*, 6 March 2015. www.intpolicydigest.org/2015/03/06/india-s-daughter-the-latest-episode-in-new-delhi-s-fraught-relationship-with-the-bbc/.

Frascina, Francis. 'Institutions, Culture, and America's "Cold War Years": The Making of Greenberg's "Modernist Painting"'. *Oxford Art Journal* 26, no. 1 (1 January 2003): 69–97. doi:10.1093/oxartj/26.1.69.

Fraser, Nancy. *Rethinking the Public Sphere: A Contribution to the Critique of Actually Existing Democracy*. Milwaukee: University of Wisconsin-Milwaukee, Center for Twentieth Century Studies, 1990.

'Frequently Asked Questions'. *Essential*. Accessed 11 March 2007. www.essentialmanchester.com/faqs.php.

Freud, Sigmund. *Civilization and Its Discontents*. Translated by James Strachey. Standard ed. New York: W.W. Norton, 1961.

———. 'Mourning and Melancholia (1917)'. In *The Standard Edition of the Complete Psychological Works of Sigmund Freud*, translated by James Strachey, Vol. XIV, 1914–1916. London: Hogarth Press/Institute of Psycho-Analysis, 1957.

———. *Totem and Taboo: Resemblances between the Psychic Lives of Savages and Neurotics*. Translated by Abraham A. Brill. Harmondsworth: Penguin Books, 1938.

Fuss, Diana. *Essentially Speaking: Feminism, Nature & Difference*. New York: Routledge, 1989.

Gad, Amira. 'Blurring the Boundaries'. In *A Formal Film in Nine Episodes, Prologue and Epilogue: A Critical Reader*, ed. Susanne Gaensheimer and Bernd Reiss, 133–56. Leipzig: Spector Books, 2013.

Gaensheimer, Susanne, and Bernd Reiss, eds. 'In Conversation: Susanne Gaensheimer and Mario Pfeifer'. In *A Formal Film in Nine Episodes, Prologue and Epilogue: A Critical Reader*, 62–95. Leipzig: Spector Books, 2013.

Gaensheimer, Susanne, and Bernd Reiss, eds. 'In Conversation: Shuddhabrata Sengupta and Nikolaus Hirsch with Mario Pfeifer [New York, September 30, 2012]'. In *A Formal Film in Nine Episodes, Prologue and Epilogue: A Critical Reader*, 182–215. Leipzig: Spector Books, 2013.

Gandhi, Mahatma. *The Collected Works of Mahatma Gandhi*, vol. 87. New Delhi: Publications Division, Ministry of Information and Broadcasting, Goverment of India, 1983.
Gates, Jr, Henry Louis. *The Signifying Monkey: A Theory of African-American Literary Criticism*. New York: Oxford University Press, 1988.
Genocchio, Benjamin. 'The Details Are in the Beauty'. *The New York Times*, 6 May 2007, sec. New York/Region / New York/Region Special. www.nytimes.com/2007/05/06/nyregion/nyregionspecial2/06artsnj.html.
Gentleman, Amelia. 'Austerity Cuts Will Bite Even Harder in 2015 – Another £12bn Will Go'. *Guardian*, 1 January 2015, sec. Society. www.theguardian.com/society/2015/jan/01/austerity-cuts-2015-12-billion-britain-protest.
Getsy, David. *Abstract Bodies: Sixties Sculpture in the Expanded Field of Gender*. New Haven, CT: Yale University Press, 2015.
———. 'The Unforeclosed'. In *FLEX*. Brochure for Exhibition of Same Name. New York: Kent Fine Art, 2014. www.kentfineart.net/attachment/en/5374fae0a9aa2cd3748b4568/TextOneColumnWithFile/53d287e252d850f22a6f02eb.
Gilroy, Paul. *The Black Atlantic: Modernity and Double Consciousness*. Cambridge, MA: Harvard University Press, 1993.
Glimcher, Arne. *Agnes Martin: Paintings, Writings, Remembrances by Arne Glimcher*. London and New York: Phaidon Press, 2012.
Glissant, Édouard. *La cohée du Lamentin*. Paris: Gallimard, 2005.
———. *Poetics of Relation*. Translated by Betsy Wing. Ann Arbor: University of Michigan Press, 1997.
———. *Traité du Tout-Monde*. Paris: Gallimard, 1997.
'Glossary of Art Terms'. *Museum of Modern* Art. Accessed 15 January 2016. www.moma.org/learn/moma_learning/glossary.
Goethe, Johann Wolfgang von. *Theory of Colours*. Translated by Charles Locke Eastlake. Cambridge, MA: MIT Press, 1970.
Gohil, Neha Singh, and Dawinder S. Sidhu. 'The Sikh Turban: Post-911 Challenges to this Article of Faith'. *Rutgers Journal of Law and Religion* 9, no. 2 (Spring 2008): i–60.
Goodyear, Sara Suleri. *The Rhetoric of English India*. Chicago: University of Chicago Press, 1992.
Gopinath, Gayatri. 'Archive, Affects, and the Everyday: Queer Diasporic Re-Visions'. In *Political Emotions*, ed. Janet Staiger, Ann Cvetkovich and Ann Morris Reynolds, 165–92. New York: Routledge, 2010.
———. 'Chitra Ganesh's Queer Re-Visions'. *GLQ: A Journal of Lesbian and Gay Studies* 15, no. 3 (1 January 2009): 469–80. doi:10.1215/10642684-2008-032.
———. *Impossible Desires: Queer Diasporas and South Asian Public Cultures*. Durham, NC: Duke University Press, 2005.
———. 'Queer Regions: Locating Lesbians in *Sancharram*'. In *A Companion to Lesbian, Gay, Bisexual, Transgender, and Queer Studies*, ed. George E. Haggerty and Molly McGarry, 341–54. Malden, MA, and Oxford: Blackwell, 2007.
Gordon, Avery. 'The Work of Corporate Culture: Diversity Management'. *Social Text* 44 13, no. 3 (Fall/Winter 1995): 3–30.

Green, Charles, and Heather Barker. 'The Watershed: Two Decades of American Painting at the National Gallery of Victoria | NGV'. *National Gallery of Victoria*. Accessed 19 October 2015. www.ngv.vic.gov.au/essay/the-watershed-two-decades-of-american-painting-at-the-national-gallery-of-victoria/.

Greenberg, Clement. 'American-Type Painting'. In *Art & Culture: Critical Essays*, 208–29. Boston: Beacon Press, 1961.

———. 'Louis and Noland'. In *The Collected Essays and Criticism. Volume 4: Modernism with a Vengeance, 1957–1969*, ed. John O'Brian, 94–100. Chicago; London: University of Chicago Press, 1993.

———. 'Modernist Painting'. In *The Collected Essays and Criticism. Volume 4: Modernism with a Vengeance, 1957–1969*, ed. John O'Brian, 85–94. Chicago; London: University of Chicago Press, 1993.

———. 'Post-Painterly Abstraction'. In *The Collected Essays and Criticism. Volume 4: Modernism with a Vengeance, 1957–1969*, ed. John O'Brian, 192–6. Chicago; London: University of Chicago Press, 1993.

Grewal, Inderpal. *Transnational America: Feminisms, Diasporas, Neoliberalisms*. Durham, NC: Duke University Press, 2005.

Gruen, John. 'A Thing of No Beauty'. *New York Magazine*, 6 April 1970.

Gupta, Atreyee. 'In a Postcolonial Diction: Postwar Abstraction and the Aesthetics of Modernization'. *Art Journal* 73, no. 3 (Fall 2013): 30–46.

Gupta, Subodh, Nicolas Bourriaud, S Kalidas and Dan Cameron. *Subodh Gupta: Gandhi's Three Monkeys*. New York: Jack Shainman Gallery, 2008.

Gutiérrez Rodríguez, Encarnación, and Shirley Anne Tate. 'Introduction: Creolizing Europe: Legacies and Transformations'. In *Creolizing Europe: Legacies and Transformations*, ed. Encarnación Gutiérrez Rodríguez and Shirley Anne Tate, 1–11. Liverpool: Liverpool University Press, 2015.

Guzman, Alissa. 'Kehinde Wiley's "Politics of Perception"'. *Hyperallergic*, 22 April 2015. http://hyperallergic.com/200742/kehinde-wileys-politics-of-perception/.

Habermas, Jürgen. *The Structural Transformation of the Public Sphere: An Inquiry into a Category of Bourgeois Society*. Translated by Thomas Burger with the assistance of Frederick Lawrence. Cambridge, MA: MIT Press, 1989.

———. *The Theory of Communicative Action. Vol. 1*. London: Heinemann, 1984.

———. *The Theory of Communicative Action. Vol. 2*. Cambridge: Polity, 1987.

Halberstam, Judith. *The Queer Art of Failure*. Durham, NC: Duke University Press, 2011.

Hall, Stuart. 'Créolité and the Process of Creolization'. In *Creolizing Europe: Legacies and Transformations*, ed. Encarnación Gutiérrez Rodríguez and Shirley Anne Tate, 12–25. Liverpool: Liverpool University Press, 2015.

———. 'Cultural Identity and Diaspora'. In *Identity: Community, Culture, Difference*, ed. Jonathan Rutherford, 222–37. London: Lawrence & Wishart, 1990.

———. 'Introduction: Who Needs "Identity?"' In *Questions of Cultural Identity*, ed. Stuart Hall and Paul du Gay, 1–17. London; Thousand Oaks, CA: Sage, 1996.

———. 'Maps of Emergency: Fault Lines and Tectonic Plates'. In *Fault Lines: Contemporary African Art and Shifting Landscapes*, ed. Gilane Tawadros and Sarah

Campbell, 31–49. London: Institute of International Visual Arts, Forum for African Arts, Prince Claus Fund Library, 2003.

Hatt, Michael. 'Race, Ritual, and Responsibility: Performativity and the Southern Lynching'. In *Performing the Body/Performing the Text*, ed. Amelia Jones and Andrew Stephenson, 76–88. London; New York: Routledge, 1999.

'Hattenstone, Simon. 'Into the Deep'. *Guardian*, 22 September 2006. www.theguardian.com/artanddesign/2006/sep/23/art.

'Haus der Kunst – FAQs'. *Haus der Kunst*. Accessed 26 July 2016. www.hausderkunst.de/en/research/history/faqs/.

Heidegger, Martin. 'The Age of the World Picture'. In *The Question Concerning Technology and Other Essays*, translated by William Lovitt, 115–54. New York: Harper & Row, 1977.

———. 'The Origin of the Work of Art'. In *Philosophies of Art and Beauty: Selected Readings in Aesthetics from Plato to Heidegger*, ed. Albert Hofstadter and Richard Kuhns, translated by Albert Hofstadter, 649–701. Chicago: University of Chicago Press, 1964.

Hobbs, Robert. 'Kehinde Wiley's Conceptual Realism'. In *Kehinde Wiley*, 16–83. New York: Rizzoli, 2012.

Hochdörfer, Achim. '"Blue Goes Out, B Comes In": Cy Twombly's Narration of Interminacy'. In *Cy Twombly: States of Mind. Painting, Sculpture, Photography, Drawing*, 12–39. Munich; Vienna: Schirmer/Mosel Verlag; Museum Moderner Kunst Stiftung Ludwig and Wien, 2009.

Holly, Michael Ann, and Marquard Smith, eds. *What Is Research in the Visual Arts?: Obsession, Archive, Encounter*. New Haven, CT: Yale University Press, 2008.

Hom, Alice Y., and David L. Eng, eds. 'Transnational Sexualities: South Asian (Trans) national(alism)s and Queer Diasporas'. In *Q & A Queer in Asian America*, 405–22. Philadelphia: Temple University Press, 1998.

Horschak, Amy. 'MoMA and the World: The International Program: An Interview with Jay Levenson, Director, International Program, The Museum of Modern Art'. Blog. *Inside/Out: A MoMA/MoMA PS1 Blog*, 30 August 2010. www.moma.org/explore/inside_out/2010/08/30/what-is-momas-international-program/.

Huyssen, Andreas. *Present Pasts: Urban Palimpsests and the Politics of Memory*. Stanford, CA: Stanford University Press, 2003.

'International Program: Timeline and Map'. *The Museum of Modern Art*. Accessed 19 October 2015. www.moma.org/learn/intnlprograms/timeline.

Israel, Matthew. 'A Magnet for the With-It Kids: The Jewish Museum, New York, of the 1960s'. *Art in America* (October 2007), 72–83.

Jackson, Brian Keith. 'Quiet as It's Kept'. In *Kehinde Wiley*, 110–55. New York: Rizzoli, 2012.

Jackson, Brian Keith, and Kimberly Cleveland. *Kehinde Wiley: The World Stage: Brazil = O Estágio Do Mundo*. Culver City, CA: Roberts & Tilton, 2009.

'Japanese American National Museum And Fisher Gallery, USC Present "Asian Traditions/Modern Expressions: Asian American Artists And Abstractions, 1945–1970"'. Press release. *Japanese American National Museum*, 1997. http://visualarts.britishcouncil.org/exhibitions/exhibition/anish-kapoor-delhi-mumbai-2010.

Jhaveri, Shanay. ' "Inside" and "Outside" a Frame of Historical and Cultural Referentiality?' In *A Formal Film in Nine Episodes, Prologue and Epilogue: A Critical Reader*, ed. Susanne Gaensheimer and Bernd Reiss, 38–59. Leipzig: Spector Books, 2013.

Jones, Amelia. 'Introduction'. In *Otherwise: Imagining Queer Feminist Art Histories*, ed. Amelia Jones and Erin Silver, 1–13. Manchester: Manchester University Press, 2016.

———. '"Presence" in Absentia: Experiencing Performance as Documentation'. *The Art Journal*, 56 no. 4 (Winter 1997): 11–18.

———. *Seeing Differently: A History and Theory of Identification and the Visual Arts*. London: Routledge, 2012.

———. *Self/Image: Technology, Representation: and the Contemporary Subject*. London and New York: Routledge, 2006.

Jones, Amelia, and Andrew Stephenson. 'Introduction'. In *Performing the Body/Performing the Text*, ed. Amelia Jones and Andrew Stephenson, 1–10. London; New York: Routledge, 1999.

Jones, Caroline A. 'The Mediated Sensorium'. In *Sensorium: Embodied Experience, Technology, and Contemporary Art*, ed. Caroline A. Jones, 5–49. Cambridge, MA: MIT Press; MIT List Visual Arts Center, 2006.

Judd, Donald. 'Cy Twombly'. *Arts Magazine* 38, nos 8–9 (May–June 1964).

Juhasz, Alexandra. 'Video Remains: Nostalgia, Technology, and Queer Archive Activism'. *GLQ: A Journal of Lesbian and Gay Studies* 12, no. 2 (2006): 319–28.

Jury, Louise. 'Anish Kapoor: "The Government Doesn't Understand the Importance of Culture"'. *Independent*, 13 October 2002. www.independent.co.uk/news/people/profiles/anish-kapoor-the-government-doesnt-understand-the-importance-of-culture-140025.html.

Kant, Immanuel. *The Critique of Judgement*. Translated by James Creed Meredith. Oxford: Clarendon Press, 1973.

Kapoor, Anish. *Anish Kapoor*. London: Thames & Hudson, 1996.

———. Transcript of the John Tusa Interviews with the Sculptor Anish Kapoor, 6 July 2003. www.bbc.co.uk/programmes/pooncbc1.

Kapur, Geeta. 'In Quest of Identity: Art & Indigenism in Post-Colonial Culture with Special Reference to Contemporary Indian Painting'. *Asia Art Archive*, 1973. www.aaa.org.hk/Collection/CollectionOnline/SpecialCollectionItem/15579.

Katz, Jonathan D. 'Agnes Martin: Sexuality of Abstraction'. In *Agnes Martin*, ed. Lynne. Cooke, Karen J. Kelly and Barbara Schröder, 170–97. New Haven, CT: Yale University Press and Dia Art Foundation, 2011.

———. ' "Committing the Perfect Crime": Sexuality, Assemblage, and the Postmodern Turn in American Art'. *Art Journal* 67, no. 1 (March 2008): 38–53. doi:10.1080/00043249.2008.10791293.

———. 'John Cage's Queer Silence; Or, How to Avoid Making Matters Worse'. *GLQ: A Journal of Lesbian and Gay Studies* 5 (1999): 231–52.

———. 'Passive Resistance: On the Critical and Commercial Success of Queer Artists in Cold War American Art'. *Queer Cultural Center*. Accessed 7 May 2015. www.queerculturalcenter.org/Pages/KatzPages/KatzLimage.html.

Katz, Jonathan D., Presentation on Agnes Martin for 'Hide/Seek' Exhibition Symposium, 2011. *YouTube*. Accessed 7 May 2015. www.youtube.com/watch?v=BbFLur5zdAI&feature=youtube_gdata_player.

Kaufmann, Thomas DaCosta, Catherine Dossin and Béatrice Joyeux-Prunel, eds. *Circulations in the Global History of Art*. Studies in Art Historiography. Farnham and Burlington, VT: Ashgate, 2015.

Kavuri-Bauer, Santhi. 'Colors in Motion: The New York Paintings of Natvar Bhavsar'. Unpublished manuscript, San Francisco State University, 2015.

Kee, Joan. 'The World in Plain View: Form in the Service of the Global'. In *Contemporary Art: 1989 to the Present*, ed. Alexander Blair Dumbadze and Suzanne Perling Hudson, 95–106. Chichester, West Sussex: Wiley-Blackwell, 2013.

Kehinde Wiley: The World Stage: China. Sheboygan, WI: John Michael Kohler Arts Center, 2007.

Kehinde Wiley: The World Stage: France 1880–1960 = La scène mondiale: La France 1880–1960. Paris: Galerie Daniel Templon, 2015.

Kennedy, Randy. 'Cy Twombly, Idiosyncratic Painter, Dies at 83'. *The New York Times*, 5 July 2011. http://artsbeat.blogs.nytimes.com/2011/07/05/cy-twombly-idiosyncratic-painter-dies-at-83/?_r=0.

Kester, Grant H. *Conversation Pieces: Community and Communication in Modern Art*. Berkeley and London: University of California Press, 2004.

'Khan Appeals for Trouble-Free Eid'. BBC, 2 November 2005, sec. Manchester. http://news.bbc.co.uk/2/hi/uk_news/england/manchester/4401138.stm.

Khullar, Sonal. *Worldly Affiliations: Artistic Practice, National Identity, and Modernism in India, 1930–1990*. Berkeley: University of California Press, 2015.

Kim, Christine Y. 'Faux Real: Interview with Kehinde Wiley'. *Issue Magazine*, December 2003. http://issuemagazine.com/kehinde-wiley-faux-real/#/.

King, Jamilah. 'The Art of Masculinity'. *Colorlines*, 24 February 2015. www.colorlines.com/articles/art-masculinity.

Kirmani, Nida. 'Rusholme'. In *A Postcolonial People: South Asians in Britain*, ed. Nasreen Ali, Virinder S. Kalra and S. Sayyid, 327–8. New York: Columbia University Press, 2008.

Kley, Elisabeth. 'Mystical Cosmetics: Oliver Herring, Stephen Dean, Berni Searle'. *PAJ: A Journal of Performance and Art.*, no. 72 (2002): 101–4.

Kosnick, Kira. 'Selecta at the Door'. Digital commons. *openDemocracy*, 29 November 2004. www.opendemocracy.net/arts-multiculturalism/article_2248.jsp.

Krauss, Rosalind. 'Cy Was Here: Cy's Up'. *Artforum* 33, no. 1 (1994): 70–5, 188.

Kristeva, Julia. *Powers of Horror: An Essay on Abjection*. Translated by Leon S. Roudiez. New York: Columbia University Press, 1982.

Kunz, Martin. 'British Sculpture Now'. In *Englische Plastik Heute = British Sculpture Now: Stephen Cox, Tony Cragg, Richard Deacon, Anish Kapoor, Bill Woodrow, Kunstmuseum Luzern, 11.7. – 12.9.1982*, ed. Martin Kunz. Luzern: Kunstmuseum Luzern, 1982.

Kwint, Marius. 'Color Immersion: Natvar Bhavsar in Conversation'. In *Natvar Bhavsar: Poetics of Color*, 9–26. Milan: Skira Editore S.p.A., 2008.

Kwon, Miwon. *One Place After Another: Site Specific Art and Locational Identity*. Cambridge, MA: The MIT Press, 2002.

Lambert-Beatty, Carrie. 'The Academic Condition of Contemporary Art'. In *Contemporary Art: 1989 to the Present*, ed. Alexander Blair Dumbadze and Suzanne Perling Hudson, 457–66. Chichester, West Sussex: Wiley-Blackwell, 2013.

Lamoureux, Johanne. 'From Form to Platform: The Politics of Representation and the Representation of Politics'. *Art Journal* 62 no. 1 (Spring 2005), 64–73.

Landi, Ann. 'Living On and Off the Grid'. *The Wall Street Journal* (Online), 24 July 2015. www.wsj.com/articles/living-on-and-off-the-grid-1437768845.

Lang, Karen. 'Anish Kapoor's Svayambh'. *X-Tra: Contemporary Art Quarterly* 11, no. 2 (Winter 2008): 60–3.

Lant, Antonia. 'Haptical Cinema'. *October* 74 (1995): 45–73.

Leeman, Richard. 'Roland Barthes et Cy Twombly: Le "Champ Allusif de L'écriture"'. *Rue Descartes* 34, no. 4 (2001): 61–70.

Lefebvre, Henri. 'Right to the City'. In *Writings on Cities*, translated by Eleonore Kofman and Elizabeth Lebas, English translation. Oxford; Cambridge, MA: Blackwell, 1996 [1968].

———. *The Production of Space*. Oxford; Cambridge, MA: Blackwell, 1991.

Lewin, Tamar. 'Report Takes Aim at "Model Minority" Stereotype of Asian-American Students'. *The New York Times*, 10 June 2008, sec. Education. www.nytimes.com/2008/06/10/education/10asians.html.

Lewis, Reina. 'Cross-Cultural Reiterations: Demetra Vaka Brown and the Performance of Racialized Female Beauty'. In *Performing the Body/Performing the Text*, ed. Amelia Jones and Andrew Stephenson, 56–75. London; New York: Routledge, 1999.

Lewis, Sarah Elizabeth. 'De(i)fying the Masters'. *Art in America*, April 2005.

Lewison, Jeremy. *Anish Kapoor: Drawings*. Millbank, London: Tate Gallery, 1990.

———. ' "Bilderstreit" and "Magiciens de La Terre". Paris and Cologne'. *The Burlington Magazine* 131, no. 1037 (August 1989): 585–7.

Leylveld, Joseph. 'Modern U.S. Art Stirs New Delhi'. *The New York Times*, 10 April 1967.

Lott, Timmy. 'Black Cultural Politics: An Interview with Paul Gilroy'. *Found Object* 4 (1994): 46–81.

MacDonald, Iain B. 'Argi Bhaji'. Episode. *Cutting Edge*. Channel 4, UK (1999).

Machida, Margo. 'Reframing Asian America'. In *One Way or Another: Asian American Art Now*, ed. Melissa Chiu, Karin M. Higa and Susette S. Min, 15–20. New Haven, CT: Yale University Press and Asia Society, 2006.

Machida, Margo, Vishakha N. Desai, John Kuo Wei Tchen, and Asia Society Galleries. *Asia/America: Identities in Contemporary Asian American Art*. New York: Asia Society Galleries; New Press, 1994.

Maddox, Georgina. '"Inspiring, Even Daring" Anish Kapoor in Delhi'. *The Indian Express*, 28 November 2010. http://archive.indianexpress.com/news/inspiring-even-daring-anish-kapoor-in-delhi/717199/2.

Malkani, Gautam. *Londonstani*. New York: Penguin Press, 2006.

'Manchester Is Favourite with "New Bohemians"'. Press release. DEMOS (*London-Based Cross-Party Think Tank*), 26 May 2003. www.demos.co.uk/media/pressreleases/bohobritain.

'Manchester Wins Double Accolade as UK's Top Gay-Friendly Local Authority'. Press release. *Manchester City Council*, 9 January 2007. www.manchester.gov.uk.

Marketing Manchester. *Greater Manchester Destination Management Plan: The Visitor Economy Action Plan, 2008–2011*, 2008. www.marketingmanchester.com.

———. *Leisure Tourism*. Accessed 22 August 2008. www.marketingmanchester.com.

———. *Manchester: A Guide for LGBT Visitors, 2006/07*, brochure.

———. *Manchester: Where to Stay 2006/07*, brochure.

Marks, Laura U. 'Haptic Visuality: Touching with the Eyes'. *Framework: The Finnish Art Review* 2 (November 2004). www.framework.fi/2_2004/visitor/artikkelit/marks.html (no longer available).

———. *The Skin of the Film: Intercultural Cinema, Embodiment, and the Senses*. Durham, NC: Duke University Press, 2000.

———. *Touch Sensuous Theory and Multisensory Media*. Minneapolis: University of Minnesota Press, 2002.

Mathur, Saloni, ed. *The Migrant's Time: Rethinking Art History and Diaspora*. Williamstown, MA: Sterling and Francine Clark Art Institute, 2011.

McClintock, Anne. *Imperial Leather: Race, Gender, and Sexuality in the Colonial Contest*. New York: Routledge, 1995.

McEvilley, Thomas. 'Darkness Inside a Stone'. In *Anish Kapoor: British Pavilion, XLIV Venice Biennale, May–September 1990*. London: Visual Arts Deptartment. of the British Council, 1990.

———. 'Opening the Trap'. In *Art & Otherness: Crisis in Cultural Identity*, ed. Thomas McEvilley, 57–72. Kingston, NY: Documentext/McPherson, 1992.

———. 'The Global Issue'. In *Art & Otherness: Crisis in Cultural Identity*, ed. Thomas McEvilley, 153–8. Kingston, NY: Documentext/McPherson, 1992.

McEvilley, Thomas, William Rubin and Kirk Varnedoe. 'Doctor Lawyer Indian Chief: "'Primitivism' in 20th Century Art" at the Museum of Modern Art'. *Artforum* 23 (1984): 54–61.

Meikle, James. 'The Colour of a Curry May Make It Look Better – but Is It Good for You?' *Guardian*, 24 March 2004, sec. UK news. www.theguardian.com/uk/2004/mar/24/foodanddrink.

Mellor, Rosemary. 'Hypocritical City: Cycles of Urban Exclusion'. In *City of Revolution Restructuring Manchester*, ed. Jamie Peck and Kevin Ward, 214–35. Manchester; New York: Manchester University Press, 2002.

Mercer, Kobena. 'Iconography after Identity'. In *Shades of Black: Assembling Black Arts in 1980s Britain*, ed. David A Bailey, Ian Baucom and Sonia Boyce, 49–58. Durham, NC: Duke University Press, in association with the Institute of International Visual Arts and the African and Asian Visual Artists' Archive, London, 2005.

Merleau-Ponty, Maurice. *Phenomenology of Perception*. Translated by Colin Smith. International Library of Philosophy and Scientific Method. New York: Humanities Press, 1962.

———. *The Visible and the Invisible; Followed by Working Notes*. ed. Claude Lefort. Translated by Alphonso Lingis. Northwestern University Studies in Phenomenology & Existential Philosophy. Evanston, IL: Northwestern University Press, 1968.

Meskimmon, Marsha. *Contemporary Art and the Cosmopolitan Imagination*. London; New York: Routledge, 2011.

———. 'Corporeal Theory With/In Practice: Christine Borland's Winter Garden'. *Art History* 26, no. 3 (1 June 2003): 442–55.

———. 'The Precarious Ecologies of Cosmopolitanism'. *Open Arts Journal*, no. 1 (2013). doi:10.5456/issn.5050-3679/2013s03mm.

Meskimmon, Marsha, and Dorothy C. Rowe, eds. *Women, the Arts and Globalization: Eccentric Experience*. Manchester: Manchester University Press, 2013.

Miller, Nancy K. *Getting Personal: Feminist Occasions and Other Autobiographical Acts*. New York: Routledge, 1991.

Moraga, Cherríe, and Gloria Anzaldúa, eds. *This Bridge Called My Back: Writings by Radical Women of Color*. 2nd edn. New York: Kitchen Table, Women of Color Press, 1983.

Morgan, Robert C. 'Natvar Bhavsar's Threshold of Purity'. In *Natvar Bhavsar: Five Decades*, ed. Irene Cassina, Marco Cassina and Akaash Mehta, 5–9. New York: Cara Gallery, 2015.

Morin, Roc. 'India's "Third Gender" Is Marginalized and Sanctified'. *VICE*, 29 June 2015. www.vice.com/read/indias-third-gender-is-marginalized-and-sanctified-456.

Mosquera, Gerardo, and Jean Fisher. 'Introduction'. In *Over Here: International Perspectives on Art and Culture*, ed. Jean Fisher and Gerardo Mosquera. New York and Cambridge, MA: New Museum of Contemporary Art; MIT Press, 2004.

Mouffe, Chantal. 'For an Agonistic Public Sphere'. In *Democracy Unrealized: Documenta 11_Platform1*, ed. Mark Nash, Carlos Basualdo, Susanne Ghez, Octavio Zaya, Sarat Maharaj, Okwui Enwezor and Ute Meta Bauer, 87–97. Ostfildern-Ruit, Germany: Hatje Cantz Publishers, 2002.

Mukherji, Parul Dave. 'Whither Art History in a Globalizing World'. *The Art Bulletin* 96, no. 2 (2014): 151–5.

Mundy, John. *Popular Music On Screen: From Hollywood Musical to Music Video*. Manchester: Manchester University Press, 1999.

Muñoz, José Esteban. 'Ephemera as Evidence: Introductory Notes to Queer Acts'. *Women & Performance: A Journal of Feminist Theory* 8, no. 2 (1996): 5–16.

———. 'Feeling Brown: Ethnicity and Affect in Ricardo Bracho's *The Sweetest Hangover (and Other STDs)*'. *Theatre Journal* 52, no. 1 (2000): 67–79.

Munroe, Alexandra. 'Buddhism and the Neo-Avant-Garde: Cage Zen, Beat Zen, and Zen'. In *The Third Mind: American Artists Contemplate Asia, 1860–1989*, ed. Alexandra Munroe, 199–216. New York: Guggenheim Museum, 2009.

———, ed. *The Third Mind: American Artists Contemplate Asia, 1860–1989*. New York: Guggenheim Museum, 2009.

Munroe, Majella. 'Zen as a Transnational Current in Post-War Art: The Case of Mira Schendel'. *Tate Papers*, no. 23 (Spring 2005). www.tate.org.uk/research/publications/tate-papers/zen-transnational-current-post-war-art-mira-schendel.

Murray, Derek Conrad. *Queering Post-Black Art: Artists Transforming African-American Identity after Civil Rights*, London: I.B. Taurus, 2016.

National Commission on Terrorist Attacks Upon the United States. 'Executive Summary of "9/11 Commission Report: Final Report of the National Commission on Terrorist Attacks Upon the United States"'. Accessed 22 July 2004. www.9–11commission.gov/report/911Report_Exec.pdf.

Nayak, Anoop, and Steve Drayton. 'Charvers Webchat'. Q and A with public. *BBC Inside Out*, 21 February 2005. www.bbc.co.uk/insideout/northeast/series7/webchat_charvers.shtml.

Negt, Oskar, and Alexander Kluge. *Public Sphere and Experience: Toward an Analysis of the Bourgeois and Proletarian Public Sphere*. Translated by Peter Labanyi, Assenka Oksiloff and Jamie Owen Daniel. Minneapolis: University of Minnesota Press, 1993.

Nesbit, Molly. 'Fourteen Years Ago at Yale'. In *Kehinde Wiley: A New Republic*, ed. Eugenie Tsai, 63. New York: Brooklyn Museum in association with DelMonico Books & Prestel, 2015.

'New York Centre of World Art, Feels U.S. Critic'. *Times of Delhi*, 28 March 1967.

Newman, Michael. 'Anish Kapoor'. In *Englische Plastik Heute = British Sculpture Now: Stephen Cox, Tony Cragg, Richard Deacon, Anish Kapoor, Bill Woodrow, Kunstmuseum Luzern, 11.7. – 12.9.1982*, ed. Martin Kunz. Luzern: Kunstmuseum Luzern, 1982.

Nickas, Bob, Bruce Hainley, George Baker and Saul Anton. 'Mild About Larry: 2002 Whitney Biennial'. *Artforum* 40, no. 9 (2002): 162.

'Nighat Awan Wins "Outstanding Contribution" Award'. *Redhotcurry*, 12 October 2004. http://redhotcurry.com/food_and_drink/other/nighat_awan_award.htm.

Nobelstiftelsen. *Physiology or Medicine, 1901–1921*. Amsterdam, London and New York: Elsevier Publishing Company, 1967. www.nobelprize.org/nobel_prizes/medicine/laureates/1904/pavlov-bio.html.

Ofield-Kerr, Simon. 'Cruising the Archive'. *Journal of Visual Culture* 4, no. 3 (1 December 2005): 351–64. doi:10.1177/1470412905058353.

Oguibe, Olu. 'Whiteness and "The Canon"'. *Art Journal* 60, no. 4 (1 December 2001): 44–7. doi:10.1080/00043249.2001.10792093.

Ohnuki-Tierney, Emiko. *The Monkey as Mirror: Symbolic Transformations in Japanese History and Ritual*. Princeton, NJ: Princeton University Press, 1987.

Oliver, M. Cynthia, and Mike Rogge. *Kehinde Wiley: The World Stage: Haiti = Sèn mondyal la Ayiti*. Culver City, CA: Roberts & Tilton, 2015.

Onians, John, ed. *Compression vs. Expression: Containing and Explaining the World's Art*. Williamstown, MA: Sterling and Francine Clark Art Institute, 2006.

Ooms, Herman. *Tokugawa Ideology: Early Constructs, 1570–1680*. Princeton, NJ: Princeton University Press, 1985.

'Osama Becomes a Pain for American Sikhs', *The Financial Express*, 10 July 2006. www.financialexpress.com/old/latest_full_story.php?content_id=133438.

O'Sullivan, Simon. *Art Encounters: Deleuze and Guattari: Thought Beyond Representation*. Basingstoke: Palgrave Macmillan, 2006.

Pakis, Elisavet. 'Playing in the Dark: Performing (Im)possible Lesbian Subjects'. PhD dissertation, Lancaster University, 2010. http://ethos.bl.uk/OrderDetails.do?uin=uk.bl.ethos.547939.

'PANTONE® Formula Guide Color Palette History'. *myPANTONE™*, 19 March 2013. http://pantone.custhelp.com/app/answers/detail/a_id/1327/~/pantone-formula-guide-color-palette-history.

'Pantone Publishes 1998 Color Trends for Graphic and Web Design; *Pantone Celebrates 35 Years of the PANTONE MATCHING SYSTEM® with Authoritative ColorTrends Guide and Software*'. Press release. PANTONE ®, 1997. www.pantone.com/pages/pantone/pantone.aspx?pg=20127&ca=10.

Patel, Alpesh Kantilal. 'Open Secrets in "Post-Identity" Era Art Criticism/History: Raqib Shaw's Queer Garden of Earthly Delights'. *Darkmatter: In the Ruins of*

Imperial Culture 9, no. 2 (29 November 2012). www.darkmatter101.org/site/2012/11/29/open-secrets-in-post-identity-era-art-criticism-history-raqib-shaws-queer-garden-of-earthly-delights.

———. 'Queer Desi Visual Culture Across the "Brown Atlantic"'. PhD dissertation Manchester University, 2009.

Patel, Gieve. 'The Decades and the Seminar'. *CONTRA'66*, nos 5–6 (June 1967): 5–6.

Patel, Vibhuti. 'New Explorations in a Universe of Color; Natvar Bhavsar Talks About a New Show of His Dry-Pigment Canvases'. *Wall Street Journal* (Online). 28 May 2013, sec. New York.

Patriot. 26 March 1967.

Pearlman, Ellen. *Nothing & Everything: The Influence of Buddhism on the American Avant Garde 1942–1962*. Berkeley, CA: Evolver Editions, 2014.

Pfeifer, Mario. *A Formal Film in Nine Episodes, Prologue and Epilogue: A Critical Reader*. Ed. Susanne Gaensheimer and Bernd Reiss. Leipzig: Spector Books, 2013.

Phillips, Kevin. *American Theocracy: The Peril and Politics of Radical Religion, Oil, and Borrowed Money in the 21st Century*. New York: Viking, 2006.

Pietz, William. 'Fetish'. In *Critical Terms for Art History*, 2nd edn. ed. Robert S. Nelson and Richard Shiff, 306–17. Chicago: University of Chicago Press, 2010.

Pile, Steve. 'Memory and the City'. In *Temporalities, Autobiography and Everyday Life*, ed. Jan Campbell and Janet Harbord, 111–27. Manchester; New York: Manchester University Press 2002.

———. *The Body and the City: Psychoanalysis, Space, and Subjectivity*. London; New York: Routledge, 1996.

Pinder, David. 'Arts of Urban Exploration'. *Cultural Geographies* 12 (2005): 383–411.

———. 'Ghostly Footsteps: Voices, Memories and Walks in the City'. *Ecumene* 8, no. 1 (2001): 1–19.

Piotrowski, Piotr. 'The Global NETwork: An Approach to Comparative Art History'. In *Circulations in the Global History of Art*, ed. Thomas DaCosta Kaufmann, Catherine Dossin, and Béatrice Joyeux-Prunel, 149–65. Studies in Art Historiography. Farnham and Burlington, VT: Ashgate, 2015.

Piper, Adrian Margaret Smith. 'The Color Wheel Series', 2002. www.adrianpiper.com/art/docs/2004TheColorWheelSeries.pdf.

———. 'News'. Artist website. *Adrian Piper*, 26 September 2012. www.adrianpiper.com/news_sep_2012.shtml.

———. 'Removed and Reconstructed en.Wikipedia Biography'. Artist website. *Adrian Piper*. Accessed 18 August 2015. www.adrianpiper.com/removed-and-reconstructed-en.wikipedia-biography.shtml.

———. 'Whiteless'. *Art Journal* 60, no. 4 (1 December 2001): 62–5.

Plagens, Peter. 'This Man Will Decide What Art Is: But Will Anyone Else Agree? The Whitney Museum's Larry Rinder Is out to Break Down the Traditional Boundaries in His New Biennial Exhibition'. *Newsweek*, 4 March 2002. www.highbeam.com/doc/1G1-83283918.html.

Pollock, Griselda, ed. *Generations and Geographies in the Visual Arts: Feminist Readings*. London and New York: Routledge, 1996.

Prabhupada, His Divine Grace A. C. Bhaktivedanta Swami. *Bhagavad-Gita As It Is*. The Bhaktivedanta Book Trust, 1989.

Prashad, Vijay. *The Karma of Brown Folk*. Minneapolis: University of Minnesota Press, 2000.

Pratt, Mary Louise. *Imperial Eyes: Travel Writing and Transculturation*. London: Routledge, 1992.

Preziosi, Donald. *Rethinking Art History: Meditations on a Coy Science*. New Haven, CT: Yale University Press, 1989.

———. *The Art of Art History: A Critical Anthology*. 2nd edn. Oxford and New York: Oxford University Press, 2009.

Princenthal, Nancy. *Agnes Martin: Her Life and Art*. New York: Thames & Hudson, 2015.

Pritchard, Annette, Nigel Morgan and Diane Sedgley. 'In Search of Lesbian Space? The Experience of Manchester's Gay Village'. *Leisure Studies* 21, no. 2 (2002): 105–23.

Puar, Jasbir K. *Terrorist Assemblages: Homonationalism in Queer Times*. Durham, NC: Duke University Press, 2007.

———. ' "I Would Rather Be a Cyborg than a Goddess": Intersectionality, Assemblage, and Affective Politics'. European Institute for Progressive Cultural Policies. *Transversal*, 2011. http://eipcp.net/transversal/0811/puar/en.

Puar, J. K, and A. S. Rai. 'The Remaking of a Model Minority: Perverse Projectiles under the Specter of (Counter)Terrorism'. *Social Text* 80 (2004): 75–104.

Quilley, Steve. 'Constructing Manchester's "New Urban Village": Gay Space in the Entrepreneurial City'. In *Queers in Space: Communities, Public Places, Sites of Resistance*, ed. Gordon Brent Ingram, Anne-Marie Bouthillette and Yolanda Retter, 275–92. Seattle: Bay Press, 1997.

———. 'Entrepreneurial Turns: Municipal Socialism and After'. In *City of Revolution Restructuring Manchester*, ed. Jamie Peck and Kevin Ward, 76–94. Manchester and New York: Manchester University Press, 2002.

Raman, Sita Anantha. *Women in India: A Social and Cultural History*, vol. 1. ABC-CLIO, 2009.

Raqs Media Collective. 'An Ephemeris, Corrected for the Longitudes of Tomorrow: Speculations on the Orbit and Motion of Objects and Processes in Contemporary Art Today and Tomorrow'. In *Art History in the Wake of the Global Turn*, ed. Jill H. Casid and Aruna D'Souza, 3–19. Clark Studies in the Visual Arts. Williamstown, MA: Sterling and Francine Clark Art Institute, 2014.

———. Artist website. *Raqs Media Collective*. Accessed 13 January 2016. http://raqsmediacollective.net/.

Ratcliff, Carter. 'Natvar Bhavsar: The Purpose of Looking'. *Art International* 16, no. 8 (October 1972): 17–20.

'Re-envisioning American Art History: Asian American Art, Research, and Teaching'. Accessed 7 November 2015. www.nyu-apastudies.org/research/NEH/?page_id=9.

Reilly, Maura, and Linda Nochlin, eds. *Global Feminisms: New Directions in Contemporary Art*. London and New York: Merrell, 2007.

Rendell, Jane. *Site-Writing: The Architecture of Art Criticism*. London and New York: I. B. Tauris, 2010.

Research, Development and Statistics Directorate. 'Defining and Measuring Anti-Social Behaviour'. Development and Practice Report. London: Home Office, 2004. www.gov.uk/government/uploads/system/uploads/attachment_data/file/116655/dpr26.pdf.

Richards, Jeffrey. *Films and British National Identity: From Dickens to Dad's Army*. Manchester: Manchester University Press, 1997.

Riegl, Alois. 'Late Roman or Oriental? (1902)'. In *German Essays on Art History: Winckelmann, Burckhardt, Panofsky, and Others*, ed. Gert Schiff, translated by Peter Wortsman. New York: Continuum, 1988.

Riley II, Charles A. *Color Codes: Modern Theories of Color in Philosophy, Painting and Architecture, Literature, Music, and Psychology*. Lebanon, NH: University Press of New England, 1995.

Robertson, Vida A. 'Gossip as Testimony: A Postmodern Signature'. In *The Feminism and Visual Culture Reader*, ed. Amelia Jones, 268–76. London; New York: Routledge, 2003.

———. 'The Racial Pharmakon: Investigating Albinism in African American Literature'. PhD dissertation, Miami University, 2006. https://etd.ohiolink.edu/ap/10?0::NO:10:P10_ACCESSION_NUM:miami1146224861#abstract-files.

Rogoff, Irit. '"Smuggling" – An Embodied Criticality'. European Institute for Progressive Cultural Policies. *Transversal* (August 2006), http://eipcp.net/transversal/0806/rogoff1/en.

———. 'De-Regulation: With the Work of Kutlug Ataman'. *Third Text* 23, no. 2 (2009): 165–79.

———. *Terra Infirma: Geography's Visual Culture*. London; New York: Routledge, 2000.

———. 'What Is a Theorist?' In *The State of Art Criticism*, ed. James Elkins and Michael Newman, 97–109. New York: Routledge, 2007.

Roth, Moira. 'The Aesthetic of Indifference'. *Artforum*, November 1977.

Roth, Moira, and Jonathan D. Katz. *Difference/Indifference: Musings on Postmodernism, Marcel Duchamp and John Cage*. Amsterdam: G+B Arts International, 1998.

Rushbrook, Dereka. 'Cities, Queer Space, and the Cosmopolitan Tourist'. *GLQ: A Journal of Lesbian and Gay Studies* 8, no. 1 (2002): 183–206.

Ryan, Gary. 'City Which Spawned Queer as Folk and Canal Street Wins Ultimate Gay Student Accolade'. *Guardian*, 10 August 2005, sec. UK news. www.theguardian.com/uk/2005/aug/11/gayrights.highereducation.

Sampath, Rajesh. 'India Has Outlawed Homosexuality. But It's Better to Be Transgender There than in the U.S.' *The Washington Post*, 29 January 2015. www.washingtonpost.com/posteverything/wp/2015/01/29/india-has-outlawed-homosexuality-but-its-better-to-be-transgender-there-than-in-the-u-s/.

Sandler, Irving. *Natvar Bhavsar: Painting and the Reality of Color*. Sydney: Craftsman House; G+B Arts International, 1998.

Scheerhout, John. 'Force Wins Praise from Gay Group'. *Manchester Evening News*, 18 March 2007. www.manchestereveningnews.co.uk/news/greater-manchester-news/force-wins-praise-from-gay-group-985583.

Schjeldahl, Peter. 'Do It Yourself: Biennial Follies at the Whitney'. *The New Yorker*, 25 March 2002. www.newyorker.com/magazine/2002/03/25/do-it-yourself-2.

Schreyach, Michael. 'The Recovery of Criticism'. In *The State of Art Criticism*, ed. James Elkins and Michael Newman, 3–26. New York: Routledge, 2007.

Schwendener, Martha. 'The Diaspora Is Remixed'. *The New York Times*, 22 March 2012. www.nytimes.com/2012/03/23/arts/design/the-diaspora-is-remixed.html.

Serota, Nicholas. 'History behind the Thought (interview with Twombly)'. In *Cy Twombly: Cycles and Seasons*, ed. Nicholas Serota, 42–53. London: Tate Publishing, 2008.

———. 'Interview: US Artist Cy Twombly Talks to Tate Director Nicholas Serota'. *Guardian*. Accessed 27 May 2015. www.theguardian.com/artanddesign/2008/jun/03/art1.

Shone, Richard. 'Contemporary British Sculpture. Madrid (Review)'. *The Burlington Magazine* 128, no. 997 (April 1986): 308–10.

Shukman, Henry. 'CHOICE TABLES | LONDON; Where Indian Cuisine Reaches for the Stars'. *The New York Times*, 4 March 2007. www.nytimes.com/2007/03/04/travel/04Choice.html?_r=0.

Sims, Lowery S. 'The Paintings of Natvar Bhavsar'. *Arts Magazine* (December 1984).

Singh, Devika. 'A Modern Formation?: Circulating International Art in India, 1950s-1970s'. In *Western Artists and India: Creative Inspirations in Art and Design*, ed. Shanay Jhaveri, 46–57. Mumbai: Shoestring Publisher, 2013.

Sinha, Gayatri. 'Archaeology & Subversion: Kehinde Wiley in India'. In *Kehinde Wiley: The World Stage: India, Sri Lanka*, 4–15. Chicago: Rhona Hoffman Gallery, 2011.

Sinha, Gayatri, and Paul D. Miller. *Kehinde Wiley: The World Stage: India – Sri Lanka*. Chicago: Rhona Hoffman Gallery, 2011.

Sinha, Mrinalini. *Colonial Masculinity: The 'Manly Englishman' and the 'Effeminate Bengali' in the Late Nineteenth Century*. Manchester: Manchester University Press, 1995.

Smith, Hazel, and R. T. Dean, eds. *Practice-Led Research, Research-Led Practice in the Creative Arts*. Edinburgh: Edinburgh University Press, 2009.

Smith, Neil. 'Giuliani Time: The Revanchist 1990s'. *Social Text* 57 vol. 16, no. 4 (Winter 1998): 1–20.

Smith, Roberta. 'A Hot Conceptualist Finds the Secret of Skin'. *The New York Times*, 4 September 2008, sec. Arts / Art & Design. www.nytimes.com/2008/09/05/arts/design/05stud.html.

———. 'Review: "Kehinde Wiley: A New Republic" at the Brooklyn Museum'. *The New York Times*, 19 February 2015. www.nytimes.com/2015/02/20/arts/design/review-kehinde-wiley-a-new-republic-at-the-brooklyn-museum.html.

———. 'Sculptor as Magician'. *The New York Times*, 30 May 2008. www.nytimes.com/2008/05/30/arts/design/30kapo.html.

Smith, Terry, Okwui Enwezor, and Nancy Condee. *Antinomies of Art and Culture: Modernity, Postmodernity, Contemporaneity*. Durham, NC: Duke University Press, 2008.

Solomon, Deborah. 'Kehinde Wiley Puts a Classical Spin on His Contemporary Subjects'. *The New York Times*, 28 January 2015. www.nytimes.com/2015/02/01/arts/design/kehinde-wiley-puts-a-classical-spin-on-his-contemporary-subjects.html.

'Sonia Gandhi Inaugurates Anish Kapoor Retrospective at NGMA'. Indo-Asian News Service (IANS). *Sify News*, 27 November 2010. www.sify.com/news/sonia-gandhi-inaugurates-anish-kapoor-retrospective-at-ngma-news-national-kl1uOlehaaj.html.

Sorabella, Jean. 'The Grand Tour'. In *Heilbrunn Timeline of Art History*. New York: The Metropolitan Museum of Art, 2003. www.metmuseum.org/toah/hd/grtr/hd_grtr.htm.

Spivak, Gayatri Chakravorty. 'Can the Subaltern Speak?' In *Marxism and the Interpretation of Culture*, ed. Cary Nelson and Lawrence Grossberg, 271–313. Basingstoke: Macmillan, 1988.

———. *In Other Worlds: Essays in Cultural Politics*. New York: Routledge, 1988.

———. 'Interview with Elizabeth Grosz: Criticism, Feminism, and the Institution'. In *The Post-Colonial Critic: Interviews, Strategies, Dialogues*, ed. Sarah Harasym, 1–16. New York: Routledge, 1990.

———. 'Three Women's Texts and a Critique of Imperialism'. *Critical Inquiry* 12, no. 1 (Autumn 1985): 243–61.

———. 'World Systems and the Creole, Rethought'. In *Creolizing Europe: Legacies and Transformations*, ed. Encarnación Gutiérrez Rodríguez and Shirley Anne Tate, 26–37. Liverpool: Liverpool University Press, 2015.

Stanek, Łukasz. 'The Production of Urban Space by Mass Media Storytelling Practices. Nowa Huta as a Case Study'. Boston, MA: Massachusetts Institute of Technology, 2005. http://web.mit.edu/comm-forum/mit4/papers/stanek.pdf.

Stromer, Mark. 'Combating Hate Crimes against Sikhs: A Multi-Tentacled Approach'. *The Journal of Gender, Race & Justice* 9, no. 3 (2006), 739–66.

'Success Story of One Minority Group in US'. *US News & World Report*, 26 December 1966.

Sullivan, Herbert. 'Zen Buddhism: An Ancient Eastern Religion, It Is Gaining Popularity as a Philosophy in the Western World'. *Duke Alumni Register*, April 1961. https://ia800307.us.archive.org/5/items/dukealumniregist471961/dukealumniregist471961.pdf.

Sullivan, Randall. 'The Unsolved Mystery of the Notorious B.I.G.' *Rolling Stone*, 15 December 2005. www.rollingstone.com/music/news/the-unsolved-mystery-of-the-notorious-b-i-g-20110107.

Summers, David. *Real Spaces: World Art History and the Rise of Western Modernism*. London and New York: Phaidon Press, 2003.

Sylvester, David. 'Cy Twombly (2000)'. In *Interviews with American Artists*, 171–81. New Haven, CT: Yale University Press, 2001.

Tan, E.K. 'A Queer Journey Home in "Solos": Rethinking Kinship in Sinophone Singapore'. In *Queer Sinophone Cultures*, ed. Howard Chiang and Ari Larissa Heinrich, 130–46. New York: Routledge, 2013.

Taussig, Michael T. *What Color Is the Sacred?* Chicago; London: University of Chicago Press, 2009.

Tawadros, Gilane. 'A Case of Mistaken Identity'. In *Shades of Black: Assembling Black Arts in 1980s Britain*, ed. David A. Bailey, Ian Baucom and Sonia Boyce, 123–32. Durham, NC: Duke University Press in association with the Institute of

International Visual Arts and the African and Asian Visual Artists' Archive, London, 2005.

Taylor, Ian R., Karen Evans and Penny Fraser. *A Tale of Two Cities: Global Change, Local Feeling and Everyday Life in the North of England: A Study in Manchester and Sheffield*. International Library of Sociology. London; New York: Routledge, 1996.

'The Art of Negative Sensation: Modernism In American Painting On View'. *Times of India*. 28 March 1967.

'The PANTONE MATCHING SYSTEM®: Always Show Your True Colors'. PANTONE®. Accessed 26 August 2015. www.pantone.com/the-pantone-matching-system.

Thompson, Krista 'The Sound of Light Reflections on Art History in the Visual Culture of Hip-Hop', *Art Bulletin* 91, no. 4 (December 2009): 48–50.

Thompson, Krista A., Thelma Golden and Robert Hobbs. *Kehinde Wiley: The World Stage: Africa, Lagos-Dakar*. New York: Studio Museum in Harlem, 2008.

'Three Exhibitions Opening at the Museum'. The Jewish Museum, n.d., press release.

Tomlinson, John. *Globalization and Culture*. Oxford: Polity, 1999.

'Top Boxer's Speed Charge'. *Manchester Evening News*, 13 August 2007. www.manchestereveningnews.co.uk/news/local-news/top-boxers-speed-charge-990680.

Trapp, Elizabeth J. 'Cy Twombly's Ferragosto Series'. Master's thesis, Ohio University, 2010. www.ohiolink.edu/etd/view.cgi?ohiou1276609006.

Tsai, Eugenie. 'Introduction'. In *Kehinde Wiley: A New Republic*, ed. Eugenie Tsai, 10–19. New York: Brooklyn Museum in association with DelMonico Books & Prestel, 2015.

'Tupac Shakur Biography'. *Rolling Stone*. Accessed 3 January 2016. www.rollingstone.com/music/artists/tupac-shakur/biography.

Turner, William B. *A Genealogy of Queer Theory*. Philadelphia: Temple University Press, 2000.

'Two Decades of American Painting 1946–66'. *Hindustan Times Sunday Magazine*, 26 March 1967.

'Two Decades of US Painting: Rabindra Bhavan Gets Ready for Exhibition'. *Statesman*, 8 March 1967.

'UNITED STATES: "WE ARE NOT THE ENEMY": Hate Crimes Against Arabs, Muslims, and Those Perceived to Be Arab or Muslim after September 11'. *Human Rights Watch* 14, no. 6 (G) (November 2002): 1–42.

'US Representation in 3rd International Contemporary Art Exhibition, India'. Press release. *The Museum of Modern Art*, 18 February 1957. www.moma.org/momaorg/shared/pdfs/docs/press_archives/2156/releases/MOMA_1957_0014.pdf?2010.

Vali, Murtaza. 'The White Slave'. In *Kehinde Wiley: A New Republic*, ed. Eugenie Tsai, 102. New York: Brooklyn Museum in association with DelMonico Books & Prestel, 2015.

Vanilla. Accessed 7 March 2007. www.vanillagirls.co.uk/html/gossip.php.

Varnedoe, Kirk. 'Your Kid Could Not Do This, and Other Reflections on Cy Twombly'. *MoMA*, no. 18 (Autumn–Winter 1994): 18–23.

Velpandian, T., K. Saha, A. K. Ravi, S. S. Kumari, N. R. Biswas and S. Ghose. 'Ocular Hazards of the Colors Used During the Festival-of-Colors (Holi) in India

– Malachite Green Toxicity'. *Journal of Hazardous Materials* 139, no. 2 (10 January 2007): 204–8. doi:10.1016/j.jhazmat.2006.06.046.

Vendler, Helen. 'The Medley Is the Message'. *The New York Review of Books*, 8 May 1986. www.nybooks.com/articles/archives/1986/may/08/the-medley-is-the-message/.

Very Deadly Kali. 'Deadly Kali: Look Out India! Anish Kapoor Is Here!!!' Blog. *Deadly Kali*, 30 November 2010. http://deadlykali.blogspot.com/2010/11/look-out-india-anish-kapoor-is-here.html.

Vidal, Denis. 'The Return of the Aura: Anish Kapoor, the Studio and the World'. In *Arts and Aesthetics in a Globalizing World*, ed. Raminder Kaur and Parul Dave Mukherji, 39–60. London: Bloomsbury Academic, 2014.

Vidler, Anthony. 'Reflections on Whiteout: Anish Kapoor at Barbara Gladstone'. In *Anish Kapoor: Whiteout*. Milan: Charta, 2004.

Villiers, Nicholas de. *Opacity and the Closet: Queer Tactics in Foucault, Barthes, and Warhol*. Minneapolis: University of Minnesota Press, 2012.

Volpp, L. 'The Citizen and the Terrorist'. *UCLA Law Review* 49 (2002): 1575–1600.

'Vrishchik'. Asia Art Archive. Accessed 2 March 2016. www.aaa.org.hk/Collection/CollectionOnline/SpecialCollectionFolder/2133.

Ward, Frazer. 'Haunted Museum: Institutional Critique and Publicity'. *October* 73 (Summer 1995): 71–89.

Warner, Michael. 'Publics and Counterpublics'. *Public Culture* 14, no. 1 (2002): 49–90.

Waters, Florence. 'Anish Kapoor Saves His Best for India'. *The Telegraph*, 3 November 2010. www.telegraph.co.uk/culture/art/art-news/8108384/Anish-Kapoor-saves-his-best-for-India.html.

Wechsler, Jeffrey. 'From Asian Traditions to Modern Expressions: Abstract Art by Asian Americans, 1945–1970'. In *Asian Traditions/Modern Expressions: Asian American Artists and Abstraction, 1945–1970*, 58–145. New York: Harry N. Abrams in association with the Jane Voorhees Zimmerli Art Museum, Rutgers, the State University of New Jersey, 1997.

Wechsler, Jeffrey, and Marius Kwint. *Natvar Bhavsar: Dimensions of Color*. Ed. Jeffrey Wechsler. New Brunswick, NJ: Jane Voorhees Zimmerli Art Museum, Rutgers, the State University of New Jersey, 2007.

Weiner, Julia. 'Interview: Anish Kapoor Is the Biggest Name in Art'. *Jewish Chronicle Online*, 24 September 2009. www.thejc.com/arts/arts-interviews/interview-anish-kapoor-biggest-name-art.

Wells, Karen. 'Melancholic Memorialisation: The Ethical Demands of Grievable Lives'. In *Visuality/Materiality: Images, Objects and Practices*, ed. Divya P. Tolia-Kelly and Gillian Rose, 153–70. Farnham and Burlington, VT: Ashgate Publishing, 2012.

White, Hayden. 'Historiography and Historiophoty'. *The American Historical Review* 93, no. 5 (December 1988): 1193–9.

Whitney Museum of American Art. *1969 Annual Exhibition: Contemporary American Painting. December 16, 1969–February 1, 1970, Whitney Museum of American Art*. New York: Whitney Museum of American Art, 1969.

———. *1973 Biennial Exhibition: Contemporary American Art. Whitney Museum of American Art, New York, January 10–March 18, 1973*. New York: Whitney Museum of American Art, 1973.

———. Oral history interview with Kehinde Wiley, Archives of American Art, Smithsonian Institution. Interview by Anne Louise Bayly Berman. Recorded and transcribed, 29 September 2010. www.aaa.si.edu/collections/interviews/oral-history-interview-kehinde-wiley-15882.

Wiley, Kehinde. 'Frequently Asked Questions'. Artist website. *Kehinde Wiley*. Accessed 11 June 2015. www.kehindewiley.com/faq.html.

Williams, Raymond. *Marxism and Literature*. Marxist Introductions. Oxford: Oxford University Press, 1977.

Winther-Tamaki, Bert. 'The Asian Dimensions of Postwar Abstract Art: Calligraphy and Metaphysics'. In *The Third Mind: American Artists Contemplate Asia, 1860–1989*, ed. Alexandra Munroe, 145–98. New York: Guggenheim Museum, 2009.

———. 'Japanese Margins of American Abstract Expressionism'. In *Art in the Encounter of Nations: Japanese and American Artists in the Early Postwar Years*, 19–65. Honolulu: University of Hawaii Press, 2001.

Yau, John. 'Please Wait By the Coatroom'. In *Out There: Marginalization and Contemporary Cultures*, ed. Russell Ferguson, Cornel West, Martha Gever and Trinh T. Minh-Ha, 133–41. New York; Cambridge, MA: New Museum of Contemporary Art; MIT Press, 1990.

Zeleza, Paul Tiyambe. 'Rewriting the African Diaspora: Beyond the Black Atlantic'. *African Affairs* 104, no. 14 (2005): 35–68.

Zijlmans, Kitty, and Wilfried Van Damme, eds. *World Art Studies: Exploring Concepts and Approaches*. Amsterdam: Valiz, 2008.

Zimmermann, Michael F., ed. *The Art Historian: National Traditions and Institutional Practices*. Williamstown, MA: Sterling and Francine Clark Art Institute, 2003.

———. 'Introduction'. In *The Art Historian: National Traditions and Institutional Practices*, ed. Michael F. Zimmermann, vii–xxvii. Williamstown, MA: Sterling and Francine Clark Art Institute, 2003.

Index